Books by BLAKE EHRLICH

PARIS ON THE SEINE

RESISTANCE
France 1940–1945

LONDON ON THE THAMES

LONDON
ON THE THAMES

LONDON ON

S. PAULES CHURCH

Bow Church

Cheap Crosse

Three Cranes

The Stiliard

The Gally fuste

Schipes

HAMESIS

The Bear Gardne

The Globe

THE THAMES

by BLAKE EHRLICH

LITTLE, BROWN AND COMPANY · BOSTON · TORONTO

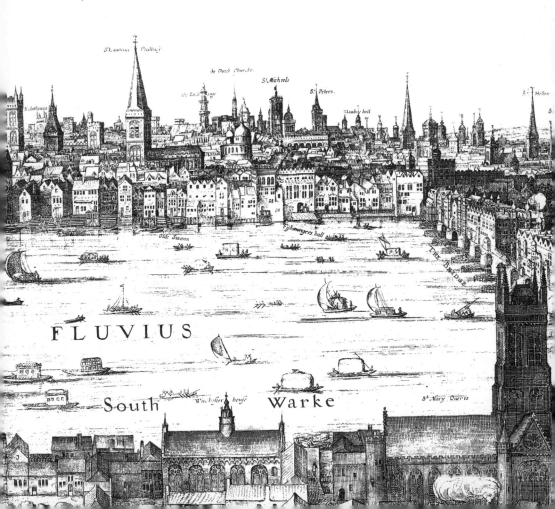

We are grateful to Harcourt, Brace & World, Inc. and to Faber and
Faber Ltd. for permission to reprint lines from "The Waste Land"
from *Collected Poems 1909–1962* by T. S. Eliot.

*Published simultaneously in Canada
by Little, Brown & Company (Canada) Limited*

PRINTED IN THE UNITED STATES OF AMERICA

To the two native sons of London
I cherish most, my father, William,
and my son, Luke

CONTENTS

LONDON
ON THE THAMES

A PREFATORY
RAMBLE

THE measure of cities, like the measure of women and the measure of wealth, cannot be encompassed by statistics alone. The intangibles, the invisibles, are as significant as the palpables.

The dome of St. Paul's is 365 feet from the floor of the cathedral to the top of the cross; the Vickers Tower, a 1963 riverside skyscraper, is 387 feet tall; Big Ben's tower is 320 feet high: the towers of Ilium were topless.

Amsterdam is more beautiful than London, Rome more antique, Tokyo bigger. Manhattan's Homicide Squad solves as many murders as Scotland Yard's Criminal Investigation Division. The Seine is infinitely more seductive than the Thames.

London is not compounded of superlatives. It is not all past (Venice), nor all present (Los Angeles), nor subjunctive (Istanbul). But London is uniquely and gratifyingly London and not any other city in the world. The thing that makes it singular can be called style, or tone or — possibly more British-sounding — character.

Greater London has grown great out of a tiny Caesarean implantation made in 55 B.C. Across from the original settlement grew the borough of Southwark, possibly in order that there be *something* at the far end of London Bridge. Eventually upstream there emerged the royal city of Westminster, and building began along the riverbank, the strand, between the two cities. The open fields between the metropolis, as the swamps were filled and the forests felled, were gradually built over, reaching toward the nearby villages, and then the villages themselves were incorporated.

3

Thus, in April 1965, when the seventy-five-year-old London County Council became the Greater London Council, the city was suddenly enlarged again, stretching fifteen miles from the center, embracing six hundred square miles with a population of nearly eight million. The London Transport Board, which runs the mass transportation systems, continued to act on its quarter-century-old assumption that London really reaches out twenty-five to thirty miles from the center and covers two thousand square miles.

Essentially, London is a gray city under essentially gray skies (or skies that the inner eye persuades the outer eye to see as gray). The grayness is relieved — or, depending on the mood, accentuated — by public splashes of bright color. These are predominantly scarlet and green, with flashes of gold and silver and white.

To these colors is keyed the London one sees from the bus-top recommended to tourists by Prime Minister Gladstone. To be sure, physical London is a matter of shapes, their proportions and relationships, but the street-level assortment of colors provides a kind of personal identification. It provokes recognition: "That must be London" or "That looks like London."

London 1588: lower left, the Abbey; upper right, the Tower; between, that broad highway, the Thames.

4

GREEN

London as a cartographer's amoeba is speckled with green blotches. These represent not a blight but a blessing. They are the parks, the squares and the churchyards of London, and they spread their verdure over more than a sixth of the city's surface.

Year by year the municipal government chips a bit here and a bit there from the gray cityscape to broaden the green patches. Most squares are built around gardens which belong not to the public but to the surrounding houses. They contribute twelve hundred acres of city-girt glade to the outward aspect of the town.

There are more thousands of acres of greenery secreted behind the housefronts in hundreds of thousands of back gardens. The one-family house is still, in spite of the banks of apartments pushing out of the overpriced soil, the typical London dwelling. The Englishman still seeks to gratify the bone-bred wish for his own castle with grounds. In this respect, as in practically every other, the Royal Family sets a Good Example, and occupies a one-family residence with walled garden (of forty acres).

Before Buckingham Palace lies St. James's Park, and directly to the north of the Palace lies Green Park, immediately west of which is the huge green parallelogram shared by Hyde Park and Kensington Gardens. These are royal parks, ex–hunting grounds still administered by the Crown, and they make a swath of green two and a half miles long and more than half a mile wide through the center of town.* They are very possibly the most beautiful, most mysterious and most restorative city parks in the entire world.

The royal parks retain a certain amount of cachet, both as places distinguished to live close to and as places to go disport oneself. One still rides in Rotten Row (Hyde Park) and bowls upon the inches-thick turf of the bowling green, or sails miniature yachts on the Round Pond of Kensington Gardens, or troops to Sunday service at the Guards Chapel off Birdcage Walk, St. James's.

* Another royal park, Regent's Park, lies a mile north of Hyde Park.

The royal parks make use of their green Victorian-Edwardian bandstands which have green cast iron columns rising like slender stalks to blossom into seriocomic parasol roofs. The brass bands of the London regiments appear throughout the summer in these bandstands:

> Their tunics red, their faces pink
> Who loudly render Humperdinck.

There is music too in twenty-two of the seventy-four municipal parks, and not just the traditional brass bands, but also jazz and symphony concerts, pipers, balalaika bands. There are plays and ballets. There are facilities for all the major British sports and in the really large parks athletic contests including equestrian jumping and automobile racing.

When the summer sun consents to shine, those Londoners not involved in creating historic traffic jams on the inadequate highways converge upon the parks, strip off their outer garments and prostrate themselves in the sunlight. The parks burgeon brilliantly with large and loving displays of flowers. There are also large displays of loving: where the woodbine twineth there also do amorous couples.

There is also a delightful thronging of birds: 134 species were identified in the royal parks of inner and outer London in 1964. These included great crested grebes, cuckoos, kestrels, plovers, nightingales and a Free Flying Ferruginous Duck. Concomitantly, the place throngs with persons avid to identify the great crested grebe and such. In addition to the visitors, the park ponds have permanent pensioners, such as those pelicans at St. James's (the Czar presented a pair to Charles II in the late seventeenth century, and that's how those things start here).

In addition to entertainment, repose or exertion, the parks also offer fresh though not instantly discernible supplies of oxygen, for which London is famished.

GRAY, WITH SAD VARIATIONS

The air of London often hangs over the streets like dirty washing. When it is bad it is sordid and at its worst it is quite literally murderous.

6

The motes in the air can make for marvelous sunsets. During an almost sunny day the light that filters through the overcast has an effulgence that softens the strictures of the stone, and the sky becomes an illumined dome.

The moisture in the air of this river-bottom town can magically transform the towers and the trees and the street lamps into a fairytale array. There are moments when it is a matter of some dismay that the helmet does in fact belong to a policeman and not to a pikeman. During the day there are often moments of wonderful opalescence. But while opalescence is to be admired, opacity is to be deplored.

A gray day in London can change color as the fog comes, for the fogs are yellow and brown. Viscid and vicious, they scorch the eyes, sludge the throat and wrack the chest. They seep into the house and stain the walls, they smell, and from time to time they kill.

The fog of December 1952 killed 4000 Londoners, and ten years later another half-week of December fog killed 396. On an ordinary London day, the inhabitant inhales some five milligrams of dirt, on a foggy day, about fifty. The fog kills by irritating the inside of the lungs and provoking excess secretion of mucus. The lodged mucus becomes infected, the tissues break down. Unable to get enough oxygen, the patient dies.

This disease is catalogued as bronchitis by British doctors, obviously not the ailment which bears the same name in America. Some thirty thousand people die of it each year and Britain annually loses twenty million working hours.

The plague of fog and polluted air has infected London since the smoke-obscured dawn of the fourteenth century at least. And spasmodically London has tried to do something about it. In 1306 the burning of oily-smoking sea coal was forbidden on pain of death, and one poor householder was actually hanged for this transgression. His fellow citizens, if discouraged briefly from poisoning the air, were not converted to the use of smokeless fuel. More than 350 years later diarist John Evelyn was telling King Charles II about the horrors of the smog problem. He also set forth his strong views in strong language in a monograph, *Fumifugium*.

He deplored with "just indignation" that London should "wrap her head in clouds of smoke and sulphur, so full of stink and darkness." He railed against the "poysoned air which obscures our Churches and makes our Palaces look old, which fouls our Clothes and corrupts the Waters."

A century later Benjamin Franklin, Agent in London to the General Assembly of Pennsylvania, wrote, "The whole town is one great smoky house and every street a chimney, the air full of floating sea-coal soot, and you never get a breath of what is pure . . ."

Lord Byron in 1820 described London as "a wilderness of steeples peeping tip-toe through their sea-coal canopy." Not long after, Elizabeth Barrett, a new arrival in town, wrote, "London is wrapped up like a mummy in a yellow mist, so closely that I have had scarcely a glimpse of her countenance."

From November 1879 to March of 1880, London was blinded and paralyzed by a single, unremitting four-month blanket of fog. Yet in 1880, a lecturer to the Society of Arts had a good word to say for fog, which, he said, by pressing down reduced the stench from the sewers.

By 1956, the 1306 Clean Air Act was held to be outdated, and Parliament passed a new one. It specified smokeless fuels, although most rooms in London — including the homes and offices of most Members of Parliament — were still heated by fireplaces. But as the British slowly emerge from a long Puritan purgatory which equated comfort with sinfulness, or worse still, unmanliness, central heating is being installed. During this period there has been a sharp rise in crimes of violence (500 per cent) and convictions for drunkenness (58 per cent), but any relationship to central heating remains unexplored.

As a result of the Clean Air Act, the air samples collected atop St. Bartholomew's Hospital show a reduction in the amount of smoke in the air. Unfortunately, there has been an increase in the amount of poison found in the samples, with new agents of air pollution such as polycyclic aromatic hydrocarbons.

It will be at least the year 2000 before London gets back to just plain old fog, the experts estimate. Perhaps that may tie up the city less than today's pea-soupers, when buses inch through the streets following a conductor walking along the curbline holding a light.

SCARLET

The red double-decker bus is not peculiar to London, and can be seen in almost every other city in the British Isles, but in London it seems to take on special local characteristics. Here it is especially noticeable that they seem to travel in schools, so that when the time for ten buses to have passed has elapsed with no bus at all, ten suddenly thunder on — and sometimes by. They have a distinct reluctance to recognize bus stops in the rain.

The evolutionary process which produced the contemporary RM (for Routemaster) began early in the century, and today's behemoth is recognizably a refinement of the 1908 monster. They are 14 feet 5 inches high, and appear about to fall over when traffic permits them to round curves at more than a crawl. In virtually every instance, they do not fall over. This stability is useful, because in spite of the use of fiberglass, aluminum alloy and other weight-saving materials, the thing still weighs ten tons with its crew of two, sixty-four passengers, and a limited number of ground-floor standees (in the case of the very tall, crouchees).

The driver is still isolated in his cabin, as was the coachman, cut off from all contact with the human cargo. The conductor is obliged to mingle with the passengers. He clatters up and down the interior iron spiral stairway selling tickets on both decks, transmitting signals for the bus to stop and start, advising those clustered at the bus stop that there is room for one more on top (smoking is allowed on top), explaining why this is the wrong bus for Shepherd's Bush. He works off his exasperation through a form of insolence apparently cherished by fare-payers under the title of Cockney Wit. Lady bus conductors are known as Clippies.

Passengers board through the doorless rear platform, some of them by dint of dangerous and illegal acrobatics as the bus groans by. Every now and then a leaper misses, with untidy results.

Each bus is a rolling signboard, bearing brightly colored posters on a strip along each side, and also fore and aft. Each bus carries not only its route number and destination, but an illumi-

9

nated list of way stations. The names are a roll-call of places familiar by hearsay to the visitor: No. 19 passes through Bloomsbury and Chelsea to Tooting Bec; No. 24 trickles down through Charing Cross from Hampstead Heath on its way to Pimlico; No. 176 goes along the Strand en route for Elephant & Castle. In 1965, the L.T.B. sneaked a few single-deck no-conductor "experimental" vehicles onto some routes, possibly a discouraging augury.

The passenger pays only for the distance he travels, unlike the American single-fare. Of course, the further he goes, the more he pays, very unlike the American single-fare. The same system operates on the Underground, where ticket-sellers are helped out by slot machines which deliver tickets and change. Guards at the entrances and exits punch and collect tickets.

It is almost impossible to get lost on the Underground. There are crystalline explanations posted at every gate, turning, and platform to tell the rider where he is and where he can get to from here. Every car has a list of stations served and maps of the system grow underground like mushrooms. The transport authority has taken the position that any of the two million daily riders may suddenly find the subterranean world alien and bewildering.

In addition to being one of the most intelligible of all subway systems, the London Underground is certainly one of the most comfortable. Noise and bad smells are at a minimum. Seats and lighting have been designed with the passenger's comfort in mind rather than the company's overhead. In some cars on each train, smoking is permitted.

The first underground trains between Paddington and the City were steam trains. That was in 1863. But even today, about the time of the last train of the evening, at one of the remote, misty stations leading to the Thames tunnels, one may see — without entirely believing it — a small steam locomotive trundling a group of toy boxcars along the tracks.

On the long, long escalators carrying passengers into and out of the deeps and in the underground corridors there are occasional signs instructing the pedestrian to Keep Right. The trains below, however, like the buses above, keep strictly to the left.

This is one of repeated indications that England is the land of the Other Hand. Despite the firmness with which prejudices are aired (". . . should be horsewhipped") and the frequency with which they are applied ("Rooms — Europeans Only"), this remains a country founded on compromise, of seeing the other fellow's side, of saying But of course on the other hand, of the battered but still functioning mechanism of Fair Play.

The foreigner utilizing the Underground may think the platform employees are speaking in patois. But it is English they speak. The cry "Her own peas!" is really "Hurry along please," followed by "My gnaws!" which means "Mind the doors," which in turn means not to look after them, but to watch out for them.

A few trains on some lines are painted silver, but most of the rolling stock is the same satisfying scarlet as the buses, Guards' uniforms, telephone kiosks, Royal Mail vans and the pillar boxes.

A pillar box is where one mails letters. It is a cast-iron pillar planted on the pavement, and bears the royal cipher to indicate in whose reign it was erected. Introduced from abroad by Anthony Trollope in 1855, they were at first hexagonal (Kensington High Street and York Gate of Regent's Park retain some of these handsome pioneers), then rather oval, and now cylindrical. They are between four and five feet high, and many of them are too fat for a man to encircle with his arms (not a recommended procedure in London).

Telephone boxes are sometimes referred to as "kiosks," but never, unless someone is humoring a transatlantic visitor, "booths." For a local call, older models require four pennies (known locally as "coppers"), and one should not use the phrase "spend a penny" in reference to them, since this is a local euphemism for going to the (pay) toilet. The new telephone apparatus, installed as prices everywhere are rising, cost a penny less per call, since they accept a single coin worth threepence and called a "thrip'ny bit," brass, with a twelve-sided edge.

There are twelve pence to the shilling, and twenty shillings to the pound. Attempts to decimalize British currency, urged by a Royal commission in 1841, is now announced for application in 1971. The Mother Country will thus catch up with her brood: Canada has long used the decimal system; Australia and New

11

Zealand put it into effect in 1966, and Pakistan, India, South Africa and Burma have gone decimal as well. The pound will remain, but the traditional coins will be replaced. The new 5-cent coin will equal the old shilling (14 cents U.S. in 1966), the 2-shilling piece will be replaced by a 10-cent piece, and the 10-shilling note ($1.40 U.S.) exchanged for a new 50-cent coin.

The familiar crossed L (£) originally represented the Roman *libra*, for pound, when money represented an actual weight, and the *s* for shilling and the *d* for penny are *solidus* and *denarius*, of the same derivation. Visitors have found it difficult, especially when adding up items in a bill, or trying to calculate a 12 per cent tip on £7 13*s* 8*d*. The traditional British coins do have the attribute of perceptible weight, conveying a sense of enduring British values and also wearing holes quite quickly through trousers pockets.

One doesn't need a coin at all to call from a public booth to the police or fire department or for an ambulance. The emergency number, 999, has the special advantage of being dialable not only free of charge but in the dark and under conditions of stress.

Equally sensible is the number for dialing to find out the time — TIM. The weather report comes from WEA 2211. The number ASK 9211 yields information on public events for the day. ASK 9311 gives the same information in French, an effective means of reassuring the non-French-speaking tourist that he is glad not to be in Paris. MAY 5414 will reach a government-supported hotel information service which helps the helpless to shelter, but only if they are overseas visitors.

On long-distance ("trunk") calls, the operator (whose male voice may astound those foreigners accustomed to all-girl operators), may ask, "Are you through?" before you've begun to talk. Neither rudeness nor stupidity, the phrase means "Have you got through to your number?" and not "Are you through with your conversation?"

Telephones in London do not simply go *ring*. They go *ring*, *ring*. Perhaps this is because the telephone system belongs to the Post Office, and the postman historically rings twice.

The Post Office does rather better on telephones and telegraph than on mail. Although in 1963–1964 the GPO made a profit of 30.7 million pounds, they lost heavily on packages and printed matter. The profit from telecommunications alone was 38.5 million pounds and on first class letters 10 million.

London has eight postal districts, split up around the compass to give designations such as South West. These are divided into delivery districts, yielding addresses such as London E.C.4, and London S.W.3. Although it has pretty well obliterated the old village place names from addresses, the Post Office has kept them as the names of its substations — e.g., Knightsbridge.

The old names are disappearing from all sorts of official nomenclature. Under the Greater London Council, fifty-eight local boroughs have vanished, to be absorbed into thirty-two new units of local government. The wealthy and ancient City of Westminster (Abbey, Parliament, Buckingham Palace) has engulfed the populous, depressed borough of Paddington (railway station) and the prim, prosperous St. Marylebone (Regent's Park with zoo, medical Harley Street, Oxford Street with department stores). The rumbustious East End boroughs of Stepney, Bethnal Green and Poplar have vanished to bloom anew as Tower Hamlets. In the district, the old neighborhoods of Limehouse, Isle of Dogs, Whitechapel, Mile End and Shadwell long ago ceased to exist except in the minds of the inhabitants.

One of the problems still to be satisfactorily arranged after the union of various boroughs is the matter of heraldic shields. When a borough without any coat of arms absorbs one which has a shield, does the old emblem now represent the new entity? Amalgamation of boroughs all of whom have arms will probably give rise to devices as inclusive as those of the Royal Family.

OF MANY COLORS

The Royal Arms are to be seen literally everywhere in London, not only on vehicles and establishments of Her Majesty's Government, but also on shopfronts. In fact, those affixed to stores are more apt to be painted in the full heraldic white, azure, gold, silver, and red. They indicate that at some time in some reign this shop or corporation has been purveyor of its wares to one of Their Majesties, and is the holder of a royal warrant which thus so names them.

13

In Park Place, a rather shabby but nonetheless discreet and costly cul-de-sac off St. James's, are the premises of T. B. Carlin, Ltd., founded 1825. They allow the public to know that they are Cigar Merchants to Her Majesty the Queen. There are also warrants from Edward VII, George V and George VI. And Napoleon III.

These emblems do brighten the street scene, as do many shining shields which give an air of royal favor without actually claiming it. Almost in the same class as spirit-lifters are shop signs and shopfronts. Umbrella repairmen often have little red and white umbrellas open above their doorways, as shoemakers will have big shoes (usually just the outline of shoe painted on wood, but sometimes a great gilded shoe) and locksmiths large keys. Victorian shopfronts, still present in surprising number, started out rather vulgar, but have been gentled by time. Still, they are rich in colored glass and gilt lettering, swathed in scrollwork and abounding in brass. Rarer are the riotous fronts of Victorian pubs, especially the Gin Palaces, apogees of the gaslit era. These too are guilty of lilaceous lettering and brass and etched glass, bespeaking interiors even more florid.

The virtues of brass are still esteemed for mail slots in doorways and for business nameplates. One can spot doorway after doorway, especially in fine old houses cut up into offices, where six to ten polished brass letter slots make bright abstracts across the paneling. The nameplates which firms, especially solicitors, seem to prize most highly are those completely illegible after years of assiduous buffing.

Doorways themselves have recently begun to add color to the scene, especially in those areas (Chelsea and Kensington, for example) where workmen's cottages have been converted into Bijou Dwellings at an ever-stiffening sales price. Pink, green, red, orange, blue they shine, sometimes abetted by shutters and flowerboxes of matching hue. They are mutually canceling shouts of individuality in rows of duplicate houses cheaply built to contain cheap labor.

Orange too are the globes which blink to let drivers know about pedestrian crossings. The crossings are painted black and white (known as "zebras," locally pronounced "zebbras"), as are the posts on which the blinkers are mounted.

Streetlight posts are not the same color all over town, and conspicuously not of the same design. They compose a history of streetlighting in themselves, from the torch to the mercury vapor lamp, and are made of wood, iron, steel, bronze, copper, aluminum and concrete. And often they are painted, differently in different districts, the two favorite schemes being pale blue and white or all silver.

Of all the blobs of color in London, the two most stirring wake echoes of pride and glory: the flag and the uniform. London is the center of government, and the seat of international commercial empires, and there is hardly a point from which the Union Jack cannot be seen flying. The uniform is that of the Guards — scarlet, black, white with dazzling flashes of burnished metal — at Buckingham and St. James's Palaces, at the Horse Guards in Whitehall, and at the Tower of London.

For more than two centuries the dome of St. Paul's dominated the skyline of London.

THE LONDON OF
PATER TAMESIS

The Thames really the father of London — Downstream and up — Oxford-Cambridge Boat Race — The river as a highroad — The Pool of London — River Police vs. Mudlarks and Pirates — London Bridge, past, present and future — Thames drinking water — The Great Stink of 1858 — Bridges — Tunnels — Wharves — Barges — The Docks

LONDONERS have every reason — and obligation — to call their river Father Thames. Without the Thames there could be no London. In England there are older cities on other rivers, and other seaports closer to the sea. Yet none became London, whose history is based on the old capital city story of being in the right place, on the spot where important roads cross an important river.

From the least hazardous of the island's southern sea inlets, the Thames gave the Roman founders of the city safe passage to the agricultural interior of the country, a calm fifty-mile voyage to the head of tidewater. Here the river was fordable and bridgeable, and the main Roman roads to the principal cities converged on walled Londinium.

Tacitus, in the Year One, called it a "busy emporium for trade and traders."

The Venerable Bede in the eighth century described it as "the metropolis of the East Saxons . . . the mart of many nations."

King James I, eight hundred years later, carried on in the same vein: ". . . the river of Thames is so necessary, commodious and profitable to the said City of London and without said River our said City would not long subsist, flourish or continue."

17

The river made London and today London repays its filial obligation. What makes it unique today — it is otherwise an unremarkable verdigrised bronze stream — is the reflection of London upon it. The metropolis, for all its thrusting implacability, its fits of sad seediness, its gnawing urban anonymity, for all its big and small hells, noise, crime, smells, grime, is nevertheless a romantic city. And it is much the same with its river.

The romance arises from mystery, beauty and history. The stream is thick with mystery and history and the flotsam and jetsam of dreams. The gull's cry and the hull's wake make far voyagers of us all, but here the provocation is extreme: from the parapet of London Bridge it is a quick clatter down the steps to the quay where a ship loads to be off across the furthest seas. Sir Francis Drake, Sir Walter Raleigh, Captain John Smith, the first Hudson's Bay traders, the first tea clippers, the explorers had their home port here and their feet walked these banks. Even Pocahontas, who did not want to go home and who died here on the eve of boarding ship for her return. Captain Kidd was hanged at Execution Dock near Wapping Old Stairs. Captain Bligh is buried just by the river at Lambeth.

The riverbanks still boast palaces, royal and episcopal. The rich sunsets and cloud masses silhouette ancient spires and domes and the new shimmering towers of commerce. There are exciting waterscapes in Dockland where the tugs hoot and barges swing and the cranes and warehouses loom spectrally out of the smoke and mist on the obscure waters.

On summer nights the lights along the embankments are gay in a genteel, shareable Edwardian way. All the little parks sprinkled in growing profusion by the river are lushly green and studded with statuary charmingly inept as art but unassailable in the goodness of their causes. They are strewn with tuppence-a-stretch deck chairs where one can encourage the band to oompah forever. The press of traffic — which may be just on the other side of the hedge — is far, far away and there is relief from whichever of its curses the big city has laid upon the recumbent possibly-listeners. The Embankments are parklike, heavy with trees through whose leaves the tubbiest barges sail with seeming grace upon the Thames.

Along the river's upper reaches there are still reminders of the sylvan way that once embraced the whole of London's Thames. The Mall at Hammersmith and the Strand on the Green in Chiswick are riverside village streets. They have a very real sense of union with the river, occasionally consummated by moderate flooding — doorsills along the Strand are eighteen inches high to keep the river out of the living room. These spots also have a happy though false sense of isolation from the giant metropolis.

From the upstream side of Putney Bridge underneath the Hammersmith Bridge to Mortlake just before the Chiswick Bridge, churns the annual Boat Race. There is no other Boat Race in all of England, though to be sure there are other races between boats, but they are called something else. The Boat Race, instituted in 1829, is between eight-oared shells representing Cambridge and Oxford universities, and takes place in late March or early April. "Provided," says a British Travel and

Along the Strand, lords and bishops built palaces still celebrated by street names.

19

Holidays Association pamphlet, "that neither boat has had the misfortune to sink. In 1912, both boats sank."

A London Transport booklet observes that the race "provides many thousands of spectators with a few minutes' free thrill and sixteen oarsmen with twenty minutes' expensive agony." And the first brochure adds that "the whole of England holds its breath on the day of the boat race until the result has been given." Which national concern is manifest, it says, "for no apparent reason."

In spite of the brochure writers, the race goes on and ends below the Ship Inn, one of the several snuggeries along this section of the river. Pleasant and unselfconsciously picturesque, they reject quaintness. In the lower river reaches there are other pubs with views over the river. Most of these establishments date from the days when smuggling, thieving, press-ganging and sailor-swindling were their principal sources of revenue. Today, as combination restaurants and bars, they still flourish amid the smells and sounds and personnel of an international port, though most of their custom is drawn from non-seafaring sections of the city.

Despite the physical inseparability of the two, there was a long moment of disaffection and the life of the river and the rest of the city became divorced. After centuries of having been London's glittering main street, it became something of a drab back alley to be bridged over or tunneled under. It was walled in by warehouses, factories, breweries, decaying shipyards, weedy railroad sidings, palisaded dockyards, gasworks and power stations. These were buffered by slums more melancholy and insalubrious than the polluted ribbon of river.

But the river was a moonlit beacon for the German bombers and the port a prime target. The Blitz made a shambles of the waterfront. When, across the flattened rubble, Londoners saw their river again, they found that the old love had not really died. Slowly, the banks of the Thames are being won back to the people and to the scale of their city.

As a high road the river was a lively place, beautiful with swans and sails, gay with awnings and pennants. Near London Bridge there is still a Galley Quay where the oars of the Venetian and Genoese galleys came to rest. There used to be a Galley Dock, too. Other than such tiny indentations, and once the River Fleet became too choked with refuse to be navigable, all loading and unloading was done at quays or else the cargo was taken from the anchored vessel in lighters to the shore. There were no embankments until Queen Victoria's day.

The Tower of London and the other castles and great houses along the bank had water gates (one is preserved in Victoria Embankment Gardens, still in its original place, but rather far from the river's edge now). From the river ends of streets there were stairs to the water's edge, and some few still exist, and the names stick, as at Temple Steps and Horseferry Stairs. From here one

The City's proud towers drew life and wealth from the river (1616).

hailed boats to the other bank or to other parts of town. The cry was "Oars!" Two-man small boats made short trips, but for a haul of any distance there were six and eight-oared wherries with upholstered benches and bright awnings against sun and rain. There were private boats then as there were private coaches later. Each of the guilds and civic and state officials had carven, gilded, many-oared barges. Several of these rich and graceful craft are preserved at the Greenwich Maritime Museum.

From the time of Dick Whittington (fifteenth century) until the time of Queen Victoria, the Thames remained "the great street paved with water." As carriages, sedan chairs and hackney coaches appeared in greater and greater numbers, and as the number of bridges grew, the watermen, those maritime cabbies, diminished.

They were the bawdy public wits of their long day, saucy and salty. Ben Jonson talked about them in Shakespeare's time, as

Through the Pool of London's forest of masts, St. Paul's (center) and the Tower (right

22

did Pepys a century later and Sam Johnson a good half-century or more after that.

Boswell reports: "It is well known that there was formerly a rude custom for those who were sailing upon the Thames to accost each other as they passed in the rudest language they could invent, generally however with as much satirical humor as they were capable of producing. Johnson was one eminently successful in this species of contest. A fellow having attacked him with some coarse raillery, Johnson answered him thus, 'Sir, your wife under pretence of keeping a bawdy house is a receiver of stolen goods.' "

In the eighteenth century the port became so crowded for lack of dock space that small ships could not make their way across the Pool of London (Upper Pool — London Bridge to Wapping; Lower Pool — Wapping to Limehouse). At moorings allotted to 545 ships in the Upper Pool, 775 were jammed plus some 3000 barges, some of which were used as floating warehouses.

There was often a week's wait for a ship to be allowed into the Pool, and an even longer wait for unloading. When pack ice came down the river, it was a menace to the massed shipping. Finally, in 1796, Parliament set up a committee to look into the matter. Three years later, Parliament granted permission for London's first real dock to be built, the West India Dock at the Isle of Dogs.* It was opened in 1802.

One of the remarkable advances it marked was a measure of protection from river thieves. The shipowners of the West Indian trade, whose sugar and rum cargoes were regularly pillaged, had not waited for Parliamentary action. In 1798 they formed a river patrol of their own, and so effective it was that the government took it over in 1800 as the River Police Office, with three magistrates attached to handle the pirate traffic. This was London's first regular police force, still very much in existence as the Thames Division of the Metropolitan Police, which was founded only in 1829.

The thieves had then (as now) picturesque classifications: Heavy Horsemen, who stole in the daytime, were usually Lump-

---

* Choice of derivations — possible site of a royal kennel; bend in river where mariners were guided by barking from shore; corruption of Isle of Ducks.

*Before the building of modern docks, the Pool became so crowded u
come up to the wharves and unload.*

pping that vessels had to wait weeks downstream for a chance to

ers (laborers) who had specially constructed big pockets for stolen goods; Light Horsemen worked at night, their numbers said to include ships' officers and Revenue men; Scuffle Hunters prowled the quays, hiding under their long aprons whatever they could snatch; Mudlarks who ranged the foreshore at low tide ostensibly looking for coal spilled from barges, often worked in cahoots with lumpers who heaved booty overside to be picked out of the mud later.

The real Pirates worked either by night or day, cutting lighters adrift to plunder when they drifted onshore, cutting ship's cables to sell secondhand and even stealing the anchors, going boldly on board and rifling the crew's quarters.

The big docks are sealed off from the river by systems of locks because of the tides. As the tide drops (and in the Thames it drops twenty feet, exposing the unlovely foreshore muck), the water in the dock areas behind the locks is kept at constant level. There are five dock systems from Tower Bridge downstream to Tilbury, twenty-six miles away, and they provide thirty-six miles of deepwater quays for ocean vessels.

In the days of the Romans, the river level was a dozen feet lower, and the tide, which now pushes seventy miles inland, used to spend itself at the piers of London Bridge.

There has been a London Bridge for close to a thousand years. The wooden bridge was renewed over the centuries, always built up again after being knocked down by ice, thrown down by flood, torn down by besiegers, burned down by accident. In 1176 *the* London Bridge was built and stood for almost 650 years. Although it has been gone since 1823, it is still lamented. It was demolished to be replaced by the current bridge designed by the great nineteenth-century engineer John Rennie, who had earlier built the lovely Waterloo Bridge. London Bridge was, alas, his "least inspired design."

By 1970 Rennie's bridge, cracking and settling into the river bed an inch every eight years (falling down, as it were), will have been replaced by history's third London Bridge. It will be one of those sleek concrete spans, resting its lightly bowed arches on but two piers. It will be one hundred feet wide, thirty-five feet broader than Rennie's bridge.

26

The new London Bridge won't cost today's taxpayers a penny. The $6,720,000 comes from the funds of the Bridge House Estates, accumulating since City men paid levies for bridge construction and maintenance under twelfth-century Lord Mayors.

London Bridge is still a thronging thoroughfare, and twice a day literally swarms with commuters. T. S. Eliot was once of their number, when he toiled in the foreign department of one of the big banks, Lloyd's. He observed the twice-a-day caterpillar procession with a cold camera eye:

The river under London Bridge (1597) roared in fearsome rapids.

27

And each man fixed his eyes before his feet.
Flowed up the hill and down King William Street,
To where Saint Mary Woolnoth kept the hours
With a dead sound on the final stroke of nine.

London Bridge, *the* London Bridge, was a far more bustling and boisterous passage. Its nineteen arches spanned the three hundred yards between the City and Southwark. The roadway down the middle was flanked on both sides by shops, and above the shops, houses three to seven stories high (138 of them in 1350). The inhabitants of these houses made up one of the wards of the City, and there were four Bridge Guilds to look after the structure. One-third of the houses were lost in the Great Fire of 1666, and all were removed in 1760 at the same time the gates of London City Wall were dismantled. (In Paris, the houses were ordered removed from the Seine bridges in 1769.)

There was a chapel on the bridge dedicated to St. Thomas à Becket, martyred six years earlier and canonized shortly before the bridge was done. The bones of Peter of Colechurch, the monk who designed and built the bridge, were interred in the chapel.

The bridge was a miniature city and a bastion in itself, with drawbridges at either end and fortified gates shut nightly. When Simon de Montfort, Earl of Leicester, tried in 1264 to force political reason on his brother-in-law King Henry III, he was deserted in Southwark by his fellow rebellious nobles. The people of the City of London, defying their aristocratic aldermen, broke open the gates of London Bridge and led Simon inside to safety. Simon died in battle a year later, else his head might have decorated that same gate.

In one of the gate towers at the south end of the bridge was a morbid kitchen where the heads and quarters of executed traitors were parboiled and then dipped in pitch. After this preservative treatment, the pieces were dispatched to be hung as warning on the gates of other cities of the realm, the heads usually retained in London, often fixed on the bridge gate spikes.

The first head thus affixed was that of Sir William Wallace,

Scots patriot executed in 1306. Aubrey's *Lives* tells of Sir Thomas More's head: "There goes a story in the family, viz, that one day as one of his daughters was passing the bridge, lookynge at her father's head, sayd she, that head haz layn many a time in my lapp, would to God it would fall into my lap as I pass under. She had her wish, and it did fall into her lappe and is now preserved in a vault in the Cathedral Church at Canterbury."

The bridge was also the triumphal way into the City and to the royal residence at the Tower, even after the Court had been long established at Westminster. In 1369 Richard II brought his child bride, eight-year-old Isabella of France, across the gaily decorated bridge. To welcome the return of Henry V from Agincourt there were figures of lions and antelopes and a giant effigy of St. George surrounded by angels. When Catherine of Aragon was brought to be the bride of Arthur, Prince of Wales, the bridge was bedecked for her passage. (Arthur died and she married his younger brother, Henry VIII. Their divorce signaled the end of papal power in England.)

Entry in pomp was made across the bridge not merely for the brave display, but also because going over it spared one the painful necessity of passing beneath it, a dangerous adventure.

The rip of the river through the narrow arches was made into a roaring rapids by the "starlings," the wooden platforms bowed out into the water to protect the piers. An especially hardy band of watermen, the "bridge-shooters," were authorized to take boats through the cauldron of waters. A German, Zacharias Conrad von Uffenbach, told how "we got into our boat and were rowed Londonwards with the tide; and we risked passing right through the center of the bridge, where the eddy and the waves were so violent that when we were under the arch, the water piled up on either side of us."

Into this seething flood one day in 1536, an apprentice plunged to rescue the little daughter of Sir William Hewett, a wealthy merchant. The child had fallen from a window of her father's house on the bridge. Osborne, the apprentice, was eventually rewarded with the hand of the daughter and the extremely good offices of her father. He became Lord Mayor of London, and so

Bustling, beautiful London in 1616, with Southwark Cathedral in the foreground. The fortified gate of London Bridge is decorated with the heads of 14 traitors. Forty of the City's hundred churches are visible.

well did his progeny continue the family rise that in 1694 one of them became the Duke of Leeds, of whom there have been eleven since.

The traders and stallholders on the bridge bellowed to out-shout the noise of the passing crowd and the constant roaring of the river. To this clamor was added, during the reign of Queen Elizabeth, yet another unabating racket, the sound of forciers (water mills) installed by a Dutch engineer to raise Thames water up to the City for the use of the citizens.

Although private water companies had laid conduits to bring pure water from the surrounding hills, and although there were some wells and springs in the town, most of the water for daily use came from the Thames, which got filthier year by year.

Toward the end of the eighteenth century, eighty-two million gallons of river water were being taken every day into the homes and workshops of London, although the "silver streaming Thames" had become almost black. Modernization and new con-cepts of public health and hygiene made it worse instead of bet-ter. Thirty thousand cesspools were abolished as the new main sewers were installed (1847–1853), but the sewers drained into the Thames, except at high tide, when the river backed into the sewers and prevented drainage at all. The summer of 1858 was the Year of the Great Stink.

Everyone who came anywhere near the river, or in whose di-rection the wind blew from the river, suffered a horrible odor. June was exceptionally warm with an equally exceptional low rainfall. Most of the river steamers (there was a water-bus, similar to those in Paris, Lyon and Venice) were taken out of service: their paddle wheels churning the fetid river made it impossible for passengers to stay aboard.

The windows of the Houses of Parliament were hung with sheets soaked in chloride of lime, and near the sewer outlets 250 tons of lime were dumped daily. The stench was so overpowering that at times the House was forced to adjourn for the day.

One such day they appointed a Select Committee to investigate the Great Stink and "find means for its abatement." However, the next summer was almost as bad, and it took 4281 tons of chalk lime, 478 tons of chloride of lime and 50 tons of carbolic acid plus some fortuitous rainfall to combat the odors.

At the moment of worst distress there came forward a Mr. Gurney who declared that sewer gases were to blame, and these could easily be piped away and burned off. Parliament gave him permission to pipe gas to the Clock Tower at the House, but engineers forbade the demonstration on the grounds that Mr. Gurney would simply complete the plans of Guy Fawkes and

By 1593, the City had already pushed beyond its encircling walls.

blow up Parliament. It was a perfectly feasible idea, however, and today a four-sided sewer-gas lamp burns atop a fluted silver column in Carting Lane next to the Savoy Theatre off the Strand. It is stamped "Patent Sewer Ventilating Lamp."

The stench problem was solved not too long afterwards by construction of huge mains to carry the effluvia of London far from the metropolis — and there dump it into the Thames again. Eventually, treatment plants were erected at these distant outfalls and the Thames gradually lost its offensiveness.

Until 1750 London Bridge was the only bridge across the Thames in London. The ferocious opposition of the watermen, the bargemen, the Corporation of the City of London, the Council of the Borough of Southwark and the inhabitants of the London Bridge houses beat down proposition after proposition for any new bridge. Finally, Westminster Bridge was built in 1734, Blackfriars in 1769, Battersea in 1773, and between 1816 and 1819, Vauxhall, Waterloo and Southwark. Not including the railway bridges, there are now fifteen spanning the Thames at London.

Innocent visitors have no trouble at all pointing out to one another ancient London Bridge, a majestic structure which supports its central span from two massive spired Gothickal towers 150 feet high. They point, and they are mistaken, for this is the 1894 Tower Bridge, last downstream bridge across the Thames. No one blames them for being misled. After all, it is a Victorian drawbridge with center bascules weighing one hundred tons each, raised and lowered several entertaining times a day — if that is one's notion of entertainment — for the passage of largish ships.

Between the upper stories of the towers there is a spidery footbridge flung, and the answer to the inevitable question is: "No. You are not allowed to walk across."

Further downstream one is permitted to walk or drive underneath the Thames. In addition to the train tunnels there are the Shadwell–Rotherhithe (1908), the Isle of Dogs–Greenwich Footway Tunnel (1902) and the Blackwall–Greenwich Tunnel (1897). Past Greenwich, there's another tunnel at Woolwich, and a Free Ferry, too.

The docks of London — which is still the greatest port in the world — are not the only places that ocean vessels do business. There are wharves such as those at Queenhithe, Rotherhithe, St. Saviour's, whose sites have been stations of call almost since the beginnings of commerce here.

Most of these, because the tide goes so far out when it does go out, are served by barges and lighters which have picked up their loads from ships further down the river. Still, a few lines with vessels of lighter tonnage have their ships tie up at the company wharf without benefit of locks, to sink gently upon the exposed bosom of the Thames at low tide.

It is one of the marvels of the machine age that the lighters, dropped by their towing tugs, arrive at the wharf without engines, using wind and tide and two great sweep oars. The lightermen at the sweeps employ instead of machinery the skill of centuries to make their adversaries, the currents and breezes, work on their behalf.

The set of docks closest to the heart of the city are the St. Katherine Docks (1825–1828), named after the Royal and Collegiate Chapel of St. Katherine which they displaced. Just alongside downstream are the London Docks (1805). These two are now administered as one unit by the Port of London Authority, which is in charge of virtually everything on the river. The warehouses which serve these docks house a marvelous miscellany: wool, tea, wines, rubber, hides, elephant tusks, rhinoceros horns, marble, spices, perfumes. Ostrich plumes, cigars, carpets and curios all share one building together. In the iodine warehouse dark lumps of the raw product sit in small casks, but the seeping fumes stain the walls a bright yellow. Most of these goods are in bond and there are showrooms where buyers (they will do their buying at Plantation House auctions for the most part) come to inspect samples. The wine vaults have bottling rooms. Downstream a bit and on the other side of the river (the only docks on the south bank) are the Surrey Commercial Docks in Rotherhithe (still known to old-timers as Redriff, a rougher, more seagoing name). The softwood trade dominates here, although the biggest dock of the complex, Greenland, was once the center of the whaling trade. Downriver on the Isle of Dogs are the India and Millwall (there were windmills) Docks. The West India docks are the oldest in the port (1802) and are still important for sugar. Some of the Georgian warehouses survived the blitz. Millwall is the place to unload grain. The East India Dock (1806) is at Blackwall, where the East India Company had offices and a fitting-out dock in 1614, and their nineteenth-century granite gateway remains as a souvenir of the departed private empire. Tucked away in all this welter of water and wealth is the unseen (no admission to the docks) 1951 memorial to the 105 adventurers who sailed from here in 1606 to found the first permanent British colony at Jamestown, Virginia.

Next, edging past the boundaries of London, are the Royal Docks, named Victoria, Albert and King George V (which King George V opened himself in 1921). Tobacco and frozen meat predominate. Tilbury Docks are further down East. The phrase, except among rivermen, is dying out, but until World War II, residents of the East End spoke of going "up West" to see the bright lights of Piccadilly, and anyone headed downstream was literally going down East. Perhaps the immemorial coupling of *down* with *East* among London-based mariners (including the Rotherhithe captain of the *Mayflower*) gave New England its perennial etymological problem — why Maine, the northernmost state, should be "down East."

The CITY ARMS.

THE LONDON OF
DICK WHITTINGTON

The City, its name, its Roman rise and Saxon decline — Legend of Gog and Magog — The Lord Mayor — A long circuit of the Wall and its gates with some churches along the way — Risen from the ashes — Barbican, the model plan — The Book of Martyrs and the Newgate Calendar — Temple Bar — City independence — The Tower, aspect, history, Yeomen, ravens, crown jewels and the man who stole them, notable prisoners and martyrs — Dick Whittington — How to become Lord Mayor — City government — Lord Mayor's Show — The Guilds and their Halls — Swan Upping — Free Vintners — Trial of the Pyx — Guildhall precinct — The Bank of England, fiscal, physical and spiritual — Lombard Street and its bankers — The Royal Exchange — Bedlam — Mr. Peabody of Massachusetts — Stock Exchange — Lloyd's, what it does and how — John Company — Commodity Exchanges — The Hudson's Bay Company — Tea as a commodity rather than a ritual — Tower Hill — Trinity House — Royal Mint — Glimpse of Dockland — Billingsgate — The Monument — Cityscape with Alleys — Blackfriars Bridge — The Mermaid Theater — The College of Arms, with Kings, Heralds, Pursuivants — The Temple of Mithras — Wine Houses and Chop Houses — Leadenhall Market — The Bow Bells — The Honourable Artillery Company — John Wesley's house and chapel — "Pop Goes the Weasel" — Brewery tour, how to order English beer — Grub Street — Gin — Charterhouse — St. Bartholomew's hospital and fair — Smithfield meets, meats and martyrs — Ely Place, perhaps — Hatton Garden, street of diamonds — An early movie mogul

THE City of London was founded upon the banks of the river Thames and upon the assumption that the sun would never set upon the Roman Empire.

The name was Celtic, and there is a splendid choice of boggy origins amid the mists of antiquity: *Llyn-din*, fort on the lake; *Llhwdinas*, town among the woods; *Lhongdinas*, town of ships, and even *Luan-din*, city of the moon (from Roman worship of Diana).

The Romans came in A.D. 43. They builded upon two hills (now Leadenhall and St. Paul's) with a creek running between them (Walbrook). They stayed for more than four hundred years. After the Legions were recalled to defend the beleaguered Empire, no one knows what happened to London or to the Romans' London Bridge, though it is romantically agreeable to envisage the horn-helmed hairy tribesmen wandering the deserted agora and forum, puzzling over the tiled baths, hallooing down the colonnades of empty temples. It is not so agreeable to consider the fate of those Romanized Britons who had not departed along with the troops.

After Boadicea (or Boudicca), Queen of the Iceni, successfully sacked the invaders' settlement in A.D. 62, the colonizers built bastions, then a town wall. When the next foreigners came a-conquering, they carried no torch of culture, just a torch. These were the Saxons, seeking lebensraum. They pulled down the marble halls and alongside the ruins erected their wooden huts, thus demonstrating their superiority and contempt for comfort.

The first solid date in the obscurity is 886, when Saxon King Alfred retook the site from marauding Danes and put the town back together, building a new wall on the Roman foundations.

By the time the Normans appeared, not quite two centuries later, to accept in their turn the burden of English government, Londoners had forgot the origins of their city and most of them believed the story that it had supernatural beginnings. Brute (Brutus), the son of Aeneas and Venus, had searched the world over for a land fair enough on which to lay out *Troam Novem*. This was the spot he picked after defeating the local landlords, the giants Gog and Magog. Later, King Lud repaired and improved New Troy, adding a fortified gate (still called Ludgate). Still later, King Bellinus "built a tower of prodigious height and a safe harborage for ships" (Billingsgate). General belief in this fable did not expire until the seventeenth century.

Within its walls London prospered as a trading and processing center, and within its walls it pretty well remained. The Royal City of Westminster flowered further upstream just before the Norman conquest, the old Danish siege site of Suthvirke (Southwark) across London Bridge also grew, and settlements sprang up downstream to the East, but the City of London remained aloof — and wealthy — within its walls.

When Londoners speak of "the City" they mean not the metropolis as a whole, but this ancient enclave of 677 acres. The City is the smallest local government area in England. It has its own police force (faint vestige of the Roman crest on the helmets, gold buttons) and fire brigade, distinct from those serving the rest of London.

The Lord Mayor of London is head only of this square mile (an irregular crescent rather than a square) and not at all of the

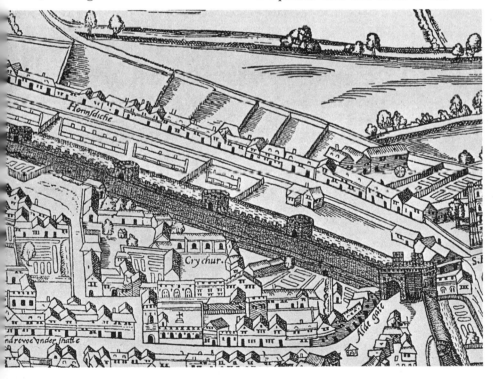

Chaucer dwelt on Aldgate two centuries before this drawing was made in 1570.

39

metropolis which surrounds it. While a million persons a day ebb and flow through the City, only 4800 really live here,* as compared with the eight million in the rest of London. Nevertheless, the rest of the world persists in regarding the chief official of this tiny municipality as — as, well — the Lord Mayor of London.

Within the confines of the City are those banks, stock and commodity exchanges, insurance and shipping companies which make it the working center of the Commonwealth and one of the great commercial centers of the world. Its borders were marked out anew in 1964 by twelve aluminum dragons mounted on six-foot-high columns. They follow, of course, the line of the old city wall.

The names of the old gateways survive: Aldgate, Aldersgate, Bishopsgate, Cripplegate, Ludgate, Moorgate, Newgate, Temple Bar, plus Dowgate and Billingsgate on the river. The actual gates have been down since the mid-eighteenth century, but their spirit persists, and there is often a sharp difference on the other side of the gate, in the pace of life and work and the appearance of the streets and buildings.

A few paces past the Aldgate Pump and one is abruptly out of the City and into the East End, where the dealing is just as sharp, but the dealers are not. On the City side of the gate, toward the west, one is aware that something is cooking; on the east side one is aware that something is frying.

The Aldgate Pump has not been there forever, but a well, reputedly with healing powers, was there in Magna Carta time, and a pump in the 1590's. When the street was widened in 1866, the pump's location was altered by a few feet, but official proposals for its removal were met with hostility by the natives. Ten years later tests showed the well to be hopelessly polluted, and the sage city fathers filled it in almost by stealth and hooked the old pump to the urban water supply. It is still there, with its bronze dog's head for a spout, though the handle is permanently hooked and rusted fast.

For years it was a City witticism to call a worthless check "a draught on the Aldgate Pump." Geoffrey Chaucer, many of

* With completion of the Barbican project, the City population will jump 200 per cent.

whose jokes are still funny, lived in the house atop Aldgate from 1374 to 1385. Last rebuilt in 1609, it was torn down in 1761.

In Aldgate High Street there is a pub, Ye Hoop & Grapes, which claims to date from before the Great Fire of 1666 and to be the oldest licensed premises in London. Lounging back from plumb, the place looks too good to be true or vice versa: the building is an authentically listed Ancient Monument, and the claims to both truth and goodness are amply sustainable.

Aldgate High Street is met by Middlesex Street, which slants hastily back toward Bishopsgate. On this street, the East End and the City oddly commingle. While the City sleeps on Sunday morning, Middlesex Street reverts to its original name, Petticoat Lane, site of the best-known street market in town. The only top hats to be seen here are for sale on some pushcart. The vendors are reputed to be wondrous spielers and terribly funny. If nothing else, they do give a sterling demonstration of the London equivalent of the Bronx accent, discernibly different from other area speech in the metropolis. The humanity compacted between the walls of the warehouses and wrapped in sounds of the current cheapest music (there are radio and phonograph record

ALDGATE.

stalls) is of the wildest assortment and the greatest density. So is the merchandise. Ideal shopping place for those who seriously believe something can be both the Cheapest and the Finest.

The City is planning redevelopment of its side of Middlesex Street, and the Petticoat Lane of today is bound to undergo some alteration, in surroundings if nothing else. At the end of the street is Bishopsgate, which was probably one of the four Roman gates of London. The bishop who stamped his episcopal seal on this pagan portal could be any of half a dozen historically worthy divines. The gate stood at the corner of Wormwood Street until 1760.

Moorgate, next along the circuit of the wall, was originally a postern through which City men could slip to reach the moor outside. Today's Moor Lane and the street named Moorfields recall the fens drained in the sixteenth century. Finsbury Avenue, Circus Market, Pavement, Square and Street are supposed to recall the same fen, unless they recall two sisters named Finn or Fins who deeded their property here as a public recreation ground.

The Romans made these fields a swamp by damming the waters

BISHOPS—GATE.

MOORE— -GATE.

of the Walbrook, across whose bed they built their wall. The youths of Norman London ice-skated here with bone runners tied to their feet. After the moor was drained and filled four hundred years later, it was an archery ground, and after it was further filled and leveled in 1606, trees and shrubs and benches were planted and it became the first public park in London.

At the site of what is now 85 Moorgate, John Keats was born in 1795 at the livery stables where his father was a stableman. ("Love in a hut, with water and a crust,/ Is — Love forgive us! — cinders, ashes, dust.") Keats arrived too late to see the gate at Moorgate. That foster child of silence and slow time had gone thirteen years before, its stones used to fill the widened central arch of London Bridge. The larger Cripplegate had gone too from nearby Fore Street, though the adjacent church of St. Giles Cripplegate still stood, still stands. The name came from the Anglo-Saxon "creple" and meant "covered way." St. Giles, a mid-sixteenth-century church gutted in the Second World War and now restored, has nearby a stretch of the old City Wall and the remains of an ancient bastion, probably built by the Romans, rebuilt by the Saxons, and rebuilt once more after that.

CRIPPLE–GATE.

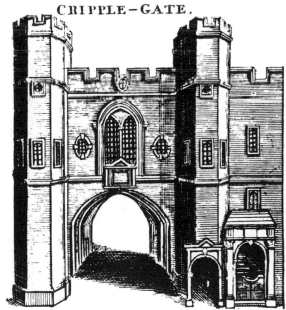

A few yards north, in the direction of the Thames, behind St. Giles, runs a street called London Wall, from almost at Bishopsgate, past Moorgate, to Aldersgate Street. It ran just inside the old City wall and is now known over much of its length as, alas, Route 11. Or worse, Route XI. Appropriately, a section of surviving medieval and later wall was destroyed to make London Wall into Route 11. However, the length of the street is still bordered by sizable sections of the wall. The buildings along the route west of Moorgate are all new, since this area was utterly devastated by bombs. Most of the buildings are in the anonymous slab style which excuses itself under the appellation "International," except for Girdlers' Hall and Brewers' Hall. Around the shattered remains of St. Alphage's Church are splendid bits of the old wall exposed to view. The last of the new buildings in this group is to be the home of the London Museum, now housed at Kensington Palace.

St. Giles Cripplegate survived the Great Fire but not the blitz, stands
restored at the edge of Barbican.

This range of buildings, connected by raised pedestrian walks, forms a whole punctuated by six office towers and makes up the southern part of the grand Barbican plan. A vast area ripped and churned by German National Socialist ambitions, it lay fallow from 1940 to 1958. Meanwhile the whole scorched area was acquired through compulsory purchase by the City of London and the London County Council, and a joint scheme worked out for some genuine coherent city planning. There evolved a complete neighborhood, with shops, schools, recreation facilities, offices, and — a revolutionary step for this period in the City's history — homes for real live people.

The name comes from a vanished street which passed beneath the barbican, or outer defense tower. Some members of the Corporation Council still manned that ghostly tower as the ninety-million-dollar project progressed, one of them, Alderman de Coucey Howard, calling it "thirty-three acres of cockeyed socialism." When in 1965 and 1966, the City and the Greater London Council were joined by Parliament in approving — They pay one-third each — a 3.5-million-dollar two-thousand-seat concert hall for the London Symphony, a 2.8-million-dollar, fifteen-hundred-seat theater for the Royal Shakespeare Company and a 5.6-million-dollar London Museum to house the collections currently at the Royal Exchange and Kensington Palace, there were about a dozen who voted No. Alderman Howard called the theater "a disaster," arguing that "Business is our business, not entertainment." Confronted with the concert hall, he altered his statement to: "It is the City's job to look after the citizens and the taxpayers and not to provide shelter for homeless orchestras."

By the early 1970's, the planners say, all the phases of Barbican building will be completed and the revivification of the City well begun. It will be the showpiece of post-bombing reconstruction (a generation after the bombardment) in all England, and perhaps as Alderman Gilbert Inglefield said, "without parallel in any other city in Europe or America."

On this northwestern border of this new neighborhood is the site of Aldersgate. Of Anglo-Saxon origin, it bore the Anglo-Saxon name Ealdred's Gate. By the twelfth century, this had been slurred to Aldredsgate, by the thirteenth, Aldrichesgate, and a century later, the name which still clings to the area, although the gate disappeared in 1761.

This gate too has its joke, from John Day, the sixteenth-century printer who lived over the arch. He roused his apprentices with the cry, "Arise, for it is Day!" The apprentices rose at one period to work at printing a book written by a house guest and presumed silent partner in the firm, John Foxe. His *Book of Martyrs*, published in 1563 as *The Actes and Monuments of These Latter and Perilous Dayes*, recounted — not with consummate accuracy — the persecution of Protestants up to the end of Mary Tudor's reign in 1533. Illustrated with sensational woodcuts of tortures and ingenious executions, it was a best-seller for almost two hundred years, and did much to keep alive anti-Catholicism in England.

Equally sensational and ostensibly as moral was *The Newgate Calendar or Malefactor's Bloody Register*, "containing Genuine and Circumstantial Narrative of the lives and transactions, various exploits and Dying Speeches of the Most Notorious Criminals of both sexes . . . ," which appeared in 1771. The cham-

bers atop the gate were a prison from the twelfth century on, and even after the gate was demolished in 1777, the adjoining prison extensions went on infamously until 1902. The Central Criminal Court — Old Bailey — now stands on the spot.

South along the sloping street called the Old Bailey to the street called Ludgate Hill, up Ludgate Hill toward St. Paul's Cathedral, one finds the medieval church of St. Martin Ludgate, rebuilt 1677–1687 by Sir Christopher Wren. Next to the church until 1760, stood Ludgate, another of London's Roman gateways. During repairs in 1210, statues of King Lud and his sons were added, and when the gate was entirely rebuilt four hundred years later, King Lud and sons were carved anew on one side, Queen Elizabeth on the other. When the gate was taken down (it had been a debtor's prison too, for three hundred and fifty years), the monarchs found employment on the façade of St. Dunstan-in-the-West, down Ludgate Hill at the far end of Fleet Street, next to Chancery Lane.

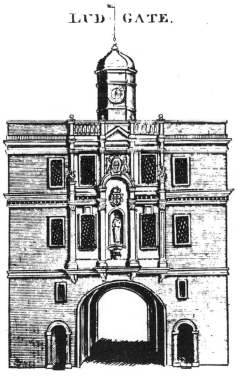

Just about at Chancery Lane stood the most westward of the City barriers, Temple Bar. Though the Bar is gone, the Temple is still there. It was built as the headquarters of the Knights Templars, whose order was dissolved in 1313.

The original gateway, first mentioned in records of 1293, was thrown down in 1381 by Wat Tyler's rebels. The last one was confected by Wren in 1672, and its stones were collected from a storage yard by Sir Henry Bruce Meux in 1878. They were re-erected at his estate at Theobalds Park, Hertfordshire — "at great expense to himself," his son reminded City authorities in 1921 when they asked for it back. It is still out to pasture.

Rather than a prison for debtors, the Temple Bar was a strong-room for creditors, rented by the City for £25 a year to the Child family, bankers.

Child's may possibly be the oldest bank in England. The goldsmith-founder began a sideline in money dealing in 1559, the second year of Queen Elizabeth's reign. Sir Francis Child, Lord Mayor of London in 1698, abandoned goldsmithing to concentrate on banking and is considered "the father of the profession." Customers included Oliver Cromwell, the Duke and Duchess of Marlborough, Nell Gwyn, Samuel Pepys, John Dryden and their Majesties William and Mary. Now part of the Glyn Mills banking corporation, Child's still clinks coins on Fleet Street.

Through all the reigns and all the permutations of political development, some of them highly hazardous, the City enjoyed a remarkable independence. There were several reasons for this and the greatest of these was money. The monarch always needed money, for wars, for building, for the upkeep of Court. He could get it through inordinate fines, by deposing a favorite and confiscating his possessions, by wracking his barons who in turn wracked their underlings, by holding enemies for ransom and foreign cities to tribute, by pawning valuables, by selling titles and charters. Henry III (1216–1272) obtained needed cash by pawning all the Jews in the kingdom to one of his earls.

Money could also be had by wheedling it out of the City. The center of British trade, of highly skilled craftsmanship, of international seaborne trade, the City always had money. But the men who earned it were of necessity no fools and could not be dealt with as fools.

Nor were they defenseless. The City had a volunteer army, not very bellicose perhaps, but numerous and well-armed. The very walls allowed Londoners to refuse embroilment in armed conflicts that often surged about them. Rulers or would-be rulers needed the goodwill of this mart, this treasure house, this armed bastion.

There was another thing that aided London to harden its privileges into rights and sustain the claim that the rights were irrevocable. This was the fact that the Court did not lodge in London. The ancient royal capital was Winchester until Edward the Confessor (1042–1066) moved it "by pious whim" to Westminster, a mile upstream from London, so that he could supervise the construction of the Abbey. Thus London did not become a royal city subject to the immediate control of the king and all the king's men.

The ancient independence is still ritually celebrated at Temple Bar. At this invisible barrier the reigning monarch halts to ask permission of the Lord Mayor to enter the City. The Lord Mayor demonstrates his loyalty by offering his Sword of State, which is immediately returned by the sovereign and then carried before the procession to show that the crowned head is in the City under the Lord Mayor's protection.

This grave mummery was once a real and significant action

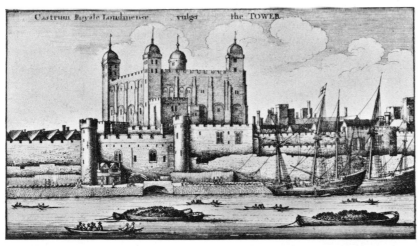

The Tower — royal might at the sill of the City's prerogatives.

which showed the City of London to be almost an autonomous republic within the king's realm.

When William the Conqueror appeared, he terrified London without directly threatening it. His troops made a wide arc of slaughter and arson through the countryside, finishing at the far end of London Bridge at Southwark, which they burned. The Londoners came out in support of the new king and in turn he gave them his: ". . . I will that ye be all law-worthy that were in King Edward's day. And I will that every child be his father's heir after his father's day; and I will not endure that any man offer any wrong to you. God keep you."

And then, for the "protection" of the City, he built the Tower of London. Glowering upon the town, it was an unremitting reminder of royal power. It rose just inside the easternmost corner of the City Wall, almost touching the Thames. The remains of a Roman bastion abut William's White Tower, which gives com-

The Tower in 1616: the wharf is now a bathing beach for local children.

fort to those who, like Shakespeare and Thomas Gray, enjoy believing that Julius Caesar put up the tower as he passed through in 55 B.C.

By today's geography, the Tower is not within the City bounds at all, but stands stolidly in the Borough of Stepney (now the super-borough of Tower Hamlets). Around William's White Tower (white stone brought from Caen in Normandy, and whitewashed besides) subsequent rulers built other towers, tracing in stone the evolution of the theory of fortification from Norman through Tudor times. The building of William's central Keep was continued by William II and Henry I, and completed about 1100. Succeeding rulers built a massive surrounding wall studded with towers, and their successors built yet another to enclose the first, stiffened it with bastions and protected it by a moat. From the original keep, one hundred feet square, the Tower of London grew to be a redoubt of more than eighteen acres. The basic fabric was finished by the time Henry VIII died, almost four hundred years after the battle of Hastings.

The White Tower still dominates the enclave. It is a square stone structure, ninety feet high, buttressed and battlemented. Three of its corner towers are square, one is round, and all wear metal bonnets topped with pennant-shaped and orange-painted weather vanes. From the middle of the roof sprouts a ponderous flagstaff (a 185-foot Douglas fir presented by British Columbia Boy Scouts and whittled down to 85 feet) from which flies a Union Jack of matching proportions.

So familiar is the silhouette, so hoary yet so hale, that it is at once endearing. It has that remarkable quality of being the real thing. The walls of the Keep are fifteen feet thick at the base, eleven feet thick at the top: only one of the four corners is a right angle, which means that the sides of the "square" are of differing lengths. This geometry attests to the authenticity, and gives the prospect the charming crudeness of early tapestries and illuminations. It evokes both the Lion and the Unicorn.

Along the riverside in front of the weighty walls is a shaded walk with antique cannon and benches and, for the wiry, self-immunized local young, a bathing beach.

As one descends Tower Hill past the quite contemporary ticket window and the cafeteria with the stone-age food, there is a shakoed sentry before his sentry box. Beyond him is the ticket taker, a member of the Yeoman Warders,* garbed in Tudor rig. The guardians are genuine military personnel in issue uniform: nothing has been got up for the occasion.

The way leads through the Middle Tower and across a bridge over the dry moat (drained in 1843). The moat is now a grassy depression about 125 feet wide in which off-duty soldiers practice soccer and in which the City of London Festival during the summer stages Gilbert and Sullivan's *Yeomen of the Guard* † on a special trestle.

It is possible to engage a not otherwise engaged Yeoman Warder to act as guide across the greenswards and among the towers of the inner and outer walls. There are sights to see other than historic stone and turf, for example the several museums of arms and armor. Nowhere else in England will you see — but since this is England, a bland land of mysteries and secrets,‡ it is wiser to say that probably nowhere else in England are you likely to see — a suit of armor for an elephant.

And there are the ravens, of which the Ministry of Public Buildings and Works official guidebook says, "The birds are not popular with everyone, they are often noisy, and will amuse themselves by removing putty from windows, causing damage to unattended cars, and by taking sly pecks at ladies' legs!"

With a daily thirty-cent ration of horsemeat and under the special care of the Warder Quartermaster, they live long. James Crow, one of the six always kept "on establishment," was on duty at the Tower for forty-four years. The ravens' main duty is to keep the Tower from falling; the ancient belief is that it will fall if the ravens depart. Clipped wings aid in minimizing the recruiting problem.

---

* There are forty Yeoman Warders, all retired career Army noncoms. They are not the Beefeaters, Yeomen of the Guard at St. James's Palace. The Warders of the Tower, jealous of the special uniforms and privileges of Henry VIII's bodyguard, got identical dress, minus the crossbelts, upon the intercession of a discharged Tower prisoner, the Duke of Somerset.

† Even a British knight can confuse the two bodies of Yeomen.

‡ Late in 1964, a *Sunday Times* reporter wrote, "In the service of this publication I have investigated such organizations as the Mafia and the Japanese Communist Party. Both were open and candid compared to the Royal Entomological Society of London."

The ravens, having been the protected scavengers of the City over many centuries, have probably always been at the Tower, and until 1834 there were other animals, too, inmates of the Royal Menagerie. The collection was begun in 1235 with a gift of three leopards of heraldic implication from Frederick II to England's Henry III. Henry also received a polar bear, from Norway, who was encouraged to fish for his own dinner in the Thames. From Louis of France came an elephant.

Another Tower attraction (extra charge, one shilling) is the shimmering mound of treasure known as the Crown Jewels. The Tower of London has been the depository for the regal bangles ever since completion of this royal stronghold.

In a huge, high glass case the regalia rises tier upon tier, glittering and dazzling. The sight could evoke greed in the most modest of sightseers and respect in the most republican. These are the trappings of wealth and power and a word which is beyond both — majesty.

There are four crowns, six scepters, two orbs, a profusion of royal plate, five maces, three jeweled Swords of State, the golden Spurs of St. George, and such curiosities as precious arm bracelets. Most of it dates from the seventeenth century, because during the six-year experiment in non-royal dictatorship by Oliver Cromwell, the six centuries' accumulation of regalia was sold or melted down. At the restoration of the monarchy in 1660, some few pieces were retrieved and new talismans of kingship contrived in imitation of the old.

Thus, the Spoon with which the monarch is anointed at his coronation and the eagle-shaped Ampulla containing the oil are the only two authentically ancient pieces in the group. And even those were restored for Charles II, as was in fact the monarchy itself.

The Imperial State Crown, made for Victoria in 1838, holds the oldest of the pedigreed jewels, plus three thousand other gems, mostly pearls and diamonds, including the second largest of the "Stars of Africa" cut from the Cullinan stone (the largest, the biggest cut diamond in the world — 530 carats — decorates the Royal Scepter). In the center glows the enormous uncut ruby given by Pedro the Cruel to England's Black Prince in 1367 as a thank-you gift after the battle of Najera, which restored Pedro to the throne of Aragon. Pedro also gave his daughter — gave her in marriage — to Edward III's other son, John of Gaunt.

The ruby is not all that Edward Prince of Wales (the French called him the Black Prince from his armor) brought to the Tower. In 1356 at the battle of Poitiers he captured King John II of France. When they pranced over London Bridge, the regally accoutered, charger-mounted King of France came first, and slightly behind was the Prince, plainly dressed, on a small black pony. This was to avoid humiliating the captive King* and to avoid any unchivalric appearance of gloating.

Many of the respectable millions who have viewed the Crown Jewels have mused lightly on the notion of theft. Many thieves have mused thereon as well. One man, Colonel Thomas Blood, did steal the Crown Jewels — in broad daylight, May 9, 1671. He succeeded in stealing the crown, but .was caught when his horse fell during the getaway. Both Blood and the loot were returned forthwith to the Tower where Keeper of the Jewels Talbot Edwards lay near to death.†

Blood's life story was a succession of similar near-successes. Rewarded by Cromwell with Irish estates for his Civil War actions, he lost his lands at the Restoration. To get them back he prepared nothing less than a Puritan counterrevolution in Ireland, mounting a skillful plot to seize Dublin and the British Viceroy. Its daring was almost a guarantee of success, but informers gave the game away before the starting signal and Blood fled.

His next try for high estate was again through conspiracy. He fell in with the Fifth Monarchy group in London. They aspired to rule England with a "republican theocracy," but their plot failed and again Blood trickled away. He then joined the Covenanters in Scotland, just in time to join them in defeat at the battle of Pentland. Chased into England, Blood not only eluded

---

* John was kept prisoner in the Tower until ransom was paid and hostages surrendered four years later. Four years after that, one of the hostages escaped, and John, to keep bright his royal *parole d'honneur*, returned to England, where he died.

† Blood's daggers, which he did not use, can be seen in the Record Room of the White Tower. The sword-stick with which he skewered Keeper Edwards is not on display, but sword sticks are still made and can be had of James Smith & Sons, 53 New Oxford Street.

his pursuers, but on the way liberated a comrade-in-arms. For this deed a price of five hundred pounds was put on his head.

Still wearing his price tag, he appeared in St. James's Street and dragged the Duke of Ormonde from his coach. With his small band of henchmen, Blood proposed to haul the Duke to the gibbet at Tyburn and hang him. Blood had not forgiven his Grace for having been Viceroy of Ireland when the Colonel's plot had failed three years earlier. The hanging party was ignominiously put to flight by the Duke's servants.

Less than a year later, Colonel Blood, disguised as a clergyman, made friends with Mr. Edwards, Keeper of the Jewels. He presently made arrangements for a wife-seeking nephew to call upon the marriageable Miss Edwards at the Keeper's quarters in Martin Tower. While waiting for the nephew to arrive on the appointed day, the clergyman suggested whiling away the wait by looking at the Crown, the Scepter and the Orb.

Once the Keeper had the chest open, the visitors struck him with mallets and Blood ran him through with his sword. The Scepter was too long to conceal, so the thieves began to file it in two. Then Blood's curse began to uncoil. His lookout was stupid enough to stop and question Edwards's son, a soldier unexpectedly home on leave. The son ran to Martin Tower to ask what was going on, and the alarm was raised. Blood popped the Crown under his cloak, one of his men stuffed the Orb into his wide breeches, and letting the Scepter clang to the bloody floor, they ran.

They got past all the guards and gates, but on Tower Hill the Orb-stealer lost his nerve and bowled the golden ball among the passersby. Blood leapt to his horse and galloped away, but not very far. Taken, he refused to say a word except to King Charles himself. Incredibly enough, the request reached the King, and even more incredibly, the King granted audience.

What happened next was absolutely beyond belief: the notorious rebel plotter, attempted assassin, fugitive with a price on his head, and most lately stealer of the Crown itself was pardoned. Not only that, but he was given back his lost estates in Ireland.

A short time later Blood was dining with the Treasurer, several French nobles including the Duc de Gramont, and diarist John Evelyn, who noted that this "impudent bold fellow" was both "very well spoken and dangerously insinuating."

His life continued in such admirable company until he was jailed briefly nine years later for conspiring against his dear friend, the Duke of Buckingham. Released, Colonel Blood went home and died in bed.

Of all the reasons advanced for his repeated ill-fortune as a marplot and his repeated good fortune in being the only man to escape, only one is reasonable: he was a spy and agent provocateur for Charles II. The theft of the Jewels? Either Charles needed money and was unwilling to do as other monarchs did and pawn them or sell off a few gems, or else Charles wanted them stolen and planted to incriminate someone else. Had Blood's escapade been a bit of private enterprise, it is not likely that Charles would have granted the remarkable interview and less likely that Blood would have left the Tower alive.

Failing to leave the Tower of London alive has been the final failure — or success — of so very many persons over the centuries. Thomas Gray called it "London's lasting shame, With many a foul and midnight murder fed."

To be sure, there have been happy times at the Tower: every monarch to James I used the Tower as a royal residence, except Elizabeth I, who was an imprisoned princess here where her mother, Anne Boleyn, was beheaded. Welcomed here by the *Water Music*, George I appointed Handel Master of the King's Musick. The War of the Roses was ended when Henry VII married Elizabeth of York here.

But in the very tower, the very room where cheerful trippers gaze at the Crown Jewels, Henry VI was murdered while at prayer. The chapel of St. Peter ad Vincula, one of the two churches in the Tower,* has a graveyard described by Macaulay as a place where death is associated with "whatever is darkest in human nature . . . with the savage triumph of implacable enemies, with the inconstancy, the ingratitude, the cowardice of

---

* The Chapel of St. John is in the southeast corner of the second and third floors of the White Tower. Built in about 1080, it is in perfect condition, a rare example of Early Norman architecture in England. It is bare of ornamentation, the stone alone breathing power, surety and mystery.

friends, with all the miseries of fallen greatness and of blighted fame . . . men who had been captains of armies, the oracles of senates, and the ornaments of courts."

Summertime, with the majestic trees in leaf and the massed tourists in bloom, is not the time to visit the Tower. To seize the terrible meaning of this place come not in the season of flowered dresses and nurtured grass and the packaged excursion.

Come instead when the winter mists wreath the gray walls and footfalls echo from the stone and the chill in the air might be the breath of specters. While it has been fashioned into a monument of much else, the Tower of London is also a monument to power and to the lust and inhumanity it can engender.

Since the eleventh century the Tower has been a fortress, with garrison and armory. It is commanded by the Constable, seconded by the Lieutenant, though neither of these has quartered here for centuries. The Constable is always an officer of high rank. St. Thomas à Becket, the Duke of Wellington, Field Marshal Alexander of Tunis have been among those who have held the title of Constable of the Royal Palace and Fortress of London.

Until modern times, they have always had prisoners in their keeping. The White Tower was the principal place of imprisonment until the fifteenth century, when prisoners were dispersed among the buildings of the inmost ward and the thirteen towers of the inner wall. Beauchamp Tower, the Salt Tower, Wakefield Tower, the Bell Tower, the Bloody Tower. ("Oh, Beefeater, which is called the Bloody Tower?" "All of it, madam, all of it.")

The first prisoner was Ralf Flambard, Bishop of Durham. He was also the first man to escape, one of the very few who ever did so. In 1101 he went out a window gripping his crozier, which he managed to retain along with his liberty. Another celebrated escape was engineered by the prisoner's wife. Lord Nithsdale, captured at the collapse of the 1715 Stuart rebellion, was paraded through the streets of London to the Tower with six other Scottish nobles. His young wife made her way from Scotland across treacherous winter roads and rivers to be with her husband. In London, her pleas for his life failed, and the eve of the beheading arrived.

During the final hours Lord and Lady Nithsdale received visits from ladies come to bid a tearful adieu. One of the weepers who departed, face muffled in kerchief, was Lord Nithsdale in wig and clothing left by the visitors. His wife stayed behind to cover the escape, carrying on a conversation by imitating her husband's voice. He lived out his life in freedom in Rome.

The last person to be decapitated at the Tower — indeed the last person to be beheaded anywhere in England — was also a Scot, one of the very many who perished here for their Scottish patriotism. As he emerged from Westminster Hall at the end of his trial before his fellow Lords, a woman from the crowd stuck her face through the carriage window and jeered, "You'll get that nasty head of yours chopped off, you ugly Scotch dog!" He replied, "I believe I shall, you ugly old English bitch." The year was 1747 and he was Simon Fraser, Lord Lovat, convicted of participation in "the '45," the uprising of Bonny Prince Charlie.

Among the Scots who languished here were Sir William Wallace (beheaded, drawn and quartered in 1305), David II of Scotland (imprisoned 1346–1357), James I of Scotland (1406–1407), and nobles captured in the long series of risings against the occupiers. Contention among Stuarts for the Crown of England led to more imprisonments and deaths. Contention among the English for the same crown led to more of the same.

Henry VI, a prisoner, was murdered here. Richard II, a prisoner, surrendered his crown to Bolingbroke here. The "Little Princes," Edward V (thirteen years old) and his brother the Duke of York (eight) are generally supposed to have been smothered to death in the Bloody Tower in 1483 by order of their uncle, Richard III. Children's bones found centuries later concealed under a stairway in the tower were interred by Charles II at Westminster Abbey.

Anne Boleyn was spared the axe to die by the sword, wielded by an executioner brought from France. Shoeless, he stepped behind her while his assistant distracted her attention, plucked his hidden sword from the straw strewing the scaffold, and whisked off her head. Henry VIII's fifth wife, Catherine Howard, was also beheaded here.

Lady Jane Grey, for nine days Queen of England on a thin but acceptable claim, died here on the same day as her husband and her scheming father, the Duke of Suffolk.

The Tower has also a long roster of religious martyrs of many faiths, most of them executed, many for political rather than theological transgressions. Quaker William Penn was released after a year's imprisonment (1668–1669), as was Samuel Pepys, who was exonerated of ridiculous charges of complicity in the Titus Oates plot. Guy Fawkes and his fellow Catholic conspirators (1605–1606) and the Knights Templars (1334–1335) were tortured and executed.

When the Lombard moneylenders who came to England in the wake of the conquering Normans were well established, Edward I saw no further use for Jews in England. He began systematic fines, taxes and confiscations and sundry persecutions. In 1278 he crammed six hundred of them (probably the whole adult male Jewish population) into the dungeons of the White Tower on charges of clipping and defacing the King's coin: two hundred of them "died where they were." In 1290, having wrung them dry, he banished them from England, and none returned until Cromwell's time, four hundred fifty years later.

Throughout the centuries, out-of-favor royal favorites languished here, some for disagreeing with the monarch, some for being bores, some for outliving their patrons, some for being dangerously rich or popular. Henry VIII's Earl of Essex (beheaded 1540) and Sir Thomas More (beheaded 1535), Elizabeth's Earl of Essex (beheaded 1601) and Sir Walter Ralegh (beheaded by Elizabeth's successor) are among the more famous.

Sir Thomas More mounted the rickety ladder to the scaffold and to sainthood. Said he to the Lieutenant of the Tower, "I pray you, Master Lieutenant, see me safe up; and for my coming down, let me shift for myself." Sir Walter Ralegh did three terms in the Tower, 1592, 1603–1616 and in 1618 before his execution. During the thirteen-year incarceration he wrote his *History of the World*. Released by James I for a new expedition to the West Indies, Ralegh was imprisoned anew on his return from a failure (King James had warned the Spaniards about Ralegh's intended incursions that he, the King, helped plan).

When he was executed a month later, he asked to see the axe, felt its edge and said to the attending officer, "This is sharp medicine, but 'tis a physician for all diseases."

The block and the axe are on view in the White Tower together with an assortment of torture implements.

During World War I prisoners were again lodged in the Tower, including Sir Roger Casement, who had been landed in Ireland from a German submarine. On the miniature rifle range near Martin Tower eleven spies were shot.

During the Second World War, Deputy Führer Rudolf Hess was held here for four days before being moved to other quarters; other enemy prisoners stayed longer — except for one spy who was turned over to the firing squad.

Traitor's Gate, under St. Thomas's Tower, is no longer used. It was the water gate for the entry of prisoners brought downriver from Westminster in Tudor times. The gates of the Tower are still locked at night, exactly at 10 P.M., with unvarying ceremony.

> Five minutes before the hour the Chief Yeoman Warder joins an escort consisting of a sergeant and three men who are detailed to help him close the three gates. When the keys return, the sentry calls a challenge: "Halt, who comes there?" The Chief Warder replies: "The keys." The exchange continues with "Whose keys?" — "Queen Elizabeth's keys." Then the guard present arms: the Chief Warder, doffing his Tudor bonnet, calls: "God preserve Queen Elizabeth"; and the whole guard respond: "Amen." The keys are finally carried by the Chief Warder to the Queen's House where they are secured for the night.

Once the Tower is secured for the night, admission is by password only. The Constable transmits the list of future passwords (changed daily) to two persons only: the Monarch and the Lord Mayor of London.

The most renowned Lord Mayor was Richard Whittington, whose story passed rightly — and incorrectly — into legend. The story has poor ragged Dick walking barefoot to London with his cat, only to find the City hostile and frightening. Despairing of finding his way into the closed circle — apprenticeships were inherited or purchased — he headed away from town. On the heights of Highgate he sat down to rest and heard the Bow Bells pealing, "Turn again, Whittington, thrice Lord Mayor of London." So he turned again, and when his cat destroyed the rats in the house of a merchant, Dick was taken in to learn the trade, rose to fortune and the Lord Mayor's chain of office.

Richard Whittington did indeed come from the country to London to seek his fortune. He was the third son of Gloucestershire country gentleman, Sir William Whittington, and with two brothers ahead of him, no hope of inheritance. The boy was apprenticed to a member of the Mercers' Guild. The landed gentry of the fourteenth century was not snobbish about "persons in trade," for they appreciated the luxury in which London merchants lived, the dowries that went with their daughters, the expectations that went with their sons, and the fortunes left to their widows.

Whittington's cat was a kind of boat used to haul coal up the Thames and the Fleet to Sea Coal Lane (still there, just by Ludgate Circus). Some of Dick's large fortune came out of the cats.

He was indeed Lord Mayor of London, not thrice but four times. He finished out the term of a Lord Mayor who died soon after taking office in 1396 and then was elected to serve (1397–1398) and reelected 1406–1407 and 1419–1420.

He added to his fortune by lending money to Henry IV and Henry V. The latter's wars in France kept open Continental markets for British wool, so that the war loans were profitable in two ways.

Whittington was lavish in his charities, which included building a College of Priests on what became College Hill, an almshouse (which his guild, the Mercers' Company, moved to Highgate near the spot now marked by a statue of waif Whittington — with cat), and the land for a new Church of St. Michael Paternoster Royal and cemetery, in which he was buried in 1423. By the terms of his will, Newgate was rebuilt. His charities, including a foundation for the purchase of apprenticeships for poor lads, continue functioning.

To become Lord Mayor today, the aspirant must pass through the same stages as Whittington before emerging in the full robes of office. Basic requisite is to belong to the species — he must be a liveryman of a City Company. The Companies descend from the ancient guilds, at first mutual societies for paying blood money ("gild" is Saxon for "money") and usually attached to a parish church. Later, the Company became a grouping of men in the same trade, gradually developing into a combination craft trade union and manufacturers' society, maintaining standards and prices and controlling the number of practitioners. They were granted the right to wear distinctive livery just about the time young Whittington came to town.

Today membership in one of the eighty-four Companies can be inherited, purchased or earned through "apprenticeship" to a member. As a liveryman, the political hopeful should probably contrive to be elected from one of the City's twenty-six wards to membership in the lower house of the municipal legislature, the Common Council.

Becoming a Common Councilman is not essential to further

These streets of Shakespeare's day still run by St. Paul's, their shops entirely rebuilt after the blitz.

progress, but becoming an Alderman is an absolute necessity. Elected from the wards for life, the Court of Aldermen is the upper house of the City with several judicial and executive functions, such as administration of Freemanship of the City, livery company membership and ward elections; each alderman is automatically a justice of the peace since the Court is also a court of justice.

It also holds the power of veto over newly elected Aldermen, who are, after all, possible future Lord Mayors. They want to know not only that he is a pleasant fellow of good repute, but also that he is or will be very rich. He must be financially and professionally so situated that he will be free to spend a great deal of time performing the unpaid aldermanic duties.

Next, the aspirant must become one of the City's two Sheriffs, one an alderman, the other not. At the end of his year's term, the Alderman-Sheriff will be qualified to be elected Lord Mayor someday.

The Sheriff's post is good apprenticeship for the Lord Mayoralty: the Sheriff pays a share — out of his own pocket — of the City's official entertainment expenses, attends meetings of both Common Council and Court of Alderman and serves as Execution Officer of Old Bailey.

There is no unseemly contest for the mayoralty: the succession is pretty well arranged among the livery companies and those members qualified for the post. However, on Michaelmas Day, September 29, the motions of election are performed. Here we see an early democracy which has evolved into a functioning plutocracy for disinterested democratic ends.

The man who is mayor has an exhilarating, exhausting and financially depleting year ahead of him. His official salary is £15,000 ($42,000) and to meet expenses he must pay something around $60,000 more — of his own money, of course. In addition (or subtraction) he loses a year away from his habitual business desk.

The Lord Mayor leaves home and for a year resides in the Mansion House, a quite magnificent residence which is also his office. Since he is Chief Magistrate of the City, it contains a courtroom (sessions twice weekly) under which are cells, giving this eighteenth-century classical building the distinction of being the only residence in London with its own jail.

During his year in office the incumbent, with his splendid Elizabethan gold collar and his four fine Swords of State, makes about 1200 speeches during his visits to the twenty-six wards, eighty-four livery companies, the schools and at the State banquets to which the Monarch and Ministers are invited. He is honorary head of the City's Army and RAF units, descendants of the community's volunteer trainbands. Although he may be a Catholic (as were Whittington and his predecessors) or a Jew (first Jewish Lord Mayor, Sir David Salomons, 1855–1856), he is trustee of the Established Anglican Church's Cathedral of St. Paul.

There is a very good likelihood that he will travel abroad on visits of civic goodwill, and there is no doubt that the Foreign Office will ask him to entertain distinguished foreign visitors. He has a seat on the Monarch's Privy Council as well. Within the City he is a sort of monarch himself, and inside its limits only the crowned head takes precedence over him. If he is not al-

The Lord Mayor's Coach rolls before the Lord Mayor's residence,
the Mansion House, in the 1750's.

ready a baronet, he will most likely be made one at the end of his term.

The Lord Mayor is installed at Guildhall, the Hall of the Corporation of the City of London. Installation takes place on the Friday preceding the second Saturday of November, and on the following day he rides in his splendiferous State Coach from the Mansion House to the Law Courts just past Temple Bar where he is received by Britain's Lord Chief Justice. Lord Mayors have been going toward Westminster to pledge loyalty to the sovereign since Whittington's time. Until 1838 this progress was a superb waterborne spectacle with all the barges of the City companies in attendance, decked with rich fancy. "Shrouds and ratlines being hung with a number of small Bells, producing a Pleasant Noise," and also "divers beautiful Virgins, singing and playing melodiously" among an "agreeable variety of Streamers and Flags."

Today the Lord Mayor's Show (that is what it is called) has marching brass bands and liveried City officers in their coaches and a profusion of floats increasingly sponsored by some trade organization such as the Wool Secretariat or by companies with which the new incumbent is associated.

There is little if any disapprobation for this sort of live singing commercial amid an ancient ceremonial drive, for the City is commerce and commerce is the City. It was the resolution of the guilds which made possible the election of Mayor Henry Fitz-Ailwin in 1192, an election recognized by the Crown. When Magna Carta was signed in 1215, the Mayor of London put his signature down with those of the other chief vassals of the king.

Twelve City companies are called Great, sixty-nine are listed as Minor and both categories are refused by two of the oldest, the Company of Thames Watermen and Lightermen and the Company of Parish Clerks. Which of the companies is the oldest is a point of contention between several of them which date from the twelfth century. The Weavers (1184) is sometimes acknowledged senior, but it is not one of the dozen Greats, although the Mercers (1393), Drapers (1364), Clothworkers (1528) and Haberdashers (1448) are. In 1964 the Corporation chartered the newest, the Worshipful Company of Scientific Instrument Makers. The

Furniture Makers received their charter the year before without apparent impingement on the Carpenters (1477), Joiners (1571) or Turners (1310).

The sword rests for the symbolic blades of Corporation officials are still in place in surviving City churches, some of which have absorbed the cures of as many as four vanished ancient houses of worship to which the earliest guilds were originally attached as lay societies under the banner of a chosen saint.

Few of the churches of Whittington's day and almost none of the Company halls survived the Great Fire of 1666. Most of the companies rebuilt at once, and those still standing more than two hundred years later were ravaged by the Luftwaffe's bombs. There were thirty-four Livery halls when the war with Germany started in 1939, and when the last of the rocket-borne bombs exploded in 1944, fourteen of them were gone and thirteen damaged, many gravely. A chuckling destiny spared four of the newest, built in the twentieth and late nineteenth centuries.

Only the Merchant Taylors' Hall at 30 Threadneedle Street retains in large part its fourteenth- and fifteenth-century rooms. Stationers' Hall remains an essentially post-Fire building of 1667, although several of its historic chambers had also to be reconstructed after bomb damage. The hall is tucked away in an alley called Stationers' Hall Court, near Ave Maria Lane and Amen Corner in the precinct of St. Paul's Cathedral.

Ironmongers' Hall, in Shaftesbury Place off Aldersgate Street north of London Wall, was also a victim of German bombing — by zeppelin in 1915. The 1924 replacement of their 1750 building emerged unscathed from World War II. To the uncataloguing eye, it is old, very old even, with its scrupulously Gothic doorway and its Tudor half-timbered upper stories, the two separated by Georgian brick walls.

The bombed-out Bakers seem to be the only guild to admit, architecturally, that this is the twentieth century. Instead of rebuilding on the fifteenth-century site in Harp Lane in nostalgic echo of Olde Tymes, they ordered a building in contemporary idiom. And it is a building which brings in a profit: the Company occupies only the first two floors and the other five are rented out. This prudent procedure of having one's house and letting it too was established long since by Kensington widows endowed with fixed incomes, high houses and rising expenses, who solved their problem by taking in paying guests. Gentlemen's clubs in the area of St. James's are following the example set by the Bakers, replacing their income-draining candy boxes with income-producing egg crates.

Having accumulated bequests — some of it in City land now measured by the carat rather than the square foot, many of the Companies are rich and annually dispense impressive amounts in charity. A surprising number still maintain almshouses, all "out in the country" beyond the City walls. Almost all contribute to schools for technical education and give scholarships to schools and universities. Some maintain schools founded by members centuries ago, and some of which have since become distinguished Public Schools: St. Paul's (Mercers), Oundle (Grocers), Merchant Taylors (Merchant Taylors), Tonbridge (Skinners).

Aside from their support of education, most of the guilds lost all connection with their trades by the eighteenth century. True, the Fruiterers every seventh of October present English fruit (including twelve bushels of apples) to the Lord Mayor to demonstrate their ancient and utterly unenforceable right to check all fruit for quality and collect a toll in kind.

And in August the new Freemen of the Watermens' Company row a race upstream 4 miles 5 furlongs from the site of the Old Swan, London Bridge to the site of the Old Swan, Chelsea, for Doggett's Coat and Badge — the coat "of orange livery," the silver badge embossed with the Hanoverian horse. Thomas Doggett, Drury Lane actor-manager, established the prize partly as theater publicity and partly to honor the accession of George I. Run since 1715, his race is the oldest continuing sporting event in the country.

Also on the Thames, the annual Swan Upping is performed in July by the Swan Masters of the Vintners and the Dyers. They mark those cygnets they are privileged to maintain upon the river, whose swans — with this guild exception — automatically belong to the Crown. The royal swans are left unmarked, but the Dyers make one nick on the beaks of their birds, the Vintners two.

The Vintners also maintain another glorious exemption from the rules: fifteen families have inherited the title of "Free Vintner," which means they may sell wine without a license and ignore the strict hours of opening and closing provided by the licensing laws for public houses. Two such houses are near the Baker Street station, Henry Emberson and the Vintage Wine House, and another, of wider renown, close to the borders of the City is Gordon's at 47 Villiers Street, W.C.2. As one authority comments, "They may close when they wish — and do, at 9.0."

There are a few guilds still performing some of their original functions. The Fishmongers are the fishmeters, who measure quality with the right to examine and condemn fish and to prosecute out-of-season sellers.

The Goldsmiths, on behalf of the sovereign, continue an examination begun in the Middle Ages, the Trial of the Pyx. Each March trial blocks of each coin publicly circulated in the kingdom are brought for assay, each in its special box ("pyx"), to the

Goldsmiths' Hall survived World War II, and the guild survives to carry out craft functions.

68

Goldsmith's Hall from the Royal Mint near the Tower of London. The Goldsmiths also control the London hallmark on gold and silver ware.

The Apothecaries' Society, which closed its retail drug business only in 1922, and whose 1673 physic garden yet blooms in Chelsea, still grants medical licenses. The Licentiate in Medicine and Surgery of the Society of Apothecaries is "a complete qualification for the general practitioner," and the Society also grants the degree of Master of Midwifery.

The Worshipful Company of Plumbers keeps the register of qualified craftsmen. Any plumber on this roll, though not necessarily a member of the Company, has the right to put after his name the initials R.P.

The sum of all these antique parts is the Corporation of the City of London, seated at Guildhall. The hall's medieval central portion has withstood the Great Fire and the Blitz, and it has kept pulled about its shoulders a Middle Ages cloak of narrow,

St. Lawrence Jewry, a Wren gem, is the official church of the City Corporation.

69

bent, short ways: Church Alley, Three Nuns Court, Fountaine Court, Dyers Court, and its own Guildhall Yard which is found behind the City of London Court, Gresham College and the Church of St. Lawrence Jewry, all facing Gresham Street.

St. Lawrence Jewry is one of the many City churches identified by its neighborhood. (There are five St. Marys — Abchurch, Aldermary, at-Hill, le-Bow and Woolnoth.) Near here is the street called Old Jewry, the district assigned to the Jews in Norman times. The church is the official church of the City Corporation, and on election eve, the retiring Lord Mayor attends services here. On the second Wednesday after Easter, the Corporation officers attend in state to hear the Spital Sermon, for which a bequest was made in the twelfth century at the Priory of St. Mary Spital (Hospital). The church, rebuilt by Wren after the Great Fire, was gutted in 1940 and restored in 1957.

Gresham College was established in 1579 under a bequest

St. Mary's Aldermanbury, bomb-torn during the blitz, has been moved to Fulton, Missouri as a memorial to Winston Churchill.

from Sir Thomas Gresham, founder of the Royal Exchange. Intended as a sort of University of London, the free public lectures were given in Sir Thomas's own mansion near Bishopsgate until they were moved to this site in 1842. The present building is from 1912. Four nights a week, at the end of the working day, the lectures are presented, but no longer in Latin.

The street that runs along the western edge of the Guildhall nest is Aldermanbury, where the "bury" or court of aldermen, the big city landowners of pre-Norman times, had its sessions. On the first turning to the left is Love Lane (and Little Love Lane) where stood the churches of St. Mary Aldermanbury and St. Alban, both ravaged by German bombs. The stones of St. Mary (a Wren church but not a masterpiece) have been numbered and transported for re-erection at Fulton, Missouri. In this American town Winston Churchill paused long enough in 1946 to make a speech on deteriorated Russian-Allied relations and fired a *mot* heard round the world — "the iron curtain."

Although the church has gone, the remains of parishioners remain, notably those of Judge Jeffreys, "the most hated judge in the history of criminal law," and those of Heminge and Condell. The names of these two last are probably unknown to the average reader, yet they should be celebrated. Flowers should heap their resting place. To them, his fellow actors, we owe the works of William Shakespeare. John Heminge and Henry Condell alone collected Shakespeare's plays and published the First Folio edition of his dramatic works, out of love for Shakespeare and the plays. They incurred debt in their venture, and in turn we are forever indebted to them.

St. Alban, restored in 1960 after being bombed, was one of the last Gothic churches built in London. The replacement of a gone-to-seed fourteenth-century Gothic structure, the 1633 church retained the style as a matter of "survival rather than revival," according to Dr. Pevsner.* Wren gave it a new tower after the Great Fire.

Atop the Guildhall is the City shield with its motto, *Domine*

* Dr. Nikolaus Pevsner, in his incomparable two-volume Penguin edition of *London* (part of his *Buildings of England* series), rich in pungent, pithy and penetrating observations, honest and antipedantically expert. The author is grateful for this architectural guide.

dirige nos — Lord, direct us. This is an appropriate petition to a higher power, when one considers the complexities of finding one's way mid the streets, courts, alleys, passages, lanes and ways of the district.

Four very tall stories high, Guildhall was completed about 1440. It was damaged by the Great Fire and hurt by the Nazi Air Force, and "improved" and "restored" here and there over the centuries, but it is still in bone and spirit out of the Middle Ages.

It is a brave and dignified façade with some inherited Gothic fancy in the thirty pointed paned windows and the fluted buttresses. The entrance is the original stone fifteenth-century porch, the rest of the front as remade by George Dance the Younger in 1789. The front door opens directly into the fifteenth-century

Seat of the primitively democratic government of the City, Guildhall.

72

great hall, more than 150 feet long, almost 90 feet high. Here the great formal feasts are tendered by the City to royalty and statesmen, and here the Sheriffs are annually elected with ancient ceremony and with brand-new hustings set up at one end of the hall.

It was here that Anne Askew, the Protestant martyr, was tried and the poet Earl of Surrey, Henry Howard (1547), and Lady Jane Grey and Archbishop Cranmer (1547) were all found guilty. The shields of the City companies decorate the cornice and the embroidered banners of the twelve Great Companies.

Attached to the building are the Guildhall Library and Art Gallery (the Museum collection is provisionally housed at the Royal Exchange). Next to St. Lawrence Jewry is an early nineteenth-century house, the Irish Chamber. This is the seat of the Honourable Irish Society, formed in 1613 under pressure from James I, who, to finance his Ulster Plantation, obliged each of the twelve Great Companies to buy vast tracts of Northern Ireland,

St. Margaret's Lothbury, another surviving Wren gem.

73

and the Corporation through its Hon. Irish Soc., to buy the City of Limerick.

A few yards east Gresham Street becomes Lothbury (not Lothbury Street or Avenue or Way, just Lothbury, a singularity not too rare in the City where lie Cheapside, Poultry, Eastcheap, Moorfields, Bishopsgate and the rest). To the left is St. Margaret Lothbury, another Wren church, completed 1701. Its interior, enriched by furnishings from several vanished churches, is especially fine, the most striking object being the carved wooden chancel screen stretching all the way across the church (from All Hallows Dowgate).

On the other side of the street, the Bank of England. It occupies four acres between Lothbury and Threadneedle Street, with Princes Street and Bartholomew Lane making the other sides of the square. In front of the Bank we are in one of the most closed-in open spaces in the Western world, hedged about with Corinthian columns and respectability. The dimly perceptible rustling is not the sound of acanthus leaves but the sound of money folding and unfolding.

The open space has no name. It is the intersection of ten streets: Threadneedle Street, Cornhill, Lombard Street, King William Street, Mansion House Place, Walbrook, Queen Victoria Street, Poultry, St. Mildred's Court and Princes Street.

It is palisaded by three grand buildings, not tremendously tall physically, but psychologically towering — the Bank, Mansion House and the Royal Exchange. This is one of the two great religious precincts of the City. The other temple, St. Paul's, is across the Walbrook on the other hill. The hill on this side is devoted, under a carefully Christianized overlay, to the worship of Mammon.

Along the streets branching easterly off the temple close cluster the votary chapels of banking, insurance, shipping and exchange. Their missionary work of past ages still bears fruit in the lands beyond the seas: half the world's trade is cleared in pounds sterling, and this spot is the center of the sterling area. The City has a heart of gold.

The Bank of England was the dream of a Scotsman, William Paterson, who had the simple notion of grouping City merchants as the government's creditors. They certainly had had enough practice in this role, sometimes through astuteness and sometimes through coercion, across many reigns.

Paterson persuaded Charles Montagu, later Earl of Halifax, of the excellence of this notion. As senior Treasury Commissioner, Montagu tacked the enabling act onto a Parliamentary bill for taxing ships and spirits. Thus the Bank was founded and given a Royal charter in 1694 for the specific purpose of raising £1,200,000 for William III's war against Louis XIV. Forty merchants subscribed the sum and elected a governor, a deputy governor and twenty-four directors (250 years later when the Bank was nationalized, the number of governors was reduced from twenty-four to sixteen). The procedure being a success, Montagu was made Chancellor of the Exchequer.

Members first met at Mercers' Hall, and then for forty years at Grocers' Hall. Mercers' Hall (new building 1960) is at 83 Cheapside, a short stroll from the present Bank, and the Grocers in their trimly rebuilt (1893) hall are in Grocers' Court, directly across from the bank on the other side of Princes Street.

In 1724 the Bank bought the Threadneedle Street mansion of Sir John Houblon, the bank's governor. The pink tailcoats and scarlet waistcoats of the top-hatted Bank messengers are derived from the livery of an early governor. The gatekeepers wear gowns of scarlet and gold. The vaults underground provide their splash of color too, containing as they do the gold reserves of Great Britain.

Almost as soon as the Bank was installed, the Threadneedle Street house needed enlargement and wings were added in 1765 and 1782. In 1782 more space was required and Sir John Soane was summoned. He worked for twenty years and produced a masterpiece. In 1921 the Bank needed still more space, and Sir Herbert Baker was called in. He worked for sixteen years to undo the whole thing.

If the Bank of England had made a banking error as gross as this architectural blunder, Great Britain would have gone bankrupt. "In spite of the Second World War the worst individual loss suffered by London architecture in the first half of the twentieth century," is Dr. Pevsner's estimate. The ground-level screen wall on Threadneedle and Princes Streets is Soane's.

Two years after the Bank had been chartered by the Whigs, the Tories succeeded in having a competing bank established, a Land Bank. The idea was to make it a sort of mortgage bank on the premise that the true wealth of the nation was not its gold, but its soil. Viewed with a desolating lack of sympathy by the Bank of England and its money men, the Land Bank failed within six months.

The Bank itself knew some rather breathless moments. When Bonny Prince Charlie's band was marching on London in 1745, there was a run on the Bank which was met by paying out in the smallest coin, one at a time, and slowly. The queue was salted with Bank agents who immediately paid back the money they drew.

When the City was being sacked by the Gordon rioters in 1780, a beer-wagon driver mounted on a dray horse led a midnight mob against the Bank. The staff, with the help of troops and City volunteers, beat off both attacks. Ever since, a detachment of Guards from Wellington Barracks has been stationed every night at the Bank.

By 1800 the Bank of England was supplying its banknotes to smaller houses, had become custodian of most of the national gold reserve, and had made a start toward management of the public debt. Peel's Bank Charter Act of 1844 separated the note-issuing department from the banking department, and even though the Bank was privately owned, the profit from money-issuing henceforth went to the Government. Simultaneously, the issue of banknotes by some three hundred other banks was restricted, with no new permits given. Once a bank ceased issue, it was not allowed to resume — the last one gave up in 1921.

In 1857 the Bank was within one day of collapse, with reserves down to a half-million pounds. The explanation: "overspeculation in America." Nine years later, when the Quaker banking house of Gurney collapsed, the shock waves rocked the Bank. Legislation soon after curbed Bank investment and the directors began building up a proportionately high cash reserve.

The man who made the Bank of England into a true central

bank was Montagu Norman, a bearded and rather strange man (finally married — happily — at the age of sixty-one) whose personal peculiarities were eagerly overlooked in the brilliance of his financial wizardry. He was Governor from 1920 to 1944, the longest the office was ever held.

Today the institution is banker to the government and to other major banks and still retains some of its old private commercial customers. It still issues the banknotes, pays the interest on the national debt, repays Treasury Bills and matured government loans. Like other central banks, it greatly influences whether money will be "cheap" or "dear," credit easy or tight. This it does by money market operations and by changing the bank rate, which is roughly the interest charged on loans.

The effects of such actions are vast, since they have inflationary and anti-inflationary reactions, influence the amounts of foreign and domestic investment, industrial expansion and consumer spending.

It was William Cobbett who called the Bank the "Old Lady of Threadneedle Street," endeavoring, like Mrs. Partington, with her "financial broom to stem the Atlantic waves of national progress." He was also the man who termed London "the great wen."

The name Threadneedle Street was probably "Three Needle Street" originally, after the shield of the Needlemakers' Company, a still-extant guild. There are other banks on Threadneedle Street, but many of the major houses persist in maintaining headquarters in Lombard Street, one of those radiating from the space before the Bank.

This street was the repair of the thirteenth-century Italian moneylenders who took over from the banished residents of Old Jewry down the road. Narrow, short, and gently winding, Lombard Street is mildly picturesque because the austere buildings are softened by a profusion of flowerboxes and because the banks have the courage of their conservative convictions and maintain medieval street signs hanging bannerlike over the street.

The multicolored shields represent two of the three main kinds of money-handlers in the City: the "ordinary" banks and the discount houses. The other type, the merchant bankers (such as Morgan Grenfell, Rothschild, Baring), make their own neighbor-

77

hoods, as is fitting to the longtime princes of the financial world, still princely but with painfully diminished sovereignty.

There are only eleven "ordinary" banks in England maintaining those familiar neighborhood branches for deposit and withdrawal. They are few because they are enormous, the two largest each with more than two thousand branches.

There are only twelve member houses of the London Discount Market Association. They trade in commercial paper, buying it for cash at a discount, a fraction less than its face value.

The merchant bankers are seventeen in number, functioning primarily as investment banks, floating stock and bond issues and acting as acceptance houses guaranteeing the postdated bills of exchange drafted by commercial traders, usually in foreign trade. The closest to Lombard Street is Rothschild's, just a few steps from the corner where it meets King William Street. Down St. Swithin's Lane is a 1965 glass and concrete office building with only the granite-carved name "New Court," a name with a golden aura in knowing circles, to indicate what is behind the façade. There is nothing to show that from this spot flowed the money that helped shape the nineteenth century's history and geography. One might suspect that there are many institutions in London today with a great deal more money to invest, and one's suspicions would be correct. However, much of the old magic clings to the old names which still ring like solid coins on the counters of all the houses in the City.

Lombard Street is not all that modest. Coutts's red disc sign swinging over the pavement is graced with three golden crowns. Martin's bank is identified by a golden grasshopper. Glyn Mills sports a golden anchor and also shows the marigolds of Child's bank which they absorbed (Child began lending money at the Marigold Tavern). These are all "ordinary" banks. Alexander's Discount Company shows a golden thistle. The National Commercial Bank of Scotland has two signs, one with a golden cat playing a golden fiddle on a green signboard, the other a portrait of King Charles I. Lloyd's bank (no connection with the insurance Lloyd's) has a red shield on which prances a black horse. Barclays displays a black spread eagle on a golden ground.

In the middle of the block one of Wren's typical obelisk spires pokes up, typical in being different from all the others he designed. This one is short, with lightly concave sides and is set on an octagonal lantern. The church is St. Edmund the King, 1679.

Edmund was a Saxon king martyred by the Danes, and his church was slightly martyred too by a German bomb in 1917. Here Joseph Addison in 1716 married the Countess Dowager of Warwick, after which he changed his occupation from writer to drinker and within three years made her a widow again.

On the other side of the street is little Plough Court, which many people harmlessly believe to have been the birthplace in 1688 of Alexander Pope. It is said more popular phrases can be traced back to him than to any other secular writer save Shakespeare.*

* "Fools rush in where angels fear to tread." "A little learning is a dangerous thing."

Today there is an Underground station below Hawksmoor's Church of St. Mary Woolnoth.

79

At the Bank end of the street the intersection with King William Street forms a triangle in which sits St. Mary Woolnoth, designed in 1716 by Nicholas Hawksmoor, a Wren pupil. The Lombard Street elevation is rather grander than that fronting King William Street. Tucked in under the prow of the church are entrances to the Underground, one of which leads past a sealed low doorway into the church and on the arch of which is graven "Lift Up Your Hearts." This probably refers to religion rather than to banking or underground travel. One of the more satisfying things about St. Mary Woolnoth is the name: here in the City where everything has a history and an explanation, there

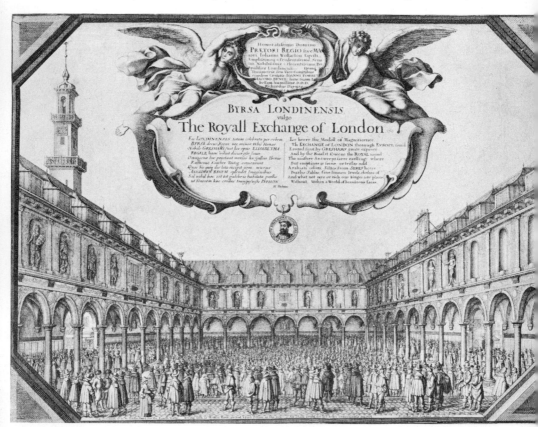

Thrice destroyed and thrice rebuilt, the Royal Exchange still graces the City.
Courtesy, Museum of Fine Arts, Boston (Harvey D. Parker Collection)

is none — not even a guess — about what or who or when or why "Woolnoth."

Back in the open space, one is menaced anew by the plethora of pediments, the most overwrought of which belongs to the Royal Exchange.

In front of the Exchange is a concrete island containing two statues and one of the many exits for the Underground station named simply Bank (there is another named Mansion House, but it lets you onto the pavement a quarter of a mile from here on Queen Victoria Street). Off the station below ground is a rather remarkable blue-tiled crypt, dating from the last half of the twentieth century. The crypt has a tubular approach, with a gradual downward incline. A moving sidewalk rolls through the glowing tunnel down to the crypt, depositing the traveler on a pavement of blue and white tesscrac under the vaulting of a warm blue grotto, spacious and with a reassuring feeling of enormous strength. Inside the crypt are the station platforms of a railway which conducts the passenger to yet another railway station. The railway is called *The Waterloo & City Line* (*Weekdays Only*). At commuter time it is the arena of the normal carnage, but in the off hours it is a place of calm beauty, possibly the best small architectural achievement of the postwar City.

Above on the surface there are wooden benches for the wilted who have made it safely to the island, there is a memorial shaft to Londoners who served in both World Wars, and an equestrian statue of the Duke of Wellington, toga-clad, bare-legged, riding without stirrups. Although he is known as the Iron Duke, the statue is bronze.

His Grace was present at the unveiling of his statue in the autumn of 1844. He stood at the head of the steps of the new building (the previous one had been destroyed by fire), distantly acknowledging the huzzahs of the hats-off crowd, gazed without comment at his effigy and then turned and entered to watch Queen Victoria ceremoniously declare the new Exchange open. Charles II had laid the cornerstone for the preceding building, which replaced the original, lost in the Great Fire, and which had been ceremoniously declared open by Queen Elizabeth in 1565.

The founder of the Royal Exchange was Sir Thomas Gresham,

who set it up in imitation of the Exchange at Antwerp, where he had been Elizabeth's financial agent. Also in imitation of the Flemish establishment, the building had a campanile to which Gresham added a weathervane in the shape of his trade symbol, a golden grasshopper. The succeeding Exchanges have all had bell towers and golden grasshoppers (or grasshopper — the one up there now may well be the original). Sir Thomas is respectfully remembered in London for his financial astuteness, his founding of the Exchange and the endowment of Gresham College. Outside England he is known as the author of Gresham's Law: Bad money drives out good. Gresham's Law is assailable only on one point — it was formulated long before his time and there is no evidence that Sir Thomas ever even repeated it.

Announcements of Gresham College free courses are still posted at the Royal Exchange, and a statue of Sir Thomas stands in a niche in the tower.

The ground floor, formerly arcaded booths around an open court and now a large hall roofed in glass, is used for exhibitions and is also the current home of the Guildhall Museum. Among the objects ancient, historic, curious and beautiful, one exhibit is especially arresting: a work sculpted in the seventeenth century by Caius Gabriel Cibber. The two figures are Raving Madness and Melancholy (or, some say, Acute Mania and Dementia). For more than a century and a half they reclined over the archway into Bedlam. One of the oldest institutions in the world for the care of the insane, the hospital was originally at the Priory of St. Mary of Bethlehem, founded in 1274. When Henry VIII dissolved the monasteries, he gave the property to the City of London to use as a madhouse. In 1647 a huge new hospital was finished at Moorgate and London Wall, its name by then contracted to be officially Bethelm, popularly Bedlam. In 1815 the hospital transferred to an eighteen-acre park in Lambeth, where its buildings are now occupied by the Imperial War Museum. The hospital still carries on near Croydon.

Until 1770 Bedlam was one of the great sideshows of London. It was open to sightseers who, for the price of a small tip to a warder, could tour the cells and laugh at the antics of the inmates. One of the sequences in Hogarth's *The Rake's Progress* takes us into Bedlam. Cibber's sculptures show the terror and pity of madness. The Raver is in chains, the Melancholic is in his own lost world. Made from drawings of a powerful inmate, they are a remarkable evocation — both clinical and compassionate — of mindlessness.

These days little is exchanged at the Royal Exchange save civilities. Two insurance companies, Lloyd's and the Royal Exchange Assurance, moved into the building in 1796. Three years later, they and the East India Company and the Bank paid to have a firefighting pump installed on a well originally provided by Mayor Henry Wallace in 1282. It was quite a while later, almost forty years, that fire did break out. The Exchange was totally destroyed, but the pump survived and is still there, alongside at No. 9 Cornhill.

Right behind the Royal Exchange is a paved open street for pedestrians. Called Freeman's Court, it is dominated by a statue of George Peabody, a self-made multimillionaire American who established a London brokerage and in 1854 took in an American partner, Junius Spencer Morgan. The firm is now known as Morgan Grenfell, merchant bankers, with a building at 23 Great Winchester Street, off Old Broad Street, which begins just over the way from this passage.

Peabody's statue graces this spot not simply because he was an eminent City man, but because he gave millions to clear slums in the East End and to erect model low-rent dwellings. His housing trusts still function. He died in 1869 and was interred in Westminster Abbey. Later he was removed to his home town of Peabody, Massachusetts, which, at the time he left it to seek his fortune had borne the name of South Danvers.

The Royal Exchange is not to be confused with the Stock Exchange, although early in the seventeenth century, the stock dealers hoped it would be. However, the Royal Exchange, feeling that stock-jobbers lowered the tone ("rascally" was the conventional term), threw them out. They simply went across the street, Cornhill, and congregated in Change Alley. They became an institution after a 1773 meeting in Jonathan's Coffee House, deciding on the name Stock Exchange, "which is to be wrote over the door."

Twenty-nine years later they abandoned the coffeehouse for their own premises. The new place was in Capel Court, across Bartholomew Lane from the Bank of England. This original entrance can still be seen through the slit in the buildings, but the present ingress is around the corner on Throgmorton Street, in later buildings. Physically, the place just growed, additions being hitched together to cover expansion.

"No one ever accused the London Stock Exchange of architectural distinction," wrote the late Sir Oscar Hobson, eminent financial editor. "No one, indeed, ever pointed to the Stock Exchange and said: 'What is that building?' — for no stranger looking at it from the outside could possibly recognize the Stock Exchange as being a single building, so thoroughly camouflaged is it by its outer coating of shops, cable offices and insurance companies."

Visitors are invited to step inside, however, and watch the Exchange in action from a glassed-in gallery. It is sort of a free replacement for the visits to old Bedlam.

In 1964, the Exchange's senior deputy chairman declared the quarters to be "absolutely out of date, grossly inadequate, and in places slightly biblical." The Exchange proposed to erect a 26-story tower block, mightily altering the heart of the City.

It is not just in building cramp that the Exchange has felt the press of change and growth in the City. Its members have been involved with the share sales in the merger and take-over battles. Some of the most resounding struggles have concerned the operations of American capital looking for major investment in British concerns. Such moves evoked chauvinist right-wing splutterings about the Union Jack becoming the tail for the Yankee kite, and left-wing anguish about subjugation of the British workingman to the dictates of Wall Street.

Investigation shows that in reality, Britain owns more of the United States than vice versa. Most of the British money is in oil, chemicals, textiles and consumer goods such as food, drink, tobacco. Her Majesty's Government is believed to hold a $200,000,000 piece of Detroit's General Motors, which in 1960 bought out minority shareholders of Vauxhall Motors, one of Britain's big automakers.

All these changes, architectural and financial, are felt too at the Royal Exchange, which is much more than a decorative souvenir shell. After 132 years in the building, Lloyd's moved out to its own installation in 1928, but the Royal Exchange Assurance Company stayed on. One of the largest non-life insurance companies in the country, it is one of the new financial giants. Insurance companies and pension funds in the British Isles as in North America, have millions in individual payments flooding in every week. They cannot sit on it; they must invest it. This endless stream of money looking for a home gives them enormous power in the City, where once the merchant banks were the grand masters.

Lloyd's buildings, the new one finished 1957, stretch down Leadenhall Street (a continuation of Cornhill) and on both sides of Lime. The name Lloyd's is not that of the founder; it is not a corporation in the usual sense, since the company itself takes no risks and pays no claims, although its members do. Lloyd's was the name of the coffeehouse hangout of merchants daring enough to insure ships and cargo in 1689. The coffeehouse was first in Tower Street, then in Lombard Street, and owner Edward Lloyd posted shipping information for the benefit of his customers. In 1696 he began publishing *Lloyd's News*, a single sheet out twice a week. It flourished for seventy-six issues until the House of Lords took offense at an erroneous parliamentary report, and the paper did not appear again until almost forty years later under the name *Lloyd's List and Shipping Gazette*. Still going, it is London's oldest daily newspaper.

Edward Lloyd died in 1712, and his son-in-law carried on as host. In 1769 one of the waiters quit and set up on his own in Pope's Head Alley, which still runs between Lombard Street and Cornhill. Name of his place was New Lloyd's Tavern, and the insurance men followed. By 1771 the customers formed a committee to regulate operations, and in 1796 deserted the coffeehouse for the Royal Exchange. However, they kept the word "coffeehouse" in their name until well into the nineteenth century.

The underwriting room, which in the mid-1960's was earning about a billion dollars a year in premiums, is open only to staff (the scarlet-uniformed runners are still called "waiters") and members and guests. The core of the enterprise is composed of five thousand "names" made into 140 syndicates. It is they who issue the policies and assume unlimited liability. Admission to membership means that six members have recommended the applicant, that the Committee, after careful scrutiny and a long interview, has been satisfied as to the man's character and ability. About his finances they are less probing: if he were not certifiably worth more than a quarter of a million dollars, his name would not be proposed.

The apparently mad congress on the floor of the Room (the Rothschild's reception office is also called the Room, whereas the Stock Exchange is called the House) is in essence a simple and orderly process. In the center of the scrimmage is the red-robed Caller on his rostrum, calling the names of brokers through his microphone. At a series of pews ranged along the sides of the room, the underwriters sit four in a row on benches. Between these desks ("boxes" at Lloyd's) perambulate the brokers, carrying long folded slips of paper. On the top of each is the broker's name and the details of the proposed policy. He goes from desk to desk securing shares of insurance from various underwriters — at an acceptable rate — until the whole hundred per cent is subscribed. Each risk-taker writes his initials under the broker's résumé, giving insurance to the broker's customer and the word "underwriter" to the rest of us.

At times the Caller interrupts business by ringing the bell which hangs from the clock over his head, once for bad news, twice for good. This is the bell of the *Lutine*, a frigate which sank off the entrance to the Zuider Zee in 1799, her cargo seven million dollars in gold and coins insured by Lloyd's.

Lloyd's older building stands on the site of East India House, headquarters of the East India Company. The building, outlasting "John Company" by seventy-seven years, was not demolished until 1924. The Company was chartered by Queen Elizabeth on the last day of the year 1600, and it endured until the Sepoy Mutiny of 1857. It was granted the monopoly of British trade with the Eastern Hemisphere, taking to the Indian subcontinent when driven out of the East Indies by the Dutch East India Company. The Company had its own armies and virtually its own empire, out of which it squeezed untold riches. A poor boy could go out to

India and come back a rich man, which is what happened in the cases of Robert Clive and Warren Hastings who saved the Company in the 1760's and 1770's. They saved it both from uprisings and from the consequences of the greed and corruption of its employees.

They were repaid for their services with obloquy. Clive, by then Lord Clive of the Irish peerage, was called home from his reform activities in Bengal to submit to investigation by the House of Commons. Exonerated, but hurt beyond bearing, he went home to his house in Berkeley Square and shot himself.

The stain had been removed, but the brightness was marred, and more than 170 years later, Edmund Clerihew Bentley could comment:

> What I like about Clive
> Is that he is no longer alive.
> There is a great deal to be said
> For being dead.

Warren Hastings, as Governor General of India for ten years, aggressively reformed the finances and the judiciary and codi-

From this building the East India Company took, governed and plundered an empire.

fied local law. Disgusted with opposition from other Englishmen, he quit in 1784 and arrived home to find himself under impeachment on charges of high treason and misdemeanor. The charges had been instituted by personal enemies, including Edmund Burke. Hastings spent his fortune defending himself through the eight incredible years of the trial, and was acquitted. He outlived Burke, Charles James Fox and Richard Brinsley Sheridan, his principal inquisitors, and died a cheerful old man of eighty-six.

Long after Clive and Hastings, Thomas Snodgrass had his innings with the Company. Envious fellow workers reported that Snodgrass had left his post and was living "in princely style" by the seaside, and he was ordered to return to London and bring his accounts with him. He showed up in Leadenhall Street empty-handed, having lost his ledgers in a shipwreck (boat upset in four feet of water). Justly stricken from the rolls and denied his pension, he returned next day to East India House in rags and installed himself as a crossing sweeper.

It was a scandal: "Having ruled 100,000 people and served the Company with distinction, he is reduced in the evening of his life to gain his few pitiful crusts as a sweeper." The Court of the Company was not insensible to the mutterings in the clubs. They offered Snodgrass his pensions with payments in arrears if he would only please remove his wretched person and his revolting broom. He accepted.

Next day he drove up in a coach and four, swanked into the Court Room in his frock coat, swept off his top hat with Oriental grace and gave thanks to the august governors: "You have now made up my income to five thousand pounds a year."

Charles Lamb, James Mill and his son John Stuart Mill all labored as clerks for John Company.

Across on the other side of Leadenhall Street, Lime Street becomes St. Mary Axe (locally, "Simmery Axe"), after the church which once stood there. The church counted among its relics one of the three axes used by Attila the Hun to slay ten thousand indubitably Christian fifth-century virgins at Cologne.

The church on the corner of Leadenhall is St. Andrew Undershaft. To ponder the path to beatification of Andrew Undershaft, or of Benet Fink, whose church is gone, is bootless: this St. Andrew is the standard holy man, patron saint of Russia and Scotland. The church name comes from the neighborhood's towering Maypole, slung out of season from the eaves of the houses in Shaft Court, which is still there. The pole is not. The pastor, during the Reformation, condemned the Maypole as a heathen totem and the parishioners chopped it to bits.

The fifteenth-century tower has a nineteenth-century top on it, but the rest is pretty much 1530. Here the Lord Mayor appears every April at the funerary monument of John Stow, poor sixteenth-century tailor who spent his life compiling his *Survey of London*, the invaluable stone-by-stone story of the City. On the monument a life-sized figure of Stow sits at his desk, writing. Each year the Lord Mayor puts into his stone hand a new goose-quill pen.

At No. 24–28 St. Mary Axe is a permanent animated display of Lloyd's customers — the members of the Baltic Mercantile and Shipping Exchange, one of the world's great shipping markets, air freight and charter markets, barley and maize futures markets. In 1965 the wheat pit (called "ring" here) was still waiting for postwar government permission to resume operations. The name Baltic comes both from a coffeehouse where shippers and grain merchants met, and from the fact that grain, oilseeds and tallow, still traded here, were staples of the ancient Anglo-Baltic trade.

The cereal trading at the Baltic is only part of the London grain exchange, for over near the Thames on Mark (Mart) Lane there is the Corn Exchange and the concentration of most other London commodity selling. There are two important markets outside the cluster: metals and furs. The London Metals Market, one of the world centers for buying and selling copper, lead, tin and zinc, is tucked away in Whittington Avenue among the butchers' shops surrounding the produce market at Leadenhall. The fur trade lurks further west in the periphery of the Hudson's Bay Company at Beaver Hall on Garlick Hill.

Hudson Bay's main face (red brick with thick Georgian accent, 1927) is turned to Great Trinity Street atop the hill, and the salesrooms are downhill toward St. James Garlickhithe (locally, "Jimmy Garlic"), a church founded in 1170. Rebuilt by Wren in 1687 and carrying one of his most graceful spires. The church owns a mummy in a glass case, who is not St. James. St. James is the Apostle (Santiago da Compostela) whose tomb in northern Spain was, along with Rome and Jerusalem one of the great places of pilgrimage in the Middle Ages.

Through shop windows and open loft doors along the hill hanging sheaves of animal pelts are visible. The auctions at which raw furs are sold take place at four general sales a year, although from time to time there are special sales devoted to one kind of fur. At the sales, the Hudson's Bay Company gets first turn, the others drawing lots for theirs.

The Hudson's Bay Company was chartered in 1670 as "Governor and Company of Adventurers of England trading into Hudson's Bay." It gave the company "the sole trade and commerce" of the Hudson's Bay territory (three million square miles) made them its "true and absolute Lordes and Proprietors" with full power to govern. This handsome document was obtained in the space of two weeks from King Charles II by Prince Rupert, the monarch's German cousin and counselor who showed his faith in the New World by investing £200 and being the first to accept the post of Governor. During the two hundred years that the company maintained its privileges, the validity of the charter was frequently, if not quite continuously challenged.

The company still recruits young Scots (apparently congenitally immune to effects of isolation) to man its two hundred trading posts in the Northwest. The trade whose frontier traditions these young men carry on opened up one-fourth of the North American continent. As the Grand Seigneur of the Company, Winston Churchill, wrote in a foreword to the official history, it is an "epic of British enterprise* interwoven with the growth of the great country that Canada has become."

The fur traders congregated at Garroway's, a teahouse in Change Alley, and they held their fur sales on days when the tea traders weren't using the big room upstairs. Thomas Garroway in 1657 served the first publicly sold cup of tea in England. As he said in his first advertisement:

---

* Based entirely on French vision, the idea outlined to Prince Rupert by its authors, M. C. Groseilliers and P. E. Radison.

Tea in England hath been sold in the leaf for £6 and sometimes £10 the pound weight and in respect of its former scarceness and dearness it hath been only used as a regalia in high treatments and entertainments and presents made thereof to princes and grandees.

Garroway's price was between sixteen and fifty shillings a pound. To his place flocked the rich who wanted to taste the new beverage and be seen doing so. When the tea trade developed into a regular business, the traders gathered at Garroway's and did their trading there as well, a habit they did not break until the building was razed in 1866.

Today's tea auctions (in 1964 the British consumed nine pounds per capita) take place three days a week: Monday and Wednesday, sales of tea from Northern India, Pakistan, Africa and Indonesia; Tuesday, tea from Ceylon and Southern India.

The auction room is in the evocatively named Plantation House on the charmingly named Mincing Lane. It can be disappointing to learn that Mincing is a corruption of the feminine form of the Anglo-Saxon word for "monk," *mychene*. And it can be disillusioning, after thoughts of punkahs, stengahs and wallahs, to see that Plantation House is a ponderous, barefaced 1937 thing stretching down the Lane from Fenchurch Street (which was Lombard Street a couple of blocks back — both Fenchurch and Gracechurch refer to an ancient haymarket — grace for grass and fen for *faenum*, hay). There is a new extension which pushes all the way to Mark Lane, the next street east. This addition was constructed after the plans had matured for fifteen years in a dark, dry place, a 1954-built building designed in 1939 — not a vintage year.

At Plantation House are auction rooms for the sale of rice, rubber, wool cocoa, sugar, spices, shellac, bristles, jute and ivory. Down Mincing Lane is the post-bombing neo-Georgian hall of the Clothworkers' Company, with the fifteenth-century tower of All Hallows Staining just behind in Mark Lane leaning against the hostile bulk of postwar Dunster House.

Also in Mark Lane, the Corn Exchange, founded in 1749 by customers from the Old Ship Inn and Jack's Coffee House. The exchange deals with grain in job lots instead of in whole crops as does the Baltic Exchange. The big market day is Monday, and the Lane takes on a rather bucolic tinge with farmers showing bakers and brewers handfuls of grain as they stand in the street to do their examining in broad daylight.

The next street east is the Seething Lane of Samuel Pepys, who is buried in the church of St. Olave on the corner of Hart Street and the Lane. It is a fifteenth-century church with a thirteenth-century crypt, the tower retopped in 1732 and most of the structure pasted back together after World War II. St. Olaf, Olav, Olave was a martyred ninth-century King of Norway and patron saint of that land, who tried to help Ethelred the Unready. There were once five churches named for him in London, and only this and the one across the river in Bermondsey remain. One of Bermondsey's ancient highroads, bears a name which is St. Olaf transmogrified — Tooley Street.

Mother Goose was interred at St. Olave's Hart Street in 1586.* Pepys attended services regularly after becoming Secretary at the Navy Office, with his pew in the Navy Officers' Gallery. He moved into Seething Lane in 1660, but moved out again later into the Navy Office in Crutched Friars (a street name left behind by the Friary of the Holy Cross — "Crutched" = "Crossed"). Every Trinity Monday, the members of Trinity House attend services at St. Olave's, where they have a chapel in the South Aisle.

Seething Lane leads on to Great Tower Street, which gives onto Tower Hill and the precincts of the Tower of London. On the edge of the hill is the ancient church of All Hallows Barking by the Tower, whose fabric was knit through the ages, from Roman bricks in the seventh-century arch in the unbombed seventeenth-century tower, to the 1959 steeple. The church was founded by the Abbey in the town of Barking in Essex, as a sort of mission to the heathen of London. In the undercroft are remains of Roman mosaic pavements, and excavations to clear bomb damage brought to light two extremely rare Saxon crosses (aside from place-names there are few remains of Saxon London).

William Penn was born on Tower Hill, baptized at All Hal-

---

* Mother Goose is also buried at the Old Granary Burying Ground in Boston, Massachusetts, her tombstone there bearing an eighteenth-century inscription. There are those who believe her to be immortal.

lows in 1644, imprisoned in the Tower twenty-four years later, and at the age of thirty-five quit the district to go found Pennsylvania. The year John Adams became second President of the recently United States of America (1797), his son John Quincy Adams was getting married at All Hallows Barking by the Tower to a London-born American, daughter of the United States Fiscal Agent in Britain. Ten years earlier, J.Q.'s mother Abigail had endured snubs at the Court of St. James's, where her husband was the first accredited Minister sent by the ex-colonies.

To the east of the church a broad open space is marked at the spot where at least seventy-five condemned men from the Tower of London were executed between 1388 and 1747. One postwar plan completed was the removal of many of the architectural eyesores from Tower Hill.

From the hill there are splendid views on the Tower. Lower, near the Tower entrance is a small pagodafied brick structure, the entry to the first tube railway in London. An iron tube seven feet in diameter runs from here under the river 1340 feet to Southwark, and in 1870 the railway was open to passengers, twopence first class, a penny second class. Steam engines pulled cables to which fourteen-passenger cars were attached. Within a few months this pioneer venture was abandoned, the machinery removed and the tube opened as a halfpenny pedestrian tunnel, used by twenty-five million patrons until the Tower Bridge (free) was opened to traffic in 1894. The tunnel now carries two fat water mains.

Atop the hill is Trinity Place, swaggeringly dominated by the 1912 (completed 1922) Port of London Authority building. Its movie-palace fulsomeness is genteelly ignored by the elegant little Trinity House of 1794, restored after bombing. The Port Authority was created in 1909. The Trinity Corporation, after centuries of service to navigation, was chartered in 1514 by Henry VIII. It was then the Brotherhood of the Most Glorious and Undivided Trinity. When the Puritan Commonwealth was terminated, the brotherhood emerged from its forced service as a government bureau and became the Corporation of Trinity House, still directed by nine Elder Brethren who elect two hundred Younger Brethren, who must be Merchant Marine Captains or Navy Lieutenants. Trinity House, which built its first lighthouse in 1680, was given control of all English lighthouses in 1836. It also controls a number of buoys and all the lightships in English waters, and supplies the pilots at the Thames mouth.

The Port Authority, housed in its exuberant assemblage of uplift, with giant columns, giant statues, giant tower, administers the Thames and its docks from mouth to the head of tidewater sixty-nine miles upstream.

The granite grove on the east side of Trinity Square honors Britain's merchant seamen who died in World War I (twelve thousand) and in World War II (twenty-four thousand "who have no grave but the sea"). Further along the curving road at the top of Tower Hill is a brave little splinter of a park through which steps lead to a platform overlooking an excavation from which rears an impressive piece of City Wall, twenty feet high, made largely of reused Roman material.

Further along the curve and lower down the hill is the Royal Mint, whose 1808 offices have been retained in recent rebuilding. The Mint was in the Tower until 1809 and then moved here, which is only across the way. The complex now covers almost as much ground as the mother fortress.

Visitors are permitted to enter and to witness something not readily visible at the Stock Exchange or other City institutions: how money is really made. It is really quite simple to pass the guarded portals: just write to the Deputy Master of the Royal Mint for permission to enter, making the request some six weeks before the intended visit.

A further stroll past the Mint along the street called East Smithfield with a right turn at Thomas More Street offers a quick, deep taste of Dockland. Sir Thomas More, that saintly man, loved the riverside, but he loved it at his green, agreeable estate in Chelsea, and this street is probably the least appropriate the authorities could have found to name after him.

The street twists and sulks between towering, curving brick walls, St. Katherine Docks on one side, London Docks on the other. At night it is a walk through a series of not wholly credible stage sets, especially as the street makes its way over the small bridge across the ship basin to Wapping High Street amid river smells that can be tasted and the snorting and hooting of water traffic.

Tracking back toward the City underneath Tower Bridge, around the Tower and to the road running along the river the length of the City, one is in Lower Thames Street. The excursion boat pier is on the left, flanked by a river terrace provided by one of the new half-glassed buildings of the district. Leading off uphill to the right are cobbled ways named Beer Lane, Water Lane, Harp Lane and Idol Lane.

Nearly five hundred feet of Lower Thames Street (and riverfront) is occupied by the 1817 Custom House. It is a low, gray structure whose amiable exterior belies the stern functions of its occupants. This spot has been infested by Customs agents since the fourteenth century. The new executive headquarters of the Customs and Excise is up the hill now in the huge 1956 King's Beam House in Mark Lane.

Next door to the Custom House is Billingsgate Market, designed in 1877 by the same man who did Tower Bridge and two other City markets, Smithfield and Leadenhall. Billingsgate is thought to be the very first wharf in regular use on the Thames. Its merchandise has for almost a thousand years been impregnating the neighborhood with the smell of fish. Business got a boost from Queen Elizabeth, who declared Wednesdays and Fridays to be meatless days, not out of an interest in diet or religion, but from a desire to keep British seamen and ships employed and seaworthy.

To watch the market at work, it is best to observe from a distance, say from above, hanging over the railings of London Bridge Approach. To observe at closer range is to participate, although involuntarily, with a strong possibility of bumps, bruises and other outsiders.

Here Lower Thames Street and its tributary lanes are alive with fish folk going about their pressing business with pushcarts, trucks, horses and wagons, and on foot. The celebrated fish porters wear long white coats and flat-topped wooden hats, broad-brimmed, ridged and covered with tough leather. Called billy-cocks, the hats are said to be a little-changed version of the helmets worn by the British archers at Agincourt. Atop their head-

Billingsgate is not quite so picturesque today, but just as crowded.

gear, the porters balance a stack of five or six wicker fish baskets, supposed to hold a hundredweight, and speed to their destinations. Anyone getting in their way is apt to be roundly cursed, but alas not with the sulfurous imagery which made "billingsgate" the word for what the Oxford Universal Dictionary characterizes as "vituperative language" and "violent abuse."

The high tide of business is 6 to 9 A.M., and the interior of the arcaded market building is heaped with the silver, green-blue and coral of the undersea world, aglitter under a merciless man-made light.

There's a street running uphill just across from the center of the market building, and a few steps along it is the Watermen's Hall of 1780 whose narrow, gray and rather unkempt exterior is graced with the sense of just proportion which so happily prevailed in its period. At the church of St. Mary at Hill (for which the street is named) the Billingsgate merchants celebrate their harvest festival — fish harvest — every October. The church is decorated with boats and nets and lobster pots and hundreds of pounds of fish on beds of fern. The church was designed (1670–1676) by Wren to replace the fire-raked earlier structure, but twenty years later someone else rebuilt the west wall in yellow brick, and eighty years later someone redid the side walls. Its chief point of interest is technical, with a square domed center resting on four free-standing columns, derived, says Dr. Pevsner, from the Byzantine quincunx plan.

St. Magnus the Martyr, another Wren church — with one of his best steeples — is just west on Lower Thames Street, very close to London Bridge and almost touching the walls of the modern, overblown Adelaide House. This juxtaposition, which sounds hopeless, really works out well visually: further west the Victorian vastness of Cannon Street Station makes a vivid contrast with the surrounded low-crouched buildings. In demonstration pieces of this sort, non-planning can be seen to have its own virtues. The happy happenstance has a good deal more life and vigor than the over-nice plan. Moved by the free-swinging, good (though admittedly accidental) result, one might wish to echo the Royal College of Art student who recently said upon graduation, "To hell with Good Taste."

West past Pudding Lane, the next hill street is Fish Street Hill, at the top of which stands the Monument to the Great Fire of 1666. A 202-foot high fluted Doric column designed by Sir Christopher Wren, it would, if toppled in the right direction, fall on the spot in Pudding Lane where the fire began in a bakehouse. The Monument stands on the site of the church of St. Margaret, consumed by the flames. On top there is a balcony (enclosed in wire 1842 to halt the procession of suicides), and above that a bulbous urn of brass emitting brass flames, very much not Wren's original idea. The pedestal is laden with allegoric reliefs, such as a disheveled, languishing London seated on ruins and being slowly raised up by winged Time. Science, Architecture and Liberty are being dispatched to her aid by a

Wren's monument to the Great Fire of 1666.

Roman-clad Charles II. Below the King is Envy, literally eating her heart out. It costs sixpence to climb the 311 steps. The panting and vertiginous tourist can add humility to discomfort by reflecting that tavern boys used to race up and down in the eighteenth century in 2 minutes 32 seconds for the round trip.

Lower Thames Street scuttles under London Bridge Approach to emerge on the other side as Upper Thames Street. On this far side of the Approach, Fishmongers' Hall rears up like a bridge house of old. It is an elegant Greek Revival building of 1831 with none of the extravagance of that other Grand Manner company hall, Goldsmiths' Hall, built in the same period. This comely building has a terrace looking out over the river.

Upper Thames Street would be worth a visit if only to see with one's own eyes the thirty alleys leading down to the river under such names as Angel Passage, Red Bull Yard, Dark House Lane, Stew Lane, Broken Wharf and White Lion Wharf. After London Bridge, the street takes another plunge to get under Cannon Street Station, a harrowingly busy commuter dump,* exterior reckless Victorian, interior streamlined 1964. The station

---

* One hundred trains in sixty minutes during each rush hour. Traffic studies for modernization revealed that 42,000 commuters arrive in the morning, but only 40,000 depart at night. Next morning 42,000 arrive again.

Fishmongers' Hall in the early nineteenth century.

was the site of the Steelyard of the Hanseatic Traders, deeded to them by Henry III in the mid-thirteenth century. The Hanse merchants did not relinquish their property title even after they were banished from the country by Queen Elizabeth, and their legal successors (what a protracted feast for lawyers) finally disposed of the plot in 1835.

On the west side of the station runs the street of Dowgate Hill, on whose left-hand ascending side are three City Company Halls: Tallow Chandlers' (1670, with 1880 alterations), Skinners' (1790 on street side, 1670 on courtyard), and Dyers' Hall (1840). Just behind them on College Hill is St. Michael Paternoster Royal, Wren replacement of an earlier church (first mentioned 1219). Wrecked by a rocket-borne bomb in 1945, it has been restored. Dick Whittington lived and died next door and was buried here. The paternoster in the name refers to the neighborhood rosary trade, and the royal to La Réole, a Bordeaux wine district. The area below here around Upper Thames Street was for centuries the center of the wine trade and was known as the Vintry.

Geoffrey Chaucer, son of a vintner, was born here about 1340. The Hall of the Worshipful Company of Vintners is still in the neighborhood, right after Southwark Bridge (the bridge is a 1921 replacement of the Rennie 1819 structure). Rebuilt after the Fire, the Hall was altered on the outside a couple of hundred years later to please Victorian taste, and once again to please Edwardian taste, and once again in 1948, to restore the whole thing to its original appearance.

Up the street is another Wren church (1677–1683), St. Benet Paul's Wharf, very Dutch, very sweet in red and bluish brick with white quoins. This is the sort of endearing doll's-housey sort of thing associated with Wren's name by those who overlook his mastery of the grand Baroque, his good hand at Gothic, and his infinite variety.

At the end of Upper Thames Street sits Blackfriars Station (the Dominicans were here from the 1200's to the 1543 Dissolution). Blackfriars Bridge is here too, originally named upon completion in 1769, for William Pitt, Earl of Chatham. For a dozen years the public paid the halfpenny toll, penny on Sunday, and then suddenly rioted and burned the tollhouse. Impressed by so forthright an argument, the Government bought the bridge and made it free, though they didn't liberate Southwark Bridge downstream until 1864. Blackfriars was demolished in 1860 and replaced in 1890 by the present structure.

Just before the bridge is Puddle Dock, where flies the flag of the Mermaid Theater, proof of the dedication of actor-producer Bernard Miles, who restored theater to the City after a three-hundred-year drought. Converted in 1959 from a warehouse whose cast iron columns remain at the entrance, the theater is identified by so many visitors as "the original Shakespeare Mermaid" that the management no longer argues.

Queen Victoria Street, cut through in 1867–1871, leads back from the riverbank to the heart of the City. Apothecaries' Hall, 1670, partly 1786, is up Blackfriars Lane, just above Playhouse Yard, where the last City theater was, back in Queen Elizabeth's day. To the left, the august *Times*. Its 1964 buildings astonish many who expected something more in keeping with *The Times*'s immutable front page. This is at least the original address, where the paper was born in 1785 as the *Daily Universal Register*, taking its rightful name and vocation three years later.

Further along on the same side of Queen Victoria Street, and restored in 1961 after bombing to its 1695 Wren appearance, is St. Andrew by the Wardrobe: the King's storehouse (Great Wardrobe) was nearby for two hundred years until the Great Fire. A congenial neighbor is the British and Foreign Bible Society, founded in 1804 to circulate Bibles, which it has done in 865 languages through seven hundred million copies. Beyond is the offensive Faraday Building, London long-distance telephone central.

The College of Arms, on the other corner of Godliman and Queen Victoria streets, decides who has the right to what coats of arms if any. Three Kings of Arms head the College, with Clarenceux and Norroy & Ulster seconding the president, Garter King of Arms. They are assisted by six Heralds (York, Richmond, Windsor, Somerset, Lancaster, Chester) and four Pursuivants (Portcullis, Rouge Dragon, Rouge Croix and Bluemantle). They are all subject to a royal officer who is not a member of their college, but who has the duty of appointing Kings of Arms,

101

Heralds and Pursuivants. He has a throne in the Court Room of the building, being the Duke of Norfolk, hereditary Earl Marshal of England.

The college assists His Grace in arranging royal ceremonies — the opening of Parliament for example — and assists those in search of pedigrees and armorial bearings. Office hours for those who wish to consult the unparalleled records and collections are 10 till 4, except Saturdays when Bluemantle, Rouge Dragon and all depart for the weekend at 1 P.M. They wear tabards and cloaks only on state occasions. Their building, although constructed anew after the Fire, was *not* designed by Sir Christopher Wren.

The 1964 building across the street is the headquarters of the Salvation Army, and across the street from it is St. Nicholas Cole Abbey, another Wren church, also bombed and restored. There is another, after Queen Victoria Street crosses Cannon Street, St. Mary Aldermary, first mentioned in 1080, and so named because it was "elder than any church of St. Marie in the Citie," according to Stow. It is one of the most surprising and exciting of Wren's works. It is Gothic, and built in this style because Henry Rogers left money for its reconstruction under proviso that the 1511 structure be copied. The tower is from the original, re-topped by Sir Christopher. The whole ceiling is plaster fan-vaulting, the whole interior rising and joyous.

On the right side of the street by Walbrook (the brook still runs underneath through conduits) is the hulking Bucklersbury House of 1958, one of a welter of new buildings which deliver a stale message in modern idiom throughout the district. But Bucklersbury House has one thing which distinguishes it from the rest, a remarkable architectural feature — a real Roman temple. Unearthed during foundation digging, the remains have been reassembled and exposed to view in front of the modern building. It was a Temple of Mithras, used from the year 90 to 350, a basilica 60 feet long. To the inexpert eye, it is an assemblage of flagstones, column bases and wall fragments. But still, it is a relic of a London in which the visitor must perforce believe but into which he finds it almost impossible to project himself.

Diggers have been finding pieces of Roman London here for a

A cast-iron cathedral of commodities, Leadenhall Market still thrives in the City.

long time. In 1889 a few steps from here in Bond Court they found a sandstone slab with a high relief of Mithras slaying the bull (now in British Museum), and in 1869 near the corner of Bucklersbury was unearthed one of the finest Roman mosaic pavements yet found (now at Guildhall). When the Temple of Mithras was first revealed in 1954, there appeared a magnificent marble head of Mithras in Phrygian cap, and small figures of Minerva, Serapis, Mercury and Bacchus. Mithras, a Persian deity attendant to Ahuramazda, the Sun God, was considered invincible and was adopted by Roman legionnaires and voyaging merchants and brought by them to Britain.

The most important place in the City for Roman finds has not been here on the banks of the Walbrook, however, but up on the hill to the east, Cornhill, where Leadenhall Market now spreads its iron wings. If one crosses the open space at Bank, the center street of those radiating from here, the one laid toward the rising sun, is Cornhill, which at the next main crossing changes its name to Leadenhall Street. Off Cornhill to the right, burrowing into the cheese-wedge between it and Lombard Street, are alleys, and lodged among them are three places of special interest. These are exemplars of two City institutions — the Wine House and the City Tavern or Chop House. Here, if the hour is right, are food and drink and — is this what the traveler seeks? — atmosphere.

The ambiance is not imposed, not decorator-arranged. So deeply steeped in time are these institutions that it seeps out of the old beams and permeates the place and the people. The Wine Houses and Chop Houses conform to a pattern, but it is a pattern not conformed to anywhere else any more. The pattern includes a management which acts according to the ancient innkeeping tradition, i.e. by managing. Customers find life smoothed and pleasure deepened by according themselves to this tradition, whose invariables include copious portions of good cooking and potables of high standard swiftly and deferentially served. Prices are moderate to downright modest.

The Jamaica Wine House in St. Michael's Alley is the site of London's first coffeehouse, opened by a Dalmatian named Pasqua Rosee in 1652 at "the sign of my own head." When it later became the Jamaica Coffee House, it was the center for merchants in the West Indian trade. There are today four mahogany-walled bars, known to intimates as "traps," and each trap known by its number. "Ladies and beer drinkers, downstairs."

Simpson's Tavern is at 38 Ball Court, and the George & Vulture at 3 Castle Court. However, they can be arrived at through any of the passageways into the interior from Cornhill or Gracechurch Street or Lombard Street: Birchin Lane and Castle Court, St. Michael's Alley, Ball Court, George Yard. On the ground floor of both houses are grill rooms where clients may select the morsel to be grilled on the open-fire grill by the grill chef. The ground floor of Simpson's is paneled and the seating is mostly in high-backed stalls very like stable loose-boxes. The George & Vulture has horse boxes as well, and etched on the glass of its main doors, *Thomas's Chop House*. Originally — circa 1150 — under the name of the George, it had a considerable success, so that two hundred years later that eminent Wool Gatherer (collector of customs at Wool Quay, that is) Geoffrey Chaucer could have been a customer. After complete transformation of the premises by the Great Fire, the five-hundred-year-old George moved in with another tavern called the Live Vulture. Where Thomas came in is not certain, but probably through the door. The City Pickwick Club has its headquarters here.

Among the amiable buildings backing onto this series of courts (they include the churches of St. Michael and St. Peter) is the former City of London Club, now at 19 Old Broad Street, where it maintains a large, unshowy two-story clubhouse on some of the most expensive real estate in the world. The City has the distinction of being the most expensive club in London (entrance fee £100), but lacks not for fully subscribed members.

Across Gracechurch Street, and also approachable through any one of a dozen tiny byways, is Leadenhall Market (the City in 1411 acquired an old lead-roofed manor house here). The market buildings of 1881 show us Sir Horace Jones, architect on the way to his 1886 apotheosis at Tower Bridge. Having worked up his courage and imagination on Smithfield market, Billingsgate market, Marshall & Snelgrove's department store, Temple Bar Memorial and the Guildhall School of Music on Victoria Embankment in a thirty-year career, Sir Horace finally began to take

105

flight in the path blazed at this period by *Alice in Wonderland*.

Leadenhall Market is a soaring and flowering, the glorification of cast iron and the celebration of abundance. From a central dome, three arms branch out to cover the market with a great high glass-roofed *galleria*. The color scheme is cream and deep red, so that the giant Corinthian columns are cream, the plinth marked with the City flag painted in red, the lower third of the fluting in red, and the elaborate capitals in red and gilt, with gilded red gryphons sitting atop the capitals. The upper stories over the shops are embellished with leafy plaques. The richest

Goose, pheasant and other fowl still hang high at Leadenhall Market.

decoration comes not from Sir Horace, however, but from the market men who festoon their spaces (wholesale and retail) with chickens and rabbits hung by the hundreds.

The notices about licensing ("A Special Session will be holden at the Guildhall Justice Room") are posted in the market pursuant to laws of William IV (1820–1830). An ordinance of 1345 directed all strangers to sell their poultry in Leadenhall and Londoners to sell in Westcheap (that stretch of Cheapside since known as Poultry). The market has oozed out of its official Victorian carapace and shops occupy the nine lanes straggling as far as Lime Street.

Today's market site was the center of Roman London. Here was a basilica thought to measure 505 feet in length, longer than many a basilica in Rome at the time. It was a huge aisled hall on an east-west axis, and south of it toward the river was the Forum (public square) 500 feet across, surrounded by shops and offices. Around this center clustered the centrally heated, marble-paved, tile-roofed town houses of officials and rich merchants.

The other big City produce market, for meat, is Smithfield, completely at the other end of the Square Mile, bordering on Finsbury and Clerkenwell. If one passes the Bank again and pauses before turning down Princes Street, one gets a view down Poultry and Cheapside past the church of St. Mary-le-Bow through a growing avenue of glass walls westward toward St. Paul's.

That whole area was once covered with markets. Cheapside was formerly called Westcheap to tell it apart from Eastcheap which still exists just by the Monument. The Saxon word *chepe* meant market. Side streets still wear their market names: Bread Street, where the Mermaid Tavern was and where John Milton was born, 1608; Milk Street, where Sir Thomas More was born, 1478; and Wood Street. Cattle and fish were sold at the Stocks Market, the site of Mansion House.

Three streets down is the rebuilt bombed Wren church of St. Mary-le-Bow. The steeple is "Wren's proudest." Atop a broad, square tower, the belfry is framed in pilasters and topped by an open balustrade girding the first of three tiers of the steeple, two of which are circled in pillars. The whole is capped with an obe-

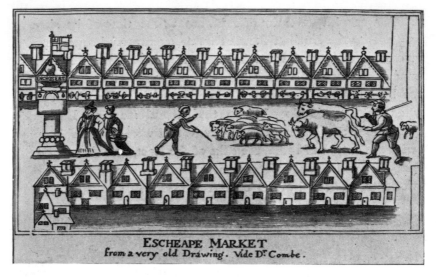

ESCHEAPE MARKET
from a very old Drawing. Vide Dr Combe.

lisk spire crowned with a nine-foot-high weathervane, a copper gryphon. In words it sounds labored and even topheavy, but in being it is quite noble.

The early Norman crypt is one of the oldest pieces of church architecture in London. Its groined arches ("bows of stone") are thought to be the origin of the church name. The bells which called to Dick Whittington perished three hundred years later in the Great Fire of 1666, and their replacements smashed to earth in World War II bombing, but the fragments were melted into the metal of the new ones (first rung 1961), cast by the same company that made the 1680 set. Anyone born within the sound of Bow bells is a true Cockney, which at the City's current decibel level means that Cockneys have ceased to be born. Although Whittington would have been able to hear them six miles away on the hill at Highgate in the fourteenth century, six streets away would probably be the record in the mid-twentieth.

After contemplating the view down Cheapside, to reach Smithfield, one continues down Princes Street which becomes Moorgate to change its name again after it passes the invisible old City gate to become Finsbury Pavement. At Finsbury Square, one is outside the City proper and can gaze northward up City Road through a neighborhood changing from a mean mélange of mouldering mansions and tenements to a bright, clean, airy corner of town. To the left of this spot, the works of the New Barbican triumphantly rise.

Immediately up City Road is the parade ground of the Honourable Artillery Company of the City of London, Britain's oldest military body. Like the guilds and Trinity House, it functioned long before it was officially incorporated (1537) to supply officers for the City's trainbands of volunteer soldiers. This site has been its headquarters since 1642, and Wren and Pepys were both members here. The H.A.C. fires all the salutes from the Tower of London for royal birthdays and such, and its captain-general is always the Prince of Wales or the Sovereign.

ver London Bridge and through the City was the way to Westminster's Royal City (1639).

North of the parade ground is another stretch of green, Bunhill Fields, a cemetery unused since 1852. Here lie Daniel Defoe, William Blake, John Bunyan. A notice on the gate says that from 1685 until its closing, more than 120,000 bodies were buried here. Another notice of more than two dozen regulations specifies (No. 3) that no "gipsy, hawker, beggar, rogue or vagabond shall enter or remain in the Burial Ground."

Across the street at No. 47 City Road is John Wesley's modest four-story yellow brick house. Wesley (1703–1791) spent the last twelve years of his life here. In the same grounds is the Chapel, opened in 1778 to — as the signboard says — "continue the work begun at the Foundery near this site in 1739 . . . The Reverends John and Charles Wesley ministered here. It is the mother church of World Methodism." John Wesley is buried in the churchyard.

Still further north on City Road, past Old Street and East Road, in a region still bleary with blight, is Shepherdess Walk (the laurels are cut down). Here, some recall, was 1881 Salvation Army headquarters. But most would be more likely to cite it as the site of the old Eagle Tavern, translated from simple tavernity in 1825 to become "the mother, father and wet nurse of the music-hall." Both of these headquarters were on the same spot, in the same building in fact, now vanished. There is a friendly pub with keepsakes of the original Eagle Tavern carrying on the name a few yards closer to City Road. The Eagle Tavern is a paramount feature of the true, non-nursery, original version of "Pop Goes the Weasel":

> Up and down the City Road,
> In and out the Eagle,
> That's the way the money goes —
> Pop! goes the weasel.

When the song was composed at the end of the eighteenth century, *pop* was a verb meaning "to pawn." It still means the same thing in London, although the pawnshops are disappearing. A weasel is a tailor's flatiron (still small clothing factories in the crumbling old terrace houses) as well as a leather-working tool or, in Cockney rhyming slang, a coat ("weasel and stoat"), all of which are hockable in thin times at poor places.

110

Across City Road from the Eagle is the Eagle Dwellings, built in the late Victorian era to improve the lot of the working class. Gray brick with the general cheer of a penitentiary, it is hard to imagine it an improvement on anything, which God knows it was.

Back at the beginning of City Road at Finsbury Square, there is a street going off to the left and leading in the direction of Smithfield market. This is Chiswell Street, on which the London County Council built (1965) the main portions of an estimable project, one of many going up around London at the same time. It is part of the upgrading of technological schools and the creation of a campus around the new buildings. This one, with three million dollars' worth of new buildings, is the Northampton College of Advanced Technology and the New City Day School, which will include schools of drama, engineering and dispensing optometry. The buildings, connected by flying bridges, are set in an automobile-free park.

There is another advantage to the location: it is but forty paces from an unquenchably flowing bowl of fellowship, the Whitbread Brewery, part of which is within City boundaries. Samuel Whitbread began brewing in 1749, and there is still an early eighteenth-century building that was there when he bought the property. Soon after the grand opening King George III and Queen Charlotte inspected Watt's "stupendous engine" for grinding malt. The whole range of buildings seems honorably ancient, made of soot-softened brick, and the enormous Porter Tun Room is definitely from 1774. However, the visitor can see for himself, since there are guided tours one and a half hours long, at 10:30 and 2:30, followed by a restorative free sample of the company's wares.

Founder Whitbread was the first Member of Parliament to speak against the evils of the slave trade. There is a Reynolds portrait of him. Samuel Whitbread II was Richard Brinsley Sheridan's patron. When the Drury Lane Theatre burned in 1809 (Sheridan, guzzling bumpers of port at the blaze: "Surely a man may take a glass of wine by his own fireside!"), Sam Second built a new theater. Today the firm is one of the backers of the

111

Mermaid Theater at Puddle Dock.* Following an old tradition which dates clear back to 1954, Whitbreads provides the six horses (with appropriate handlers) to draw the Lord Mayor's coach in the Lord Mayor's Show. Until the coach is lodged in the still-building new London Museum, it and the horses are on view at the brewery.

This firm has turned ten of its London public houses into "theme houses," making them small museums of personalities or institutions. This is a boon to lore-hungry tourists and seems equally well viewed by the natives. The Sherlock Holmes, for example, is actually frequented by Scotland Yard detectives.

Almost every pub in the kingdom is owned by brewing companies. Not more than one in a hundred is a free house. The tied house generally sells no draught beer other than that of its brewer. Lately more pubs seem to have an extra tap with a special non-company brew, but it most often less a sign of tolerance than of shrewdness, since a postwar phenomenon of the brewing industry has been amalgamation, and the "foreign" beer is probably a product of a subsidiary company.

The nomenclature of British beers is simple: the cheapest is called *bitter*, a pale beer heavy with hops; the cheapest is "ordinary," the "best" or "special" costing a bit more, and the order, "one of the best," provokes a half-pint of the more expensive bitter. To get a pint, one must order a pint. The other common tap beer is *mild*, darker, sweeter, dearer. And a *mild and bitter* is half-and-half.

There are special brews on draught, but not everywhere. These include Guiness's stout, and a dark bitter called "Scotch ale," and one sold only in the winter, "Burton," a very dark, rather sweet and often strong brew. Almost every type of beer and ale is available at pubs in the bottle, and often iced, which the draught drink is not.

Although the tax is 8½d per pint, Britons drink one out of

---

* In 1965, for the first time in modern history, the City Corporation commissioned a play. To mark the 750th anniversary of the Magna Carta sealing; John Arden was commissioned to do a drama on the theme of the charter to be presented at the Mermaid. The Corporation also bought out the house for a week (for school pupils) and guaranteed half the production costs.

112

every nine or ten pints of the eighty million brewed in the world (1963 figure). This makes them fifth in the international swill-stakes, after Belgium, West Germany, Australia and New Zealand.

Half way along Chiswell Street is bomb-blasted Milton Street, once that river of agony called Grub Street. Its name was changed in 1829 to something of a higher literary assay by petition of the non-literary inhabitants. From the 1650's its name was associated with hack writers. In 1775 Dr. Johnson defined it in his dictionary as "A street in London much inhabited by writers of small histories, dictionaries and temporary poems."

When they could get it, Grub Streeters prized the inspirational qualities of gin over those of beer. They had to wait until 1725 to lay their hands on any, for it was not introduced into England until then. But when it came, it came with a shout, and besides the grocery shops and street barrows which dispensed the fiery dram, there were 17,000 gin shops in London where the miserable lower classes could drown their very real misery. The distillers of this elixir settled upon Clerkenwell (the Clerk's Wells were bought up by a Dr. Sadler), as a place with pure water, a good grain supply, a labor pool and an unslakable market. John Rocque's 1746 map of London shows distillers both north (Nicholson's is still there) and south (Booth's still there) of Clerkenwell Green. Gordon's ("A tower of strength in a changing world") did not come to Goswell Road until 1769, but it has stayed, benefiting perhaps from the publicity spread by an old adage: "On a wet Sunday the shortest way out of Manchester is through a bottle of Gordon's Gin."

Gin is triple-distilled. Once to obtain alcohol from grain, once to work off the "feints" such as fusel oil, and once to infuse the botanicals, which are invariably juniper berries, coriander seed, and other herbs and seeds usually dubbed Secret Ingredients. The name "gin" is an abbreviation of the French or Dutch for juniper.

The tax on alcohol is somewhat higher than the 5s 8d the gallon of beer. In 1729 it was two shillings a gallon, in 1736 it was twenty shillings and in 1964 well over two hundred shillings the proof gallon. According to one distiller, "The Government

113

has a financial interest four or five times greater than the Company has in every drop of gin distilled."

Leaving the brewery and proceeding in a more or less straight line westward, one comes to Aldersgate Street. A short jog to the right and first corner on the left puts one in Carthusian Street then into Charterhouse Square. Off the square are the Charterhouse and St. Bart's (for Bartholomew) Medical School.

A priory of Carthusian monks was established here in 1372. Dissolved in 1537 (its members cruelly exterminated), the Charterhouse was literally stripped, and Lord North used the remains to build himself a mansion which seemed for the rest of the century to carry a lethal curse. North died soon and the heir, the Duke of Northumberland was beheaded in 1553, and the property passed to the Duke of Norfolk who was decapitated in 1572. The Earl of Suffolk entertained Queen Elizabeth and James I here, but the big house was too big for his purse and he sold it in 1611 to Thomas Sutton, who made the mansion into a house of charity.

Charterhouse became a hospital for eighty impoverished "bretheren" and a school for forty poor boys. It became one of England's leading public schools (i.e., private, being public in the sense that they are not state schools) and in 1872 removed to Surrey. Three years later it was occupied by the Merchant Taylors' School (founded 1561) until it too moved to the country. The bomb damage to Charterhouse was restored by 1961, and the brethren — Church of England bachelors or widowers over sixty — are once more installed. The gatehouse is fifteenth-century, but beyond this visitors can go only by prior arrangement with the Registrar, and then only in groups and only on Saturday.

Bart's is the offspring of yet another priory, whose site lies one street south of Charterhouse Square, back inside the City line. This is Smithfield, one of the secret places of London, though it seems open and banal enough to look at. It's a wide lake of pavement churned by traffic complicated by the activity of a giant meat market, and there are the walls of a hospital and some narrow lanes disappearing behind some sagging buildings. Appearances are misleading, for the stones have tales to tell and the walls conceal considerable beauty.

A St. Paul's prebendary named Rahere returned from a pilgrimage, and in 1123 here founded an Augustine priory and London's first hospital, thus obeying a vision which had ended a desperate illness on the road from Rome. There is a legend that he was once jester to the King and he is recorded as "a pleasant witted gentleman" who accomplished his mission through "the engaging charm of his manner." The hospital and cloister rose with rapidity. Of all the great hospitals St. Bart's is the only one still on its original City site.

The priory was suppressed in 1545. The Lord Mayor, Sir Richard Gresham, pleaded successfully for retention of the hospital, the City matching the King's endowment of five hundred marks a year. Thus, the King who closed the hospital gets credit for reopening it with the inscription, "Founded by Rahere, refounded by Henry VIII."

Rahere may well have been the founder of St. Bartholomew's Fair, held on Smithfield (smooth field) every August 23–24–25 for the saint's feast day. It ran every year from Rahere's time until 1855, at a pleasant profit to St. Bart's.

It was a horse and cattle fair, a cloth fair, a puppet-show–peep-show–sideshow–wirewalking–boxing–wrestling–eating–drinking–musical–athletic fair. Ben Jonson wrote a play called *Bartholomew Fair*. After the priory was dissolved the fair went on, Sir Richard Rich having bought the rights along with the property. Lord Mayors and Aldermen came in coaches and robes for the opening. Everyone who was anyone attended, as Evelyn and Pepys noted in their time, but gradually it became more and more disreputable. The Lord Mayor ceased to open it in person, then finally ceased to announce it, and it dribbled to an end. But it was fun while it lasted, for at least six hundred of its seven hundred years.

Even the Puritans, who shut the theaters and stopped the dancing elsewhere, did not close the Fair. Only one thing could cause suspension of the Fair in its heyday — the Black Death. The plague of 1348–1349 left alive only two out of every three Englishmen. During the resulting labor shortage, wages rose, despite a Royal decree freezing them. New taxes were imposed to feed on the unusual prosperity. Resentment against all the guild and feudal restrictions simmered among the craftsmen of the

115

small cities and the countryside. In 1381, after thirty years of slow ebullition, it suddenly boiled over into open revolt.

The town of Dartford was taken, and under a workman called Wat Tyler, Canterbury was seized on June 10. The rebels, whose ranks swelled at every village, streamed toward London. They sacked the Archbishop's palace at Lambeth, invaded the City, burned the houses of officials, broke open and then burned Newgate and Fleet prisons, damaged the Temple and other public buildings. This action won Tyler the audience he had been demanding of King Richard II. At Mile End, the King promised the end of serfdom, feudal obligations, market monopolies and all restrictions on buying and selling (these last two would have put an end to the Guild system). To underline the urgency of his

Meat is still the main business of Smithfield Market, but no longer on the hoof.

116

claims, Tyler walked into the Tower of London and hanged several officials.

Then he and the King met again, in Smithfield. It was only the fourth day of the rebellion, which was spreading throughout the country. As he faced the King, Tyler heard a catcall from the crowd and made as if to reach for his dagger. Before he could unsheath it, he was mortally struck by the cutlass of the Lord Mayor, Sir William Walworth. It is usually said that Walworth acted to protect the King against what he thought was an attack from Tyler. It is even more possible that he saw an excuse to end the talks successfully for his side and he took it.

The King stayed bravely and outfaced the enraged rebels, who were dispersed when reinforcements arrived. Over England the uprising was remorselessly beaten down. King Richard took back his promises.

Seventy years later another group of revolting countryfolk were assembled in Smithfield. These were the men of Kent and Sussex under Jack Cade. They were protesting against the same old Statute of Laborers and against the high taxation and general misrule of Henry VI (who went mad three years later). They were furious too that the King's policy-makers should have lost the war and the English-held provinces in France. Equally discontented Londoners opened the gates of London Bridge to Cade's men, but they did not prevail and Cade was killed in battle soon after.

Not long after, the execution stake was set up here. Many of the condemned men from the Tower of London were executed here. The biggest season for executions, always a popular public spectacle, was under Mary Tudor, starting in 1554. During her reign at least 270 Protestants were burned alive at this spot.

When the Augustinian order was suppressed, most of the main church of St. Bartholomew the Great was torn down. What remains to us now is the choir of the church and a thirteenth-century portal topped by an authentic half-timbered Tudor upper story. The half-timbering was revealed when a 1915 zeppelin bomb blasted off the tiles which had concealed it for centuries.

Around the remaining portions of the choir, a small house of worship was completed in the nineteenth century, matching the original Norman manner. The brooding, massive quality of the twelfth-century construction is strong in today's church. The mysticism and toughness of the Crusaders who brought this style home with them from the East is strongly evident.

The hospital has its own little church, St. Bartholomew the Less, which retains its tower from the fifteenth century. The hospital's historic buildings, no longer tenable, were replaced 1730–1759, to become historic in their turn. The Great Hall (no admittance) is one of James Gibbs's finest pieces.

William Harvey, after studying Cambridge under a student of Vesalius, went to Italy and studied under Gallileo. Applying the master's principles of dynamic motion, Harvey discovered that the heart pumped blood through the body, circulating the same fluid over and over. He proved his theory in 1616 while chief physician at St. Bart's.

The individual blood circulation might be improved by a pause on Charterhouse Street, which runs along the northern edge of the market area. Here at No. 15 is the Fox & Anchor, a public house which could claim special distinction, but doesn't bother. For the special needs of market porters, it's open at 6 A.M. (your average pub opens at 11 A.M.) and stays open straight through until 3 P.M., serving breakfast and tea and coffee as well as the Usual until eleven, and then lunch from noon to 2:30 P.M. This is an unusually hospitable and intelligent arrangement.

Crossing the next road, Farringdon Road, where a V–2 rocket exploded at high noon on this street corner in March 1945, killing a hundred persons, you come to Ely Place. At least, early in 1965 it was Ely Place, an eighteenth-century private close with gates tended by top-hatted beadles who not long ago were relieved of crying the hour. By now they may be relieved of all their duties, since the plan is to pull down Ely Place and shove up something less old-fashioned.

The Bishops of Ely had their town house here, of which long occupation there remains only the tiny fourteenth-century chapel. Since its purchase by a religious group in 1874, the chapel has been known as St. Etheldreda's Church (she is the patron saint of Ely). The purchasers were a traditionalist denomination known as the Roman Catholic Church, and this church is the only pre-

Reformation house of worship to be reacquired by a Catholic congregation.

The chapel is not to be confused with the sweet little St. Ethelburga's Church (1430) in Bishopsgate. St. Etheldreda is the one who gave us, involuntarily, the word "tawdry." We have it from Blount that the saint "thought herself punished for wearing rich Necklaces of Jewels; and therefore women after that wore neck laces of fine silk." Since her English name was Audrey, these became Sain Taudrey's Laces. By the seventeenth century the quality of such frills greatly declined — they became tawdry. But suppose she had been known only by her Saxon name, what word would we have instead of "tawdry"? Tetheldredful?

Through a passageway called Ely Court one can squeeze out into Hatton Garden (a street, not a park), past Ye Olde Mitre. This pub in the passage sports a stone graven with the Bishop of Ely's mitre and dated 1546. The stone is authentic. The pub is Terriblie Gotte Uppe.

Hatton Garden is named for Sir Christopher Hatton, a man everyone but Queen Elizabeth seemed to find unbearable. She initially admired his dancing, later made him her Lord Chancellor, dispossessed the Bishop of Ely and gave Hatton Ely Place for an annual rent of £10, ten loads of hay and a red rose plucked at midsummer. The bishop was reluctant to give up his mansion. The Queen urged him to do so: "Proud prelate, you know what you were before I made you what you are! If you don't immediately comply with my request, by God! I will unfrock you."

He was a good target for jinglers:

> Sir Christopher Hatton lives here.
> He has a great house, but no cheer,
> A large cellar but no beer.

Even after he was dead, he caused comment. When his ornate monument was placed between memorial tablets for Sir Philip Sidney and Sir Francis Walsingham in old St. Paul's, this was written:

> Philip and Francis have no tomb
> For Great Sir Christopher takes all the room.

119

Hatton Garden, which has buildings dating from 1720 to 1964, doesn't care too much about appearances. It doesn't have to: this street is a river of diamonds, with eddies of sapphires, pools of emeralds and rubies and shoals of pearls. And there are the associated precious metals as well (through cellar doors and gratings one may glimpse the ardent glow of crucibles). There are buildings called the Diamond Bourse and the Diamond Club, and that is exactly what they are.

However, it is not entirely true that Hatton Garden is "the center of the diamond trade," as it is usually called in the press. The center of the diamond trade is the De Beers company, which has a world monopoly on diamond production, and their subsidiary Diamond Trading Corporation is not in Hatton Garden but around the corner on Charterhouse Street. About a dozen times a year, having selected the diamonds it cares to release, the Corporation announces a "sight." Here ten to twelve million dollars' worth of stones made up into price-tagged packets are offered to those persons on Diamond Trading's Buyers List whose applications to attend have been accepted. The lots of raw gems will not be split — if you want one, you take the whole bunch. And the price is marked on the packet — no higgling. The unwritten (and certainly unspoken) motto of the firm is Take It Or Leave It.

Since there is no other legitimate source of raw stones in town, the dealers take it. Their profit will come from skill in cutting the raw gems and from disposing of stones they didn't really want in the first place.

A foggy day in Hatton Garden ruins the diamond trade, because then even choice blue-white stones look as yellow and cheap as some of the peripheral curbside traders.

There are other businesses in the Garden, though. One is scientific instrument making, and the craftsmen here can claim fraternity with Robert W. Paul, whose name should be writ large in every Executive Wash Room.

In 1894 two Greek showmen came to Mr. Paul's Hatton Garden shop and asked the twenty-five-year-old instrument maker to reproduce for them Edison's Kinetescope, a sort of crank-operated peep-show motion picture viewer. The deal was legitimate, inasmuch as Edison had no British patents. Paul made not the six machines that had been ordered, but sixty, devising improvements as he worked. In February 1895 he produced a workable projector for the Kinetescope roll. Having no pictures to show, he made one of his own on the roof of the Alhambra Music Hall. One of the first fictional films, it ran for eighty feet and was called *The Soldier's Courtship*. Afterwards, Robert Paul married the heroine. The following year he shot the first newsreel made in Britain, the 1896 Derby.

To supply the demand for his projectors, he expanded his workrooms, trained projectionists, bought an estate at Muswell Hill and made it the nation's first film studio. He introduced film tricks — ghosts, fairies, giants. He built a high-speed camera to take movies in slow motion. He made animated cartoons.

Robert W. Paul was a pre-Hollywood Boy Wonder, Movie Mogul and Cinematic Genius. One day he took his entire stock of film, worth a gold-standard fortune, piled it all up in the yard and set fire to it.

Then he went back to making scientific instruments. He never made any explanation and he died in 1943 a rich and evidently contented man.

122

THE LONDON OF
SIR CHRISTOPHER WREN

Sir Christopher himself — The Great Fire — His plan for reconstruction — Rebuilding St. Paul's and fifty-one City churches — Wren's reward — St. Paul's tombs, towers, bells — The blitz — The new Cathedral precinct.

SIR CHRISTOPHER WREN was a Renaissance man, and his masterpiece, St. Paul's Cathedral, is one of the great architectural achievements of the Renaissance. It was undertaken in 1675: the Renaissance came late to London.

Noted as a mathematician, anatomist, and more especially as an Oxford professor of Astronomy, he did not look into architecture until he was thirty-four years old. By the time he was fifty, he had left his personal stamp more indelibly upon London than any other individual, and London has harbored some impressive individuals in the past two thousand years. He left St. Paul's, fifty-one City churches, three elsewhere in town, and a number of major public buildings.

Born in Wiltshire in 1632, he was the son of a clergyman who was later Dean of Windsor. Christopher was a student at Westminster, but the Civil War put the Royalist family in an uncomfortable position, and the boy was placed in the London house of Sir Charles Scarborough (later physician to Charles II) where he learned mathematics and anatomy.

John Evelyn recorded meeting "that miracle of a youth, Mr. Christopher Wren, nephew of the Bishop of Ely," and called him "that prodigious young scholar." At fifteen he had begun making inventions, doing etchings and engraving and making scientific investigations, mostly medical. At seventeen, he entered Oxford and at twenty was a Fellow of All Souls.

Five years later he became Professor of Astronomy at Gresham College, a post he filled for four years before returning to Oxford as Savilian Professor of Astronomy. He was there when he solved the problem Pascal sent to challenge the scholars of England — determine the arc made by a nail in a coach wheel turning on a perfectly flat surface. Although Wren solved the problem he never got the promised purse of pistoles. He wrote the constitution for the newly formed Royal Society of London for Improving Natural Knowledge, still the premier scientific society of Great Britain.

Then the desire to build overcame him. "'Beauty is from Geometry," he wrote, and "Firmness, Commodity and Delight, Beauty and Strength depend upon the geometrical Reasons of Opticks and Staticks." He made his only trip to the Continent in 1665. Most of his six months were spent in Paris, where he met Mansard and the visiting Bernini and saw the building of Versailles.

The Gothic cathedral of St. Paul's was tottering before the Great Fire.

His first architectural work was the Chapel of Emmanuel College, Cambridge. Upon request he submitted in May 1666 a plan for rebuilding the crumbling Norman edifice of St. Paul's Cathedral (there had been a Saxon St. Paul's before that) which Inigo Jones had already patched up. But then the Great Fire spewed forth and destroyed the Cathedral and most of the City in five days of September.

"God's Terrible Voice in the City" had begun trembling the walls in 1665 with a nine-month scourge of plague which killed 100,000 Londoners. Now four-fifths of the City was scoured out by flame: 436 acres ravaged, 13,200 houses burned, 88 of the 108 churches (108 in one square mile!) consumed, including St. Paul's.

The day after the fire, five complete plans for rebuilding the cindered City were submitted to the King. One of these was Wren's, another John Evelyn's. Wren specified avenues along the Fleet River and a wide quay beside the Thames. He also pro-

SPECT OF THE CITTY OF LONDON, AS IT APPEARED, IN THE TIME OF ITS FLAME

Southwarke

On the 2 of September in y⁰ Yeare 1666 (being the Lords day) in the morning, there hapned a dreadfull Fire, in y⁰ house of one Mⁱ Farmer a Baker in pudding lane, which Continued till about 5 at night the Wednesday following, in which time it burnt 89 Chur-ches, thirteene thousand & two hundred houses, 656 acres, of 97 Parishes within y⁰ Walls, there was but 11 left intire, One Robert Hubert of Roane in Normandy, vpon examination, Confessed he was that fired the first house (viz) Mʳ Farmers in Pudding lane, for which fact he was Shortlie after hanged at Tiburne,

posed a grid system for the streets, overlaid by thoroughfares radiating from five *rondpoints*, in the French fashion. Evelyn's plan was along the same general lines, but with a more rigid grid. Some of the other proposals were more radical, but all were doomed because all required a redistribution of land which the owners would not accept. Wren sat on the commission which evolved the final plan. The medieval street plan remained, along with the City gates. Wren got his quays, but the Fleet was too filthy and the Thames waterfront too desirable for either improvement to endure very long. Street booths were forbidden, and building permitted only in stone and brick (a few timber and plaster houses of the old style were built anyhow, vide the Hoop & Grapes at Aldgate).

The government levied a special tax on coal, one-third of the proceeds to rebuild St. Paul's, one third for the parish churches, one-third to assist householders in rebuilding private houses and shops. The rubble was dumped outside the walls, and some of the mounds in Whitechapel, half a mile outside Aldgate, weren't removed until 1803. The domes of debris were higher than the three-storied London Hospital (moved here 1748), and the old ash pile is now the site of Mount Place, Mount Street and Mount Terrace.

In 1669 Wren was made Surveyor General of Works and was knighted the following year. He designed seventeen of his fifty-one parish churches in 1670, only seven in the next four years since he was somewhat busy with the building of the previous seventeen and getting the St. Paul's project approved and launched, and then he resumed his old pace. For his work on St. Paul's he received an annual stipend of two hundred pounds. For his work on the parish churches, nothing.

His first design for St. Paul's was too radical for the Commissioners (the ground plan in the shape of a Greek cross, for one thing) and it was rejected. His second design was accepted with Royal permission to change it as he deemed needful, and change it he did. No matter what other compromises he was forced to make, he got his dome, his swelling, peaceful dome which until the 1960's dominated the skyline of London.

With approval of the design in 1672, Wren began removing

old St. Paul's, using gunpowder until complaints obliged him to stop blasting. He then invented the forerunner of today's steel wrecker's ball to batter the stubborn ancient stones. There were 47,000 wagonloads of old St. Paul's carted away.

Commented E. C. Bentley three centuries later:

> Sir Christopher Wren
> Said, "I am going to dine with some men,
> If anybody calls
> Say I am designing St. Paul's."

Before the Great Fire and Christopher Wren, this was the interior of old St. Paul's.

Eight years before the Great Fire, the Choir of St. Paul's looked like this.

There is a legend that as the walls of St. Paul's rose, Wren had himself hauled aloft in a basket to oversee the work. This rather endearing legend has the added charm of being absolutely true. And during all this physical labor, this huge managerial task, this solving of engineering problems (there are flying buttresses concealed between inner and outer walls, and a brick cone between inner and outer dome), this creation of a majestic work of art, Wren wrought his remarkable city of parish churches. Not one is like another, yet all are unmistakably Wren.

He marshals space, architectural orders, window shapes, vaultings, galleries, pillars and arches with a virtuosity that deals in fundamentals, not superficials. For example, his fifty-one churches have seven different basic styles of steeple, but each one is an individual of its type, with its own characteristics. There is in all an infinite variety and vigor.

In addition to this work, he did the three parish churches outside the City, made a new Temple Bar, worked on rehabilitation of the Temple and of Westminster Abbey, built the huge Greenwich and Chelsea Hospitals and Kensington Palace, put the superb Fountain Court and Garden Front on Hampton Court Palace.

The churches standing about St. Paul's are sited and pinnacled in harmony or in counterpoint with the dome and towers of the cathedral, which was started in 1675 when Wren was forty-three, opened for worship in 1697, when he was sixty-five, and the final stone laid on the cupola 1710, when Wren was seventy-eight.

Yet the Commissioners were unhappy. For several years they withheld his annual pittance to drive him to finish the cathedral faster. These were not the commissioners with whom he had battle over the plans. Those had been appointed by Charles II. James II and William and Mary had reigned and gone, and Queen Anne was now on the throne. When the Cathedral and the awesome sweep of his thirty years' labor were finished, the Commissioners rewarded Wren by firing him ignominiously from his post.

On the cathedral wall the inscription says, "*Lector, si monumentum requiris, circumspice*" ("Reader, if you seek a memorial, look about you"). Since in London one is exposed to grandeur

The view on the next two pages of Sir Christopher Wren's Cathedral of St. Paul was made early in the eighteenth century, soon after the church was finished.

either Gothic or Classic, the magnificence of baroque on the grand scale is stunning.

There are many, many, many monuments to the dead, and many of these are overbearing and just plain bad. But John Donne's posthumous half-joke is here against the south wall of the choir. He was Dean of St. Paul's for ten years more than a quarter of a century before the Great Fire, and his monument is one of the few to survive. Donne is not esteemed on his own side of the Atlantic as one of the great poets of the English language, at least not as generally or as profoundly as he is on the North American side.

Admiral Lord Nelson's tomb in the crypt of St. Paul's Cathedral.

132

In his poems Donne often saw himself clearly as the Poor Sinner, but without bathos, and often with a strong sense of how ridiculous he — and all humans — can be. His monument shows him wrapped in his winding sheet and standing on his burial urn. It was his idea. He had a painting made of himself thus, kept it by his bedside until death, and the monument sculptor used it for his model.

Sir Christopher's ashes are interred in the crypt, to which a sixpenny admission charge is made for upkeep. The Chapter should raise the prices and improve the upkeep, unless they feel that the dust and deliquescence engender beneficial intimations of mortality. But as it is, the crypt of St. Paul's is sort of a bargain-basement Valhalla. Here are buried two of the most revered heroes of British modern history: Arthur, Duke of Wellington, and Horatio, Viscount Nelson. Wellington's porphyry-and-granite tomb is flanked by marble columns holding flame-shaped electric lamps. Nelson is pickled in alcohol (the only body so preserved in St. Paul's) inside a coffin fashioned from the mainmast of *L'Orient*, French flagship at the battle of the Nile. *L'Orient*'s captain, Louis Casabianca, had his ten-year-old son along on the voyage, the boy who stood on the burning deck whence all but he had fled. It was at this battle that Nelson said (according to Southey), "Before this time tomorrow I shall have gained a peerage or Westminster Abbey." And here he is, a peer, in St. Paul's. His wooden coffin is lodged inside a mammoth black marble sarcophagus atop which is a carved red-and-gold cushion bearing a red-and-gold coronet. This rather garish envelope was perpetrated in 1529 by Benedetto da Rovezzano for Cardinal Wolsey, later reserved for Henry VIII, both of whom avoided it, even in death. Nelson was put inside in 1805.

At the far end of the crypt is one of the more astonishing public exhibits in London: the ornate funeral car of the Duke of Wellington. Its six wheels, richly ornamented, are made of the metal of Waterloo cannon. On the body of the vehicle the names of Wellington's victories are lettered in metal. Twelve black horses, three abreast, drew this ponderous, rumbling, eighteen-ton vehicle, apparently inspired by the Car of Juggernaut, all across London from Chelsea Hospital to St. Paul's. Behind the British shield affixed to the front of the car is a panoply of arms of Wellington's epoch: rusting lances, dusty rifles and bayonets, rotting banners, kettledrums with split heads, tarnished helmets and breastplates, corroded swords. The penetrating symbolism may be intentional.

There are other military and naval leaders buried down here, and here too is a "painter's corner" with the bones of Benjamin West, Sir John Millais, J. M. W. Turner and Sir Joshua Reynolds. Sir Max Beerbohm, Walter de la Mare and Sir Arthur Sullivan are laid here too, as is Sir Alexander Fleming, who discovered penicillin.

High above, on the west front are twin baroque towers. The right-hand one, with the clock, houses "Great Paul," the biggest bell in England (16¾ tons, cast 1882) and "Great Tom" (5½ tons) from Westminster Palace, recast in 1709 for St. Paul's. Great Paul rings for five minutes a day, at 1 P.M., and Great Tom sounds only the funeral knell, and only for members of the royal family, the Archbishop of Canterbury, the Bishop of London (whose church this is), the Dean of St. Paul's, or the Lord Mayor.

This porticoed west front was cleaned for the first time in 1964, and for the first time in almost two centuries, Wren's architectural ideas were clearly visible. The lower half of the façade was a deep black, the upper half a smudgy gray, each ledge and projection was a little guano mine. Cleaning restored the balance to the building, with no noticeable divisions other than those made by the architect. The weekly *Observer* observed, "The whole assumes a lighter, more attenuated and vigorous character."

The sense of proprietorship Londoners feel toward St. Paul's was heatedly revealed in the controversy which preceded the cleansing. There was not really any room for controversy: the Dean and Chapter and the Church Commissioners had decided to have their cathedral cleaned. But the people, those for and those against the decrustation, felt in their hearts that St. Paul's was in fact *their* cathedral, as it had been in one form or another since A.D. 604. The press frothed with reader correspondence, as it traditionally does on occasions of public moment. One letter to

Cleanliness is next to godliness; St. Paul's was cleaned in the 1960's despite objections.

135

the *Architects' Journal* said the writer had direct word of Wren's endorsement of the cleaning through the *Psychic News*. However, a considerable group put their money, as the transatlantic saying goes, where their mouths were, and the face-washing fund was soon fully subscribed. Of course, there was no competing fund to keep the face sooty.

Some of this possessiveness toward St. Paul's was engendered, or at least stimulated, by the cathedral's survival of the Blitz. St. Paul's did more than escape destruction: it was defiant. It was the City, it was London, it was even England as it stood alone in a sea of flames. The bombs fell, the air and the earth shook, the streets were lanes of wreckage in the smoke and fire. But St. Paul's was there, dear and familiar and reassuring. The night sky was really bright as day as the City crashed in flames, and from all the vantage points of London you could see Wren's dome. Always a symbol of shelter and steadfastness, its symbolism was enriched and renewed. The Londoner's world was literally collapsing, but St. Paul's stood.

For millions of first-time visitors, just as for millions of young Londoners, the Blitz is almost impossible to envisage. The worst scars were gone within ten years of the end of the war. Twenty years after there are virtually no traces left. The wartime tags about "valiant London" and "heroic Londoners" are not fully comprehensible to those who come after. The statistics have hardened into lines of type and columns of numbers: 30,000 killed, 50,000 injured, 100,000 houses destroyed, 1,650,000 damaged. These do not explain the heroism of London or its people.

Germany, having thrown the British Expeditionary Force into the sea, was master of Europe by the middle of June 1940. England, alone and defenseless, was next. First step in the invasion of England was a three-pronged attack: against the Royal Navy and its bases, against the Royal Air Force and its bases, against London to disorganize the government and the national defense by terrifying the populace. To prostrate London by bombing might be Guernica again, Rotterdam again. The British might even sue for peace.

From June 18, the Germans prepared their newly won attack bases, reconnoitered the British coasts, moved up their bombs and planes. The Battle of Britain began August 8. London was hit and hit again by day and by night, but not with the full fury that was to come. At the end of August the German News Bureau announced, "The attacks of our Luftwaffe are only a prelude. The decisive blow is about to fall."

And it fell. On a fine September Saturday, 375 bombers came at teatime. At their leisure they dropped their bombs. It took only an hour. They ripped apart and set fire to Woolwich Arsenal, the Beckton gas works, the docks at Millwall, at Limehouse, at Rotherhithe, at Tower Bridge, and dumped the remainder into residential Kensington.

Ordinarily, a thirty-pump fire is a very big fire indeed, but on this first large raid there were nine fires at once rating over a hundred pumps. From a Ministry of Home Security summary of this first heavy attack:

> It set alight the wooden blocks in the roadways, a thing without precedent . . . The flames were so long and their heat so great as to blister the paint on fireboats that tried to slip past under the lee of the opposite riverbank 300 yards away. At Woolwich Arsenal men fought the flames among boxes of live ammunition and crates of nitro-glycerine . . . There were pepper fires, loading the surrounding air heavily with stinging particles so that when firemen took a deep breath it felt like breathing fire itself. There were rum fires, with torrents of blazing liquid pouring from warehouse doors and barrels exploding. A rubber fire gave forth black clouds of smoke so asphyxiating it could only be fought from a distance. Sugar, it seems, burns well in liquid form as it floats on the water of dockland basins. Tea makes a blaze that is sweet, sickly and very intense.

When the daylight raid ended, there was a pause, and the night bombers came, guided by the fires. Until 4:30 the next morning, they dropped high explosive and incendiaries. Sunday night they were back, and Monday night and every night for fifty-seven nights from September 7 to November 2, 1940.

There were raids after this, shattering raids bitterly costly in lives and supplies and homes. The City's major devastation came on Sunday night, December 29, with the water mains smashed and a fifty-mile-an-hour wind to insure destruction. Inside St.

137

Paul's, twenty-eight incendiary bombs caught fire and were extinguished by the firewatchers. Hundreds more bounced off the roof. In a later raid (known as "the Wednesday"), April 16, 1941, one bomb whistled through the roof and exploded on the high altar. In the same night strike more than a thousand were killed and over two thousand injured. Eighteen hospitals and thirteen churches were hit, and the Houses of Parliament were bombed again. Worse was the five-hour raid on the night of May 10 that year, with 1436 killed and 1792 injured, and vast damage including the destruction of the House of Commons Chamber. That night the RAF and antiaircraft fire brought down thirty-five of the three hundred attacking bombers.

That was the final great, furious raid on London by bombing planes, though there were other occasional bashes to follow. It was after the D-Day invasion was safely away that the buzz-bombs began. In June 1944, the V–1 flying bombs began dropping and in September the V–2 (the "V" was for "vengeance") began to ravage London anew. The last one of these fell in March 1945. The V–weapons killed 8938 and injured 24,504.

The strain of living through this is easily understood in general terms — the frightening noise and concussion, the presence of death and calamity, the yawning uncertainty. But to live through it every day and every night, that is not easily understood now, to carry on with the work at the shop or the office, to worry about members of the family, to try to cook meals ("Potatoes are very warming and invigorating and protect you from illness" — Ministry of Food) when the gas was out, the water was out, and very possibly the windows were out as well, the grocery store smashed to flinders, the milkman buried under a falling wall. How to explain how it was to come home and find no house, sometimes no street, nothing but a churned and smoking stretch of broken brick? There was no section of London that was not hit, no lane without its gaunt, gutted building, no street without the evidence of shattered lives, the bathtub hanging in space from its pipes over a long slide of masonry with wallpaper and broken furniture showing among the debris. "One walked, hearing the familiar, brittle crunch of glass."

There was always the problem of getting to work in the morning by ripped railways and through streets blocked by fallen walls. The roadway has collapsed into the bombed subway station and the lost bus lies on its side in the crater. The office has been bombed. You must go round the other way, and the other way is a long clamber over rubble and around half buried burned automobiles.

The winter of 1940–1941, every night a hundred thousand Londoners slept in the bunks arranged (finally) in the deepest underground stations, at Southwark, at Clapham, at Hampstead. There were other hundreds and hundreds of thousands who did not seek shelter, but went out to fight: firewatchers, air-raid wardens, ambulance drivers, rescue crews, the personnel of the rolling kitchens, the auxiliary firemen and policemen, first-aid crews were all volunteers. They were attacked and they fought back.

"London is facing riots, the authorities prove to be helpless, and everywhere there is the wildest confusion," said an October third broadcast in Germany. A collaborationist French broadcast said, "The legend of British self-control and phlegm is being destroyed. All reports from London concur in stating that the population is seized with fear, hair-raising fear. The seven million Londoners have completely lost their self-control. They run aimlessly about in the streets and are the victims of bombs and bursting shells." This sort of message came from experts in terror. They could have been right, and they were wrong only because London was valiant and its people heroic.

Almost everything around St. Paul's, including the publishing center of Paternoster Row (four million books lost) was wiped out. Slowly, to a new plan, the entire precinct is being rebuilt. It will be completed about thirty years after the bombings, the same amount of time it took Sir Christopher Wren to build the cathedral and six dozen other remarkable London landmarks.

Descending the hill toward Fleet Street you will still find Canon Alley, Dean's Court, Creed Lane, Ave Maria Lane, Pilgrim Street and Amen Corner.

THE LONDON OF
DR. SAMUEL JOHNSON

His street, Fleet — Newgate Prison, penalties and executions — Old Bailey, some historic trials — The Fleet River and prison — Newspaper row — Press Lords — Penny press and responsible journals — Drink — Johnson's house and his life — The Temple, its gilded history and tenants — Inns of Court, how to tell a barrister from a solicitor — Chancery Lane — The priceless papers of the Public Records Office — Treasure Vaults of London — Lincoln's Inn and Lincoln's Inn Fields — The Law Courts — London School of Economics — The Embankment — Waterloo Bridge — The embellishments, amusements and population of Victoria Embankment Gardens — The Arches — The Strand — Lost palaces — Dr. Johnson's church, oranges and lemons and St. Mary-le-Strand — Somerset House — Bow Street villains and heroes — The London Police then and now — Drury Lane, Covent Garden opera, square and market — Savoy palace, chapel, hotel, theatre — The Adelphi and the brothers Adam — Trafalgar Square, Horatio Nelson's career and column, National Gallery, St. Martin's-in-the-Fields — Charing Cross, center of London

D R. SAMUEL JOHNSON (1709–1784), novelist, playwright, satirist, lexicographer, biographer and conversationalist, is esteemed — deeply if not widely — for his recipe for cucumber salad.

> A cucumber should be well sliced, and
> dressed with pepper and vinegar, and
> then thrown out, as good for nothing.

This spirit of scrupulous analysis and meticulous prejudice based on general irreverence still prevails in Fleet Street, the newspaper row of London. Dr. Johnson lived most of his London life in this district and spent a good deal of his time in its taverns which persist in murmurous multitude down to our day.

On the way down Ludgate Hill from St. Paul's to Fleet Street, the first main street on the right is Old Bailey. Where it meets Newgate Street there sits the Central Criminal Court, also called Old Bailey (the name most likely from the Latin *ballium* — enclosure — of the City Wall between Newgate and Ludgate).

The present Court building, in Civil Service Baroque, dates from 1907, but the twisted history of this spot goes back to the twelfth century. The prison which began in the City gate overflowed into other buildings. After George Dance the Younger, Corporation Architect, supervised the demolition of the gate — along with the other gates and the London Bridge houses — he built a new prison here in 1783. It was frightening, even from the outside, an almost solid wall of granite broken only by low, nar-

Newgate — outside, a model prison built in 1783, inside, "a prototype of hell."

141

row slits at the center. Inside was what Magistrate (and novelist) Henry Fielding called "a prototype of hell." It was surely one of the worst prisons in England, and was deeply and abidingly hated.

Newgate's bad reputation began early. An official investigation in 1354 confirmed that the jailers were extortioners and that misdemeanor offenders were thrown into the deepest dungeons with the most dangerous criminals. Wat Tyler's men wrecked the place in 1381, and the Gordon rioters wrecked it again four hundred years later. A century after this last invasion, another official investigation determined that the jailers were extortioners and that 340 debtors, for example, were jammed into space provided for 100.

Apart from debtors, and a few special criminal cases, prison was but a way station on the road to exile or execution. As late as 1800 there were still more than two hundred crimes punishable

The Gordon Rioters of 1780 put horrendous Newgate to the torch.

142

by death. Picking a pocket of more than one shilling, theft of goods worth more than forty shillings from a house, theft of goods worth more than five shillings from a shop, or breaking a pane of glass after five P.M. for the purpose of stealing, were among the capital offenses. Save in the matter of treason, the defendant on a capital charge had no right of counsel.

There were lesser penalties than death — flogging, branding (abolished in the 1750's), transportation (to Australia after the Americas would have no more; abolished in 1857), exposure in the pillory (last used in London 1830, dropped in 1837).

For the prisoner, Newgate provided nothing but chains, bread and water. (In other prisons, the prisoners beat hemp, picked oakum or turned treadmills which produced nothing.) The cheapest bed was two shillings a night — otherwise there was the damp stone floor — and prices for any necessity were equally high; for comforts, astronomical. Those who would not or could not pay what the jailers demanded were thrown into the darkest, filthiest holes where they would be most likely to die. The only item that was cheap — relatively — was gin, easier to get from the warders than water.

In 1783 the spot outside the jail door became the site of the gallows. Previously, every six weeks, the condemned, each wearing a halter around his neck and accompanied by his coffin, were taken in carts the three miles from Newgate to Tyburn. Dr. Johnson was among the London figures who protested the halting of the morbid carnival (which he never attended) because he considered it a deterrent to crime.

To open proceedings before the Old Bailey, ten men were hanged in one morning. At this event the new neck-breaking drop was introduced as an improvement on the standard method of simple strangulation. In the year 1785 there were ninety-six executed here, twenty of them on one day. It was always a festive occasion for the mob. As many as twenty thousand would turn out for the sport, as they did in 1789 for the partial hanging of a female counterfeiter who was then cut down and burned at the stake — the last to suffer this fate in England. Public hangings ceased in 1868 with the death of Michael Barrett, a Fenian who tried to blow up the Middlesex House of Detention.

143

Hearing criminal cases from Greater London, the court sits at Old Bailey Monday through Friday at 10:30 and at 2:00 (except in August) and the public is admitted to seats in the galleries. The first two days of each session sweet herbs are strewn on the courtroom floors and the judges carry nosegays of posies, reminders of the years when the pervading prison smell choked those unused to the odor, and when there was ever-present fear of jail fever, an especially virulent form of typhus which killed far more people than the hangman.

The judge presides in red robe and full-bottomed wig. The attorneys in black robe and short wig address him as "M'lud." The prisoner mounts to a raised, railed platform, the dock, through a short stairway from a cell below the courtroom.

Old Bailey has heard some of the most celebrated murder trials of all times, crimes which the rest of the world prefers to consider "classically English," as well as treason trials and at least one historic trial for indecency.

This last was the trial of Oscar Fingal O'Flahertie Wills Wilde, sentenced in 1895 to two years at hard labor on a 25-count indictment of committing acts of gross indecency with various male persons. The indictment had been handed down after Wilde sued the Marquess of Queensberry for libel and lost. The Marquis — the boxing-rules man — with whose son, Lord Alfred Douglas, Wilde had been involved, had sent a card to the Albemarle Club addressed to "Oscar Wilde posing as a sodomite," and the libel action followed. Since calling Wilde a pederast was no libel, it followed that he must be guilty of the crime (and it is still a crime in England) of being such — thus the indictment. The day of his release in 1897, Wilde crossed to France where he died in 1900. Between his sentencing and his death he published but one thing, a poem, *The Ballad of Reading Gaol.*

The traitors tried here included William Joyce, who enraged Britons with his sneering "Lord Haw-Haw" broadcasts from Nazi Berlin during World War II. At his trial in 1945 Joyce proved that he had been neither born nor naturalized a Briton, having been born to Irish parents — naturalized Americans — in the United States. He further submitted that he had been a German citizen since 1940.

144

But the Crown contended that he was subject to British law in that he had, through fraudulent statement, obtained a British passport to leave England for Germany. Until the passport expired in July 1941, the Crown considered Joyce British to the extent that asking for the protection of the Crown (which is what a passport gives) is to proffer allegiance, and in giving its protection, allegiance is demanded by the Crown.

The court found this reasoning sound and the broadcasts treasonable. The verdict of guilty was upheld by the Lords, four to one, and Joyce was hanged. Many Britons now question the proceedings and the sentence.

For giving Russia atom-bomb data through a Canadian spy ring, Alan Nunn May, atomic physicist, was sentenced in 1946 to ten years' imprisonment. Klaus Fuchs, the scientist who transmitted secrets of the uranium and plutonium bombs to Russia, was sentenced in 1950 and served fourteen years, after which he went to East Germany.

The multiple murders in the post–World War II period included the well-spoken, sullenly handsome lady-killer George Neville Cleverly Heath (1946), the dim-witted trucker Timothy Evans, convicted of murdering wife and child (1950), and, two years later, the state's star witness against Evans, meek, middle-aged strangler and necrophile John Reginald Halliday Christie, who murdered his own wife and at least five other women in the same house and in the same manner as he had killed Mrs. Evans, whose slaying he confessed at the trial. All three of these men were hanged.

Brian Donald Hume did not hang. As his third trial began, the prosecution dropped its murder charge. At the first trial the judge fell mortally ill, at the second the jury disagreed and at the third Hume accepted a plea of accessory after the fact. He admitted that he had hired a plane the year before and had dropped into the ocean the bundles a hunter found floating. They contained the remains of a black-market dealer named Stanley Setty. Hume said he had been paid by mysterious strangers to dump some bundles without knowing what — or, as it turned out, whom — they contained.

The prosecution could show that Hume had had a carving

knife sharpened the night of the murder, had had his rug cleaned the day after. The defense could show that there was not one Setty fingerprint in the apartment, and that no neighbor had heard the penetrating and singular sound of thigh bones being sawed. Hume served eight of his twelve-year sentence, then sold a story to the *Sunday Pictorial* headlined, I KILLED SETTY . . . AND GOT AWAY WITH MURDER. The following year Hume shot and killed a policeman during a Zurich bank robbery and was sentenced to life in a Swiss prison.

The church of St. Sepulchre across the way is also sometimes called Old Bailey. Poised between Smithfield and Newgate since 1137, it has seen some of the best in man and much of the worst. The parade of the condemned from Newgate used to pause here on the way to Tyburn Tree to receive a bouquet and a blessing. Now one can sit in the garden of the church and contemplate Old Bailey and the site of Newgate through the traffic fumes. The church was rebuilt in the fifteenth century and has a heavily restored tower of the date. The interior has been redone many times, once by Wren, traces of whose work are still visible. Captain John Smith is buried here, although his statue stands outside the church of St. Mary-le-Bow.

Sea Coal Lane and Fleet Lane, which enter the street called Old Bailey as one goes back toward Ludgate Hill, once led to the busy quays of the Fleet River, which was thrust underground in 1737 as far as Ludgate Circus, the remainder in 1765, much to the relief of all. All except perhaps those who tossed in so much garbage and debris that the river was literally choked with it.

Shortly before it was put down out of sight and smell, Alexander Pope described it:

> Fleet Ditch with disemboguing streams
> Rolls the large tribute of dead dogs to Thames,
> The king of dikes! than whom no sluice of mud
> With deeper sable blots the silver flood.

The first special commission to consider the foulness of the waters was convened in 1356. Conditions had not improved in 1593 when a petition appealed for action, the river "being a congregation of unwholesome smells of the town." The Fleet

Prison on the riverbank suffered epidemics of pestilence attributed to the stagnant corrupted waters. By the eighteenth century, the prison was reserved almost exclusively to debtors. Until an Act of Parliament abolished the practice in 1753, the prison was one of the spots noted for instant, no-questions-asked marriages. In the days of banns, dowries and sword-bearing relatives, this was a thriving business. The prison was closed in 1842. In 1875 the Congregational Memorial Hall rose on the site, and is still here, not unprisonlike in appearance, in Farringdon Street.

Fleet Street, reaching from Ludgate Circus to Temple Bar, is only a quarter of a mile long. Like the quarter-mile square in the center of the City and the half-mile of Whitehall, this small parish is the seat of international power. In this quarter are lodged the daily newspapers of London, and because the United Kingdom is small, they are national newspapers as well.

Off the main street scurry about three dozen lanes, alleys, courts, passages and small streets blossoming into tiny squares, all of which fit into "Fleet Street." As a matter of fact, three of the most important houses are not on Fleet Street at all: *The Times* is almost on the riverbank at Printing House Square, far east on the other side of Blackfriars; Thomson House, almost as distant, is northward on Grays Inn Road, and the new red edifice of the *Daily Mirror* is off on Holborn.

The British read more newspapers than any other people in the world, 51.4 copies per hundred of population, a proportion nearly twice as high as that prevailing — and declining — in the United States. Although readership continues undiminished, the number of newspapers lessens in Britain as it does everywhere else in the Western World. In 1910 there were 190 dailies, and in 1965 there were 124. In Fleet Street today there are 2892 members of the Central London Branch of the National Union of Journalists, but in the welter of mergers and take-overs which began in the late 1950's, more of these newspapermen are working for fewer and fewer owners.

The first of the modern press empires was built by Alfred Harmsworth, who owned the *Evening News*, the *Daily Mail*, the *Daily Mirror* and *The Times* by 1908. He became Lord Northcliffe in 1917, and his brother Harold became Lord Rothermere.

Those who called Northcliffe a megalomaniac in his final years were proven correct in their diagnosis upon his death (of megalomania) in 1922.

The nephew of Northcliffe and Rothermere is one of the major figures of the Fleet Street of the 1960's. The mergers he contrived in 1961 were the biggest in British press history. His Daily Mirror group had 24 per cent of the daily and 42 per cent of the Sunday circulation of the entire nation.

With the death of Lord Beaverbrook (daily and Sunday *Express*) in 1964, the Canadian influence in Fleet Street is maintained by Roy Thomson, who took his seat in the House of Lords in 1964 as Baron Thomson of Fleet. "Example" is perhaps more the word than "influence." Beaverbrook was the son of a Scottish Presbyterian parson at Newcastle, New Brunswick. After a village school education he went forth into the world, which he very soon conquered. After amassing millions through acumen in controlling and developing corporate power, he departed for England, politics and journalism. He displayed as much genius for mass journalism as he had for moneymaking. He was probably the most vilified and deplored but nonetheless respected and loved boss in Fleet Street.

Roy Thomson came from a poor family too: his father was a Toronto barber. He made his fortune in the United States and Canada with radio stations and thirty small-town newspapers. In 1953 at the age of fifty-nine he crossed to Scotland, land of his (and Beaverbrook's) forebears, and in eight years was the second largest newspaper proprietor in the Kingdom, and one of its television moguls. Among other properties, the posh *Sunday Times* is his. His secret, like Beaverbrook's, is remaining himself, and keeping the individuality and energy which are as common on the far side of the Atlantic as they are rare on this.

The largest single readership belongs, as it has for a generation, to the *News of the World*, a weekly which specializes in libel-proofed summaries of spicy or scabrous court cases.* The details would be salacious — were they printed, which they never

---

* British libel laws are among the most severe in the world and are responsible for phrases in print such as "a man was being sought by police to aid in their inquiries" and "a weapon was found in the room where the body was discovered."

are — but the more than six and one-half million readers seem satisfied with the stark trellis of carefully bleached fact. Occasionally there is departure from the formula: in 1963 *News of the World* outbid all the great combines for the "confessions" of Christine Keeler, the pretty prostitute about whose friendship the Secretary of State for War lied to the House of Commons.

The sensational press of Fleet Street is about the most lurid — but dreary — in the world. Yet, the responsible publications produced here are among the brightest and most reliable anywhere.

There is a toothless Press Council to hear charges of unethical conduct. In matters of national security, the press obliges the government in deferring publication of ticketed items. But even beyond the secrets of defense, the government, no matter which party is in power, shows a growing tendency to have nobody looking over its shoulder.

There is the business of Crown Privilege, for example. When the company operating the Victoria Station hotel sued to get a clear yes or no on lease renewal before renovating the premises, the Minister of Transport invoked Crown Privilege. He forbade anyone from the nationalized British Railways to appear in court, declaring that Her Majesty's servants on Her Majesty's service could not be compelled, could in fact be prevented from testifying regarding said service.

Other services were, at the beginning of 1965, invoking the same immunity from due process of law. In regard to information generally, not things stamped Secret or Confidential, the machinery of government was increasingly screened from view. Under such circumstances, the role of newspapers as public watchdogs was greatly altered. It consisted largely of barking at shadows or howling after decisions were already made.

Physically, Fleet Street is a mess, but an exciting mess, of architecture lunging along a narrow street, ranging wildly from authentic seventeenth-century to bogus twenty-first-century — which is just about the way everyone wants it. It is a public street, to be sure, but with very much an air of being open to members only. In invisibly enforced sense of exclusivity, the Street is genuinely part of the City, but in other ways it is in but not of the

City. As one reporter pointed out, "You'll never hear a newspaperman say, 'I work in the City.' "

The pubs of this district have always been celebrated, and many still merit celebration. They do not lack for celebrants. Despite the fact that since the 1940's journalism has become an increasingly respectable calling and pays virtually a living wage (though union scales indicate it is not a wage printers and engravers could live on) to men who commute to families who want a Whiter Wash and bigger TV screen, reporting and editing remain among the most thirst-provoking of honest labors.

The Fleet Street tradition of publishing began when printing began in Britain and Caxton's assistant, Wynkyn de Worde, set up press at "London in Fletestrete at the Signe of the Swanne." The tradition of drinking is even older, obviously, since there was already a Swan where de Worde could establish his press. Dr. Johnson proclaimed on March 2, 1776, "There is nothing which has yet been contrived by man, by which so much happiness has been produced as by a good tavern."

Dr. Johnson also said, "When a man is tired of London, he is tired of life," thereby demonstrating that he was a small-town boy (from Litchfield at age twenty-seven) who continued to find the big city a wonderland to which he continued to run away every day.

A good deal of what he found delightful about London persists in his old neighborhood. Especially among the Fleet Street taverns and their variegated clientele. The Old Bell is still swinging down by Bride Lane. It is said to have been constructed just after the Great Fire to serve Wren's workers building neighboring St. Bride's church, which has the highest steeple in the City, and in the courtyard of which John Milton once dwelt. Hard by is Salisbury Court, where Samuel Pepys was born. This opens into tiny Salisbury Square, a secluded Victorian enclave, and the pleasant stir of discovery it provides can be prolonged by finding one's way down to the Thames through a series of connecting courts, with excursions into blind alleys on the way.

The Cock is no longer where Johnson knew it. After doing business at the same spot for something like three hundred years, it found its premises about to be razed in 1887 and moved across

the street to No. 22. Before this forced displacement, the Cock
was host to both Pepys (1668) and Tennyson (1840).

The earlier customer recorded in his diary for April 13:

> By water to the Temple, and thence to the
> Cock Alehouse, and drank and eat a lobster,
> and sang, and mighty merry.

Tennyson wrote this:

> O plump headwaiter at the Cock,
>   To which I most resort,
> How goes the time? 'Tis five o'clock.
>   Go fetch a pint of port.

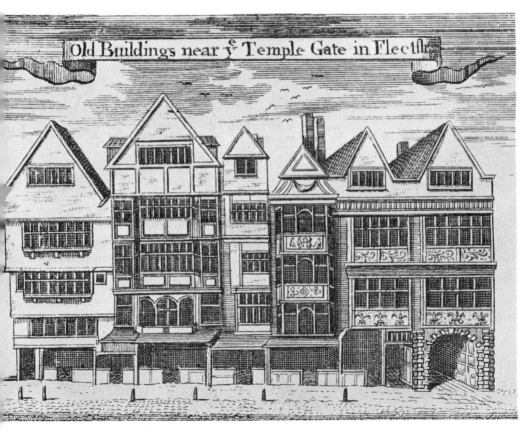

Much disguised, some of these buildings are still in use on Fleet Street.

It is said that the said headwaiter is said to have said, "I do not recall the gent."

Johnson's beloved Mitre, a medieval tavern which was scorched but not destroyed by the Great Fire, fell finally to the purveyors of progress when Hoare's Bank was enlarged in 1829. This early nineteenth-century building still stands at No. 37, and under it is the cellar (bare of bottles) of the Mitre.

Dr. Johnson lived hither and yon about Fleet Street, mostly in small courts which poke off the main thoroughfare, and for preference off the North side. He spent a dozen years at 17 Gough Square (sole Johnson house still standing), eleven years in Johnson's Court (named more than a century earlier for Elizabethan merchant Thomas Johnson), which leads into Gough Square, and died in Bolt Court, which also leads into Gough Square.

For two shillings the visitor may wander through the Gough Square house clear to the attic where the six amanuenses sat at countinghouse desks inscribing in the great folios the Doctor's definitions ("*Lexicographer.* A writer of dictionaries, a harmless drudge"). A visit can provoke not only an authentic literary *frisson*, but also one of the few apt twentieth-century occasions for uttering the word "amanuensis."

Johnson was paid 1500 guineas for the dictionary in 1755, worth then about fifteen times the $4500 the sum equals today. In addition, until the death of his wife Tetty in 1752, he brought out a twice-weekly paper, the *Rambler*. Later, he had a £300-a-year royal pension.

All this liberated him from dependence on a patron, defined in his dictionary as "commonly a wretch who supports with insolence and is paid with flattery." To Lord Chesterfield, the patron who let Johnson down, the Doctor wrote, "The notice which you had been pleased to take of my labors, had it been early, had been kind; but it has been delayed till I am indifferent, and cannot enjoy it; till I am solitary, and cannot impart it; till I am known and do not want it."

Of Chesterfield's *Letters* he said, "They teach the morals of a whore and the manners of a dancing master." Of his Lordship himself, "This man, I thought, had been a Lord among wits; but, I find, he is only a wit among Lords!"

In Johnson's Court in 1833, the *Monthly Magazine* was being published. In this "dark court in Fleet Street" where the magazine had "a dark letter box in a dark office" into which a dark young man slipped his first bright manuscript that anyone ever paid him for, and which appeared later as "Mr. Minns and His Cousin," in *Sketches by Boz.*

Although the house in which Dr. Johnson died in Bolt Court burned thirty-five years after his death, the neighboring house, No. 3, is still standing. It was for a number of years the headquarters of the London Medical Society through the generosity of its owner-occupier, Dr. John Coakley Lettsom. This physician signed his prescriptions "J. Lettsom," but with an eighteenth-century "J" that looked just like "I," which prompted this jingle:

> If any folk apply to I
>   I blisters, bleeds and sweats 'em
> If after that they please to die,
>   Well, then — I. Lettsom

Next door to Dr. Lettsom's, William Cobbett, that remarkable and useful troublemaker, began publication in 1802 of his *Political Register.*

When Johnson did move across to the other side of Fleet Street, where he had his early meetings with Boswell, he was from 1760 to 1765 at No. 1 Inner Temple Lane, a building no longer standing. The site is covered by a group erected in 1857 and named Dr. Johnson's Buildings.

The Temple embraces two of the four surviving Inns of Court — Inner Temple, Middle Temple, Lincoln's Inn and Gray's Inn — which march in stately procession, robed in green (sward) and red (brick) from the Thames northward three-quarters of a mile to Bloomsbury. They are sanctuaries buttressed by age, privilege and wealth. Their quiet (and it is astonishing how the clamor of traffic is dimmed within their gates) is enhanced by a centuries-thick layer of gentlemanly conduct and privacy.

The occupants of the Inns are something more than private gentlemen, however: they are ministers of a mystery, they are the teachers and the practitioners of the Law. The apparatus of Brit-

153

ish justice — robes, wigs, titles, conventions of address, court-room decor — is designed to confirm the awful majesty of the Law. Unlike the physician, who has lost much of his power as a healer and a social figure by doffing his priestly garb and permitting vulgarization of his arcanum, the lawyer has guarded both against the laity.

The Temple has more of the cloistral air than the other Inns, for it began in 1160 as the walled seat of the military-religious or-

The Temple in 1671 was an enclave for lawyers and students, a sheltered p
respects four centuries have not changed the place at all.

der of the *Pauperes Commilitones Christi et Templi Salomenio*, the Poor Knights of Christ and the Temple of Solomon, called the Knights Templars. Too rich, the poor knights, too powerful, too independent, they were brought down by Kings and the Pope in 1313 on charges of having substituted a pagan Mystery for that of Christ. This riverside enclave was then given to the Knights Hospitallers of St. John of Jerusalem, who allowed professors of common law to take up residence with their pupils.

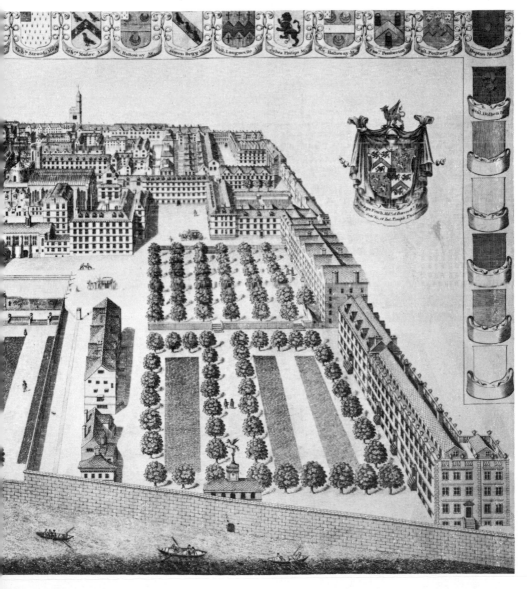

wns and trees and ancient buildings around the Crusaders' church. In these

The Inns of Court are the only institutions for the qualification of barristers in England. A barrister is a "lawyer of the highest class," recognized by judges as fit to plead in higher courts. The senior members of the Inns of Court, which are societies of barristers, call students to the bar. Those who aspire to hear this call register at one of the Inns and eat at least six dinners in hall each term for twelve terms — three years — in addition to paying their fees and passing their bar examinations. Those who are studying Law at a University need dine only thrice per term. The barrister is not engaged directly by the litigant, but takes a case "on the instructions of a solicitor."

Although a less magical figure than the barrister, the solicitor is no less a lawyer. He is a law-school graduate who has passed examinations, completed several years' clerkship and has been duly diploma'd as qualified, although not by one of the glamorous Inns of Court. The solicitor pleads in lower courts, takes care of legal matters not involving pleading (e.g., wills, probates, deeds and contracts). Indeed, as the family counselor, the solicitor is today a major factor in the investment world, since the amounts solicitors collectively are asked to invest assume enormous proportions.

In court cases, the solicitor takes charge. It is he who arranges the hearing (or the delay), collects evidence and draws up the brief. On the brief he marks the fee offered by the client and sends it to a barrister, who will either refuse the case or, on the basis of the solicitor's brief, go into court and plead. In legal-aid cases, the Court appoints barristers.

When a barrister "takes silk" he wears a silk gown and a bigger wig and after his name the initials Q.C. for Queen's Counsel. Those desirous of taking silk apply, after ten years' law practice, to the Lord Chancellor and if the application is approved, the barrister is appointed by a Royal Letter Patent, "Her Majesty's Counsel learned in the law." The Crown has first call on the services of a Q.C., services of which use is often made to obtain brilliant prosecution. In theory, the man in silk may not appear against the Crown, which would prevent his defending criminal cases, but generally he is given permission when he asks.

Taking silk is risky. A Q.C. does not appear without a junior, who receives a fee one-third less than the senior counsel. So, upon taking silk, the barrister charges higher fees than before, at the risk of having fewer cases. But if he wants a career as a judge or a Crown law officer, this is the usual road to follow.

Because the Inns of Court early established their training monopoly, judges were lawyers and servants of the law rather than "executants of the King's will."

Between the separate properties of the Inner and the Middle Temple, there is no visible dividing line. Even in the matter of the dinner call, the difference is slight: Middle Temple answers the notes of a hunting horn, Inner Temple responds to those of a silver-mounted ram's horn. Middle Temple buildings bear the sign of the Lamb and Flag, and those of the Inner Temple are marked with the seal of the Winged Horse.

The winged heralds of Hitler's Thousand Year Reich smashed much of the eight hundred-year-old Temple and destroyed parts of Lincoln's Inn and Gray's Inn as well. The damage has been repaired, although one cannot say in all cases that it has been made good.

The restoration of the Temple Church of St. Mary has been extremely well done, and in fact it proved easier to efface the ravages of the Nazi raiders than those of the Victorian "restorers."

The original church, consecrated in 1185 by the Patriarch of Jerusalem, is the nave of the present church. Circular, as are all Templar churches, in imitation of Christ's Sepulchre, it is partly Norman and partly Gothic in design. Attached to the Round is the 1240 chancel, the Oblong, which Pevsner calls "one of the most perfectly and classically proportioned buildings of the thirteenth century in England." An active serving church, it belongs to both Temples and is exempt from episcopal jurisdiction.

Middle Temple Hall was opened by Elizabeth I in 1576, and its double hammerbeam roof is still intact. Here *Twelfth Night* was presented in February 1602, probably by the author's own acting troupe. The serving table is said to have been made from the timbers of Drake's *Golden Hind*.

Another Elizabethan survival is the gateway from Fleet Street to the Inner Temple. One of the finest pieces of half-timbering to be seen in London, its second story overhangs the entry, and the third overhangs the second, with the attics tucked away behind a railed terrace. Originally there was a shop pocketed into the left-hand side of the gate, and there is a shop there to this day with proper contempt for the theory that historical monuments must be embalmed.

Directly across from this gateway is the entrance to Chancery Lane, which for a short stretch is within the City boundaries. To the right of it is the Church of St. Dunstan-in-the-West, founded in the 1200's, and whose present building was done by John Shaw at the opening of Queen Victoria's reign. Over the vestry porch looking Citywards is the statue of Queen Elizabeth made during her time to grace Ludgate. The other gateway figures of King Lud and his sons are inside. Westward, toward the Strand, is the spindly monument marking the vanished Temple Bar gateway, and on the south side of the road at No. 1 Fleet Street is Child's Bank, formerly housed in Temple Bar itself.

Chancery Lane is a narrow thoroughfare bending gently between Fleet Street and High Holborn, leading past the Law Society, the Patent Office, the Public Records Office, Lincoln's almost to Gray's Inn. This, and not the riverbank, is really where angler Izaak Walton really spent most of his time. After eight years around the corner in Fleet Street, he moved his linen-draper's shop to Chancery Lane in 1632. His friend John Donne, whose biography Walton wrote, was a reader of theology at Lincoln's Inn before becoming Dean of St. Paul's.*

Chancery Lane and its tributaries are today thronged with law students and jurists of Commonwealth and other nations once

---

* Even a brief list of those associated with the Inns is dazzling. Besides such resident nonmembers as Dr. Johnson and Oliver Goldsmith, the Temple housed such worthies as Sir William Blackstone, whose *Commentaries*, still invaluable to the law, were interrupted by the parties Goldsmith gave above him at No. 2 Brick Court at the end of the 1760's. Also, Sir Walter Ralegh, John Evelyn, William Congreve, Henry Fielding, Edmund Burke, William Cowper, Richard Brinsley Sheridan, Thackeray, De Quincy, William Wycherly, Boswell, the statesmen John Hampden and the Earl of Clarendon, and Judge Jeffreys of the Bloody Assizes.

Other than Donne at Lincoln's Inn were Sir Thomas More, William Penn, Horace Walpole, William Pitt, George Canning, Cardinal Newman, Disraeli and Gladstone.

Gray's Inn produced a host of Tudor statesmen and divines, including the Bacons, father and son, Thomas Cromwell, Sir Thomas Gresham, Archbishop Laud, Bishop Juxon, Sir Francis Walsingham and William Cecil, who became Lord Burghley and founded the line which has served England in high position ever since. Lord Macaulay was a member too.

colonies of Britain, testimony to the undiminished esteem in which British justice is held throughout the world.

Along the Lane to the right is a rather forbidding pile of gray mock-Tudor thrown up between 1851 and 1902, with the unstimulating title of Public Records Office. For those who respond to the legacy of Britain to the world, this is one of the most exciting and rewarding places open to visitors. The treasures are infinite: the records of the nation dating back as far as the Norman Conquest.

These records were first kept by the King's Chancellor who, with his fellow Royal Chaplains, constituted a reliably literate group of Court servitors. The Chancellor became Keeper of the Great Seal, which made royal documents legal and binding, and handled all State records and papers.

By the fourteenth century, the Chancery was a department of state and, weighted with paper, was unable to follow the King's Person, and thus settled in Chancery Lane. As the source of all writs, it was a center of the judicial system as well.

The search rooms are open to those who have written to obtain access, but for those who wish to browse on the high fields of history, there is a small free museum from which one can carry away photocopies of (for example) pages from Domesday Book, William the Conqueror's byre-by-thatch census of taxable English property. With an unusual awareness of the rigors of tourism, the museum is open only from 1 until 4 each weekday afternoon.

There are royal autographs and seals in profusion. Wolfe's letter to Pitt is here, saying on November 22, 1785, that he is willing to go back to America in spite of his ill health. A letter from the Comte de Frontenac assures the Governor of the Hudson's Bay Company of his desire for cordial relations. A sketch map of the Ohio River by a colonial serving with British troops in 1753 is signed "Major George Washington." This is the same Washington whose letter to his "Great and Good Friend" George III is here, written August 25, 1795, from the capital of the new United States. The letter closes, "I pray to God to have Your Majesty in His Holy keeping."

Another piece of Americana is the July 8, 1775, "Olive Branch Petition" from the Continental Congress (Georgia did not sign) seeking restoration of the former harmony between Mother Country and the colonies. The last lines say to the King, "That your descendants may govern your dominions with honor to themselves and happiness to their subjects is our sincere and fervent prayer." The first name, twice as bold as the others, is John Hancock. Ben Franklin, Thomas Jefferson and the Adamses signed too. They all signed another document 361 days later, which is on display at the Library of Congress, Washington, D.C.

Here are Drake's dispatch reporting the defeat of the Spanish Armada, Marlborough's announcement of victory at Blenheim, the log of Nelson's *Victory* at the Battle of Trafalgar, Wellington's Waterloo dispatches, and Captain Bligh's record of the mutiny on the *Bounty*.

There are documents from the hand of Chaucer, Ben Jonson, Spenser, Bacon, Milton, Locke, Defoe, Addison, Steele, Byron, Shelley, Scott.

Here is the record of incorporation on September 29, 1865, of the Industrial Newspaper Co., Ltd. Each of the founding members signed for the number of shares for which he had invested his capital. "Five shares . . . Karl Marx, Dr. Phil., Modena Villas, Maitland Park, Haverstock Hill." The company was dissolved by *London Gazette* notice May 1, 1883, and ever since May Day has been a day for major anticapitalist manifestations.

Across the way from the Public Record Office is the elegant home of the Law Society, which is to solicitors what the Inns of Court are for the barristers, a teaching, examining qualifying and dining body.

Up the Lane to the right is the Chancery Lane Safe Deposit, which started in business as a perfectly normal set of strongrooms for the protection of valuables. During World War II some jewelers who had moved their stock into the lower level asked permission to have a few select customers come below to do their shopping. Before long, the strongrooms two stories down had become a subterranean shopping arcade. Today thirty silver dealers keep shop in these walk-in safes. There's a similar non-bargain basement in two hundred-year-old vaults at 11 Charterhouse Street around the corner from Hatton Garden, and another coop-

erative Aladdin's cave just off Piccadilly Circus at the Pall
Mall Safe Deposit, 10 St. Alban's Lane.

Across Chancery Lane is the 1518 gateway to Lincoln's Inn,
marking the third site of the Inn, which was probably founded in
the fourteenth century. The oaken doors of the turreted gatehouse are the originals, and they lead into a courtyard called Old
Buildings enclosed by brick buildings which are at least elderly if
not old, dating as they do from 1518 as well. The other courts of
Lincoln's Inn date from the early eighteenth to the late nineteenth
century, and all their eaves drip time and certitude condensed
over the centuries.

New Square, now part of Lincoln's Inn, was built on Inn property as a private speculation in 1685, and remains physically unchanged except for No. 10 (1862) and No. 11 (bombed and re-

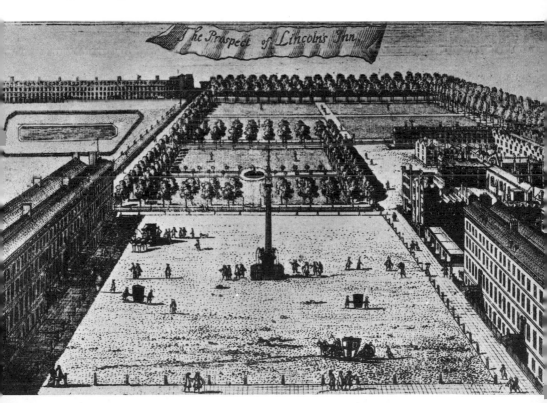

Lincoln's Inn, along with Gray's Inn and the Temple, still trains England's barristers.

161

built). One emerges from the western end of this rather large square into Lincoln's Inn Fields, which is mammoth, the largest square in central London.

Its existence is due entirely to the exclusivity of the Society of Lincoln's Inn, from the time in 1376 when they had one Roger Leget arrested for setting mantraps on the edge of one of the three fields. "He was sent to the King's Prison of Fleete, there to expect the King's grace . . . The King and councell have ever been very careful of preserving the liberties and interests of the lawyers and citizens in these fields, for their cure and their refreshment."

New Square, Lincoln's Inn, has changed little since this eighteenth-century view.

The Privy Council in 1613 instructed local justices to "restrayne and forbid" those who "doe goe aboute to erect new buildings, contrary to His Matie's Proclamation . . . and to the greate pestring and annoyance of that Society [of Lincoln's Inn]." Through direct dealing with King Charles I a builder named Newton obtained a license to erect houses with the promise to leave an open square in the center of the fields. But when, by 1641, he had finished building along the south side and most of the west side (the east side is all Lincoln's Inn), the Society thwarted his designs by appeal to the House of Commons. After a large pile of building timber stored in the center field caught fire, builder Newton signified surrender by dying.

In 1656, agreement was reached between the Society and a new group of leaseholders, and the square was completed. The tenants were permitted to enclose the central space, grade it and make a park of it in the mid-eighteenth century. Until 1894, they resisted all pressures to open their park to the public, even though the delegation of pleaders was led in 1880 by the Duke of Westminster and that of 1891 by the Earl of Meath on behalf of the Public Gardens Association.

For more than two centuries, the square was among London's most distinguished addresses. Ranged around the Fields today are a number of buildings of architectural, historical or social interest. But the lunch-hour crowds hastening to Lincoln's Inn Fields in the warm months seem unaware of these. Their interest is focused on the wonders of nature as demonstrated by girls in shorts playing tennis and netball. On Tuesdays and Thursdays from May to September the aesthetic uplift is further elevated from 12:30 to 2:00 by band concerts.

The plane trees of Lincoln's Inn Fields, aged, towering, noble, are beloved of songbirds who take over when the musicians cease. And the birds can be heard: the hectic hubub of Fleet Street and the august anguish of the Bankruptcy Buildings and the Law Courts, but a few yards distant, are here effectively effaced.

One tree in the park is little more than a sapling compared with the great grandfathers comprising most of the arboreal population. It is a Canadian maple, a gift of the people of Ottawa, and it was planted in the northeast corner in 1945 to commemorate the Royal Canadian Air Force headquarters on the other side of the street, and the park's north walk is named Canada Walk.

On this northern side the most arresting buildings are Nos. 12–13–14, designed in 1792, 1812, 1824 by Sir John Soane. Nos. 13 and 14 are the Sir John Soane Museum, memorial to his work, his taste, his influence and his personal caprice. The architecture and the decoration of the houses show off Sir John's ingenuity and individuality, the library (with twenty thousand architectural drawings, among the other things) hints at the depth of his knowledge of the past, and his collection gives a glimpse of his widely ranging tastes. Notable in the collection are two Hogarth series, *The Election* and *The Rake's Progress*, paintings by Turner and Reynolds, many antiquities of Greece, Rome and Egypt including a Pharaonic sarcophagus. And yet Soane is remembered as the "great force for the classical revival." Nos. 5–9 are mid-eighteenth, Nos. 1–2 early eighteenth-century.

Over on the west side of the square some of the notable mansions are now offices. The most important is Lindsey House. (Nos. 59–60), divided in two a century after it was built in 1640 by Inigo Jones. It is echoed in neighboring 57–58 designed by Henry Joynes in 1730. In the house which preceded Joynes's Palladian reflection, Nell Gwyn is popularly supposed to have lodged (and almost as popularly supposed not to have done so) while still a Drury Lane actress, before devoting her talents exclusively to Charles II. Here she gave birth to her first son,* and either here or at a house in Highgate where Waterlow Park now spreads, or in Chelsea, where a gasworks predominates on the site, she won the boy his first paternal recognition. There are two stories about what happened.

> STORY I: *King below in garden. Nell appears at window.*
> NELL: If you don't do something for this child's future, I'll let him fall.
> CHARLES (*dashing across garden*): Long live the Earl of Burford!

* When a local magistrate addressed Charles as "the father of his people," Lord Rochester murmured, ". . . of a good many of them . . ."

STORY II: *In nursery, Nell kneels and calls to crawling child.*
NELL: Come here, you little bastard!
CHARLES (*squatting*): Come here, Earl of Burford!

Whatever, the boy was made Baron Heddington, Earl of Burford, and in 1684 he became the Duke of St. Albans. The present Duke is the sixteenth of that line.

On the south side of the square, the stone building with the towering portico is the Royal College of Surgeons, found when the surgeons amputated themselves from the Barber's Guild in 1745. To this day, British surgeons conserve the ancient barber's title of "Mr.," rejecting with somewhat ostentatious modesty their legitimate title of "Dr." The College grants licenses and diplomas in its field.

Until it moved here in 1800, it was located in the Old Bailey, where it received for dissection the bodies of executed murderers. Bodies of those hanged for other crimes were turned over to claiming relatives or comrades and often finished in the dissecting rooms of teaching physicians, thus giving rise to many tales of revived "corpses," some undoubtedly true.

The 1800 structure has been subject to spasmodic architectural surgery, some of it conspicuously quack. The renowned eighteenth-century surgeon John Hunter, a pioneer in comparative anatomy and morphology as well as the innovator of many surgical techniques (his method of ligating aneurisms is still used) left his remarkable anatomical collection to the College. It formed the nucleus for what became the Hunterian Museum, the only part of the College to be damaged during the war. Now rebuilt, the museum may be visited (in any month but August, which of course has no "R") by writing for admittance to the Secretary.

Below Lincoln's Inn Fields to the south, are the Law Courts. After eight hundred years of dispensing justice at Westminster, they moved here in 1882 to a building which was especially designed for them (at first look, by the Brothers Grimm). Its towers, turrets, spires, arches and its labyrinthine tenebrous corridors would be ideal for ogres, a setting which at times seems to have influenced the conduct of some judges. Certainly, this stone lexicon of nineteenth-century Gothicisms inspires more dread than confidence.

Officially, the Law Courts are the Royal Courts of Justice, and a London writer, David Leitch, described them as "the embodiment of insularity and anachronism." He wrote in 1964, "The stone corridors with elaborate leaded windows exclude light and exude chill even in high summer." He also recalled that the building had been "appropriately financed by money despairing litigants had abandoned in Chancery." For those who dare ask its whereabouts, there is a public bar deep in the building.

On ordinary days the judges wear a red-sashed blue gown. On what are officially designated as Red Letter Days — Royal Birthdays, Coronation, St. George's Day — they wear ermine-trimmed scarlet robes.

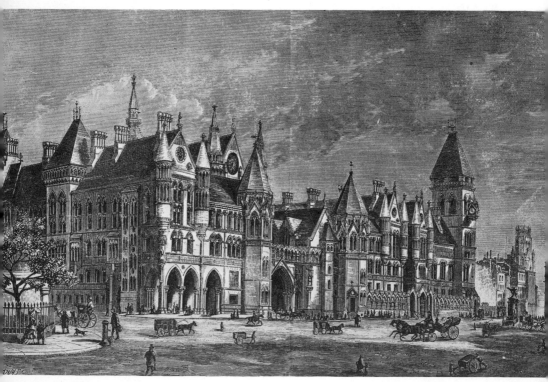

Royal Courts of Justice, the Strand: "English courts, like the Ritz Hotel, are open to all

At the end of the Lord Mayor's Show, the new Lord Mayor descends here and proceeds to the rarely used Central Hall to give Her Majesty's representative, the Lord Chief Justice, whose office is here, assurances of fealty.

Each October 23, the Corporation of the City of London sends its Solicitor to pay quitrents to the Queen's Remembrancer. The payments concern two Crown properties occupied by the City. No one can remember where the ancient properties now lie, but they do know the rent is due: for "the Forge" near St. Clement Danes Church, six horseshoes and sixty-one nails; for "the Moors" in Shropshire, a hatchet and a billhook, with which the Solicitor chops a bundle of faggots in two to prove the rentworthiness of the implements. Visitors may attend the ceremony, and after they are gone, the nails, shoes and choppers are taken back to the City for use again next year.

On October first, to open the Michaelmas session, the judges march in procession, an impressive body of jurisprudence — no English judge has been convicted of corruption since 1622, unless one counts Lord Chancellor Macclesfield, who was removed from office in 1722 for selling Chancery Masterships (at more than the going rate).

Fleet Street stops at Temple Bar, but the road continues, its name changed to the Strand. Just after the Law Courts, a street called Aldwych bows up to Kingsway (built to connect the Strand with High Holborn in Bloomsbury) and then arcs back to the Strand again. The first corner off Aldwych is Houghton Street, where almost anonymously simmers the London School of Economics, now a school of London University. The future world-changers training at this institution enjoy none of the contempletive rusticity of the neighboring Inns of Court. These students are learning to live in a world of strident realities and — as one look at their buildings indicates — the need for change.

The Strand was the road between the City of London and the City of Westminster, traced above the sloping shores of the unembanked Thames. For long this way was dominated by the palaces of nobles and ecclesiastics with handsome water gates down by the river. Many of today's Strand structures are best appreciated (or depreciated) from water level.

167

The riverfront is a creation of typically Victorian daring and imagination, a hundred-foot-wide road curving a mile and a third from Blackfriars Bridge to Westminster Bridge. This magnificent adornment to the capital, the Victoria Embankment, was wrought to cover over the new drainage system, and while they were at it, the engineers also ran a subway line under the road. The work is signed by Sir Joseph Bazalgette, engineer to the Metropolitan Board of Works. Begun in 1864, it was formally opened at high noon July 13, 1870, by the Prince of Wales as two battalions of Guards (Grenadier and Coldstream) lined the roadway.

The Embankment not only provided a splendid riverside drive but also reclaimed thirty-seven acres of festering mud flats, planted with gardens which in turn have been sown with statuary. The granite parapet along over the water's edge is also embellished with medallions and statues, the lampposts are tressed with chubby dolphins, and some of the original benches are supported by cast-iron camels and sphinxes. A tree sprouts every twenty feet on both sides of the roadway.

All this is a model of the Victorian attributes, a reminder that this period of British history was a wonderful time, or at least a wonderful time to be rich. This exemplar is assured, spacious and contrived with craftsmanship. It was built as if Queen Victoria's reign would last forever, which, in a way, it does. The Embankment cost nine million dollars, a price for roadbuilding hardly thinkable until the cloverleafed highways of nearly a century later.

Toward the easternmost end, the gardens of the Temple, which swept to the water's edge before the road was made, are visible through the fence. At the edge of the Temple grounds is a two-story crenellated, mullioned, orieled Early Elizabethan stone mansion. Its many refinements are obscured for many persons by the date: 1895. The first Lord Astor spent over a million dollars building this house as his estate office, with a flat for himself over the shop. The floors are porphyry, onyx, jasper and marble. The gallery around the great hall has ebony columns. There is an extraordinary frieze of fifty-four carved heads ranging from Machiavelli to Bismarck, from the Lady of Shalott to Anne

Boleyn, none of whom seems to influence the work of the business now occupying these premises.

Just to the west is the first bit of Victoria Embankment Gardens, with the first four statues, including John Stuart Mill and Isambard Kingdom Brunel (1806–1859), one of the illustrious animators of the age of steam. Four vessels are tethered in the Thames at this point: *President* and *Chrysanthemum*, Naval Reserve training ships; *Wellington*, livery hall of the Honourable Company of Master Mariners (founded only in 1926), and *Discovery*, the old polar explorer, open free every afternoon for visitors to inspect mementoes of Antarctic voyages and the cabin of Captain R. F. Scott.

West of this sliver of the Gardens rises the noble cliff of Somerset House, the underrated 1776 masterpiece of Sir William Chambers. When he built it, the lower arcade stood at the edge of the river, its central arch the water gate. Above this is the terrace with mighty Piranesian arches topped by a colonnade. With

The eighteenth-century replacement of this palace now houses the tax collector.

its extensions (east extension by Smirke, 1835, west by Penne-thorne, 1856), the river frontage spreads eight hundred feet.

Then comes Waterloo Bridge (just downstream is a River Po-lice station), whose good points have been much begrudged by millions who were in love with its predecessor, which stood here from 1817 until 1934. The original, a Rennie masterwork, had Doric columns and nine arches. When it began to wobble in 1924, the foundations were reinforced. And when it became a serious traffic bottleneck, plans were made to strengthen and broaden it. It was a national historical monument and it was a thing of beauty. Parliament was determined to save it and refused bill after bill which would have granted funds toward construc-tion of a new bridge. And when the London County Council, led by Socialist Herbert Morrison (later Lord Morrison of Lambeth) voted for demolition of the bridge, Parliament tried to bar the action but found it had no legal power to do so. Four years later, in 1938, it voted funds for a new bridge.

Construction of the new bridge was interrupted by the war. The temporary bridge slung alongside was taken down in No-vember 1943 and then mysteriously disappeared. It was not sold for scrap nor stored in the LCC's yards, and its whereabouts was not known until it showed up again a year later, a glowing testi-monial to British Army optimism and planning, as the Allies' new bridge across the Rhine at Remagen.

Sir Giles Scott has done well by London with his Waterloo Bridge, no matter what else Londoners may execrate him for (his power stations at Battersea and Bankside? his municipal offices next to Guildhall? his pauper's version of Gothic in re-building the bombed House of Commons?). His bridge is a twentieth-century span of five springing, shallow ellipses. Made in unadorned concrete, it is rather lean and tense. It may not be beautiful — what central London bridge is? — but handsome it certainly is.

After the bridge is the main plantation of Victoria Embank-ment Gardens, making an agreeable foreground to the London jumble pushing from the Strand toward the bank overlooking the river. Rearing up behind the municipal foliage are Savoy Hill with the Savoy Hotel (it had sun balconies across its nine stories in 1884, since windowed in to serve as bathrooms). The hotel was built by Richard D'Oyly Carte to go with his 1881 Savoy Theatre, home of the Gilbert and Sullivan operas he produced. In the matter of bathrooms, D'Oyly Carte was a pioneer. There were seventy of them in his hotel when it opened, compared with the four provided three years later for the five hundred guests by the new competing Northumberland Hotel.

The Savoy's next-door neighbor is a squarish, whitish thirteen-story building capped with an enormous squarish, whitish block-house decorated with the incontestably largest clock in London. This is now the headquarters of the Ministry of Aviation.

Next to this is a 1938 outrage, shamelessly named the New Adelphi. For this piece of commercial pomposity ("savagely ungraceful" — Pevsner) London surrendered one of its architectural treasures, the 1772 Adelphi of the brothers Adam.

The main wedge of Victoria Embankment Gardens is only about three hundred yards long and perhaps sixty-five yards wide at the fat end. But it is a garden of little marvels, especially from the end of April to the beginning of October because of the animal, vegetable and mineral flora and fauna. Like almost all London parks, it is lovingly landscaped, planted and tended, with a seeming haphazardness in the artful arrangement of nooks and crannies to give visual surprises and happy vistas even in this small space. They have even managed to work in a little pond.

In spite of the anti-litter notices, the place is littered with statuary, including a Bobby Burns who wears the rapt expression of one who hears the opening bell at the village pub, occultly balanced by a bronze Sir Wilfrid Lawson, the temperance-monger. Here too is Robert Raikes, who founded the Sunday Schools in 1780 in order that illiterate children might, under the cloak of religious instruction, learn to read.

Of all the effigies strewn here, the most compelling is the monument to the otherwise near-forgot Imperial Camel Corps. It is small, the stone topped with a bronze camel whose rider demonstrates the correct seat as used in the 1916–1918 campaigns in Egypt, Sinai and Palestine. The catalogue of their eighteen major engagements lists Hill 265, Beersheba, Hedjaz and (twice) Gaza.

Before a bust of Sir Arthur Sullivan an unidentified (bronze) nude is contorted by unidentified emotion. Across the road on the Embankment wall is a memorial to Sullivan's partner, Sir W. S. Gilbert. Nearby are benches marked "Presented by W. H. Smith, Esq., M.P., 1873." He was also known as "Pinafore Smith." The "Son" of W. H. Smith & Son, ubiquitous news-vendors and stationers, he became First Lord of the Admiralty the year after donating those benches. Subsequently he was lampooned by Gilbert ("I Am the Ruler of the Queen's Na-vee") in *Pinafore*.

Nearby is Cleopatra's Needle (really the 1500 B.C. obelisk of Thothmes III), planted here in 1871. Made of pink marble and not quite 69 feet tall, it came from Heliopolis, a rather sly needle from the Khedive to sun-worshipping, sun-spurned London. It is flanked by two nineteenth-century British Made sphinxes. A set of massive steps once led down to the water at this spot, but they were blown up in 1940, not by the raiding Germans, but by the invasion-conscious British.

There's an outdoor café in the park, with parasols and lanterns. There's a bright bandstand before which the deck chairs are marshaled for two concerts a day from May to October. A superb collection of Londoners and visitors is on display at concert time.

On the inland side of the bandstand, where the riverbank once oozed, is the water gate to York House, once the town palace of the Bishops of York, later of the Dukes of Buckingham. The gateway is generally attributed to Inigo Jones, which means he might have designed it, but there is doubt. At any rate, Jones was the Duke's protégé when the gate was erected in 1626. Nibbled by time and leading to a blank wall, it doesn't look like much standing on the grass. It must have been quite grand as the entrance to a private palace from a private galley.

The western edge of the garden is blighted by the ugly repeat ugly railroad bridge which comes over the river and the embankment to end its inglorious career in the appropriate surroundings of Charing Cross Station. However, the black-on-black scene is not without its poetic side. There are passages under the bridge and bolt-holes leading to the Underground and tea stalls and

The obelisk is authentic antique Egyptian, the Sphinxes genuine Victorian.

tiny food shops and peddlers and newsstands to give a rather raffish onion-flavored resort touch to the area. Further up are the Arches, once the resort of London's dispossessed, the marks of whose fires are still visible on the walls. If you like your misery romanticized, there is a song more rollicking than "Sous les Ponts de Paris" called "Underneath the Arches."

For centuries the Strand was the elegant big city street, before Piccadilly was more than a path through the fields. With its many theaters (three left), its palatial hotels (three left), its island churches and remaining fine buildings such as Somerset House, its magnetism ("finest thoroughfare in Europe" — Disraeli) ran strong well into the twentieth century. But for some time it has been a commercial street with elegance and/or gaiety defended by very few bastions.

The first streets off the Strand after Temple Bar are Devereux Court and Essex Street, a reminder that the Devereux family won the earldom of Essex. Twining's tea shop, which moved here in 1700 after twenty-five years at other locations, is still here, the point of departure for a worldwide tea trade. One can go out through the back door of the tiny shop into Devereux Court. Devereux Tavern hiding here is the 1834 reconstruction of the Grecian Coffee House frequented by Addison, Steele, Isaac Newton and Sir Hans Sloane, one of the great establishments of the seventeenth- and eighteenth-century coffeehouse period.

The second Earl of Essex was Queen Elizabeth's favorite. He became a national hero in 1596 for his capture of Cadiz, and increased his glory by fighting in Portugal and raids on the Azores. His enemies, the Cecil family, maneuvered him into position as "the only man for the job" of subduing the perennial Irish rebels. Lured into a protracted truce by the astute Irish leader, Tyrone, Essex was enraged by English rumors that he was conniving to become King of Ireland himself, and went roaring home. In one of English history's high romantic moments he forced his way into the Queen's bedroom. Haggard and travel-stained, he flung himself at her feet. Apparently she forgave him, despite the fact that he had disobeyed orders in giving command of his cavalry to Southampton and the fact that technically he was a deserter, having abandoned his Irish post in time of war.

But in the end, a special tribunal arranged by the Cecils stripped him of his Crown offices. He was not to appear at Court and the Queen refused to renew his monopoly on the importation of sweet wines, worth a huge fortune annually.

Kept idle at Essex House, surrounded by unemployed comrades in arms, the Earl's restiveness solidified into revolt. Part of the plan included a payment of forty shillings to the Globe Theatre troupe to play *Richard II*, a play Elizabeth disliked because of its revolutionary implications. The uprising fizzled dismally, with virtually not a blow struck.

After their trial for treason the Earl of Southampton begged the Queen's mercy and was later released. Essex, urged to do the same, was told he would find Her Majesty merciful. He refused. But at the last moment he sent the Queen the ring she had given him, a gage of affection and mutual loyalty. It was intercepted on the way to the Queen and Robert Devereux died at the Tower February 25, 1601 (inside the walls, for fear of a popular uprising). Shortly after, the ring was delivered to his widow.

In 1751 the Countess of Essex made a gift of the ring to the Viscountess of Weymouth, in whose family it stayed until 1911, finally bestowed upon the Dean and Chapter of Westminster Abbey in 1927. It can be seen at the Abbey now.

About seventy-five years after Essex's execution, one of the town's earliest building speculators, Dr. Barbon (or Barebone, but not he of the Barebones Parliament) built Essex Street across the site of Essex House, and of his labors Nos. 11, 14, 19 and 34 remain in their neat stone-dressed red brick. Henry Fielding lived in this street, where in 1783 Dr. Johnson established a club. Essex Hall, rebuilt after bombing, was in 1774 the site of the original Unitarian church and is still the headquarters of the Unitarian and Free Christian churches.

Out in the middle of the Strand stands the church of St. Clement Danes, and a few streets westward toward Trafalgar Square is its "twin," also on an island in the center of the road, St. Mary-le-Strand. St. Clement's probably started in Danish times. The medieval church that stood here was rebuilt in 1640, and when Sir Christopher Wren came along to re-rebuild forty years later, he used the still-extant tower of the fifteenth-century church, giving it simply a new facing. Above the bell stage, James Gibbs in 1719 finished the tower and made the steeple.

Among the distinguished parishioners was Dr. Johnson, whose statue is behind the church facing Fleet Street. And there was Joe Miller the jokesmith, a Drury Lane comic deceased in 1738. Miller's tombstone was preserved indoors until the bombers dropped the first of several loads which reduced the church to a shell in 1941. Miller's jokes have proved less perishable.

St. Clement's was rebuilt in 1958 as the church of the Royal Air Force. In the floor slates are the 735 crests of the RAF units and on the rolls of honor the names of 125,000 men and women of the Force who died in both World Wars. The Commonwealth air forces are also remembered, and there are furnishings given by the USA, Netherlands and Norwegian Air Forces.

In 1920 the rector started a children's service which concluded with the gift of an orange and a lemon for each child, in souvenir of the old rhyme. When the church was bombed, the bells which rang "oranges and lemons" were cracked, and so was the heart of Rector W. Pennington Bickford, who died.

The same firm that had cast the 1588 sanctus bell recast the old metal into new bells in 1957, and now over the streets lilt the first lines of the song every school child in London once knew: *

> "Oranges and lemons,"
> Say the bells of St. Clement's
> "Lend me five farthings,"
> Say the bells of St. Martin's,†
> "When will you pay me?"
> Say the bells of Old Bailey.
> "When I am rich,"
> Say the bells of Shoreditch.
> "When will that be?"

* In all likelihood, the St. Clement's of the jingle was that in Eastcheap, the age-old fruit market district. The St. Martin's referred to, on Martin's Lane in the City, was destroyed in the Great Fire and not rebuilt. Old Bailey stood next to the debtors' prison, Shoreditch was notoriously poverty-stricken, and Stepney's shipping was bringing prosperity. Bow, in the financial and market center of Cheapside, was too rich to worry about five farthings.

† A 1964 edition of nursery rhymes keeps British kiddies apace with inflation by changing this couplet to: " 'You owe me ten shillings;'/Say the bells of St. Helen's." The farthing has not been minted since 1952.

Say the bells of Stepney.
"I'm sure I don't know,"
Says the big bell of Bow.

St. Mary-le-Strand, first mentioned in 1147, was rebuilt by James Gibbs on a new site as one of the fifty new churches ordered by Queen Anne's Act. It is a small masterpiece, built to be admired — and indeed admirable — from all sides. Gibbs, a Scot recently returned from studies in Holland and Italy, blended in it the Italian style with the Wren style. There's a story that the Young Pretender, Prince Charles Edward Stuart, staying on Essex Street, was (for political rather than religious motives) admitted into the Church of England here in 1750.

Next door to the old Devereux place, the Howards, who lost and regained the Dukedom of Norfolk, had their London residence, Arundel House. Arundel, Norfolk, Howard and Surrey Streets remind us that the Howards, Earls of Arundel and Surrey as well as Dukes of Norfolk still own this piece of real estate.

Somerset House also began as a palace, eventually replaced by the present structure. The Duke of Somerset — Somerset the Protector — was regent during the minority of Henry VIII's ailing heir Edward VI. Ambitious as well as able, the Duke built himself a palace, using the stones from St. Mary-le-Strand and other ecclesiastical buildings which stood where he wanted his house to stand. After five years of progress, building was halted in 1552, owing to the unforeseen execution of the Duke. Princess Elizabeth lived here next, for part of her sister Mary's reign. Later the place became the Dower House for Stuart Queens: Anne of Denmark (James I), Henrietta Maria (Charles I), Catherine of Braganza (Charles II). The archenemy of the Stuarts, Oliver Cromwell, lay in state in the palace in 1658.

In 1776 the ex-ducal mansion was razed and replaced by something which set an architectural precedent — very possibly the Western world's first government office building, designed and constructed for the specific purpose of sheltering administrative machinery.

There were quarters for the Exchequer, Privy Seal and the Tax Office, and rooms for the Royal Academy, the Royal Society and

177

the Society of Antiquaries. These last three subsequently moved to Burlington House in Piccadilly, where they may be found to-day. The tax man, once installed, stuck, to coin a phrase, like a leech. He is now in the west wing, built in 1856.

The Navy Pay office was here as well, and among its employees one John Dickens who, on the thirteenth of June in 1809 went down the road to St. Mary-le-Strand and married Elizabeth Barrow. The couple's son Charles was born three years later, though it is not likely that this event was recorded at the General Register Office, now in the north wing, since civil registration of births, deaths and marriages was not instituted until 1836.

In the South Wing the Probate & Divorce Registry has records which go all the way back to 1382, and for a two-shilling fee anyone may examine any will, including that of Charles Dickens.

The east wing, by Sir Robert Smirke, 1835, contains King's College, founded in 1829 by the Duke of Wellington and a group

Bureaucratic architecture in 1776 — Somerset House.

178

of Anglican Tories as a riposte to the Whigs' foundation of University College on Gower Street. Both these institutions are now part of London University. Additions planned for King's caused in 1965 the departure from the Strand to Lancaster Place around the corner of the shirtmakers Thresher and Glenny, who have held Royal appointments to every succeeding monarch since George III ordered gloves and hose in 1783. Two former opulent town houses, now with shops on the ground floor and offices above, standing in the way of the college expansion were offered to the Victoria and Albert Museum and to the London Museum who manifested "no interest" in dismantling and re-erecting elsewhere at least the façades. They were the two oldest buildings on the Strand, timber-framed and plastered and dating from the 1680's.

If one crosses the Strand just after passing Somerset House and ascends Wellington Street, in a very few minutes the walker has entered a very different London. Wellington Street has become Bow Street, with the Drury Lane Theatre on the right, Covent Garden on the left, and straight ahead Bow Street police station, chief of London's fourteen police courts.

The present building, for all its mien of centuries-old authority, was built in 1899. The court opens at ten in the morning (the most variegated session, examining the previous night's haul) and the visitor's gallery, open to all, often is filled to capacity. After the luncheon recess, sittings resume until 5 P.M. This is a clear peek under the prosperous and orderly surface London presents to the casual visitor (save those who fall victim to the pickpockets or hustlers on parade in morning court).

This is the spot that saw the first unsteady steps in 1749 toward a police department for London. Sixty years earlier, bounty-hunting had been established under an Act for Encouraging the Apprehending of Highwaymen. It offered a reward of £40 for the arrest and conviction of a highwayman. The thieftaker, as he was called, also got the malefactor's horse, harness, arms and any money not proven stolen. This was not so that the informer could set up in business as a highwayman for himself, but rather to discourage inns and livery stables from hiring out horses to known badmen.

Following this, the number of highwaymen hanged increased

179

noticeably, but then so did the number of highway robberies. Eventually all sorts of wanted men could be turned in on a set schedule of tarrifs, down to £1 for an army deserter.

The most notorious thieftaker was Jonathan Wild (1682–1725), who came to London as a youth, was jailed for debt, and in jail met the prostitute who would later introduce him to London's leading thugs.

Operating as a thieftaker who also specialized in the recovery of stolen goods, he became in a few years king of the London underworld. He planned the crimes, organized London into territories with one gang assigned to each. All refusing to join his syndicate were hunted down (Wild was a good detective) and convicted with evidence Wild produced.

Bow Street Runners pursued criminals in pre-police days.

He took a house near the Old Bailey and advertised himself as "Thief Taker General of Great Britain and Ireland" and carried a crown-topped baton as the emblem of his nonexistent authority. Robbery victims came to his office to claim stolen goods delivered at the back door by Wild's thieves. It was known what Wild was doing, but it was impossible to get anyone to inform on him. There was no police force to collect evidence.

Sir William Thompson, a City official who became Solicitor General in 1717, brought in a bill ("Jonathan Wild's Act") making it a capital felony to accept a reward under the pretense of helping return stolen goods. Wild found ways to stay within this law and went on to open a branch office and a warehouse for his loot. He had a country house with servants, and his sloop took otherwise undisposable merchandise out of the country, returning with contraband.

In 1723, pointing out the sixty criminals he had sent to the gallows, Wild petitioned the Lord Mayor for the Freedom of the City.

Convicted on evidence furnished by the syndicate he refused to join, a highwayman called Blueskin seized Wild in the courtroom and cut his throat, but not fatally. Dean Swift wrote an elegy, "Blueskin's Ballad."

Wild was not brought low until 1725, when, "for procuring the return of some stolen lace," he was sentenced to death under the terms of "Jonathan Wild's Act." The judge was Sir William Thompson. Wild, whose suicide was foiled, was stoned and pelted with filth on his way to Tyburn.

When Henry Fielding — lawyer, theatrical producer, playwright, satirist, novelist — became magistrate for Westminster in 1748, he instituted the Bow Street Runners. He shared the bench with his sightless half-brother, Sir John Fielding, who was known as "the Blind Beak" (judges are still called "beaks" by underworld traditionalists). There were always two Runners on duty at Fielding's, ready to set out anywhere a robbery was reported. They were so successful in breaking up London's biggest gangs that the government paid them a guinea a week (in ratio to living costs, more than policemen are paid today) out of Secret Service funds and allowed them to accept thieftaker's rewards. While at Bow Street, magistrate Fielding also wrote *Tom Jones*.

After an attempted assassination of George III in 1786, two Runners were assigned to His Majesty's protection. In 1820, it was a Runner named George Ruthven who captured the Cato Street Conspirators in a stable off the Edgeware Road in Cato Street. Led by a man with the undesperate name of Arthur Thistlewood, the conspirators plotted to force a change of administration by assassinating Lord Castlereagh and his entire Cabinet.

It was more than obviously time for a municipal police force: riots were not uncommon (the 1780 "No Popery" riots were broken only by troops deployed in street warfare), street traffic was uncontrolled, after dark the town was infested with footpads ("Who goes home?" is still the cry at the close of business in Parliament, a cry born in the days when safety on the way home lay in numbers) and citizens were literally murdered in their beds.

Yet, a commission studying the matter in the 1820's overrode chairman Sir Robert Peel to say they saw no way to "reconcile any effective system of police with that perfect freedom of action and exemption from interference which is one of the great blessings and privileges of society in this country."

But when Peel became Home Secretary in 1829 he put through a bill giving him the police force he wanted. The police were dubbed "peelers" and "bobbies" and, because of their badges and buttons, "coppers." The members of the new force were insulted, jeered at and assaulted. In the first two years eight thousand men joined and four thousand were dismissed, many for drunkenness and incompetence. Even King George IV made fun of them. They were murdered, beaten, kicked, tossed into the river and impaled on spiked railings. Since there was no public prosecutor, an arresting policeman brought the charges himself, and if the case was lost, had to pay court costs. And if he couldn't pay, he went to debtors' prison.

However, when the force was but a year old, it had a chance to prove its worth. Rumors of impending mob action in the City (which had no police force until 1839) were so persistent that the Lord Mayor's Show was canceled. Outside the City gates, the Metropolitan Police formed up. The mob, looking for some authority to smash, streamed out toward them. The sixty policemen proceeded with the first baton charge in London's history, and dispersed the rioters with no further trouble.

Since there were no detectives, the Bow Street Runners stayed in being until 1824. In 1878, the police set up the Criminal Investigation Division, modeled on the French Sûreté.

With the advent of the high-wheeled pram and the starched and goffered nursemaid, the London bobby entered into the happy folklore of the period. He was brave (which he still is, being one of the few unarmed policemen in the world), endlessly patient, gravely polite — sort of an outdoor butler, everybody's ideal family retainer. It was evidently painful to him to be pushed to physical execution of his duty, arresting suffragettes and the like. The policeman Knew His Place and such things were almost tantamount to Rising Above One's Station.

Along with the loveableness of its patrolmen, London could enjoy the tenacity and brilliance of its detectives. These reaching, protecting arms of British justice were as sure and selfless as the judges.

But soon after World War II, the bobby began losing his traditional authority. British youth took the lead in demonstrating that the high-humped helmet was empty of tribal magic. Policemen were attacked by errant adolescents as well as by professional criminals (murderous crooks are another new development). Policemen were killed.

Indictable crime in the United Kingdom doubled in the decade 1953–1963. In London, it more than doubled, rising from 95,000 a year to 230,000 a year, with the percentage of solved crimes dropping. Things were worse than statistics showed because the records were watered down or dissipated at stationhouse level, with files disappearing in the ever-mounting mountain of paperwork and with crimes being logged in the least serious possible category (e.g., "trespassing" instead of "burglary"). Also there were relatively small crimes which were really symptoms of major criminal movements, movements not appearing on the charts: for example, an acid splashing or a vengeful bit of incendiarism registered as assault or attempted arson in reality bespeak the opera-

183

tion of a protection racket and indicate developing big-time gang-sterism.

Public confidence in the police ebbed. The government's Social Survey in 1960 showed that 42.4 per cent of the public thought that some policemen took bribes, that 34.7 per cent thought police used unfair methods in questioning, and that 32 per cent believed police might distort evidence in court.

There were proven cases of police corruption in the provinces and some police brutality in London. The 1964 investigation to discover how a detective obviously suffering a nervous breakdown could go on working for months revealed stories of planted evidence, strongarm methods and harrassment. Three young men jailed on police-fabricated evidence were given free pardons.

It was simultaneously revealed that because the public attitude had changed and because criminality was becoming big business, the police were finding it increasingly harder to police the metropolis. In 1964 the force numbered eighteen thousand, which was five to six thousand under strength. The Police Commissioner felt that full strength might be achieved by 1976. Only about ten per cent of the force could be assigned to detective work, and putting in a sixty-hour week, each detective was dealing with 250 to 300 new cases a year, double the caseload a detective is deemed capable of handling.

When Britons were aghast at a woman's death from stab wounds on a New York street while thirty-eight neighbors ignored her calls for help, the British *Police Review* said, "It can happen here. It has happened here." Cases in point were cited. The policeman-editorialist whose work is conducted on the back side of traditional British civic virtue wrote, "Everybody expects the game to be played according to the rules, but nobody will help to enforce the rules."

Commented a Member of Parliament, W. F. Deedes, "Policemen today are working in a society where the sense of right and wrong is less to be relied upon than ever before." Another observer wrote, "Our society is becoming increasingly criminal and criminals increasingly professional."

Lord Shawcross, Q.C., one of the noted British lawyers and on occasion a devastating prosecutor, said that the law favored the criminal. "Crime pays. Crime is booming," he said. "Most criminals are not caught. We, the public, have not enabled the law and the police to keep pace with the growing number and efficiency of criminals."

The annual report of the Metropolitan Police Commissioner said that the detective staff evinced "a growing feeling that the odds are stacked against them and the barriers protecting the suspected and accused are being steadily reinforced in a way which hampers the detection of crime and the conviction of criminals whilst the latter prey upon their more deserving fellow citizens with greater confidence."

The British problem is identical with the American problem: how to achieve the fine balance between the protection of society by the police and the protection of society's members from violation of their individual rights by these same protectors. Just how much liberty can society forfeit in exchange for safety? And safety from which danger? Londoners may be edging closer to the end of the circle begun in 1829, a preference for risk from criminals rather than interference from the police.

The daily dramas played out in Bow Street police court are for the most part truer to life and less believable than those offered in the half dozen playhouses in the immediate neighborhood — the Aldwych, Strand, Fortune, the Royal Opera House at Covent Garden and the Theatre Royal, Drury Lane.

The entrance to the Theatre Royal is really on Catherine Street, and its long colonnade runs along Russell Street almost to Drury Lane, where the original theater stood in the seventeenth century. This was a converted cockfighting hangar and was known as both the Cockpit and the Phoenix. In 1663 it was replaced by a real theater on this present site, the one Pepys attended so assiduously and where Nell Gwyn got her start. Burned out in 1672, it was rebuilt by Wren, and John Dryden was the principal playwright. Here in 1747 Garrick began his Shakespeare revival, prologue by Samuel Johnson. Garrick had with him the bewitching Peg Woffington and the powerful Charles Macklin, pioneer of the new naturalistic style Garrick later perfected.* Garrick also had

* When, as Macbeth, he said to the First Murderer, "There's blood upon thy face," the other actor clapped his hand to his cheek and cried in horror, "Is there, by God!"

185

Woffington and Macklin at home with him, ménage-à-trois, at 6 Bow Street.

The Wren theater, after the brilliance of Mrs. Siddons and her brothers the Kembles, was torn down in 1791, rebuilt by architect Henry Holland for Richard Brinsley Sheridan, who watched it burn in 1809. It was rebuilt by architect Samuel Wyatt in 1812, with the opening-night prologue by Lord Byron. The fortunes of the theater, foundering when the Kembles left for the Covent Garden Theatre, were restored by the incredible performances of Edmund Kean, who in turn crossed Bow Street to play in the competing house.

The columned porch on Catherine Street and the long row of cast iron columns along Russell Street were added in 1831, but the interior of the theater remains enchantingly Georgian, airy, elegant and truly theatrical. The existence of a ghost has been attested to by hundreds of witnesses. He emerges in from a wall at the left of the circle, walks past the seats in the back of the house, and melts through the opposite wall. He appears mostly at matinees, mostly during hit shows, and is presumed to be the ghost of the man whose skeleton was found, a knife between the ribs, in a secret chamber discovered in 1840 behind the wall from which he appears.

The theatrical monopoly enjoyed for 115 years by Drury Lane was broken by John Rich, the famed Harlequin, who procured a Royal Patent for his Covent Garden Theatre. Peg Woffington and Garrick were here before going to Drury Lane. When Kemble assumed management, he raised the prices. There were riots night after night until Kemble, experienced showman that he was, made the psychological thrust that stilled the rioters: he lowered the prices.

Handel's *Messiah* had its first night here in 1744, and all his later oratorios were introduced in this house. After the Siddons-Kemble company left, the theater languished, was seized by the parish for nonpayment of taxes, and was saved from the wreckers in 1829 by public subscription. Subsequently Edmund Kean pulled himself out of bitterness and alcoholism long enough to give his farewell performance here, followed not long after by Charles Macready in his last appearance onstage. It became the

Royal Italian Opera House not long before it was burned down for the second time. The present house is E. M. Barry's 1858 rebuilding, a three thousand-seat theater. All the great names of nineteenth- and early twentieth-century opera shone here. In 1928 the Russian ballet burst into flower on this stage, opening a whole new world of music and dance for the British. But by 1941, the huge old barn had become a dance hall. After World War II it regained all its former glory with its own ballet and opera companies, Command Performances, tiaras, ermine and subsidies.

Covent Garden was in the Middle Ages the vegetable garden of the Abbey of St. Peter at Westminster, the Abbey's convent garden. When religious establishments were seized in 1535, Henry VIII gave the land to Sir John Russell. In 1631 one of Sir John's descendants, the fourth Earl of Bedford, asked King Charles I for permission to put buildings on the ground at the bottom of Bedford House garden. The King said yes, providing the buildings were planned by Inigo Jones. The Earl had something in

The beginning of the market and the end of Covent Garden's "piazza."

mind like Henri IV's Place Royale (now Place des Vosges) in Paris. Inigo had something in mind like the Piazza d'Arme in Livorno. At any rate, it turned out to be marvelous and was the first square laid out in London. Tall arcaded blocks of houses closed the north and east sides, the gardens of Bedford House the south side, and Inigo's church of St. Paul the west end.

The word *piazza*, imported from Livorno along with the idea, was immediately adopted by Londoners. It rang with distinction upon the average ear, and many little English girls found themselves going through life named Piazza. As Londoners applied the word to architecture, they meant it to refer not to the square, but to the arcades. To this day in many parts of America almost anything with columns — usually a front porch — is to the natives a piazza.

Except for the church, known as the actors' church, because Drury Lane and Covent Garden stars were and are parishioners, it is all gone now. The last of the original buildings was torn down in 1890. The piazza dazzled the wealthy as well as simpler folk, and Covent Garden became instantly and utterly fashionable. It remained so for more than a century, which is something of a surprise, for the Earl (the Bedfords didn't become Dukes until 1694) obtained permission from always-needy Charles II to have a vegetable market in the square. At first it was simply a matter of early morning carts, choruses of street cries and early evening cabbage leaves and late evening footpads. By the eighteenth century there were stalls and sheds. In 1828 the Duke had a stone market building erected, sold in 1913 by a later Duke, but still there and still operating.

A principal preoccupation of marketmen in 1965 was to remain a little longer in their present location. Authorities have been trying to move them out for quite a few decades. In 1923 Lord Linlithgow's committee found the site "wholly inadequate" for London's central fruit and vegetable market, and recommended its removal. The idea came up with regularity after that, and was regularly blocked. Finally in 1960 Parliament passed a Covent Market Bill by only 58 votes after a stormy debate. The Bill established the Market Authority, empowered in conjunction with the London County Council to choose a better location. Just where this better location might be must in the end be agreed upon by many groups including traffic and transport people. It is apt to be quite a while before the smell of pears ceases to mantle the neighborhood.

The market is at its most blooming at 6 A.M., at which thought-

Only the flowers smile in Covent Garden market in the spring of 1867.

189

ful hour the surrounding pubs open like morning glories for which the sun will set at 9 A.M.

It was under the columns of St. Paul's porch that Professor Henry Higgins discovered Eliza Doolittle. The two corner columns are square, the two center Tuscan columns are round, and the porch, like the eaves, very deep. It is plain, a parallelogram with no interior subdivisions and no obvious fuss on its brick exterior.* The big doorway under the porch is a sham, the real entrance being around on the other end, down a narrow, tree-lined lane off Bedford Street called Inigo Place whose benches are peopled on sunny days with market porters feigning exhaustion.

Slipping (probably on some discarded vegetable) down Southampton Street, one is again on the Strand, on the south (river) side of which is the site of Savoy Palace, the London home of Peter of Savoy. Peter came in 1241 to visit his niece, Eleanor of Provence, who happened to be Queen of England at the time. Her husband, Henry III, gave Peter the manor whose grounds reached from today's Adelphi to the Temple, between *La Straunde* and the Thames. Peter left twenty-one years later to go rule Savoy, and at the London palace began the succession of inheritances, seizures, bestowals and snatchings back which continued through its cycle of splendor, decay and restoration as palace, hospital and hospice until the construction of Waterloo Bridge 550 years later. The building serving as German Lutheran Chapel held out until 1877. All that remains today is the 1516 chapel, the personal property of the Duke of Lancaster, who is also usually the monarch of Britain. John of Gaunt, Duke of Lancaster, occupied Savoy Palace until his death in 1399, and his son, Henry IV, then attached the estates and titles to the Crown. The national anthem sung in the chapel begins, "God save our gracious Queen/Long live our noble Duke." Often rebuilt, the chapel was adapted in 1940 for the Royal Victorian Order, the sovereign's personal Order of Chivalry. The building is open to all, and there are services every Sunday.

---

* Standard apochryphal anecdote for this church: Bedford instructs Jones to cut costs for this parish church, "something more like a barn." Jones replies, "You shall have the handsomest barn in England."

The chapel is almost overwhelmed by the buildings of the Savoy Theatre and Savoy hotel, which are threaded with a number of passages and small streets, some of which have a surprisingly steep slope for an area so long built upon and rearranged.

The hotel's restaurant is one of those fashionable places which has never gone out of fashion. It successfully ignores (one of those small triumphs of the British way of life) the fact that its next-door neighbor at 100 Strand is one of the rare temples of British gastronomy, Simpson's.

Simpson's is exactly what a foreigner wishes the distinguished London restaurant to be — elegant Edwardian decor, portions and service. The renown of Simpson's emanates from its huge roasts of beef rolled up to the table and carved to the customer's specifications (a bob to the carver). The saddle of mutton is equally revered. Simpson's does not discourage the legend that it grows its own beasts to assure supplies of incomparable meats. There is another legend that ladies are not served in the downstairs room at lunchtime, a legend one does well to believe, since it is true. After sundown mixed feeding is tolerated all over the house.

Past the Savoy complex (note a pub below stairs called the Coal Hole where Sydney Chaplin worked as barman to feed his mother and kid brother Charlie) is the clock-ridden Ministry of Aviation which they will obviously never get off the ground.

Fleeing from this, one could dodge across the street into Exchange Court, a rather dusty passageway leading to a bow-fronted, pilastered and columned eighteenth-century house whose bow-front, pilasters and columns are quite new. This has been since 1895 the headquarters of the Corps of Commissionaires, who in their military uniforms and blindingly polished military leather, serve as doorkeepers and in general decorate the town's office buildings. They are all ex-servicemen, often hung with medals. The Corps was founded by Captain Edward Walter to provide dignified employment to veterans spurned by civilian employers who had habitually shown their gratitude by applauding at parades. The Captain's efforts were supported by *The Times*, which by a happy coincidence belonged to his brother John.

Back across the Strand and down Adam Street are the remains

of one of London's urban wonders, destroyed in 1936. This was the Adelphi. The *adelphoi* were the brothers Adam, three of them architects, one a banker, who pooled their resources to achieve a masterwork. The two most noted, Robert and James, were responsible for the design and execution of the project. They just about lost their shirts on it, but Parliament granted permission for a lottery, and they were saved from financial ruin.

In the beginning they rented Durham Yard, a slummy hillside above the smelly Thames-side from the Duke of St. Albans for ninety-nine years, starting in 1768. Since Robert had the post of Sole Architect to the King and Board of Works they had little trouble in obtaining all the Parliamentary licenses needed for their undertaking.

They straightened the riverbank and built a pier and a quay. Then they tore open the hillside and built a series of vaulted cellars with arched gateways facing the Thames. Seven subterranean streets ran inland from the river gates and were bisected by others running from Robert Street to Adam Street. This monumental concept was probably influenced by Robert Adam's studies of ancient Rome (his drawings of Diocletian's palace had been published four years earlier). High above, on a terrace of brick, Adelphi Terrace was shaped, with a central block of houses making one wide sweep of windows above the river, balanced by separate wings to either side.

But to rear this island of luxury on a manmade escarpment 265 feet over the Thames was enormously costly. The expected steady revenue from rental of the underground warehouses was not forthcoming because the river at flood pushed in over the floors of the great brick caverns. There were difficulties in renting the houses, too, despite their desirability, their exclusivity and undoubted beauty (Adam entries, Adam windows, Adam fireplaces, Angelica Kauffmann ceilings). Still, when the financially pressed brothers were obliged to raffle them off, there was a scramble for tickets.

David Garrick took the center house on the Terrace, and Dr. Johnson and Boswell and Sir Joshua Reynolds came to dine and to sit about in the Chippendale furniture for which Garrick owed one thousand pounds to the makers. Persuaded at last that the theatrical genius couldn't pay, they accepted less . . . "the Chippendales were out of pocket and much displeased."

Thomas Hardy studied architecture at Sir Arthur Blomfield's house. Bernard Shaw lived in the Terrace from 1896 to 1927 (Mrs. Shaw gave the two top floors to the London School of Economics) and Sir James Barrie lived opposite.

Surprisingly, in the streets off the vanished Terrace,* there are more than half a dozen surviving Adam houses. In Adam Street, Nos. 7, 10 and 18. Number 7 is the home of the *Lancet*, the medical journal, and No. 18, the interior of which is resplendent with Adam work brought from country houses, is the home of the mysterious Institute for Strategic Studies. Thomas Hood, John Galsworthy and Robert Adam himself lived in Robert Street, where Nos. 1 to 3 survive, though threatened with demolition. On John Adam Street Nos. 4, 6 and 8 still stand, the latter constructed in 1774 for the Royal Society of Arts, which is still there and which admits visitors.

The Adam structures are really rather much like the red brick Palladian rectangles every other builder was sprinkling around London at the time. The difference between the Adams and the rest is the difference between one ballerina's *Swan Lake* and another's — touch, taste, talent.

John Adam Street passes out of the Adelphi project and goes across the grounds of what was once York House. When the Duke of Buckingham gave up his forty-eight-year old house off the Strand in 1673 and allowed the grounds to be built over he provided that the new streets spell out his name and title. (He had just lost his military command and his favor at the Court of Charles II.) Today John Adam Street crosses three of these streets which until the 1920's were *George* Street (now York Place), *Villiers* Street, *Duke* Street (gone), *Of* Alley (now York Buildings), *Buckingham* Street.

At No. 43 Villiers Street Rudyard Kipling had his first and last London residence, three small rooms over the shop of Sausage King Harris, opposite Gatti's Music Hall. Kipling stayed for

---

* Pevsner demands, "Would Paris have demolished Gabriel's buildings fronting the Place de la Concorde, or Nancy its squares? As a composition and as part of the architectural setting of London the Adelphi was on the same level."

less than a year from September 1890. He left when his health began to break down, but not before writing *The Light That Failed*.

On the west side of Villiers Street is Charing Cross Station, squatting here with its hotel since 1864. All over London esteemed, handsome and historic buildings are being torn out by the roots, but these unesteemed, unhandsome and not very stirringly historic structures remain, along with their painful railway bridge over the Thames. In front of the station is what they feigned to believe was an Eleanor Cross. The real Charing Cross was some distance west and south of here, at what is now the top of Whitehall, and it was a real medieval memorial cross, not a Victorian town pump.

Before the Strand reaches Trafalgar Square, one should throw a glance at least to the opposite side at what was still called in early 1966 Southern Rhodesia House, and at Coutts's Bank. The first is notable because Charles Holden had the temerity in 1907 to choose Jacob Epstein as the sculptor to decorate the second story of the new British Medical Association building. It was Epstein's first major British commission, and the remains of it are still there, nude figures minus their heads and other bits of anatomy. This mutilation was necessary not to protect a sense of prudery, as is often said, but to protect passersby: the stone was quarried wrong and cut wrong, could not withstand the invisible scourges of the clement London weather, and began to crack and fall. The bank building is interesting because of the name Coutts, which entails a tale to be recounted further on.

Toward the river after the station runs a narrow eighteenth-century street called Craven Street, and craven it seems to be. Its many original houses huddle timorously and untidily. Many of them are now small hotels, one rejoicing in the nearly-great name of the Waldor. Ben Franklin lived at No. 36 from 1757 to 1762, left when his widowed landlady remarried, but returned 1764–1772. At No. 32 Heinrich Heine passed three months of 1827 in an orgy of poetic sensitivity — London was all right in its way, but far too expensive and there was snow in April.

Trafalgar Square is a huge sloping traffic bowl, its road junctions broadening into lakes of asphalt, and its surrounding buildings arguing fruitlessly with the wide open spaces. In the center a big flat area has been gouged out and made into a lively sort of necropolis. It is best seen at night in the Christmas season when the illuminated tree (gift of the gracious Norwegians) briefly brings its brilliance and beauty to the square.

But in truth, this place has no best season, unless one is partisan for some cause being upheld at one of the mass meetings peculiar to this spot — they started as riots put down by police and soldiery in the 1880's. It succeeds in being big, but fails to be grand, one of those out-of-focus focal points.

The English sense of the dramatic is evident in their superb pageantry both indoors and out, and in their landscaping. Their great cityscapes, however, are compounded of surprise or intimacy or both. But when it comes to the Grand Style in regal avenues or *grandes places*, the British since Stonehenge have not succeeded, apparently because they don't really like the basic concept (John Nash's magnificent Regent Street quadrant was ripped out and Christopher Wren's Royal Avenue in Chelsea was never carried through).

Thus Trafalgar Square. It has seven major arteries radiating from it, it is girt with objects of interest and beauty, and from it there are several exciting vistas. It is stuffed with statuary, fitted with fountains, and endowed with the Nelson column. But . . .

There are the mendicant sidewalk artists and mendicant pigeons, throngs of distraction-seekers and wheeling of heavy traffic, but nevertheless, it remains cheerless and curiously barren. A bizarre memorial for that great romantic hero, Horatio Nelson.

The period of Nelson's heroism was an epoch of heroes, especially romantic heroes. It was the time of the American revolutionary heroes, the French revolutionary heroes, of Byron, Wellington, Napoleon, of Wolfe Tone in Ireland and Daniel Boone and young Andy Jackson on the American frontier.

"Everybody loves a winner," and Nelson won, but his grip on British affections grows out of something bigger than his success as an admiral. In his time and after Nelson compelled a love not given to other saviors of the nation such as Marlborough and Wellington. Perhaps it was because he did not repress those impulses every proper Englishman is trained to hide.

He was vain, he was boastful. A married man, he made a British Ambassador's wife his mistress, abandoning not only his wife but his post of duty to be with her.

He lost his eye, his arm and finally his life in combat and considered all three sacrifices quite in the ordinary nature of his profession (he lay long hours a-dying in the *Victory*, so we know what he thought about giving his life in battle).

The Duke of Wellington gave John Wilson Croker a penetrating sketch of Nelson, whom he had met but once, by chance:

> He could not know who I was, but he entered at once into conversation with me, if I can call it conversation, for it was almost all on his side, and all about himself, and in, really, a style so vain and so silly as to surprise and almost disgust me. . . . He went out of the room for a moment, I have no doubt to ask the office-keeper who I was, for when he came back he was altogether a different man, both in manner and matter. All that I had thought a charlatan style had vanished, and he talked of the state of this country and of the aspect and probabilities of affairs on the Continent with a good sense, and a knowledge of subjects at home and abroad that surprised me equally and more agreeably than the first part of our interview had done; in fact, he talked like an officer and a statesman. The Secretary of State kept us long waiting, and certainly, for the last half or three-quarters of an hour, I don't know that I ever had a conversation that interested me more. Now, if the Secretary of State had been punctual, and admitted Lord Nelson in the first quarter of an hour, I should have the same impression of a light and trivial character that other people have had, but luckily I saw enough to be satisfied that he was really a very superior man.

Nelson was the supreme naval genius. One of his innovations in sea fighting was "crossing the T," bringing his ships at right angles, instead of parallel to the enemy fleet. He wrote, "It was new, it was singular, it was simple. It must succeed." His major successes resulted in breaking Scandinavian armed neutrality, in sweeping the French out of the Mediterranean, in removing the threat of Napoleonic invasion of Britain, and at his last battle, the Battle of Trafalgar, making true the wishfully written words, "Brittania rules the waves."

196

Trafalgar is a cape on the southwest coast of Spain near the Straits of Gibraltar. There on October 21, 1805, Nelson signaled, "England expects that every man will do his duty." The combined French and Spanish fleets were smashed. Nelson was killed by a sharpshooter firing from the crosstrees of the French *Redoutable*.

Lady Hamilton's daughter, four-year-old Horatia, was legally given the name of Nelson and grew up to marry a clergyman and be the mother of clergymen, thus carrying on a Nelson family calling to which Horatio had been the exception.

Nelson was forty-seven when he died and Emma Hamilton was forty. Ten years later, she died too, blowsy, boozy and alone in a dive on the Calais waterfront where nobody believed her story.

Nelson on his column is 17 feet 2 inches tall, blinded in his right eye by a bullet and in his left eye by pigeon dung. The Devon granite column on which he stands is almost ten times taller than the statue: 170 feet 2 inches. Sixteen different books on London give the height as anywhere from 145 feet to 193 feet, but this is the figure in the files of the Ministry of Public Buildings and Works.

The memorial to Nelson was slow in coming. The open space was dubbed Trafalgar Square in 1830, the Nelson Memorial Committee founded in 1838, the grading of the sharply sloping ground not undertaken until 1840, when Sir Charles Barry designed the north terrace and steps.

The column and statue were erected at last in 1842, not quite forty years after Nelson's death. The four twenty-foot-long lions by Landseer took up their posts in 1867, a little late for the fiftieth anniversary. Behind the column are the two fountains and their basins (when there's a breeze, the flagstones around become a sort of thawed skating rink). On a line with Nelson's column stand Generals Havelock (statue 1861) and Napier (1855). The busts of Admirals Jellicoe and Beatty were placed on the terrace wall in 1948.

On a pedestal sits a horse and on the horse sits George IV, without stirrups, still waiting to take his place on the Marble Arch in front of Buckingham Palace. He ordered the statute himself, paid one-third down, and died. The arch, without statue, stood in front of Buckingham Palace from 1828 until 1851. However, the statue was not paid for until repeated requests to Parliament produced the money in 1843 — for the artist's heirs. And after all that, the statue was placed in Trafalgar Square, where there is another pedestal, ready for a similar windfall.

Some very handsome octagonal galleon lanterns adorn the periphery of the memorial part of the square. One is especially noticeable atop a police box done as an Early Icelandic Round Tower. Anyone in London can tell you the lanterns came from Nelson's flagship. It won't do any harm to believe it, but it won't do any good either, since it is absolutely false.

Above the terrace is the National Gallery. Many Londoners are still amusing themselves by repeating the term coined for it in 1838, "The National Cruet Stand," because of its "mean cupolas, resembling pepperpots." In the same chucklesome vein, Sir John Summerson wrote, "Wilkins set a dome over the portico and turrets over the terminal pavilions, like the clock and vases on a mantelpiece, only less useful." Just about every architect or historian writing of this building implies he could have done better than poor Willie Wilkins, who was not, in his other buildings, a bad architect.

But in this case Wilkins was striving for one sole effect: that of keeping his job. He was told, incorporate the colonnade of dismantled Carlton House in your façade. He was told, don't distract from or impede the view of St. Martin's-in-the-Fields; leave plenty room around the barracks behind your site, and don't forget we want a dome and cupolas and porticoes. He was told, don't spend more than £100,000, more like £95,000 (he spent £96,000). So he did as he was told.

At any rate the National Gallery as a gallery can't be sneered at by anybody. It is composed to a high degree of masterpieces, and probably assays less junk per square foot than any other national gallery. Admission is free.

Out front on the grass is a fine Grinling Gibbons statue of James II in Roman garb. Gibbons was whittling away one day when John Evelyn saw his work and used Court connections to have the youngster appointed Master Carver to the Crown. Practically any piece of carved wood in London is apt to be attributed

*Trafalgar Square — Prinny in the foreground, Nelson aloft,
National Gallery behind.*

199

to this great craftsman, but this statue (which is bronze and not wood and art, not craft) and the choir stalls of St. Paul's Cathedral are without question his work. First erected in Whitehall in 1688, this statue was moved four times, alighting here in 1948. James, who ran away from England in disguise, throwing the Royal Seal into the Thames, was never a vastly popular monarch.

George Washington is on the lawn too, donated by some Virginia ladies who perhaps wanted to show it was possible to make a bad copy of a good statue (Houdin's, in Richmond, Virginia). Above, on the façade of the gallery, another Marble Arch castoff, Flaxman's "Minerva," which he sold to the government as "Britannia."

Round the corner on St. Martin's Place, but scheduled to remove, is the National Portrait Gallery, foolishly overlooked by hundreds of thousands of tourists every year. It has good and bad pictures of good and bad persons, three thousand in all, who have made England — a range of personalities and physiognomies instructive, diverting and in many cases mystifying: Emma Hamilton, Lord Baden-Powell (inventor of the Boy Scouts), Florence Nightingale, Sir Francis Drake.

Over the way, St. Martin's-in-the-Fields, by James Gibbs, 1726. This work replaced a 1544 rebuilding of a church first mentioned in 1222. Gibbs's original plan was for a circular church, the sort of thing not usually approved by a Board of Commissioners. So he did something else. He moved the tower — in earlier churches built to one side or on a far end as a barely attached structure housing the bells. He planted it right over the entrance to the building which he fronted with a portico of six enormous Corinthian columns, an idea much copied since, especially in Ireland and America. Sacheverell Sitwell calls this "aesthetically the most successful of all London churches."

The bottom of St. Martin's Lane was lopped off in the making of Trafalgar Square, which leaves the church a fine position and makes the first building on the street Number 29.

A stirring picture of the north side of Trafalgar Square, of Canaletto-like flattering distortion, appeared in 1964 on an eight-yen stamp of the People's Republic of China. On a large red banner over the National Gallery and the church appeared the heads of Marx and Engels and the dates 1864-1964. The explanation was a bit obscure. It was the centenary of the founding of the First International (the International Working Men's Association). This was formed by Marx and Engels, and in London, under vigorous prompting of British trade unions, all right. But not at St. Martin's-in-the-Fields. It was rather at St. Martin's Hall, several blocks up St. Martin's Lane and turn right at Longacre. The Hall has been gone for some time. The church looks very good on the stamp.

Along towards Whitehall is South Africa House, designed in 1935 to harmonize with St. Martin's, but the architect indulged in so many cute tricks that he canceled the pretended kinship of the porticoes and found himself with nothing more than a large building. Clear across the square is Canada House, built in 1827 for the Union Club and the Royal College of Physicians. Designed by Sir Robert Smirke, it has been somewhat tinkered with, but retains the basic opulence of a gentlemen's club. Both the doctors and the clubmen have departed, leaving the premises to the High Commissioner for Canada. On the ground floor there are an information bureau, a reading room and a touch of home for visiting Canadians.

South of Canada House is Admiralty Arch, which straddles the entrance to the Mall, the pink road to Buckingham Palace. It is abutted by one of London's first drive-in banks, a bit of Scottish enterprise. Beyond is Whitehall, at the top of which is Charing Cross.

The crossroads, halfway between the Abbey and the City, has been an important one for almost a thousand years. The Royal Mews, where the hunting hawks were housed, stood at the top of the slope, and when Henry VIII, after a palace fire lodged his horses there, the term "mews" began to mean "stables." The mews were replaced by a barracks and the National Gallery. Between them and Charing Cross, a hundred hovels were cleared away to open the space to make Trafalgar Square.

The Cross at Charing was one of those erected at each spot that the funeral cortege of Eleanor of Castile, beloved wife of Edward I, stopped overnight on the journey to Westminster Abbey from Harby in Nottinghamshire in 1290. Edward erected thirteen such crosses, this final one at the charcoal-makers' hamlet (whence the name) a mile from the Abbey.

The Puritan Parliament of 1643 ordered the cross destroyed as a popish symbol. In its place was erected, in 1675, the statue which is now there. It is an equestrian figure of Charles I, the King whose head was lopped off in Whitehall by Cromwell's Puritans in 1649.

The statue was made in 1633 (the date and the sculptor's name, Le Sueur, are still legible on the horse's left forefoot) and placed in the churchyard of St. Paul's, Covent Garden, awaiting erection in Roehampton. When the Civil War broke out in 1642, it was hidden in the church crypt. The Cromwellian Council of State ordered it produced, which it finally was, in 1664. Sold as scrap to John Rivett, brazier, it was melted down by him and fashioned into Royalist souvenirs (nutcrackers, candlesticks, thimbles, knife handles) which sold briskly to Royalist sympathizers.

But after the Restoration, the statue was found intact. Rivett, a royalist like his friend, and fellow Huguenot, sculptor Le Sueur, had hidden it away, and returned it only after a series of court actions. On the spot where it was erected several of those who had voted the death of Charles I had been hanged, drawn and quartered in 1660. Chronic Stuart supporters still hang the statue with wreaths on January 30, the anniversary of Charles's death.

Behind the statue a bronze plaque is sunk into the pavement: it marks the official center of London, from which all distances are measured.

THE LONDON OF
WINSTON CHURCHILL

Historic dilemma — Parliament, its palace, its practices, its pain, Commons and Lords, Guy Fawkes — Westminster Hall — "New" Houses of Parliament, Big Ben, best club in London, the terraces — Parliament Square — St. Margaret's Church — the Abbey, its monuments and architecture — New New Scotland Yard — Queen Anne's Gate — Whitehall, Britain's most important street — The Civil Service — Whitehall Palace — The Treasury, Foreign Office, Home Office — Downing Street — Richmond Terrace — The Quadragon — Old Treasury — Dover House — Gwydyr House — Banqueting House — Horse Guards — Ex-Admiralty — St. James's Park — The Guards, an institution — Marlborough House and Clarence House — St. James's Palace — Lancaster House — Buckingham Palace — Royal Household — London on wheels — Hyde Park Corner — Apsley House — Green Park

WHEN Wordsworth loitered on Westminster Bridge composing his sonnet (this was more than twenty-five years before the London police were invented, so he wasn't told to move along there) he wrote, "Dear God! the very houses seem asleep." Although the Houses of Parliament were disposed then as they are now, just off the bridge, he was not talking about them in particular.

The scene over which he rhapsodized was entirely changed by 1850, when Wordsworth died — if Poets Laureate of England may be said to die. The centuries-old Parliament buildings were gone, and new housing for the Houses was underway. Four years later Wordsworth's bridge had been torn down and replaced by a new span.

It was another of those moments when the face of London was being changed.

> Oh they've shifted father's grave to build a sewer
> They've shifted it regardless of expense.
> They've shifted his re-mains
> Just to lay some bloody drains
> To glorify some toff's new res-i-dence.

The mid-nineteenth century was the period of ripeness and richness in the full flowering of modern England. At that moment anyone gazing from the bridge where Wordsworth had gazed ("Earth has not anything to show more fair") would have seen the capital of the world.

Victoria was on the throne and her capital was being remade in her image. The London thus fashioned is the city that foreigners have come to know through Charles Dickens, Conan Doyle, Henry James. Now Victoria's reign is finally terminating in London and the city is being remade. But in whose image? London toward the end of the 1960's is a city in transition, but transition to what?

In the 1860's there were no questions about personal national values. Even the millions who were the models for Marx's exploited masses had no questions about what England was, what the Flag represented, what the Crown meant. The meaning of "work" and "duty" was clear to all. And as Marx complained, most of the population was addicted to religion. Queen, Country, Church, Family — those were the foundation stones of Empire.

Industrialization and colonialism were carrying England ever forward and England was carrying the whole world. The British were the imitated innovators in everything solid and progressive — machine tools, colonial administration, trade unionism, international finance, democratic reforms, building construction.

But just about the time Victoria went into mourning, the fine flower of Empire began to fade. The energy and the jingoism not only went on, they burgeoned, but on a stricken stem whose malaise was undetected.

To be British was to be right. Britons were the arbiters of dress, manners and morals. *To be an Englishman is to belong to the most exclusive club there is.* They knew what was done and what was simply not done, my dear chap. *How can what an Englishman believes be heresy? It is a contradiction in terms.* Despite the earthshaking changes in the world and in Britain itself, millions of Britons continued to act out the Victorian charade through World War II. *I have not become the King's First Minister in order to preside over the liquidation of the British Empire.*

At the time the new Houses of Parliament were being completed, the greatest national virtue was Success, the product of daring, genius and courage. Borne on a tide of optimism and self-confidence, success begot success. The success has evaporated, the optimism is fabricated, the self-confidence — where it remains — petrified into smugness. Only the courage remains, but its flame is low and its keepers few. Still sturdy in the face of adversity, the British have not relearned how to live in the face of uncertainty.*

As colonists, the British have been taunted with destroying native cultures and leaving nothing in their stead. With more justice this can be charged against the British in their home islands. The wilderness in which they cry is of their own making.

They, the innovators, are now the imitators, and the physical rebuilding of the capital is a painful assemblage of secondhand ideas and palely reflected alien zest. London is not at all sure just what it is the capital of today.

This was all foreseen. Walter Bagehot wrote in the 1860's, "The characteristic danger of great nations, like the Roman or the English, which have a long history of continuous creation, is that they may at last fail from not comprehending the great institutions they have created."

About the end of the nineteenth century, Max Beerbohm drew a cartoon comparing nineteenth- and twentieth-century man. The first is comforted by a vision of the future which is an endlessly magnified version of himself. The second also sees the future in his own image, but ever dwindling, vaporizing, ending as a transparent question mark.

* "British government is inefficient, antiquated and inept . . . British purpose, in the largest sense, died after the war and has yet to be reborn." — Editorial, *The Times*, London, September 1964.

The current dilemma belongs partly to Britain and partly to the age through which her planet is passing. If history continues to favor the Island Race, history will produce someone to point the way and others will rush up behind to pivot the nation in the direction of greatness. Fumbling and groping, the famous "muddling through," are as much a part of Britain's story as are glory and achievement.

The economic and social organization have been awry before, as has been the nation's political position in the world. They have been rethought and rewrought, and as a new system has emerged, cities have been rebuilt to match. As the 1970's loom it is evident that the passions of 1905, the slogans of 1925, the planning of 1945 do not apply. A fresh analysis and a fresh impetus are needed, and at similar moments in the past, they have always been forthcoming.

One of the great sources of such impetus in the past has been the House of Commons. One of the great sources of dismay in the mid-60's is that the Commons seems incapable of creative force. Parliament seems to do little more than annotate investigations performed, plans proposed or reforms effected by experts outside the legislature — for example, in regard to highways, railways, fuel and energy production, education and governmental reorganization.

A long and rather wistful look at Parliament by its members was prompted by the decision of Winston Churchill in August 1964 not to stand again for election. He was the last Member to have served under Queen Victoria, when, in the words of Labour M. P. Woodrow Wyatt, "the British Parliament was still the center of the world. Distinction there was distinction everywhere."

Somberly and truthfully he went on to say, "Today the House of Commons is little considered in the world. Such is the evolution of the Whip system and the monolithic nature of the two mass parties that even the British Government barely takes notice of its debates."

The 1964 (sixth) edition of *Our Parliament* expressed similar misgivings. This book, now a standard, widely translated work on the operations of the legislature, is by Strathearn Gordon, historian, admirer and librarian of the House of Commons. Hardly the man to question its adequacy, yet, "Do the people trust Parliament as much they did fifty or one hundred years ago?" he asked.

"Perhaps the answer is that although our constitutional machinery has been tested through the ages," he wrote, "and enjoys high repute in the world, no machinery will run forever without periodic overhaul and redesign."

The executive branch of government has increased its power manyfold since the turn of the century, while Parliament has been slowly sapped. The influence of its debates has been vitiated because no matter what logic flashes or eloquence thunders over the debating floor, the party with the Parliamentary majority will win the vote.

Winston Churchill was, for most of his parliamentary career, a maverick. Then a political life was possible for the unshepherded individual. In his maiden speech he went against party policy to speak sympathetically of the Boers. When the House of Commons was rebuilt after the German bombing, he insisted that the rectangular shape be retained, not just to honor traditional architecture, but to honor the concept of debate in which opposing parties face one another. * For the Member who can in conscience no longer sit among his party fellows, there is the option of rising, crossing the floor and sitting with the Opposition, a walk Churchill took twice.

"I have been a member of the Conservative Party longer, but less often than Sir Winston Churchill," said one very senior Tory.

As Prime Minister Churchill said, "Two things I put above everything: God and the House of Commons." †

He also said, "I have lived nearly all my life in the House of Commons and I believe it to be the enduring guarantee of British liberties and democratic practices." However urgent or important

---

* A red line on each side of the green carpet down the center of the room separates the Government and Opposition front benches, and are so drawn that the party leaders are at least two sword-lengths from one another during debate. In the reconstructed chamber, 437 seats, as before, were provided for members who numbered 506 in the 1945 elections, 616 in 1966.

† "I hope that you treat God better than you do the House of Commons," rejoined Sir Stafford Cripps, irked by Churchillian arrogance. Sir Winston, equally nettled by Crippsian righteousness, was later moved to observe, "There, but for the grace of God, goes God."

his other work was, Churchill always put it aside to attend sittings of the House. When he sat for the last time in the chamber, the House passed a resolution of gratitude, something done only once before in Parliament's history, to thank the Duke of Wellington for winning the battle of Waterloo. To remain a Member after World War II, he refused a peerage.*

Others, born into the peerage, have renounced their titles to gain membership in the House of Commons. The House of Lords as a place of power has diminished over the years to the lowest possible current consistent with the maintenance of life. This power has not seeped away, but has been taken away. Today it has power to delay for one year any Commons bill except a money bill, which it may hold up for four weeks.

Apart from that, there is little the Lords can do, except debate — it takes three to make a quorum. Their House is still the highest court of appeal in the land, but judgment is no longer heard by the whole membership, only by the nine Law Lords, judges granted life peerages for this specific duty.

In 1948 Peers lost the right to be tried by their peers instead of by ordinary courts. They did retain their right to keep their hats on before a judge and, prior to abolition of the death penalty, to be hanged by a silken cord.

The peerage includes five ranks of nobles, starting at the bottom with baron, going up through viscount, earl and marquess to duke to Royal duke. There are twenty-six dukes and about nine hundred other hereditary peers, most of them barons. This latter title is the most frequently awarded. New earldoms, except to retiring Prime Ministers, are rare. No dukes have been created since 1874 (except for Royal relatives), although it was persistently rumored that Churchill, grandson to one Duke of Marlborough, nephew to another and cousin to another, refused the offer of a dukedom.

Other than the Law Lords, the House contains other Life

---

* The House is reserved to commoners only, in strict fact, to Members only. When the House wishes to go into executive session, a Member cries to the Speaker, "I spy strangers!" and all nonmembers are ordered out. Resignations are not accepted. If a Member wants to resign, he applies for Stewardship of the Chiltern Hundreds. The pay of £1 a year makes this "an office of profit under the Crown," and bars him from membership in the House.

Peers who will not transmit to their progeny the prestige and burdens of a title. The Church of England's two archbishops and twenty-four bishops are Lords of Parliament without being peers. Outside the House of Lords and the peerage are baronets and knights ("Sir"), who are not nobles.

The first rein on the legislative power of the Upper House was the Reform Bill of 1832, an act promoted by two peers, Earl Grey and Lord John Russell. It abolished "pocket" and "rotten" boroughs whose votes were controlled by their landlords (usually peers) and enfranchising more members of the middle class. Succeeding bills through the century adjusted parliamentary representation to population and spread the vote to larger portions of the population.

The showdown came when the Lords vetoed Lloyd George's budget in 1909, starting a two-year savage power struggle, ending in 1911 when the Upper House lost almost all of its legislative functions to become an ornamental and somewhat advisory body.

Parliament lists its own birthdate as 1265, when Henry III was forced to accept the parliament summoned by Simon de Montfort. It was an assembly not only of Simon's fellow nobles, but of representatives from the shires as well. Later kings convoked the Commons as a counterbalance to restive lords and to give token national acceptance of taxes to pay for foreign wars. It was tyrannical Henry VIII who fixed regular meetings of the people's representatives. During his reign Parliament sat longer and more often than any time before, exploited by Henry to legalize his supremacy over the church.

Under the Tudor reigns the Commons developed its rules of order for debate, established the three readings for each bill and the system of voting, not by acclamation but by division, filing from the debating chamber into the "aye" or "no" lobbies.

The chamber had also established enduring privileges, in spite of the Tudor royal despotism. They had won complete freedom of speech in their House and were immune from arrest. The Stuarts saw that whatever Parliament gained in power, the monarchy lost. They sought to restore untrammeled absolutism. Parliament fought back, rejecting the contention that taxation was a royal and

An early Parliament, King up front, Lords to the right, Clergy to the left, and Commons well to the rear.

not a parliamentary prerogative. Puritan M.P.'s seethed over royal High Church policy. Charles I actually invaded the Commons in person to arrest five members he considered traitors. In 1642 it came to open warfare in which Parliament's army defeated that of King Charles, whom they beheaded in 1649. The Commons then ruled England until forcibly ejected by their leader, Oliver Cromwell, who assumed personal quasi-royal rule as Lord Protector.

Following the 1660 Restoration, there was a pro-monarchical reaction, but when James II tried to "subvert the Established Church," there was another revolution (the Glorious Revolution of 1688) and Parliament invited William and Mary from Holland to rule. When Queen Anne died in 1714 without heirs, Parliament had already picked the House of Hanover as rulers.

At the time of the American Revolution, the king still retained a good deal of ruling power, although the Crown could no longer veto acts of Parliament. The king, almost like a modern U. S. President, picked his principal ministers and guided and influenced legislation.

It was only toward the end of the nineteenth century that the modern political parties began to emerge, and when Gladstone campaigned outside in his own constituency in the 1879 election, he shocked a great many people.

It was Gladstone who said — and he served there sixty-five unbroken years — "The House of Commons is a place where it is impossible either to work or to relax."

The Palace of Westminster hasn't changed much since his day except to become more crowded despite its one thousand chambers, eleven courtyards and one hundred staircases all connected by more than two miles of hallways. Members who complained to the Minister of Public Buildings and Works in 1965 about no working-space were reminded, "The control of the Palace of Westminster through the Lord Great Chamberlain goes back to the year 1133." *

* The hereditary Lord Great Chamberlain, the Marquess of Cholmondeley, is not to be confused with the Lord Chamberlain, whose principal occupation is censoring plays, nor the Lord Chancellor, who is Chief Law Lord and presides over the House of Lords seated upon the traditional Woolsack, a sort of elegant crimson pouf with back and armrests, stuffed with wool from the sheep-raising countries of the Commonwealth.

Nonetheless, a few months later in the same year, a compromise was effected, called by the *Telegraph* "a sound English blend of preservation and progress." Although the Queen had "graciously agreed that the control, use and occupation of the Palace and its precincts shall be permanently enjoyed by the Houses of Parliament," the building remained a royal palace. The Lord Great Chamberlain retained his functions for royal occasions and control of the Royal Gallery, Her Majesty's robing room and the staircase and anteroom adjoining it. The Speakers of each House, acting for their membership, took control of the areas used by each body. The crypt and Westminster Hall are under the joint control of the three officials. And as before, the Minister of Public Buildings and Works has the responsibility of the heating, lighting, furnishing and upkeep of the building.

As one of the principal objectives of the Norman invasion, the brand-new palace of Westminster appears on the Bayeux tapestry. It was built (1042–1066) for Edward the Confessor and remained the main London seat of the sovereign until Henry VIII appropriated Whitehall from Cardinal Wolsey in 1529. In 1557 the Commons moved into the deconsecrated palace chapel of St. Stephen, giving up the traditional meeting place in the Westminster Abbey Chapter House. The House of Lords convened in the old Chamber of Requests in Old Palace Yard, now an open space, then an inner court. This was the room designated for demolition in the Gunpowder Plot. The detonation was arranged for November 5, 1605, date of the State Opening of Parliament. On this occasion, the Commons are summoned before the throne in the House of Lords to hear the monarch's speech. They are summoned by the Gentleman Usher of the Black Rod, and to show their independence, the Commons still ritually pretend not to hear him knock the first time.

Before Guy Fawkes could light the fuses on the kegs of powder piled in the cellar below the Lords Chamber, he was collared by Yeomen of the Guard acting on information in an anonymous letter to Lord Monteagle (the letter is on view at the Public Records Office, Chancery Lane). Before every State Opening*

---

* Opening the new sitting of Parliament every October or November, this is one of the splendid moments of pageantry which brightens London. In the Irish State Coach

the cellars are searched again by the Beefeaters to this day.

The plot, conceived by Catholic exiles, exacerbated anti-Catholic prejudice in England. It was more than 225 years before Catholics were allowed to sit in Parliament and until 1829 no Catholic priest was allowed to live within five miles of any town. Until 1859 — 254 years — the Church of England Book of Common Prayer contained "A Form of Prayer of Thanksgiving to be used yearly on the Fifth Day of *November;* for the happy Deliverance of King JAMES I and the Three Estates of *England* from the most traterous and bloody intended Massacre by Gunpowder." The prayer describes those assembled in the House of Lords as "by Popish Treachery appointed as sheep to the slaughter, in a most barbarous and savage manner, beyond the examples of former ages." Now, in diminishing numbers, Britons light bonfires and immolate effigies of Guy Fawkes ("A penny for the Guy!") and set off fireworks on the fifth of November.

Fawkes and his fellow conspirators were able to stuff the cellars with gunpowder by a very simple procedure — they rented the cellars. Although huge and rambling along the river for almost a quarter of a mile, the palace was palatial only on the inside. Against its walls and within its precinct leaned shops and slum houses and a goodly number of alehouses. John Evelyn used to frequent the Turk's Head Tavern in Old Palace Yard. And in Westminster Hall, possibly the largest medieval hall in Europe, shops operated while the Courts of Justice were in session. The different courts were separated by low partitions and whatever open spaces remained were let to vendors of lawbooks, pictures, coffee, sweets, fruit until the Courts moved out of the Hall in 1825.

The Hall itself is one of the rare pieces of the medieval palace which survived the fire of 1834. The other fragments are the crypt of St. Stephen's (in reality the lower of two chapels in the original) where marriages and christenings are held for Members (Parliament's church is St. Margaret's, just across the street) and

---

the Queen comes down the Mall from Buckingham Palace, past the remains of Whitehall Palace to Westminster Palace. Crowned, robed and adorned with an enormous velvet train, surrounded by retainers, the monarch speaks from the throne which dominates the Chamber throughout the year.

the two-storied 1526 cloister, riverwards of the Hall. Because of the press for space, the cloisters serve as a cloakroom and the splendid fan vaulting is not available to the public gaze. But for the decision of Walter Elliot, Conservative M.P., Westminster Hall might have vanished in the Blitz. Mr. Elliot was on fire watch the night of May 10, 1941 as the incendiaries rained down. The House of Commons was hit and burning and the roof of the Hall was afire as well. There was fire equipment to fight only one fire. Mr. Elliot chose to save the medieval Hall rather than the Victorian House.

The lower parts of the walls are those built in 1097 for William Rufus (which is what the British prefer to call William II, son of the Conqueror. Perhaps it sounds more warrior-kinglike, obscuring the image of gentlemen-at-arms garbed as girls for his pleasure). Richard II remodeled the Hall 1394–1402, installing the hammer-beam roof, the oldest now to be found in England. With its internal trellis of yard-thick arching and projecting beams, it needs no piers to hold it aloft.

The Hall is bare except for the fourteenth-century statues of

Westminster Hall, left, first built in 1097, still serves for the lying-in-state of great Britons

kings in the window recesses and niches, and it is apt to strike the visitor as simply large (240 feet long, 61 feet wide, 92 feet high) rather than grand, which it is, and noble. The Kings of England from Stephen to James I came upriver from the Tower the night before coronation to feast, and here there was merriment and Christmas largesse as well.

And tears and venom too. In 1305 Sir William Wallace, the Scot who had always refused to accept English conquest of Scotland, was here condemned to death as a traitor, although not being an English subject or ally, he had committed no act of treason.

No sooner had Richard II finished rebuilding the Hall than he was brought here and forced to abdicate in favor of Henry IV. Sir Thomas More and Bishop Fisher (both in 1535), the Lord Protector Somerset (1551), Elizabeth's Earl of Essex (1601), Guy Fawkes and seven other plotters (1605) were tried and condemned here. Titus Oates was convicted of perjury here in 1686: eight years earlier he had invented the existence of a second Catholic plot to kill the king (Charles II this time) and provoked a wave of anti-Catholic hysteria and persecution. Later, in the reign of William III, Oates was released and pensioned off.

It was in Westminster Hall that Charles I was condemned to death in 1649, and that four years later his principal persecutor, Oliver Cromwell, was installed as Lord Protector. In 1661, although already dead (and buried in Westminster Abbey) Cromwell returned to this scene of triumphs: his head, severed from his disinterred corpse, was set up on the roof of the Hall, where it remained for twenty-three years. Today Oliver Cromwell in bronze stands alongside Westminster Hall.

When the purchase of this statue for five hundred pounds was proposed by the Liberal Government in 1895, Irish M.P.'s inquired whether the government wished to honor the great soldier who beat the King's armies, Cromwell the founder of the big navy, or Cromwell the destroyer of the House of Commons. The government's bill was withdrawn. The Prime Minister, Lord Rosebery, later paid for the statue out of his own pocket and Parliament did not refuse it. Oliver holds his hat under his arm, his sword in one hand, Bible in the other, and wears his spurs upside-down.

The seven-year (1788–1795) trial of Warren Hastings took place here, and the equally ignoble adultery hearings against George IV's pathetic Queen Caroline until dropped by the uneasy Lords.

Kings and Queens have lain in state here, as well as Gladstone in 1898 and Churchill in 1965.

In 1834 the Palace of Westminster burned to the ground as a grand finale to a fable of frugality. The Exchequer tallies, wooden sticks notched to keep accounts — the medieval forerunner of punch-card systems — were stored for ages in the palace. Eventually the remainder was stacked in the Star Chamber after

The entrance to Westminster Hall has altered since the fifteenth century, but not vastly

216

that Court had ceased to function, and eventually someone began using them for kindling.* A stove in the House of Lords, over-stoked with this antique fuel, ignited the paneling and burned the whole palace. Charles Dickens bitterly told a public meeting that the tallies might have been given as fuel to the poor of Westminster, but that "official routine required that they — worn out, worm eaten, rotten old bits of wood — should never be useful."

To the homeless Parliament, King William IV offered Buckingham Palace, but the Duke of Wellington, at that time Foreign Secretary, advised against it. His Grace believed that the legislature should never meet in a building which offered the possibility of being surrounded on all sides by a mob. The lawmakers continued to meet in patched-up portions of the ruins, and a competition was held for a new Palace of Westminster. It was stipulated the buildings be either Elizabethan (only three competitors chose

* The Court of the Star Chamber was made up of the King's Council plus other law officers. Under James I and Charles I it was debased into a secret tribunal tolerating torture to obtain evidence in pursuit of opponents to Royal policies. The room had been used in Plantagenet days to store starrs, receipts of payment — often obtained by force — from Jewish money lenders (the medieval Latin *starrum* was adapted from the Hebrew *sh'tar*, meaning a writing). The stars on the ceiling, typical contemporary room decoration found in many other rooms of the palace, had nothing to do with the name.

Westminster Abbey, Westminster Hall and the first House of Parliament in 1647.

this style) or Gothic (ninety-one designs in Gothic). The committee liked the clarity of the winning plan and were delighted with the superb drawings done in minute and lively Gothic detail. The architect's name was Charles Barry, but the unsigned drawings had been conceived and produced by Augustus Welby Northmore Pugin. The new palace was built with Barry as architect-in-chief and Pugin exercising his magic as master of the Gothic. Barry emerged with a knighthood. Pugin died in the madhouse, his due credit denied him.

These two men of vastly different personalities and artistic convictions between them contrived a building which has come to symbolize Britain and London. It is massive, but lightened by variety. It is wrought with solid craftsmanship, but its solidity is brightened everywhere with imagination. It has touches of both the lion and the unicorn. The scientists of 1835 were, alas, quite in error, selecting after tests magnesian limestone from Yorkshire which is rapidly devoured by London's emeried air.

In 1964 plans for enlarging the palace produced a controversy which echoed around the Commonwealth, involving those for and

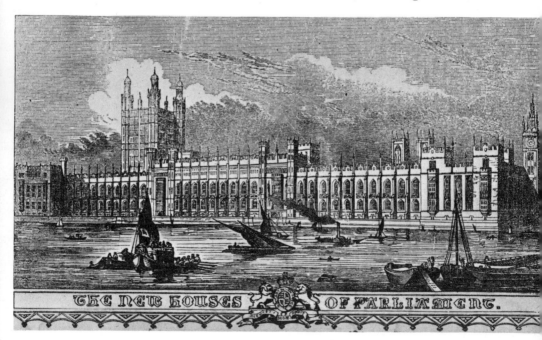

THE NEW HOUSES OF PARLIAMENT.

218

against the Gothic extension voted by a Parliamentary Committee of all parties. The proposal was quietly vetoed the following year by a new Government. However, the uproar did reveal the esteem and affection with which the building is regarded by the general public. It also showed that most architects and art historians, far from sniggering at the Victorian Gothic pile, felt that it was a good building. In general they also said there was no one left alive who could make a Gothic addition up to the standard of the original.

Among the unsolicited suggestions for obtaining more working space for Members was the proposal to make an island in the Thames, a new moated realm for the Lords. The navigation authorities thought this idea not only ingenious but also lousy.

Another suggestion, far too serious to be seriously considered, was to remove the legislative capital to some former capital city, such as York, thus relieving a great deal of the population and money pressure on London and a great deal of the London pressure on Members.

The Palace tower nearest Westminster Bridge is known all over the world as Big Ben, except to purists who call the clock Big Ben and distilled purists who call (with absolute accuracy) the bell which strikes the hours Big Ben.

There was a bell tower in the old palace of Westminster, and its major bell was called "Great Tom." Taken down in 1707, it was broken up and recast by the same foundry that later made Big Ben and it still sounds at St. Paul's Cathedral.* Although officialdom fraternally leans toward the theory that the Ben for whom the bell was named was Victoria's Commissioner of Works, Sir Benjamin Hall, it was more probably Big Ben Gault, 218-pound boxer, that people had in mind at the time.

The inscription on Big Ben reads "13 TONS 3 CWTS 3 QTRS 15 LBS." Nine feet in diameter, seven and one-half feet high, it was originally tuned to sound an "E," but it was cracked, owing to the interference of an officious M.P. who was able to insist on a

---

* The Whitechapel Foundry also made the Liberty Bell and recast the bells of St. Clement's after World War II. Not only are they still in business after all these centuries, but their secrets are still considered valuable enough to steal, which highly specialized crime was committed in 1964.

too-heavy hammer over the founders' protests. The M.P. was later ennobled. The bell is still cracked.

The clock, which has a glass face twenty-three feet across, is a Victorian wonder, keeping virtually perfect time since 1859, although occasionally stopped by the weight of snow on the fourteen-foot-long minute hand. The Ministry of Works reported that it was once halted by roosting birds, in the Ministry's words, "a murmuration of starlings." The clock works are surprisingly small, being laid out on a little-larger-than-life-size iron couch. The original makers, Dent's, who still have their shop in Pall Mall, send a man around once a week to wind it.

High above the clock a light shines when Parliament is sitting. (Sessions start at 2:30 P.M. and normally end at 10:30 P.M., although they sometimes go on all night.*) When the clock face was re-illuminated in April 1945 after six years of blackout, the switch was thrown by the Speaker of the House. Crowds gathered in the street to cheer.

Sessions of the House are also signaled by a flag flying from Victoria Tower, on the opposite end of the palace. Under Victoria Tower, the Royal Entrance gives onto the Sovereign's Robing Room, from which the Royal Gallery leads into the Royal Court, or through the Prince's Chamber into the House of Lords.

The Peers' Entrance, under an ornate porch, is toward the center of the palace. St. Stephen's Entrance, along the rear of Westminster Hall, leads to the Central Lobby and marks the division of the House of Lords (red carpets) from the House of Commons (green). Off to the left the Commons Corridor leads to the Commons Lobby and thence through the Churchill Arch to the rebuilt Commons Chamber. The Arch, made from stones of the old blitzed House, was Churchill's idea. He proposed it as a memorial to those who sat in the House through the dark days

---

* The New York *Herald Tribune* in 1964 quoted "a veteran parliamentary reporter" on the subject of "St. Stephen's widows": "The pretty wives of M.P.'s all have lovers, the prettier ones two lovers and the loveliest one has four. After all, they rarely see their husbands except on weekends." Conversely, A. J. P. Taylor mentions five adulterous Prime Ministers — the Duke of Wellington was a regular client of famed prostitute Harriette Wilson; the Reform Bill's Earl Grey had a child by the Duchess of Devonshire; Lord Melbourne twice cited as co-respondent; Palmerston had four children by Lady Cowper; Disraeli, to advance his career, shared Lord Lyndhurst's mistress. Brian Inglis adds Lloyd George, "who perjured himself to avoid exposure."

Parliament now controls its houses, but the building nonetheless re-
mains the Royal Palace of Westminster.

of the war, but the House made it a memorial to the Prime Minister.

There are towers other than the Clock and Victoria Towers. In the one overlooking the river near Westminster Bridge lives the Speaker of the House in one of the world's most covetable apartments. The Serjeant at Arms, usually a person of considerable distinction despite the title (in 1963–1964 the Serjeant was an Admiral), also resides in the Palace, as do a number of other officers of Parliament.

An apartment for the Clerk of the House has recently been carved out of the attics, where offices for M.P.'s have also been contrived (most M.P.'s must be content with a green school locker for their things and work in the library or other "public" rooms of the House).

Some find refuge across Bridge Street at St. Stephen's Tavern, at least until 11 P.M. closing time. Pubs which serve market porters have special licensing which accords their hours with those of their customers. This is not the case for legislators, but they do have several bars in their own building, which, being a royal palace, is not subject to licensing laws. The bars in St. Stephen's Tavern are fitted with Division Bells which sound to summon Members back to cast their votes. One night when they rang and the parliamentarians hurried out into the night, an old gentleman asked, "What is it? A fire? Is it a fire?"

He was told no, not at all, it was just a bell for the House of Commons.

"What's the matter, eh? One of them escaped?"

While hours in the House are long, some balance is achieved by the fact that the pay is low. It was pointed out in 1965 that if Senior Ministers' salaries (£5000) were brought up to the purchasing power of 1831, when the salary was set, the annual pay would have to be £31,250.

If there is little power in Parliament and no money, why the eagerness of so many to enter? Charles Dickens had one answer (in *Our Mutual Friend*, 1865), when Twemlow "rejoins feelingly, 'I think that it is the best club in London.' "

Sir Charles Barry was the designer of the Reform Club and the Travelers Club in Pall Mall.

Inside the Commons Chamber, the Honourable Gentlemen did not remove their hats.

Among clubby appurtenances, the river terraces are conspicuous. It is something of a social coup for the out-of-town visitor to take tea on the terrace with his M.P. or — ahem — on the Lords' Terrace. But while the interlude may be elevated, the terrace is not, and if one wishes to watch the river, one must take one's tea standing up. The trouble with this — besides the fact that everyone else is sitting at tables — is that one risks an abrupt loss of appetite. The Thames is a fairly commercial urban highway at this point, and its unctuous surface swells near. An Englishman reported, after a boat tour around Manhattan Island, "New Yorkers, from the water-borne evidence, do nothing but fornicate, defecate and eat oranges." The closeup view from the terrace does not leave quite the same impression: Londoners do not seem to be so fond of oranges.

Parliament Square was laid out by Barry to disengage the new palace, and to make this square and open New Palace Yard, a warren of squalid medieval streets was destroyed. Parliament Square was re-laid out in 1951, making a formal park with lawns and walks, benches and low white stone walls. Statues which had accumulated over the years were re-sited so that Lord Derby, Robert Peel and Benjamin Disraeli regard their beloved House, while Palmerston turns his back and Field Marshal Smuts skates urgently away in the direction of South Africa. Abraham Lincoln (copied from the St. Gaudens Chicago statue) remains neutrally to one side. Prime Minister Canning unaccountably does the same.

On the south side of the square, and just across St. Margaret's Street from the Palace of Westminster is St. Margaret's Church, the Commons' parish church ever since members walked out on the High Church services of the Abbey in 1614.

The existing structure is primarily early sixteenth-century, perpendicular Gothic, drastically restored with some additions in the eighteenth and nineteenth centuries. Americans have been partial to this small, handsome church. They have contributed a window to Sir Walter Ralegh, who was beheaded outside in Old Palace Yard (James Russell Lowell wrote the inscription), and another window to Milton, with an inscription by that Milton of Haverhill, Massachusetts, John Greenleaf Whittier. Another

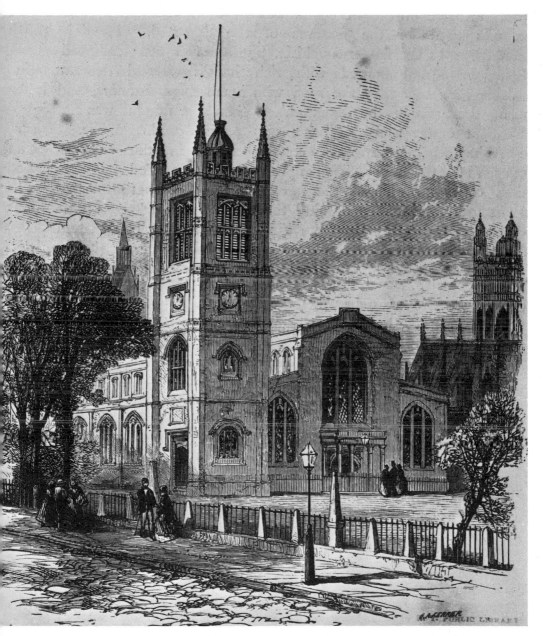

St. Margaret's, in the shadow of the Abbey, is Parliament's parish church.

225

New Englander preached here often and is remembered with a plaque — Phillips Brooks (died 1893), who was able simultaneously to be an Episcopal Bishop and a Boston Brahmin.

Almost as many ambitious people dream of being married in St. Margaret's as dream of being buried next door in the Abbey. Among those whose weddings took place here are Samuel Pepys (1655), John Milton (1656) and Sir Winston Churchill (1908).

This area was known in Saxon times as Thorney Island. The Romans did some building here by the river ford, but the fragments don't tell enough of their story. There was apparently a Benedictine community already established here when Edward the Confessor, King of England, canonized two hundred years later, arrived to build the Abbey and the Palace of Westminster (1050-1065).

The Thames veers from its east-west course just upstream of the Abbey to run almost north-south for more than two miles (roughly, Vauxhall Bridge to Waterloo Bridge). Thus, the Abbey, sitting with its beautiful back to the river, has an east-west axis.

Its official name is the Collegiate Church of St. Peter in Westminster. At the time it was built, there was already a St. Paul's Cathedral to the east, and thus the west minster (monastery).

The Abbey is not a cathedral, since it is not the chief church of a see. In fact, it is not under the authority of any prelate of the Church of England. Its "Visitor" is the Sovereign, and its designation, like St. George's Chapel, Windsor, is that of Royal Peculiar.

The monarch is "the only supreme head on earth of the Church of England," Parliament confirmed in 1534. Each bishop swears, "Your Majesty is the only Supreme Governor of Your Realm in ecclesiastical things," and also, "I acknowledge that I hold the Bishopric only of Your Majesty."

Those nominated as bishops by the sovereign are in practice named by the prime minister, no matter what his religion. Any substantial change in doctrine proposed by the church can be made only with the approval of Parliament: the 1927 Revised Book of Common Prayer was rejected by Parliament.

This is the Established Church, the official religion, but the government neither owns it nor contributes money to it. The financial authorities are the Church Commissioners, among the greatest landholders of the kingdom, with 220,000 acres, almost one-third less than Crown land acreage (both midgets compared with the Forestry Commission, which owns one-twentieth of the country). Great chunks of London belong to the church, by no means all in ecclesiastical or educational buildings. A wholly-owned subsidiary is involved in development schemes, sometimes in partnership with the new breed of high-rise speculators whom the Commissioners term "developers of high standing."

This church real estate company owns shares in twenty-eight subsidiaries and reported in 1964, 120 million dollars' worth of projects undertaken, one-third residential, the rest commercial

A Royal Peculiar, the Abbey depends directly from the monarch.

227

properties. Not one square foot, despite the legends, is used for brothels. During the preceeding year the Commissioners brought libel suits against makers of this allegation, and four times won.

The income listed in the report was fifty million dollars, about half enough for Church expenses. "The rest comes voluntarily out of the pockets of the laity."

While it is easy enough for the Church to switch from agricultural landholdings (3.6 per cent yield) to common stocks (4.75 per cent), it is thornier to dispose or even consider disposing of surplus churches which, though historical-artistic assets, are a painful financial drain. Dick Whittington's church of St. Michael Paternoster Royal was a 1965 case in point, when the Church wished to spin off the monument and spin in some revenue and found itself charged with trying to peddle a heritage it should be preserving.

Thus it is that one sees begging boards outside so many churches of this vastly wealthy organization. Even the Abbey, when it needed a million pounds for urgent repairs, was obliged to go begging. The goal was achieved within a year.

The Abbey is a religious and historic shrine, an architectural monument, an educational institution, a "national Valhalla" for the deposit of illustrious citizens, and an unsurpassed tourist magnet.*

To the Dean of Westminster and his Chapter of five Canons, the Abbey is "first and foremost a church, serving a great public. Every Sunday there are five regular services, every week day three, apart from additional services of many kinds."

Coronation is the most special of services. Every British monarch since Harold (he who was conquered by William) has been crowned and anointed in the Abbey, and since the fourteenth century the Westminster School boys have had the privilege of crying, "Vivat!" The Coronation Chair is kept on view in the Abbey. Carved by Walter, the King's Painter, for Edward I, the oaken throne has under its seat the Stone of Scone, a sandstone block on which the Kings of Scotland were crowned in Scone

---

* A survey in America on behalf of the British tourist industry showed that most prospective tourists wanted to see, first, Westminster Abbey, then, in this order, the following: Tower of London, Houses of Parliament, Trafalgar Square, Piccadilly Circus and Buckingham Palace.

Abbey from 850. Edward I bore it off to England in 1297 to indicate Scotland's subjection to Britain.

The Abbey has one of the two tombs in England still bearing the body of the saint originally buried in it. The Chapel of Ed-

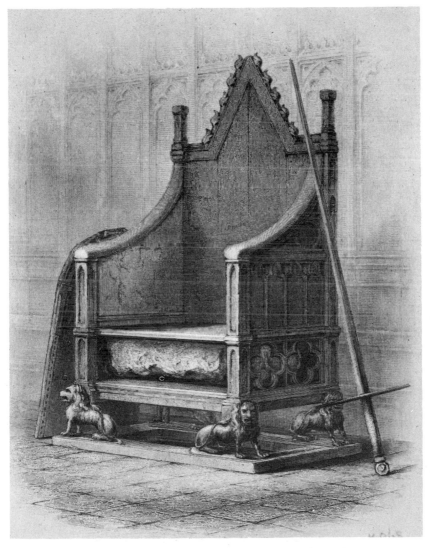

Coronation Chair of British monarchs in the Abbey.

229

ward the Confessor behind the high altar is the most sacred spot in the Abbey. To do homage to Edward, Henry III in 1245 undertook to rebuild on a more magnificent scale the church Edward built and had consecrated in 1065. Thus there is almost nothing remaining of Edward's Norman church, although there are fragments of the monastery buildings still serving.

The rebuilt church was Gothic, cruciform, with five octagonal chapels radiating from the ambulatory at the head of the cross. Another Henry, the Seventh, in 1503 began rebuilding and enlarging the 1220 Lady Chapel. He meant it as a shrine for Henry VI, whom he hoped to have canonized. After his death, his son Henry VIII finished the work in 1512, and it was named Henry VII's Chantry Chapel.

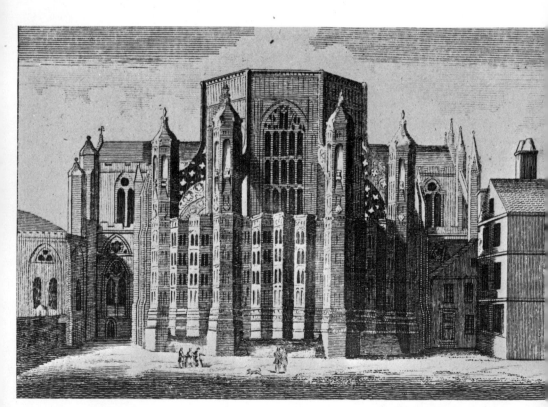

Henry VII's Chapel in the fifteenth century — not much different now.

Like the church itself, this chapel has a nave and aisles and five radiating chapels. The easternmost of these smaller chapels is now dedicated to the Royal Air Force. It was from this chapel that the bodies of Oliver Cromwell and his cohorts were wrenched at the Restoration.

Henry VII's Chantry Chapel is a marvelous creation of religious, rather than ecclesiastical, architecture:

> Make a joyful noise unto the
> Lord, all ye lands, serve the
> Lord with gladness . . .

The walls and arches are rich with carving, sculpted with foliage, flowers, birds, beasts, seraphs, cherubs, saints and — since we are all sinners here below — sinners. The ceiling of each small chapel is spun with lacy tracery of fan vaulting, and the soaring ceiling of the central chamber explodes with it, like rockets joyfully racketing into fountains of stars and cascades of comets.

The visual excitement is heightened by the brilliant banners of the Knights of the Bath. In presence of the sovereign, in crimson robes, to the sound of trumpets, the installation of new knights is made every four years here. "Bath" is a reference to the purification rites which once preceeded investiture. It is not a reference to the doctrine of total immersion, with which the Abbey does not hold.

The rest of the church is very much of a piece, which, in view of the story of its growth, is surprising. For one thing, the exterior has been mercilessly hacked about by refurbishers and painfully "enriched" over the centuries: e.g. the twin towers on the western front were built to a Hawksmoor design (1735–1740). It is surprising that the interior has not been equally ill served. Another source of wonder is that the church was built in two phases, one a century after the other. The 1245 reconstruction was halted after twenty-five years; resumed after a century's halt, it was terminated about 1500. The join across the centuries, detectable through changes in the handling of details, occurs in the nave about the fifth bay from the crossing.

However inspiring the Gothic interior of the Abbey church, it is almost impossible to find a vantage point from which to see the

The Abbey's Henry VII's Chapel, adrip with joyous fan vaulting, an anthem in stone.

building as a building. The place is deep-silted with hundreds upon hundreds of memorials deposited by the currents of nine hundred years. These range from small plaques to giant rain forests of polished stone. There are tombs of kings, queens and courtiers (George II, buried here in 1760, was the last of the monarchs). Mary Tudor, lying in the same tomb as her sister Elizabeth, has no memorial at all.

Only some of the many whose existence is subject to written notice in the Abbey church are actually buried here. Marlborough was interred here, but after his Duchess quarreled with Queen Anne, she snatched the body back to Blenheim. Nelson, Wellington, Marlborough's descendant Winston Churchill, Shakespeare, Milton, Donne, Blake, Keats, Shelley, Byron, D. H. Lawrence, G. B. Shaw, T. S. Eliot lie elsewhere. But here is the dust of Chaucer, John Dryden, Edmund Spenser, Dr. Johnson, Wordsworth, Coleridge, Dickens, Browning, Tennyson, Hardy, Kipling. And those pillars of English letters Adam Lindsay Gordon (1870) and Edward Bulwer-Lytton (1873).

The hunt along the north side of the nave is worth the discovery of the floor slab covering Ben Jonson, and which is marked: *O rare Ben Johnson*. It is noteworthy not only for the misspelling but also for the noble restraint shown by Abbey authorities who have refrained from correcting it over the centuries.

A funerary sculpture worth seeking out is in the east aisle of the North Transept past the huge monument to General James Wolfe. It is the Roubilliac 1761 monument of Lady Elizabeth Nightingale, who died in 1731. Strolling on a terrace, she was frightened into a miscarriage by a flash of lightning, and died soon after. John Wesley (memorialized but not buried in the Abbey) found the work edifying, but most moderns find it horrifying.

At floor level, directly before the onlooker, is a heavily rusticated stone burial vault whose bronze doors are ajar. With one foot in the grave and one hand grasping the ledge above him, a hideous skeleton in a slipping shroud draws back his lance to impale Lady Nightingale. She is on the level above where her husband tries in vain to ward off death's sting. The fantasy is utterly real.

At least one hundred of the hundreds of tombs and memorials have something curious or remarkable meriting scrutiny. The paneling, the bosses, the carvings, the windows of the Abbey are studded with discoveries to be made. The twenty chapels are equally fascinating.

A door in the South Nave aisle leads out to the cloisters which in turn lead one through the thirteenth and fourteenth century to the eleventh, in the Dark Cloister, the Chapel of the Pyx and the Norman Undercroft — the remains of the Abbey that Edward the Confessor built. Other honored Britons are buried here under the paving of the cloister, including one man who executed long and honorable service upon the Abbey plumbing.

The Chapter House on the left was one of the earliest works of Henry III's rebuilding, dating from 1245. The Great Council, primitive form of Parliament, convened in this lofty octagonal

Last resting place of centuries' accumulation of illustrious Britons.

chamber in 1257. From 1352 until 1547 Parliament, recognizable as such, sat here before moving to St. Stephen's Chapel in Westminster Palace. (After the Nazi blitz, Parliament moved back to the Abbey for a while, meeting in Church House in Dean's Yard, where the United Nations Security Council later had its initial meeting).

The visitor to the Chapter House is constrained by a gentle, elderly guardian to slip felt slippers over his shoes before sliding over the seven-hundred-year-old tiles. From the lovely foliage with which most of it is decorated, peep a king, a queen, a bishop. There are also depictions of a delicate rose window, probably the North Transept window of the church as it was then. Also set in the tiles is the inscription, in Latin, "As the rose is among the flowers, so is this house among houses."

The Pyx Chapel has two wooden entrance doors, one directly

To enter the Chapter House, visitors slide slippers over their shoes.

behind the other. Each is three inches thick, strapped with iron, studded with nailheads. One has three enormous locks and the other has four enormous locks. The chapel was at one time the repository of the pyx (box) holding the trial plates of the standards for gold and silver coin of the realm.

In a further chamber of the same Norman undercroft, with groined vaults and squat piers and a close-to-the-tomb underground feeling, is the Abbey museum. The collection is modest, but special, and it should be better known and frequented. In the main it consists of the wax effigies which were used in funerals and for the lying-in-state of very important persons. The figure was life-sized, earlier in wood, later in wax, clad in the clothing of the deceased, and the faces were either from death masks or from wax portrait sculptures made during life in anticipation of the funeral display. As the cortège passed through the streets, the effigy lay atop the coffin.

After interment of the person, the Abbey kept the effigy in a glass case. Eleven of the dozen displayed here are survivors of the once vast collection. The full-length figures of King Edward III (died 1377) and of Henry V's "beautiful Kate," Katherine de Valois (died 1437) are made of wood. Edward's face is distorted by the stroke that killed him.

The Essex ring is on display here, small, gold, and mounted with a blue stone bearing a cameo carving of Elizabeth I in coif and ruff. This was the ring that should have saved Essex from beheading had it not been intercepted on its way to the Queen.

And here, again, the Crown Jewels, an apparently authentic set of regalia which is entirely counterfeit. It is used in Coronation rehearsals.

King Charles II, "who never said a foolish thing, nor ever did a wise one," died in 1685. " 'Tis to ye life and truly to admiration," a contemporary wrote of the effigy. The doublet and breeches beneath the Robe of the Order of the Garter are of cloth of silver.

The effigy of Catherine, Duchess of Buckingham (died 1743) was the last to be carried in an Abbey funeral. Two of her children, in effigy, are with her: her firstborn, Robert, Marquess of Normandy, who died at the age of three, and her next son, Edmund, who inherited the Dukedom but died at nineteen. The eighteenth century in London was brilliantly multicolored, but one of the principal colors was mourning. Most children — 75 per cent of those who survived childbed — did not live past the age of five.

Buckingham Palace was built for this duchess. The inconvenience of her having been born a bastard was mitigated by the eminence of her father, generally referred to as King James II.

The official museum brochure confesses that the effigy of Horatio Nelson was set up in the year after his death "in the hope that it would attract people back to the Abbey and away from his tomb at St. Paul." Friends said the statue was a perfect likeness, and it shows us that Nelson was a remarkably handsome, well-knit man, the prototype of glory's hero. His cocked hat is interesting for its near-sombrero size and the green eyeshade which could be flapped down from the hatbrim to cover his blind eye. The tailor who made his uniform (Gieves, Old Bond Street), the hosiers who provided his silk stockings ("Be content it was an arm I lost, and not a leg," Nelson said to the commiserating shopkeeper), and his hatter, Locks of St. James's Street, are all still in business.

There are further verdant, hidden squares and courts — Farmery Court, Little Dean's Yard, Dean's Yard, the Canons' Garden. Westminster School (about five hundred boys), one of the oldest and most distinguished of public — i.e., private — schools in England,* the Chapter Library, several ancient chambers and chapels, and the perfect mid-seventeenth-century Ashburton House make up parts of the interlocking series of buildings.

Up College Mews is the Jewel Tower, a rather brooding thing of heavy stone, built 1364. The strongroom, with 1621 door, is still intact. Long abandoned as the Royal Treasury, it became the archives for the House of Lords (1621–1864), and then for seventy-five years or so, the office of the Department of Weights

---

* Some old boys are Richard Hakluyt (of *Voyages*), Ben Jonson, John Dryden, Christopher Wren, John Locke, Charles Wesley, Warren Hastings, Edward Gibbon, Jeremy Bentham, Robert Southey. It produced seven Prime Ministers and ten Archbishops.

and Measures. Its 1965 renovation was due to work on an underground parking place which removed some of its neighboring buildings.

Around on the other side of the Abbey, running in front of it and into Parliament Square is a wide way called the Broad Sanctuary. The right of sanctuary offered by the Church against abusive monarchs astonishingly persisted until the early seventeenth century. Despite the general reluctance of any king or king's officer to defy the Pope, sanctuary was not always inviolate. In 1378 the Constable of the Tower, Sir Alan Boxhull, led fifty men in pursuit of two escaped prisoners. They burst into the church itself during Mass, slew one man and dragged the other back to the Tower. The Abbey was closed for four months to purge the profanation and the sitting of Parliament in the Chapter House suspended.

Bustling into Broad Sanctuary is Victoria Street, pushed through Westminster in 1851, substituting for a shoal of nasty slums an avenue splendid with Victorian architectural exuberances being replaced in the 1960's by boxes of contemporary pallid British design. Among these are the new twenty-two-story City Hall for the City of Westminster. Victoria Street was not built to connect with Victoria Station, which rose on filled-in Grosvenor Basin more than a decade later.

The first street down toward the station from Broad Sanctuary has a name that caused considerable confusion in some sectors of British society in 1964. Scotland Yard was to be moved from its turreted gray granite stage-set on Victoria Embankment to a new building. On Baker Street. Marvelous! Shades of Inspector Lestrade! Number 221B, of course?

No, no! Not *Baker* Street, *Dacre* Street.

Oh. And where the devil is Dacre Street?

Right here. This is Dacre Street making a triangle with Victoria Street and Broadway. And here is the new twenty-story glass filing cabinet to house the headquarters of the Metropolitan Police. Smaller versions of the tower, scattered around its base like seedlings, are also for the police. A year before the late 1965 completion date, there were already cries that it was too small, that the space per person was inadequate and that the crime lab was going to have be housed across the river in Lambeth.

The Metropolitan Police were originally housed in Scotland Yard, once a part of Whitehall Palace where visiting kings of Scotland stayed. Then they were moved in 1891 to the Scottish baronial edifice constructed for them on the Embankment, more than a quarter of mile south down Whitehall on the site of the never-constructed National Opera. The grim granite quarried by Dartmoor convicts was dubbed New Scotland Yard. The New New Scotland Yard is almost half a mile west of New Scotland Yard. The original cable address remains the same: HANDCUFFS, LONDON.

At the top of Broadway is a building which was a shocker when it was made in 1929 for London Transport, which still occupies it. Today it seems a neat piece of engineering, an assemblage of cubes straddling an Underground station (St. James's Park) and rising to a height of 175 feet (another figure considerably devalued since 1929). At the time blood pressures were raised more by the exterior decorations than by the building itself: "Day" and "Night" by Epstein, and "The Winds" in eight reliefs higher on the building, by Henry Moore, F. Rabinovitch, Eric Gill, A. Wyon, E. Aumonier and A. H. Gerrard.

Just across the way is Queen Anne's Mansions, a residential structure barren of any decoration whatever and about which there is absolutely no controversy: it is an eyesore. In its guidebook to London, London Transport, obliged to live nose-to-nose with this horror, has the satisfaction of calling the Mansions "London's first and most hideous block of service flats, built in 1884." At that period of mild rents and hard money, this Late Penitentiary Style early apartment building got $1500 a year rent for its big flats.

Queen Anne's Mansions was the tallest building in London when it was erected, fourteen stories mounting 180 feet, ugly yellow brick upon ugly yellow brick. Immediately after, as a direct consequence, the laws limiting building heights in the metropolis were passed.

The negative impression of the Mansions is instantly effaced by Queen Anne's Gate, the elusive Old London one has been expecting around every corner. The charming brown brick, white-banded houses with their fanlights and wooden canopies are graced with a battered statue of Queen Anne, all dating from her day. Over the years since 1708, there have been a few structural intrusions, but most of the newer buildings are in keeping with the originals. The western part, built first, was named Queen Square by the speculator who created it, William Paterson, who is better known for another investment notion he promoted — the Bank of England. The L-shaped house where the statue stands marks the old dividing wall, and beyond it the houses are newer (Nos. 5–13 and 14–24 from 1775, Nos. 6–12 from 1836), but the calm and grace of an eighteenth-century close prevails. The suddenly narrow Old Queen Street leads into Storey's Gate and Great George Street, where one walks over the wartime bombproofed

Gracious Queen Anne's Gate awaits discovery behind the newest Scotland Yard.

Cabinet Rooms forty feet below, including Winston Churchill's concrete accommodations.

The main street ahead is Parliament Street, but is generally thought of, at least by foreigners, as the lower third of Whitehall, which comes down from Trafalgar Square to Parliament Square. Many strollers get the feeling that it runs straight down to the Thames, but in fact because of the river's jog here, it runs almost parallel to the stream. Describing a slight curve as it goes, the descending street finishes with Westminster Bridge on its left and the Abbey straight ahead across Parliament Square.

Whitehall is the most important street in Britain.

It is the seat of the Executive branch of government, of the Prime Minister, his cabinet officers and the chief departments of administration. These departments are staffed and run by the

On the right, Inigo Jones's Banqueting House, one of the few extant portions of Whitehall Palace.

241

Civil Service Establishment which in practice, more than any single force, shapes the daily life of everyone in these islands.

In the corridors of power, politicians come and politicians go, but the Permanent Secretary is permanent. Permanence requires a certain amount of suppleness, and he is thus not impervious to change. And he is changing. The technocrat, the professional expert, is gradually supplanting in the councils of decision the standard Civil Service chief, the gifted amateur from the good school. The term "civil servant" is changing meaning as the servant displays increasing mastery.

The vast and complex machinery of the Welfare State has to be run by someone, and that someone is the faceless Man from the Ministry. Whitehall is his habitat.

Government is the largest single employer in the country, the greatest getter and spender of money. One in every twenty-four employed Britons has a government job. In addition, the National Health Scheme, the nationalized atomic energy, electricity, coal, gas, rail and aviation industries, all under Civil Service control, employ eight per cent of the nation's labor force — two million workers. The Civil Service and its ancillaries spent in 1964 a sum

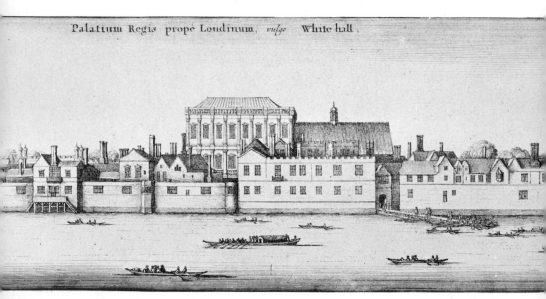

Palatium Regis prope Londinum, *vulgo* White-hall.

River view of the Royal Palace of Whitehall, another vanished glory.

242

equal to forty per cent of the country's gross national product.

The Service was taken out of the spoils system and established as a nonpolitical meritocracy in 1854. Its model was the East India Company's nonmilitary governing branch which bore the title of Civil Service. In the last half of the 1960's it was evident that Whitehall, both architecturally and organically, needed modernization. Desperately. Modernization of structure, method and communication. How this was to be achieved, by whom and by what starting and finishing dates had not been established at press time for this book. Thus, the Whitehall herein described awaits the changes which have erupted elsewhere in London.

The Abbey lands stretching north toward Charing Cross came into the hands of the Archbishop of York in 1240, and a town house was built as imposing as the other episcopal dwellings around the Court. But when Wolsey became Archbishop of York in 1514, he had the place enlarged and embellished until, Henry VIII thought, it outshone the Royal Palace of Westminster. When Wolsey fell from power in 1530, York Place became the Royal Palace of Whitehall.

At the same time Henry acquired almost two hundred acres to

St. James's Park when it was still a game preserve, the Palace in the background.

243

the west, including the Hospital of St. James, which he rebuilt as yet another palace. St. James's is still winsomely there, but almost nothing remains of Whitehall. Paintings of the period show the palace as a random collection of buildings of varying heights and styles, with two lavishly decorated archways over the street.

Later monarchs had grandiose plans for building a huge structure with grand gardens. These plans were never realized, although Inigo Jones and Wren each completed one building. Fires in the late eighteenth century swept away most of the assortment, and private houses and administration buildings began to rise on the site.

On the corner of Parliament Square and Parliament Street, the bulky late Victorian (1898) block is named New Government Buildings. This houses several departmental headquarters, but is known principally as the lair of the Treasury, the most disliked and complained-of agency in the government.

The Treasury collects the Government's revenues and has a major say in deciding how they will be spent. It has generated most of the hardly popular measures of economic restraint imposed to defend against the chronic balance-of-payments deficit. Although it has a relatively small staff, and a relatively small budget, it is the most powerful branch of the Civil Service. Since the days of absolute monarchy, it has been intimately attached to the nation's power center. Until the Prime Minister was granted a salary in 1937 (the office does not exist by any specific act of law) he was paid as the First Lord of the Treasury. The house next to the Prime Minister's in Downing Street belongs to his Minister of Finance, who bears the title of Chancellor of the Exchequer. The title descends from the days when the nation's accounts were kept by men seated at a checkered cloth across which counters were moved. The results were notched on wooden tallies (not abandoned until 1824), and in later years recorded as well in ledgers (Roman numerals not given up until 1833).

The heritage of meticulous accountancy and traditional caution remains, causing irritation. Also annoying to others is the Treasury duty of saying "No," which it does as the department directing the Civil Service apparatus. One of the Treasury's two chief officers has the title Joint Permanent Secretary to the Treasury and Head of the Home Civil Service. And as Head he runs it, overseeing budgets, promotions and placements.

Many of those who would modernize the Civil Service feel that basic change must begin at the Treasury. For example, Dr. Brian Chapman of Manchester University: "It musters under one roof several logically distinct functions. . . . In trying to be master of all and servant of none, the Treasury has developed into a mindless monster."

Across King Charles Street there is an archway (that's Clive of India at the end of the street, looking over the steps down to St. James's Park) to another aging pile, the mid-Victorian (1868) Government Offices by Sir George Gilbert Scott. Because one of the three ministries rammed into this sooty rookery is the Foreign Office and because diplomats know how to impress, the

he Treasury, outgrown Victorian pile, is slated for eventual replacement in Whitehall.

245

whole thing is known as the Foreign Office. Also here is the Commonwealth Relations Office, direct heir of the East India Company, by way of the India Office, which was later the Dominions Office.

The Home Office too is quartered here, controlling prisons, police, immigration and the registration of aliens. When Winston Churchill was Home Secretary, he went forth in top hat to direct the siege of some homicidal anarchists in the East End's Sidney Street, finally calling out the army and being criticized no end. The Home Secretary can recommend pardons, commute sentences and under certain circumstances order new trials. But the concern with regulations overshadows, in the view of many observers, the concern for justice. Anthony Sampson, in *Anatomy of Britain*, characterized the Home Office as "the most notoriously self-centered department . . . who regulate and badger aliens and visitors with little consideration of Commonwealth or foreign interests, or even of human decency."

The token central heating of the building does little more than dispel icy mists under the palazzo-high ceilings, and grave porters trundle buckets of coal to hundreds of fireplaces. The electrical circuits are so laden that only the three Ministers achieve the illusory comfort of electric heaters in their offices. Offices have been divided and subdivided as staffs have multiplied but the space remained the same over eight decades.

Architect Scott submitted designs for a building in wildest Victorian Gothic. It is easy to see what he had in mind, for with the frugality that made Victorian prodigality possible, he used the design for St. Pancras Station, still in use. Prime Minister Lord Palmerston rejected the Gothic blueprints, and said the building would be Italian. Unable to wrench himself away from the picturesque, Scott next served up an Italianate Byzantine, a sort of Turkish delight with garlic and tomato sauce. Palmerston called it "a regular mongrel affair" and refused it.

Scott, as he himself later explained, "bought some costly books on Italian architecture," boned up and produced what Dr. Pevsner calls "this florid Italian Cinquecento design." The three-year contest of wills was ended, and the Civil Service had a palazzo which would have pleased Machiavelli.

Unless there is a last-minute stay of execution, perhaps a preservation order to keep the building as a souvenir of Empire, this structure, hopelessly inadequate to its functions, is doomed.

Out in the road in front of this building is the Cenotaph

No. 10 Downing Street. "Is Prime Minister Gladstone improved today?"

247

(*kenos*, empty, plus *taphos*, tomb), from which the Queen leads the Commonwealth in the two minutes of silence on November 11, honoring the dead of both World Wars. It seems to be a simple shaft, rising in a series of setbacks, but it has no verticals and no horizontals: the seemingly horizontal lines bend toward arbitrary terminal points 900 feet underground, and the apparent perpendiculars would meet at a point just as far overhead.

The author of this architectural puzzle was Sir Edwin Lutyens, designer of the Imperial city of New Delhi, and of many of the massive office buildings of the 1920's, developing personal mannerisms of design which contemporaries found worth imitating. But if all his works were to vanish overnight, Sir Edwin would be remembered for What He Said to the Waiter.

Lunching in one of the St. James's Street clubs, he peered at his plate and asked the waiter, in tones of astonishment, "What is that?"

"Sir," said the waiter, "it is a piece of cod."

"Which passeth all understanding," said Sir Edwin.

Along the northern flank of the Foreign Office runs Downing Street. No. 10 is the residence of the Prime Minister, No. 11 that of the Chancellor of the Exchequer, No. 12 that of the Chief Whip, the administration's floor manager in Commons. The three, which are interconnected, total two hundred rooms.

Sir George Downing built this street as a speculation from about 1663 to 1682. He was a Harvard boy who made good, but not good buildings. He built hastily and shoddily on marshy soil, quickly and for profit. Earlier he had slithered from the post of Cromwell's Ambassador at The Hague to that of Charles II's Secretary of the Treasury, gaining a knighthood on the way. Owing to extensive reconstruction and reinforcement, his development, getting on for three hundred years old, is still intact, jerry-built though it was. The last rebuilding was finished in 1964 after a three-year operation costing $2,800,000.

A rather opulent new house could have been erected on the old site for the same money, but tradition prevailed and No. 10 and the others look just about as they did in the seventeenth century. (Ruskin wrote of No. 10, "Count its stones as you would jewels of a crown.") The plain brick façade is a typical British understatement, and its modesty is deceptive. The interior is quite grand and larger than one might guess from the outside since there is a second, hidden house joined onto the one seen from the street. There is even an English garden tucked away out of sight. It is not at all dim, prim and underprivileged as it seems.

In the first half-century of Downing Street's existence, it was a good private address. The street came into possession of the Crown about 1735, and George III offered the houses to Prime Minister Walpole as a personal gift. Walpole accepted them as residences for the First Lord of the Treasury and the Chancellor of the Exchequer, whoever they might be, and immediately took up residence. But during the next century and more, P.M.'s often refused to move in and used No. 10 for official receptions. With Gladstone and Disraeli it became the standard thing for an election loss to signify moving day for the old and new incumbents. Many of the tenants found the place terribly

Its elegance faded, Richmond Terrace persists among the Whitehall monoliths.

249

uncomfortable (until Lloyd George in 1916 there was no bathroom), a complaint they would hardly make in 1965.

Across Whitehall from the Downing Street opening is a small square — an oblong, really — called Richmond Terrace. A handsome terrace of Regency row houses from 1822, it now contains the Department of Education and Science and no elevators. The greensward of the Terrace ends abruptly at the white cliffs of the Defence Ministry. Some people, possibly ill-advised, call it the Quadragon. It was built after the war for the Air Ministry and Board of Trade, but on April Fool's Day 1964 became the headquarters of the armed forces combined under one Minister.

It looks out over the Thames Embankment where a riverside terrace and steps by Wren (1691) were rediscovered in 1939. The steps now lead to the inland edge of another piece of Victoria Embankment Gardens. Underneath the building is the ribbed and vaulted wine cellar of Henry VIII's palace. By a piece of engineering legerdemain greatly admired by engineers, the cellar was picked whole from the site of a demolished building and planted here. It is open to the public, but not readily.

Back on the other side of Whitehall from Downing Street to the Horse Guards, is a jumble of old buildings whose interiors were reconstructed at the same time as those of the Prime Minister's residence. This is the old Treasury, originally constructed around the remains of the Whitehall Palace Great Hall which Henry VIII had converted into a tennis court. The rebuilding uncovered a surprising amount of original Tudor brickwork — walls, fireplaces and windows. The southern flank of this building goes up Downing Street, and from the Cabinet Offices here is a passage to No. 10 and the white, green and gold room in which the Cabinet meets at a long green-covered table graced with silver candlesticks and crystal inkwells.

The complex includes what remains of Dorset House, a private mansion of 1700, the first "New Treasury" of 1736, and newer portions dating from a century later. Next door is another eighteenth-century mansion, Dover House, now housing the Scottish Office. It can be seen from the Horse Guards Parade in back, but not from Whitehall because the Duke of York, when he bought the house in 1787, had architect Henry Holland build a second house in the front forecourt.

Across the street from Dover House is Gwydyr House, a 1772 private dwelling also now in government service. Next door to it is a building which makes architectural historians drool with pleasure: Inigo Jones's 1619–1622 Banqueting House, the sole intact unit of Whitehall Palace.

At the time it was a revelation, the last word in modern architecture, the revival and adaptation of style and harmonies not seen in London since the last of the Roman buildings had been razed. Jones had been to Italy and studied all the works of Palladio, then dead about twenty-five years. He brought back with him a vision that would affect architecture forever after. With its precise proportions (the hall is an exact double cube) and its stately procession of classical orders, it made a cool, disdainful comment on the jubilant Tudor twistings of the surrounding buildings.

The stonework has been often repaired since, and in 1964 the building was reopened after restoration of the interior to the original design. The gallery which runs around the interior and the nine-panel Rubens ceiling gleam anew. The hall is a government reception center, but lacks the kitchens to serve again as the Whitehall Banqueting House.

James I died shortly before Jones completed his work, and son Charles I commissioned an "Apotheosis of James I" for the ceiling from Peter Paul Rubens. The painter had come to London on a diplomatic mission and had left with a British knighthood, a medal, a gold chain and three thousand pounds. Anthony Van Dyck was another royal protégé also knighted and given a house in Blackfriars where the King and Queen (she sat twenty-five times to the artist) visited.

Charles collected antique statues, Giorgiones, Correggios, Tintorettos, Mantegnas and some Raphael cartoons. The Puritans sold off most of the royal collection after sending Charles to his death, walking through one of the Banqueting House windows to the scaffold erected in Whitehall. In 1658 Cromwell died here, in bed.

Across the road from the newly cleansed Banqueting House is

the Horse Guards, a 1760 building replacing an earlier head-quarters. At this spot the guard was mounted for Whitehall Palace, while that palace still stood, maintained by the Household Cavalry. This is composed of the Life Guards who protected Charles II in exile, and the Royal Horse Guards ("the Blues") organized under Cromwell to keep Charles II in exile. They are still here, plumed and helmeted, booted, spurred and mounted, keeping guard.

Both regiments wear burnished breastplates. The gleaming casques of the scarlet-coated Life Guards have white horsehair plumes, and the plumes of the blue-coated Royal Horse are red.

From a window of the Banqueting House, Charles I stepped onto the scaffold.

252

Both regiments wear white buckskin breeches and very high boots. Life Guards have white lambskin saddles, Blues have black, and all, except the Trumpeter on a gray, ride black horses.

They ride to work every day, from Knightsbridge Barracks past Buckingham Palace and through St. James's Park to perform at 11 A.M. (10 on Sunday) a half-hour Guard Mount with tin soldier precision. At 4 P.M., when they rightfully should be taking tea, they devotedly submit to the further ritual of dismounted inspection. These two rites occur in the forecourt facing Whitehall in full view of a never-flagging public. Two of the guardsmen are posted motionless on their steeds in gateways at the Horse Guards entry. They are relieved every half-hour.

The low archway to the Horse Guards Parade is patrolled by dismounted guardsmen. Only royalty and a privileged few are permitted to drive through this arch (anyone is free to walk through). Prime Minister Pitt's banker, a Mr. Smith, solicited this privilege.

"I can't do that for you," said Pitt. "But I can make you an Irish peer." And within twenty-four hours banker Smith was Lord Carrington with all sorts of prerogatives save that of being allowed to drive through the Horse Guards arch.

Opposite the airy silhouette of the Horse Guards is the peevish face of the War Office, which is now but one of the hundreds of London buildings of the Ministry of Defence. The corner turrets of this 1906 edifice conceal the curious lack of any right angles.

Across the small side street called Whitehall Place are the Ministry of Agriculture and the office of the Crown Estate Agents, stretching to the original Great Scotland Yard.

Next to the Horse Guards is the former office of the Paymaster, a modest 1732 Georgian building with a parkside elevation of unwonted grandeur, the façade of a Great George Street house demolished in 1910 and too good to throw away.

With a manly tear saltier than usual, it must be stated that since April 1, 1964, the next group of buildings is no longer called the Admiralty. There is no more Admiralty since the services were all blended into the Ministry of Defence. No more First Lord of the Admiralty, no more cantankerous Admiralty Board running the Royal Navy. In order that the historic appellation of

Lord High Admiral should not perish, Her Majesty the Queen was graciously moved to accept the title for herself.

The marble screen across the front was designed by young Robert Adam in 1761. The building directly behind is the 1726 Admiralty designed by Thomas Ripley, whose position in Whitehall in those protean days was not at all architectural, but fiscal, and his title was Comptroller. It was from this building and its predecessor on the same site that Brittania ruled the waves. Alongside, riverwards, with no entrance except through the official main building, is the 1788 residence for the First Lord.* Like the Downing Street houses of a hundred years before, its exterior is deceptively plain. In 1965 the rebuilding of the interior restored its inner grandeur.

Behind these buildings, pushing toward St. James's Park, is a vulgar 1895 annex. Further into the Park is a vast but somehow unobtrusive World War II structure: a big bunker known as the Citadel. Ivy-clad, it has an acre of grass lawn on its roofs.

The rest of Whitehall toward Trafalgar Square is ordinary commercial construction, much like any city street, with, among other things, a theater and London's first drive-in bank. There are pubs in Whitehall and Parliament Street "within the verge of the Royal Palace of Whitehall," and they are licensed therefore by the Lord Steward of the Royal Household at the Board of the Green Cloth.

Behind these commercial structures the Navy pushed its buildings to emerge onto Trafalgar Square with the three-passaged Admiralty Arch. Built in 1910 as part of the national memorial to Queen Victoria, it frames the entrance into the Mall and St. James's Park.

Buckingham Palace, St. James's Palace, the Prime Minister's residence, Marlborough House, the distinguished government headquarters sit around the edge of this most favored of parks. It was a wild, boggy place until Henry VIII enclosed it as part of his hunting preserve. When it seemed that European princes under the Vatican banner might invade England in 1539, Henry manned the coastal defenses and asked the City to muster its

---

* Winston Churchill moved out in 1915, obliged to leave office after the failure of the Gallipoli landings.

trainbands. According to Stow, fifteen thousand freemen in armor and white tunics marched from Aldersgate to Westminster
and were reviewed by His Majesty in St. James's Park.

More than a hundred years later Charles II brought in an expert to study the site and make recommendations. The expert was
Le Notre, who laid out the gardens of the Tuileries and Versailles. His recommendation, the story goes, was to leave things
alone, because nature had already made a perfect park.

Charles did have the Mall laid out, a wide avenue with a border of four lines of trees (he played Paille Maille there), and had
the springs channeled into an oblong sheet of water alongside the
Mall. The locals called it "the canal." The King swam in it, and
Pepys recorded in July 1666 that he lay down in the afternoon to
nap in the grass "by the canalle." Evelyn had remarked a year
earlier, in his journal, that the pelicans were settling in nicely.

The descendants (or replacements) of these birds are still lord-
ing it over the three dozen varieties of wildfowl which hang
about the lake at various times of the year, sometimes permitting
themselves to be fed by the public. Unlike Charles II, George IV
did change the Park, and in 1829 had Nash make an irregular
lake of the springs and pools and lay out the walks through the
rural parkscape which has been little altered since then.

Birdcage Walk still runs along the southern boundary. The
refreshment booth is called the Cake House. Among the hundreds
passing along in the modern equivalent of court uniform — bowl-
ers, brollys and often Burberrys — there are sure to be some Very
Important Persons.

Many Londoners — perhaps even most Londoners — would
say that St. James's is the prettiest park or the best park or the
nicest park. However, each of the royal parks has something special of its own, each has corners which must seem to many the
most satisfying corner in the city. Each has that special virtue of
English landscaping, a matter of maintaining control but not insisting too much. The cleverness with which the landscaping is
done is concealed through even greater cleverness, so that almost the whole effect is one of happy accident. The main mood is
romantic and is evoked by architects and gardeners who know
that fairyland, to be convincing, must be made of real trees and

real grass. But the trees and grass are arranged so that they do not seem arranged, and a knight in armor could ride out from behind any oak.

All the marvelous skylines surrounding St. James's Park can be seen from the little bridge crossing the little lake (until 1957 this was a charming miniature suspension bridge, subsequently replaced by a span devoid of charm and suspense). From here the towers of Whitehall are minarets, all Oriental in a sunset of northern islands.

The big open space facing the park behind Whitehall is the Horse Guards Parade, scene of the annual ceremony of Trooping the Color. There is no more brilliant military display than this anywhere in the Western world. The Guards with all their military bands mass here to honor the Queen on her official (not the same

On the Monarch's official birthday, the Brigade of Guards annually performs the Trooping of the Color on this parade ground.

257

date as her actual) birthday. Her Majesty is Colonel-in-Chief of the Guards. All the foot soldiers of this brigade (which includes the mounted regiments, of course) wear scarlet dress tunics and black bearskin hats. The regiments can be distinguished one from the other by their hatbands, hat plumes and uniform buttons.

The bearskin became common to all regiments after the Grenadiers (1656, second oldest) beat the busby-bearing Imperial Guard at Waterloo. The Grenadiers (scarlet hatband, white goat-hair plume on the left, buttons set singly) still put black mourning bands on the sleeves of the right flank drummer, the Time Beater. The Coldstreams were a Cromwellian regiment stationed at the village of Coldstream on the Scotch border when their general, George Monck, ordered them south to persuade Parliament to reshape itself and invite Charles II to come home. General Monck became the first Duke of Albemarle. His regiment wears white hatbands, a scarlet plume on the right, and buttons set in pairs. The Scots, formed in 1642, are the oldest regiment. The Irish (1900) and the Welsh (1915) the youngest.

Some of the Guards are quartered at Wellington Barracks, right here in Birdcage Walk, and the others at Chelsea Barracks. They do guard duty at the Tower, Clarence House, Buckingham Palace and St. James's Palace, and nightly guard the Bank of England. The Scots Guards supply spear carriers of military bearing to the Royal Opera in Covent Garden.

The Brigade of Guards is the sole remaining spit-and-polish, close-order-drill-happy outfit in the New Democratic British Army. Its officers are expected to be socially acceptable by standards set before Florence Nightingale began poking her nose into things. There has been some relaxation: it is possible — though hardly encouraged — to marry an actress; resignation is no longer automatic in case of (quiet) divorce.

A private income is still essential if one is to keep up social activities and standards of living appropriate to the Guards. The Army pays the normal salary and tosses in, at a bargain rate, a personal servant from the ranks (not called a "batman" in the Guards any more than "telephone" is called "phone," or "trousers" are called "slacks"). All officers are expected to belong to the Guards Club, to ride to hounds ("gives an eye for country"), and off-duty to wear the recognizable conservative suits of a Guards officer, with rolled umbrella and bowler hat. Tipping this hat serves to return the salute of Other Ranks, who are expected to recognize mufti-clad superiors. Since a few years after World War II, the Guards officer has been permitted to travel on public transport and to carry a bundle (so long as it does not contain a human infant). He is still expected to have cigarettes in a case, not in the original plebian package.

But in spite of the unimpaired traditions, the changing times nevertheless affected the apparently impervious Guards. There appeared in 1964 a faint flaw in the enameled assurance: concern with their "image." They appointed a public relations officer.

They may have done this because volunteers for the ranks are harder to find, even though standards here have been lowered (for example, the Guardsman no longer has to be a minimum of six feet tall). The strict discipline and the ardors of public sentinel duty seem to outweigh the glory. And glory there is aplenty, of that old-fashioned sort compounded of heroism and patriotism. The Guards are still the elite of the Armed Forces, up to their

When "Prinny" demolished Carlton House, Nash filled the blank with noble terraces, still standing.

fur hats in battle honors. The mounted regiments are tank outfits when they are not playing at being cavalry, and the rest are superior infantry units. They serve around the world, almost continually in obscure and ungrateful combat, leaving token units in Britain for display purposes. When all the Foot Guards are away, the honor of palace duty goes to one of the line regiments.

The Mall (pronounced to rhyme with "pal" by the locals, who call the parallel Pall Mall "Pell Mell") is paved in pink and lined with blue flagstaffs waiting to be dressed for state occasions. From Admiralty Arch the Mall passes Carlton House Terrace, built by Nash as the starting point of his Triumphal Way to Regent's Park. It is the *back* of his terrace houses which gives onto the park, as those of Queen Anne's Gate and the rest, including Buckingham Palace.

The bottom of the terrace on Mall level is a set of squat cast iron Doric columns against a wall punctuated with halfhearted windows. Sitting atop this is a balustrade, and set back from the railing is the terrace of houses all drawn into one composition by

It is the Duke of York, not the Duke of Wellington, surveying Waterloo Place.

lines of balconies and huge Corinthian columns. The ends of the design are closed by pavilions taller than the central grouping. On the far side of the Duke of York Steps, site of the original Carlton House, there is a twin terrace pushing in the direction of Buckingham Palace.

Atop the steps sits the Duke of York's column, erected 1833. His Grace was a royal Duke, the second son of George III, and because he had been commander-in-chief of the army, every soldier was docked a day's pay as a spontaneous subscription toward the cost of the memorial. Although the Duke was dead at the time, this charity wrung from the rank and file has been added to the legend of his unpopularity along with that of his impecuniosity.

There were those who said he'd been stuck atop a column to get him out of the reach of his creditors, and others professed to believe the lightning rod above his head was a bill spike. His incompetence has been made legendary too:

> The brave old Duke of York
> He had ten thousand men;
> He marched them up to the top of the hill
> And he marched them down again. . . .

As a matter of fact (in his case, facts have often been irrelevant) he did much to reform the army and improve the poor lot of the common soldier. He was, as he demonstrated in the Lowlands campaign, an excellent commander when on his own, but when under the orders of or in harness with incompetent professionals, he necessarily shared their failures.

After Carlton House Terrace is a high brick wall concealing the gardens of Marlborough (they say Mawlbruh) House, built by Christopher Wren in 1710. His client was the First Duke of Marlborough (a national hero for repeated thrashings of the French), who supposedly sent back the bricks for building from Amsterdam as ballast in British transports returning to Deptford. Because the mansion has been heightened and enlarged from time to time, it is not considered a Wren house. The Duke lay in state here in 1722, and his imperious and unpopular Duchess, Sarah, died here twenty-two years later.

The Churchill's lease was not renewed in 1818, and the land-lords moved in their only child, twenty-year-old Princess Charlotte, heir to the Crown of Great Britain. She was the only child of George IV and his abused Queen Caroline.* Charlotte lived here with her consort, Prince Leopold of Saxe-Coburg. Mishandled by royal obstetricians, she died in childbirth, and Leopold lived on here alone until called to be first King of the Belgians. Had Charlotte survived, she, and not Victoria, would have succeeded to the throne, and the tenor of nineteenth-century England would have been quite different.

In 1863, the Prince of Wales moved into Marlborough House with Princess Alexandra of Denmark, leaving it in 1901 when he became Edward VII. The Duke and Duchess of Cornwall moved in until they became George V and Queen Mary, and Queen Mother Alexandra moved back. She died in 1925, leaving the gardens redone and tiny tombstones therein for dogs Muff, Tiny and Joss and a slab for Benny the Bunny. The Prince of Wales refused to live here, and in 1936 his mother, Queen Mary, returned to the house. It was here she had the painful interview with her son just before he abdicated as Edward VIII. Queen Mary died in 1953. The building is now a Commonwealth Center and open to the public at a shilling a go from Easter until late October.

The tour of the house includes the Queen's Chapel (open to all for Sunday services) which was here long before the house. It was designed in 1623 by Inigo Jones for the Infanta Maria of Spain (a Catholic, naturally) who was to marry Prince Charles. The marriage did not take place, but the chapel wasn't for nought: Charles frugally wed Henri IV's daughter, Henrietta Maria of France, who was a Catholic because her Protestant father be-

---

* Caroline of Brunswick, not to be confused with her grandmother-in-law, Caroline of Anspach (George II). Obliged for reasons of state to marry Caroline, the Prince of Wales was forced to put aside his first wife, Mrs. Fitzherbert, a commoner. For this interruption Caroline paid the rest of her life. She gave up her child Charlotte to escape her drunken, profligate, vengeful George and returned to the Continent. In 1806, a Commission of Inquiry looked into reports of her "misconduct" abroad and reported her "innocent but imprudent." She refused to abdicate when George became king in 1820, showed up at the Abbey for the Coronation and was locked out. The government tried her for adultery (before the House of Lords assembled in Westminster Hall) but had to drop the charges in the face of public wrath.

lieved "Paris is worth a Mass." Mass was illegal elsewhere in England when it was said for the Queen in her chapel. The too-little-known structure is beautiful, chaste, classic with baroque interior embellishments added by Wren.

Across Marlborough Road, Clarence House, a large cream-colored building, now serves as the royal dower house. Nash built it in 1825 for the Duke of Clarence, later William IV. Much altered, it is attached to St. James's Palace.

The palace was erected on the site of the Hospital of St. James the Less, which cared for "maidens that were leprous." As one expects of Henry VIII, the building is turreted and battlemented and English and romantic. Every adult possessed of a pre-atomic childhood should find here a deep satisfaction, and reassurance that his childhood fantasies were, as he remembers, of the best

St. James's Palace, to whose Court foreign ambassadors are still officially accredited.

263

sort. This palace with its tenanted sentry boxes is every bit as real as Indians or cowboys, and in better condition.

Although the monarchs moved away some time ago, ambassadors are still accredited to the Court of St. James's. The buildings have been subjected to fire, bomb damage and the wear and tear of history, but it remains a palace, endearing rather than overwhelming, red brick with white accents, and a weather-vane-tipped white wooden cupola. Chimney pots, too.

There have been additions as well as subtractions. Sir Christopher Wren came along centuries after the grand opening and added the State Rooms off Engine Court. However the Chapel Royal (open to the public for services) is Tudor, with a ceiling attributed — more by hearsay than by evidence — to Holbein. Its choristers, although quite contemporary in themselves, are garbed in Tudor dress of scarlet and gold.

When the monarch is absent from London, the guard is changed here rather than at Buckingham Palace, and it is much more intimate and less cinematic. Visitors are free to wander through most of the courtyards unchallenged by the sentries, and to observe from the small neat signboards on the ancient doors that officials of the Royal Household are discharging their functions. Some relations of the royal family live here, as others do at Kensington and Hampton Court palaces. The provision of "Grace and Favour" apartments in St. James's was started by Charles II, as a sort of repository for discarded mistresses.

When expiring Queen Caroline urged her husband, George II, to marry again, he said, in Teutonic Court French, "Never! I shall take mistresses!" * And he did, making St. James's an occidental harem. The next George (III) started the modern Grace and Favour housing for "distinguished subjects fallen on evil days."

Many heirs to the throne were born in this palace, and some monarchs and consorts died here. The Yeomen of the Guard, the Beefeaters, continue their service here, as does the Honourable Corps of Gentlemen at Arms. This latter group, all army officers with distinguished records, captained by a peer (who is also a government whip in the House of Lords), is about thirty strong.

---

* She replied, "*Ah, Mon Dieu! cela n'empêche pas*" (i.e., the one doesn't preclude the other).

White-gauntleted, with white-plumed helmets, in scarlet tailcoats with gold epaulettes, dark blue pantaloons with black Wellington boots, they sound ridiculous but look splendid as the monarch's personal bodyguard on state occasions.

On the east side of the palace is a small street running to the Mall and called with regal simplicity Stable Yard Road. Just across this street is Lancaster House, built for the Duke of York (he of the column) in 1825 and after his death taken over and completed — in 1840 — by one of his creditors, the Duke of Sutherland. It was a most lavish residence. Calling there, Queen Victoria said to the Duchess, "I have come from my house to your palace." When Viscount Leverhulme (soap and margarine) bought the house in 1912, he renamed it Lancaster House and deeded it to the nation, which uses it for conferences and receptions.

Northward of Lancaster House is one of those urban backwaters, eddying between St. James's Street and Green Park, and in whose inlets and branches there are, instead of cheek-by-jowl slums, tiara-by-coronet mansions. This goes under the general name of Cleveland Row, and it is a soothing potpourri of age and wealth, including mid-nineteenth-century Selwyn House (No. 7), late-eighteenth-century Stornoway House at the end toward the park, mating with the earlier Warwick House whose nineteenth-century owners thoughtfully updated the exterior. There is a whole row (Nos. 8–12) of houses from 1700. And in one of the coves stands Bridgewater House, in which Sir Charles Barry in 1845 had a chance to give additional flourishes to the design he had already used for the Reform Club in nearby Pall Mall. The building has for some time been a corporation head office, but at the back gates in Little St. James's Street there are two round bronze bell pulls, one marked "Coachman," the other "Groom," disconnected bells to another world.

The Mall finishes its half-mile circling about the Queen Victoria Memorial (2300 tons of First Quality White Marble) and flattens itself before Buckingham Palace.

It is very British of the British to call this Buckingham Palace (except for those terribly knowing terribly few who call it "Buck House"). The Royal Family bought the place in 1762, almost sixty years after the Duke built it for his sumptuous spouse, and the Buckingham title had been extinct since 1735. Before George III paid £21,000 for it, the Hanoverians had used it from time to time (the first George never learned English, spoke to his ministers in Latin and spent most of his reign in Germany, and the second lived at Kew and Hampton Court for the most part). Although the Regent, upon becoming George IV, had Nash redo the palace, he had plans for a bigger and better house elsewhere, and William IV stayed snug at St. James's. But nevertheless, it was a long time since the Buckinghams, enough time to rename the place. But they never did. Maybe because they never looked on it as the Royal Palace.

It wasn't until the girl Victoria arrived that it became in fact the chief of all the palaces. Three weeks after learning that she was Queen, Victoria fled the confines of Kensington and was installed in Buckingham, although painters and plasterers were

Buckingham Palace before elaborate additions formed the building we know today

still at work in half the house. The first night she arrived, she reigned at her first royal dinner party, thus establishing one of the first of those Victorian precedents which became British precepts: the sovereign lives at Buckingham, occasionally displacing to one of the other palaces, Windsor, Holyrood House, Balmoral or Sandringham. Monarchs no longer live at St. James's, Kensington, Hampton Court, Westminster, Greenwich or the Tower of London. All except Balmoral and Sandringham, which are the personal property of the family, are part of the Crown Lands administered by commissioners who in 1963 turned over to the Treasury a net profit of $6,600,000 for the year.

Victoria kept the state functions at St. James's Palace and reserved Buckingham as her home. As a home, most of the six hundred rooms (this is an estimate; nobody knows exactly how many rooms there are, but conducted by an American real estate agent who would not omit kitchens, butlers' pantries and the like, the count would be closer to fifteen hundred), are not used by the royal family. Queen Elizabeth and Prince Philip occupy the first floor, i.e., the first floor up from the ground floor, in the north wing overlooking Constitution Hill and the palace garden. The children's rooms are on the floor above.

It is sometimes a disappointment to visitors on non-state occasions to be greeted at the door, not by periwigged footmen, but by detective-sized fellows in dark blue coverall-ish uniforms. These are servants,* as distinguished from Gentlemen-in-Waiting or other splendidly titled members of the Royal Household, who are courtiers and who, for the most part, come forward to play their roles only rarely.

Once, of course, it was all very different. When at Whitehall the King's Master of the Revels had no offices to sell, he invented some and sold these, including the titles of King's Physick Taster and Royal Curtain Drawer. They were no more ludicrous than that of, say, the Groom of the Stole, who was the chief Gentleman of the Privy Bedchamber.

The Court has not existed for some time, except for the rituals

---

* Nine gardeners keep the forty-five-acre garden, twenty-six cleaners mop and dust, squads of plumbers and electricians are on duty, plus cooks, maids, grooms for the thirty horses, chauffeurs, mechanics, etc.

of Coronation, State Openings of Parliament, conferring of knighthoods and peerages and such. There are no more formal presentations at Court, no more Sovereign's Levees (there are monster informal garden parties). The private life of the monarch is private, not shared by nobles attached to the Royal Person. The Queen does have Ladies-in-Waiting who accompany her when she goes out, arrange to pay bills if she is shopping (the monarch never carries money) and who in general smooth the way, and there are secretaries and equerries handling correspondence and similar duties.

The Civil List, the amount granted by Parliament to the Queen and certain members of her family, amounts to more than $1,700,000 a year. Her Majesty works hard for the money. Not merely as a ceremonial charades player, but as an active head of state. Wherever she goes the daily red leather box of secret dispatches finds her. When she is in London, the Prime Minister calls every Tuesday night, primarily to answer questions.

Although she is in a position to be the best-informed person on the affairs of her realm, there is little action the Queen can take. But vestigial though her political authority may be, her ju-ju has enormous power. She *is* the Undoubted Queen, and the head of the government is Her Majesty's Prime Minister. She is not only a unifying force for her nation, she is for most of her subjects a force in her own right as the wearer of the crown.

Nobody in this world believes more firmly in the necessity and utility of the British monarchy than does the British monarch. Her heirs are schooled in the same deep belief. It is a faith to which hundreds of millions of people subscribe, most of them not British.

The site of the palace was originally a mulberry grove. James I imported the trees from France to found an English silk industry. The silkworms surrendered enough thread for one pair of royal stockings and then resigned their royal warrant.* Then the new Duke of Buckingham built his country house. Since the property has been in royal hands, four architects have had a bash at im-

---

* There are six hundred firms which hold the royal warrant and are entitled to display the royal arms and carry the phrase "By Appointment." They supply everything to the palace (they are paid) from dog biscuits to bagpipes.

proving, enlarging and replacing sections (the last in 1913), but the palace stubbornly remains a large country manor, especially along Nash's elevation facing the garden. (This face, which the public almost never sees, is the front of the house.)

Because tourists were teasing, pinching, kissing and otherwise tormenting the rigid sentries stationed before the gates — the center gate opened only for ceremonial occasions — the guards were moved well behind the grille and placed directly at the doors of the palace. The changing of the guard at 11:30 A.M. takes place in the forecourt behind the fence.

The palace is inaccessible to the general public except for two portions, the Royal Mews and the Queen's Gallery. The Mews, where the three magnificent State coaches are housed, may be visited from two to four on Wednesdays for one shilling plus a laissez-passer from the Superintendent, for which one applies in writing with a self-addressed stamped envelope at least two weeks in advance.

The Queen's Gallery costs two shillings sixpence. Originally the palace chapel, it was hit by bombs (the Luftwaffe's socially ambitious pilots dropped in nine times) and was rebuilt as a picture gallery, opened in 1962. From time to time — three shows from 1962 to 1965 — parts of the royal collection are shown. This is always a signal event because the family's pictures are the most valuable private collection in the world.

Charles I was the first serious collector among monarchs, although predecessors picked up works (Henry VIII kept Holbein at court) through patronage and as gifts. Charles II, after the monarchy was restored, managed to reassemble much of his father's dispersed collection, and added to it. But the founder of the Royal Academy, George III, worked hardest at acquisition. He paid twice as much for the Joseph Smith collection of Italians than he paid for Buckingham Palace. Smith, known as "Consul Smith," because he wheedled that title from the Crown, was called "the merchant of Venice" by some, but his hoard included fifty Canalettos.

On the other side of the palace runs Constitution Hill, a road dividing the palace garden from Green Park. It emerges at Constitution Arch, through whose single archway only persons of state may drive. When erected in 1846, the arch was over-topped (almost toppled over) by a giant equestrian statue of Wellington, which was eventually removed to Woolwich. In 1912, the bronze winged chariot-borne Victory appeared atop the arch. Its horses should be at least anatomically accurate, since sculptor Captain Adrian Jones was a qualified veterinarian. The arch is useful as well as ornamental: one of its uprights contains London's smallest police station, the other a flue to carry off fumes from the traffic underpass.

Here is London's busiest traffic crossing, Hyde Park Corner, which includes several crossroads, a traffic circle and an underpass. This is where Hyde Park and Green Park almost touch, where Piccadilly ends and Knightsbridge begins, their meeting pretty well drowned in concrete.

Like every other Western city, London is unable to solve its traffic problems, though it started working on them some time back. The first traffic signal, with red and green lights and extensible arms, was erected at Bridge Street and New Palace Yard in December 1868.

Traffic woes started at least two centuries before the signal was installed, and sedan chairs were imported in the 1630's to relieve traffic — they were still for hire as late as 1821. There were successive laws to limit the number of hackney coaches for hire, but the advent of the railroad in 1834 meant more people needing more transportation to and from stations. George Shillibeer started the first omnibus service (eighteen passengers) from Paddington Green to the Bank in 1829. It cost sixpence, "together with the luxury of a newspaper." Considering that the average weekly wage was then counted in shillings, sixpence was a lot of money.

In 1834 Joseph Aloysius Hansom, an architect, sold the rights to his "patent safety cab" for £10,000, but collected only £300.

In 1836, the automobile was forbidden by Act of Parliament, or at least forbidden to emerge upon the public way unless preceded by a man with a red flag and traveling less than five miles per hour. (There were still in that year six hundred stagecoaches licensed to carry passengers between London and towns within nineteen miles of it.) Karl Benz, the German inventor and pioneer manufacturer, brought one of his vehicles to London many years later, found that the law was still in force, and departed. While other nations were developing an infant automobile industry and testing and improving the machine with races, Britain had no automobiles.

Then in 1896, the Hon. Evelyn Ellis brought a four-horsepower Panhard-Levassor-Daimler from Paris and tore around London in it. The police had no idea how to stop him. His demonstration roused British car enthusiasts and they successfully lobbied to have the red flag requirement abolished and the speed limit raised to 14 MPH. The day this happened the Motor Car Club invited the brave little band of owners to assemble before Parliament and make a victory drive to Brighton. The victory — if it is still known as such — is observed every November with the London-to-Brighton antique car run from the same spot.

Londoners are learning how much truth American architectural commentator Lewis Mumford encompassed in his statement,

The seat along the top of the omnibus was called the "knifeboard."

271

"The assumed right of the private motorcar to go any place in the city and to park anywhere is nothing less than a license to destroy the city."

At this spot a concrete island rears from the sea of traffic, approached by passageways under the road. On the island are marooned two pieces of sculpture which can shake the beholder, epitomizing the attitude of the Lost Generation, the survivors of World War I in 1925.

The Royal Artillery monument is by an ex-artilleryman, Charles Sergeant Jagger, who died young and did not finish many other works. There are four bronze figures looking out away from a mortar carved in stone. They are larger than life-size, and every tiniest detail is correct, and this correctness is harrowing, in that it deprives this monument to the dead of all sentimentality, euphemism, of all pity. An officer in full gear stares south, toward France. A driver is on one side, a gunner on the other, their faces almost blank with exhaustion, their eyes lightless. None of the living looks at the fourth figure, a dead man under his greatcoat. There is nothing about victory, nothing about glory. The inscription reads: *Here was a royal fellowship of death.*

Across the island (there are trees set in the concrete, to be sure, always trees in London) there is a slender, almost girlish nude David. Derwent Wood, enthusiastically esteemed in the twenties and then virtually forgotten, wrought this apparently incongruous memorial to the Machine Gun Corps. The inscription under this willowy youth reads: *Saul has slain his thousands but David his tens of thousands.*

There is also an 1888 statue of Wellington on horseback, across the way from Wellington's house, once known as No. 1, London. The first house on Piccadilly (according to the current numbering system, the last), it was built for Lord High Chancellor Apsley by Robert Adam in 1778. Although the Wellesley family has lived here since 1815 (the first Duke from 1816 to his death in 1852), it is still called Apsley House.

In 1828 the Duke quit the army for politics, starting at the top as Prime Minister (1828–1830). In mid-term he had the brick Adam house faced with stone by the Wyatt brothers, who added a heroic Corinthian portico and the extension on the left side. That was not the Duke's only error: he also opposed Lord Grey's Reform Bill.

In 1831 as the Duchess lay dying, a pro-Reform mob — making the best possible propaganda for the other side — stoned the house, smashing windows and damaging paintings. The Duke had iron shutters put on all the windows. In 1851, as he came up Constitution Hill, on horseback as usual, another crowd gathered, this time to cheer him. He paused at his gate, pointed to the shutters, and rode inside.

In 1947 the seventh Duke of Wellington gave the house and its Wellington treasures (the Duke's portrait by Goya among them) to the nation. While the spirit of the dead Duke of Wellington is abroad in the lower chambers (admission one shilling), there is a live Duke of Wellington overhead (no admission at any price).

"Number One, London," the Duke of Wellington's residence in Piccadilly.

273

The deed of gift reserved the upper story as the seventh Duke's residence.

The first Duke had that mystical hero's ability to inspire. He could inspire obedience, devotion, valor, even awe. But not love. As an old man, when some pretty lady teased him about the galvanic effect he had on pretty ladies, he sad, "Oh yes, plenty of that! But no woman ever loved me: never in my whole life."

He was not a modest man. About Waterloo he said, "Nearest thing you ever saw in your life. . . . By God, I don't think it would have done if I had not been there." And when a stranger spoke to him, asking, "Mr. Smith, I believe?" the Duke growled, "Sir, if you'd believe that, you'd believe anything."

From here eastward, for half of Piccadilly's length, the right-hand side is all Green Park. The least dramatic and least dramatized of the Royal Parks, it is a bumpy triangular grassy slope

The openness and romantic beauty of London parks have been marvelously preserved.

with trees and benches and a bandstand. It has Hyde Park Corner at one end, Buckingham and St. James's Palaces at the other, and the Ritz Hotel at the third. With no ornamental water and no flower display, it lacks the opulence and also the mystery of its sister parks, but as the plainest sister often has, it has a charm of its own and its very plainness is appealing.

Green Park was a battlefield in 1554 when Sir Thomas Wyatt raised the men of Kent to stop Queen Mary Tudor's marriage to His Most Catholic Majesty, Philip of Spain. Wyatt's column was cut in half here and the rear decimated. In the Civil War almost a hundred years later, London Puritans dug up some of the park for earthworks around a battery of guns on Constitution Hill. After the Restoration, Charles II added a deer park on the western end and cut a strip off the eastern end for his friend the Earl of Arlington (Arlington Street still marks this spot).

Queen Caroline, wife of George II, made St. James's a royal park, and her private Queen's Walk (still there, no longer private) was traced along the eastern boundary. She loved Green Park so much she had a little pavilion, the Queen's Library, built there. On a bitterly cold January 9 (the year was 1737) she insisted on taking her breakfast there, suffered a chill, and died in ten days.

Her husband used the park for military reviews which he adored. He also ordered the first of Green Park's big fireworks displays, this to celebrate the 1748 Peace of Aix-la-Chapelle.* As at the next one, which celebrated one hundred years of Hanoverian rule in 1814, people were killed and injured and the wrong things caught fire and exploded.

In 1780 Green Park, for no discernible reason, displaced St. James's Park as the fashionable place to be seen promenading after dinner. It was noted that "houses at the back of Arlington Street with windows looking onto the park fetched high prices." They still do: the most expensive flats in London in 1965 were in St. James's Place.

---

* Handel composed a Military Overture for the occasion. There were 40 trumpets, 20 French horns, 16 oboes, 16 bassoons, 8 kettledrums, a dozen side drums and a dozen fifes. In time with the music, 100 rounds were fired, followed by a 101-gun salute.

The favored spot for strolling was the edge of the small reservoir which fed water to Chelsea. This was filled in eventually, but not before many despondent Londoners, including Shelley's first wife, drowned themselves there. When the dinner hour was changed from five P.M. to eight or nine about 1814, the postprandial parade abruptly ceased.

Robert Peel, as Prime Minister, prepared to have the park endowed with fountains and flowers and temples. But then his horse shied and Peel was thrown and fatally injured — on the edge of Green Park.

THE LONDON OF
BERTIE WOOSTER

Gentlemen's clubs, Piccadilly, St. James's, Pall Mall, Waterloo Place, Carlton House Terrace — Haymarket — Leicester Square — Spy Territory — Seven Dials — Soho — Piccadilly Circus — Nash's grand plan, Carlton House Terrace to Regent's Park — St. James's Square — The Duchess of Jermyn Street — Fortnum & Mason's — Burlington Arcade — Royal Academy — The Season — Albany — Savile Row tailors — Bond Street — Berkeley Square — Gambling — Claridge's — Grosvenor Square, U. S. Embassy, Grosvenor family — Park Lane — Hyde Park and Kensington Gardens — Tyburn Tree — Bayswater — Notting Hill, housing, color question — Holland Park — Kensington — Palace Green — Kensington Palace — Hyde Park Gate — Albert Memorial — The Great Exhibition — Albert Hall — A clutch of Royal Colleges — Knightsbridge and Harrods

BERTIE WOOSTER was a fictional clubman of the 1920's, employer of the perhaps not quite so fictional Jeeves, the perfect gentleman's gentleman. In Bertie's life Jeeves took over where Nannie had left off, and Bertie's club, the Drones, replaced the nursery. Innocent, elegant and idle, Bertie Wooster was for decades the prototype of the happy wastrel clubman, and his club was thought to be based on the Bachelors', which, like other socio-geographical landmarks which once seemed imperishable, has vanished.

As the cost of everything, including the cost of being rich, has risen, clubs have suffered. Most cannot increase the annual subscription above $100 without losing members, and few clubs have waiting lists of applicants these days. As the economic structure of British society has altered and the rhythm of urban life has

277

changed, so have the uses and benefits of the club been changed. Attendance is heavy at lunchtime, sparse at dinner, and near to nil at night.

Nevertheless, there remain scores of gentlemen's clubs in London and most of the noted ones are here along Piccadilly and within a few streets north and south of it.

How Piccadilly got its name no one knows, though the several theories of its origin have earnest supporters. A pickadil was defined in the seventeenth century as "that round hem or several divisions set together about the skirt of a garment or other thing; also a kind of stiff collar, made in the fashion of a band." A tailor who had done well out of pickadils built himself a house in 1620, near where Great Windmill Street would later appear, and it was dubbed Pickadilly Hall.

The first of many noble houses in the district belonged to Charles II's Lord Chancellor, Edward Hyde, Earl of Clarendon. In 1664 the King gave him a large tract of land north of Green Park. Clarendon sold off a part of it and built his mansion and grounds on the rest. The public was persuaded he was using materials destined for the reconstruction of St. Paul's Cathedral and that the money for furnishings came from the sale of Dunkirk back to the French. Clarendon was innocent of the Dunkirk deal at least, and the furnishings he didn't pay for at all — they were gifts from admirers who were customers in His Lordship's sideline of blackmail and protection payment. In 1667 the Earl took up residence. The mob chopped down the trees in front of the house and put up a realistic gibbet. Later in the year, fallen from power, Clarendon fled abroad, never to return.

About eight years later the second Duke of Albemarle bought the house for about half the construction value. Persuaded that he possessed the true secret map showing the location of a sunken galleon full of gold, His Grace obtained the Governorship of Jamaica. He even persuaded several men of means to invest in an expedition to retrieve the gold. He went off to Jamaica, and cloaked by his gubernatorial office, he set off to hunt the galleon. He actually found it. And it was full of treasure. Having proved his point, he died. His Duchess got the booty away from the partners intact and returned to England — mad.

Besieged by suitors, the wealthy widow said she would marry none but the Grand Turk, ruler of the Ottoman Empire. The Grand Turk duly appeared, proposed and was duly accepted. When he took off his turban he proved to be the first Duke of Montagu. He had his wife locked up and built himself another mansion in Bloomsbury (it later became the British Museum).

He sold the Albemarle property to Sir Thomas Bond and friends, who tore down the house and got more out of the salvage than they'd paid. The syndicate built Bond Street; and for Henry Jermyn, Earl of Dover, Dover Street; and for the Earl of Stafford, Stafford Street. As a thanks offering to the previous owner, they named another thoroughfare Albemarle Street.

A relative of Dover's, Lord Berkeley of Stratton, built a mansion in the new development in 1672. When he died six years later, his widow sold part of the holdings to speculative builders who fashioned Stratton and Berkeley Streets. Eventually the First Duke of Devonshire bought the house, and the widow sold the rest of her grounds to form Berkeley Square. (The "er" in Berkeley is pronounced "ar" as in Berkshire and Derby, a persistent, perhaps permanent perversity, perplexing if not perturbing. Square, oddly enough, is pronounced "square").

In 1733, the old Berkeley House was torn down and the new Devonshire House by William Kent went up, and there remained until it was razed in 1924 to give place to the present commercial building. Since that demolition, this part of Piccadilly has lost its town houses to become almost solidly commercial. Between Apsley House and Bond Street here and there a few souvenirs of ancient private grandeur remain among the hotels, banks and automobile showrooms. Many of these old luxury houses are clubs. Number 128 is the RAF Club and 127 the Cavalry Club, both in eighteenth-century buildings no longer easily recognizable as such; No. 106 is the St. James's Club, principally for diplomats, a Palladian house of 1761 with Adam ceilings and one enormous room devoted exclusively to backgammon; No. 100 is the Public Schools Club, and No. 94, the 1760 town house of Lord Egremont, stands back from the street with two gates entering the forecourt, and as anyone can see from the inscription, houses the

In and Out Club (which it is frequently called by clubmen, who know its real name is the Naval and Military).

Hard by No. 100, White Horse Street ducks off Piccadilly in an almost furtive manner. Narrowly followed, it leads into a frazzle of alleys and courts surrounded by low brick houses containing eating and drinking and some retail establishments. This is Shepherd Market, designed and built by Edward Shepherd, who was active in the construction of Grosvenor and Cavendish Squares. Londoners seem to discover it as often as tourists do, with the same delighted surprise. Many of them find it too cute for words, which is just about right. This rural market was plunked down on the site of the two-week May Fair which had been roaring every year since 1688. Like the other traditional London fairs, it was abolished because it had become an unsavory nuisance.

Somehow, transformed into a compliment rather than an epithet, May Fair grew to be the name of the whole district north of Piccadilly almost to Oxford Street with Hyde Park and Regent Street as its more-or-less boundaries. For generations, the name Mayfair has denoted wealth and, if not distinction, at least snobbery. The district is studded with luxury hotels, luxury shops, high-fashion men's and women's tailors, hairdressing establishments, antique and art galleries, and of course, clubs, night clubs, restaurants and bars.

Berkeley Street, which glides northward to Berkeley Square, is the home address of Thomas Cook & Son, a company remarkable not only for having started the travel agency business, but also for being — unbeknownst to most of its clients and some of its competitors — the property of the British Government. When the Conservatives in 1962 divested the British Transport Commission of its holdings, they spread the companies among five groups, one of which is Transport Holding. Among the ninety-odd subsidiaries of this profitable holding company is Thomas Cook & Son.

Berkeley Street does not run south of Piccadilly, because if it did, it would run right through the Ritz Hotel. Although the management of this establishment would probably handle the matter with its usual decorum, dispatch and discretion, the problem has not really arisen.

There are those who believe the Ritz to be eternal, created about the same time and with the same durability as the Himalaya Mountains. As a matter of mundane fact, the first hotel on this street corner was the Bath, succeeded by the Walsingham, after which, in 1906, the Ritz was wrought on this site. The Parisian colonnade over Piccadilly not only added a French flavor to the street, but also permitted the owners to carry their upper stories right out to the edge of the building line.

Following the Queen's Walk through Green Park makes one part of the splendid view from the Ritz dining room windows. Not very far along there is a gap in the wall to the left, deft use of which can baffle those walking behind, since the artful dodger seems to have vanished into thin air. He has really only vanished into St. James's Place. Which is a nice place to be, with two shy (but not modest) hotels, some old houses, and two new apartment houses which contain the most expensive flats in London, the leases of which sell at about $300,000 each.

St. James's Street itself is best seen from the top, at Piccadilly. The best time to look is a Sunday morning, when the traffic is lightest. At the bottom of the gentle slope, the sentries pace before St. James's Palace, their uniforms bright against the old brick. Marching from their blue-and-gold sentry boxes, the sentinel's free arm is swung straight up level with his shoulder — hup, two, three, four — pause — turn. The turn is accomplished with a maximum of snap, the black gleaming army boots are raised knee-high and slammed to the pavement — Stamp! Stamp! Stamp! The steps echo all the way up the street.

Leading to this stage set where the marvelous dolls guard their toy castle is a vista of clubs, offices and shops. Some signs: Lobb Shoes, Chubb Locks, Lock Hats. The year 1965 was the bicentenary, not of the founding of Locks, but its moving from the west side of St. James's Street to the east, to the present and unchanged establishment at No. 6.

Locks makes hats to order, and it was thus that in 1810 they made the first bowler to the order of T. William Coke, who wanted a sort of crash helmet for his hunt servants at Holkham

Hall in Norfolk. At Locks these hats are called Cokes (pronounced Cooks), elsewhere in England they are sometimes called billycocks, but certainly never derbies. Lord Derby had nothing to do with the invention of this hat; the only peer involved was the Earl of Leicester, whose name was Billy Coke.

Just down the hill is a passage leading to Pickering Place. In the paneled passage is a plaque indicating that this was the location, 1842–1845, of "The Legation for the Ministers from the Republic of Texas to the Court of St. James's." Pickering Place is tiny, flagstoned and gaslit, enclosed by four brick houses (1731) and the back of Berry Bros. & Rudd's premises. The latter are wine merchants who have meticulously preserved the eighteenth-century shop of Pickering's, a coffee merchant. One of the most interesting possessions of the present tenants is the Cutty Sark label. This was the best-selling Scotch whisky in the United States in the 1960's.

There are only six clubs on St. James's Street: White's and Boodle's on the left (east) and the Devonshire, Brooks's, the Carlton and the Constitutional on the right. Pratt's is just off the street in Park Place.

White's is the oldest club in London. It was founded by Francesco Bianco in 1693, and moved to this house (Nos. 37–38) in 1778, belonging to the proprietors rather than the members until 1927. It has an eighteen-year waiting list. George IV, William IV, Edward VII and Edward VIII were all once members, indicating the level the club likes to maintain. A wild gambling group since its inception, it has toned down a great deal since the times when there were wagers such as Lord Alvanley's £3000 bet on raindrops coming down the windowpane. Despite the hectic pace, every Prime Minister from Sir Robert Walpole to Sir Robert Peel came out of the membership.

Boodle's, the second oldest (1762) took its name from the headwaiter Edwin Boodle of Almack's coffeehouse in Pall Mall. Rather much the same high-stratum membership as White's, with a long waiting list as well. The club is just as strong on backgammon today as it was in 1762. In 1965, the club made a deal with the *Economist*, whose offices were erected next door, which included a seven-story ladies' annex for Boodle's.

Both these houses are tremendously elegant, but comparatively small. Across the way at the top of the street the Devonshire (founded 1875 as a Liberal Party club) occupies what was once "the most notorious gambling hell in Europe," Crockford's. William Crockford, son of a fishmonger, took a house cut of only 25 shillings in the £100, but so ardently did his customers gamble that he left an estate of more than five million dollars. It was here that the Earl of Sandwich, not wishing to quit the gaming table for the dining table, invented the sandwich (cold beef). In what is now the first-floor coffee room, Crockford's corpse was propped in a chair for twenty-four hours to conceal the fact that he was dead and thus prevent the disqualification of a horse he had running in a big race. The horse lost.

One of the original gambling clubs of St. James's.

Brooks's was founded in Pall Mall in 1764 by twenty-seven men, most of whom were titled, and four of whom were dukes. There are still three dukes among the members, and many high prelates of the Church of England. Though the gambling fever of the days of Charles James Fox has long since abated, it is a point of some pride that members' horses have won fifty-four Derbies. The house was built by Henry Holland for the club in 1778.

Around the corner and below the pavement at 14 Park Place is Pratt's, owned by the Duke of Devonshire. It opens at 7 P.M. and closes when empty. The dining table seats only fourteen (candlelight), and is within sight of the open kitchen range and grill. One night, after a late House session, the cooking was by W. Churchill. The only game allowed is cribbage.

One of the grander clubhouses on still-distinguished St. James's Street.

The Carlton, at 69 St. James's Street, is *the* Conservative Club, founded in 1832 to fight the Reform Bill, and until recently a den of political plot-hatching which had world importance. Until 1925, no guests were admitted. Now, they even have a ladies' dining room.

The Constitutional, which cedes nothing in Toryism to the Carlton, moved into St. James's in November 1964, the formal opening conducted by Sir Alec (who surrendered his peerage to become Prime Minister) Douglas-Home. It is quite possibly the richest club in town. When it sold its old clubhouse (but not the ground it stood upon) to a property developer, it spent $200,000 refurbishing its new home.

Most clubs were founded in the nineteenth century, with the pleasant result of making Pall Mall a street of palaces (at least on

A world apart in nineteenth-century Britain: palatial clubhouses in Pall Mall.

the south side, these days). Only eight clubs remain, six of them enjoying the luxury of waste space with enormous rooms and giant staircases, on some of the most expensive real estate in the world.

At the start of this almost-royal row, left off Pall Mall to King Street, is Crown Passage. Its old gas lamps project from the brick walls, and shop signs poke out over the alley identifying a grocer, an ironmonger, a bookshop, a pub, snack bars and cigar stores, an earthy neighborhood main street behind the elegant main streets of clubland.

There is one society on Pall Mall that differs considerably from the gentlemen's clubs: the British Legion, veterans' organization, at No. 48. This is on the left (north) side of the street, where the Army and Navy and the Junior Carlton clubs face one another across a nameless jog of pavement which leads to St. James's Square.

The Army and Navy club demolished its 1851 adaptation of Venice's Palazzo Cornaro, sold half the site to a property developer and used the money to build a new club on the other half in 1963. "With only half the space, it has more accommodation than the whole of the old morgue," commented a Sunday paper. The club also opened associate membership to women, who joined in numbers, appreciably increasing revenues from annual dues. The Junior Carlton at once began knocking down its palazzo, and while waiting for its new building accepted the hospitality of the Rag. The Army and Navy is called the Rag, one is told, because a member once compared the meager suppers to those served at the Rag and Famish, a Cranbourn Street brothel.

On the other side of Pall Mall the Oxford and Cambridge Club (Nos. 71–76) is just past Marlborough House. Open from 8:30 A.M. until midnight, it is the roost of many high civil servants and cabinet members. Number 79 is where Nell Gwyn had a house from 1671 until her death in 1687. Schomberg House at No. 80, is what remains of the Duke of Schomberg's 1698 town house, brown brick with red trim. And after that comes — as a surprise to many non-Britons — the Royal Automobile Club, a real club, with a staff of four hundred, seventy-eight bedrooms, five flats, swimming pool, Turkish bath, billiard rooms, squash

courts, rifle range, library, and fifteen thousand members who
pay a $60 entrance fee and a $63 annual subscription.

Next door, where the Carlton Club once stood wrapped in a
semblance of Sansovino's Library in Venice, there has stood since
1958 a commercial building which looks like an Occidental la-
masery, inscrutable, contemplative and silent.

And next is the Reform Club, which still requires all applicants subscribe to the 1832 Reform Act. Sir Charles Barry, who
had built the Travellers' next door, was instructed to make his
building (completed 1841) "more sumptuous than any club in
existence." He took inspiration from the Farnese Palace. Political distinctions are no longer important in this once central citadel of the Liberal party. The smoking room is said to be what

*Artistic license went too far, putting women in this drawing of the
Reform Club, Pall Mall.*

287

Jules Verne had in mind for the opening scenes of *Around the World in 80 Days*, although the establishment next door would seem more appropriate.

The Travellers' was formed in 1819 for gentlemen who had made the Grand Tour, and all applicants must have traveled out of London at least five hundred miles in a straight line. "The chief tradition of the Travellers' is that members do not speak to one another," comments Charles Graves in his 1964 book on the clubs. At meals members carry reading matter to ward off untoward chitchat. The ground floor lunchroom — "the F. O. Canteen" — in 1965 still offered an 85-cent meal. The initials F.O. stand for Foreign Office, which contributes twenty per cent of the membership.

When the club was founded it had five future Prime Ministers: the Duke of Wellington, George Canning, Lord Aberdeen, Lord John Russell, and Lord Palmerston. A later Prime Minister, Earl Balfour, resigned when smoking was permitted in the magnificent white-pillared library. The Duke of Edinburgh is patron, and members include two royal dukes, one non-royal, six earls and a clutch of viscounts. There is a waiting list.

Barry was considered a trailblazer in 1832 when he finished this building, employing Italian Renaissance instead of the Graeco-Roman hitherto standard for big clubhouses such as the neighboring Athenaeum.

On the corner of Waterloo Place, the Athenaeum is a calm, magnificent, beautiful building. Above the Doric portico stands a gilded statue of Pallas Athene. All is light and clear and open and quite the opposite of the caricature of the Pall Mall club. Around the top of the first story runs a frieze, for which John Wilson Croker paid £1280 in 1839, ignoring, since he was the man who thought up the club and took charge of the building, the icehouse which members had had put into the plans. Thus, from a member:

> I'm John Wilson Croker
> I do as I please
> Instead of an ice house
> I give you a frieze.

The club was founded at the suggestion of Croker, who was Secretary of the Admiralty, at a gathering in the Somerset House rooms of the Royal Society. Sir Humphry Davy was in the chair and Michael Faraday was temporary secretary. The club, they declared, was "for the association of individuals known for their scientific or literary attainments, artists of eminence in any class of the fine arts, and noblemen and gentlemen distinguished as liberal patrons of science or literature or the arts." Subsequent committees have hewn close to this standard.

There were seven future prime ministers among the founders (the Duke of Wellington joined, but wasn't a founder). Darwin, Dickens and Thackeray were early members. Richard Burton translated the *Arabian Nights* here, and Lord Macaulay and Matthew Arnold (among many others) wrote here. Eventually actors were recognized as "artists of eminence" and swelled the

The artist in 1827 made Regent Street and the Haymarket spotless, but balked at improving the sooty sky.

289

impressive ranks. The club is noted for its collection of bishops and archbishops (R.C. as well as C. of E.), and judges. All the dinners of the Royal Society are held here, and it has been pointed out that this is probably the only club in town which displays a map of the subway system.

Across Waterloo Place is the United Service Club, formed a few weeks before the battle of Waterloo and feared by the government of the day as a possible military junta. The vast house (by Nash in 1827, remodeled by Decimius Burton in 1842 to better match Burton's Athenaeum building) is crammed with rare military paintings, portraits and fine furniture. Officers below the rank of major or commander were not accepted until 1892. Curry on Wednesdays, boar's head on the cold buffet.

The gas-fed flambeaux of the United Service are lighted for state visits, Waterloo Day, Trafalgar Day and Battle of Britain Day. On Winston Churchill's last birthday in 1964, these torches were alight, along with those on the Athenaeum, the Oxford and Cambridge, the Army and Navy and the Constitutional.

Waterloo Place is a grove of bronze statuary, almost all without identifying inscription, thus cheating the memorialized out of much of their due. The cast of characters includes Edward VII, a king; Lord Clyde and Lord Lawrence of Indian note; two polar explorers, Scott (South) and Franklin (North). There is a Crimean War group, including a Guards memorial with captured Russian cannon from Sebastopol, plus General Sir John Burgoyne and Secretary for War Sidney Herbert, who allowed Florence Nightingale, his neighbor in bronze, to go to Scutari and poke her lamp into things, much to the annoyance of the Establishment.

Behind Waterloo Place, Carlton House Terrace and Carlton Gardens stretch to either side, running parallel to the Mall and Pall Mall. The Foreign Office and other government departments have some of these houses, and others belong to clubs, the newest arrival being the Turf (sixteen dukes) which sold its two-hundred-year-old town house in Piccadilly in 1965 to combat incipient poverty. These terraces exude the feeling of privacy purchased at considerable expense, so that the average visitor has a tendency to be somewhat self-conscious, like someone on a conducted tour of a Stately Home.

Alongside 22A Carlton House Terrace, through an iron door that says No Thoroughfare, is a flight of steps down into Carlton Mews, the stables built in 1830 to serve these houses. Wide iron-railed ramps lead to the upper rows of stables, and honest arched iron brackets support the elevated plank "road." The stable yards are cobbled, with central drainage grooves in medieval fashion, and the gas lamps must have been among the first outdoor gaslights in England. This fascinating morsel, this crumb of time left behind, is about to be swept into the dustpan of progress. Historically and architecturally, these stables probably cannot earn reprieve, but folklorically and romantically, they deserve to be cherished.

A short stumble out Warwick House Court leads to Cockspur Street (Trafalgar Square immediately on the right) where so many shipping companies are concentrated. Left is Haymarket, a broad street from which the market was removed in 1830, and which has three postwar office buildings on it. One of these, New Zealand House at this end of the street, is a very good building. (They have preserved John Nash's Royal Opera Arcade, with shops on one side only. Delicate, charming, with that special sense of fantasy made real.) Next door is Her Majesty's Theatre, opened in 1897 by that terrible and wonderful theatrical force, Sir Herbert Beerbohm Tree, who managed it until his death in 1917.

Across the way is the most (perhaps the only) ravishing theater exterior in London, the red, gilt and white colonnade of the Theatre Royal, Haymarket. When Tree was preening himself on the "House Full" signs in front of his theater, it was pointed out that similar signs were posted on the theater across the street. "Ah, but not so many!" he boomed. "Not so many!"

The Haymarket was the instrument of protest employed by Henry Fielding before he became a magistrate and before he wrote *Tom Jones*. Here Fielding wrote and staged bitter political satires directed primarily against Prime Minister Robert Walpole, who went backstage one night and thrashed, not the author-producer, but one of the actors. Fielding was eventually forced out of the theater by his powerful enemies, but his place was taken later — 1774 — by a much more redoubtable foe. This was Samuel Foote, "a gentleman by birth and education," who was a mercilessly accurate mimic of the day's celebrities. Since he could get no license for his plays and no royal patent for his playhouse (Drury Lane and Covent Garden had the only ones, and they defended their monopoly), Foote invited the public to come and have a cup of chocolate with him during "rehearsals," tickets sold at George's coffee house. Everyone in London feared Foote's malicious wit. And he was witty, as Dr. Johnson who came to sneer and stayed to laugh, attested.

> . . . it is very difficult to please a man against his will. . . . But I was obliged to lay down my knife and fork, throw myself back upon my chair and fairly laugh it out.

Foote was also an incorrigible boaster. At a country house party which included the Duke of York, he boasted of his prowess as a

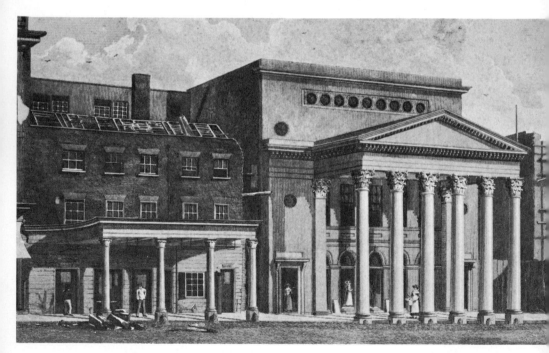

The "Royal" for the Haymarket Theatre was balm for broken bones.

292

horseman. The host produced a brute no one had been able to break to saddle. Foote mounted and was thrown. He lost not only his seat, but, since he smashed it in so many places, his leg as well. When the contrite Duke of York asked if there was anything he could do, Foote said yes, get him a royal patent for the Haymarket. The King granted the patent, and the Haymarket became Royal, though officially only for Foote's lifetime.

In 1829 the century-old theater was demolished and a replacement built next door by John Nash. Its rear elevation is on Suffolk Street, which is reached from Haymarket by Suffolk Place, which two streetlets — not entirely intact — are all that is left in this district of Nash's splendid, ill-fated triumphal route from Carlton House Terrace to Regent's Park.

Up Haymarket is an institution which has done much to impose the heroic silhouette of the Englishman on the foreign eye. This is Burberry's, where Sherlock Holmes would have bought his greatcoats and where so many World War I officers did buy their trenchcoats. Burberry's classic garments are a remarkable compound of sturdiness and elegance, casualness and correctness — in short, those British attributes which the wearers may easily lack.

Panton Street leads off Haymarket to the right to Leicester Square, one of the great rallying grounds for the entertainment-buying public. In the immediate neighborhood of the Square are half a dozen of the big first-run movie houses, three theaters, a dozen restaurants, coffee bars and pubs, two dance halls and purveyors of supposedly sexy reading matter and suppliers of contraceptive devices. This latter has been a speciality of the district since the eighteenth century, when Mrs. Philips at the sign of the Golden Fan and Rising Sun announced that she sold "implements of safety."

This was all land reserved in perpetuity to the people for seasonal grazing — until 1631 when the second Earl of Leicester got royal permission to build his town house here. It was the only house for more than thirty years, but by 1680 it was fairly well surrounded by others and Leicester Fields became Leicester Square. In 1700 Sir Joshua Reynolds built a house on the west side, painting the portraits which won him fame, entertaining

Boswell, Garrick, Burke and Goldsmith to dinner. The house remained until 1937.

Sir Isaac Newton had his house and observatory just off the square. This is where he is supposed to have cut a hole in the study door to let the cat pass in and out, and while he was at it, cut a smaller one for the kitten. This house was torn down in 1913. Hogarth's house was torn down too.

At the same time began the series of Hanover family fallings-out which made the square "the pouting place of princes." Having quarreled with his father, the son of George I moved to Leicester Square in 1718 and set up a court of his own. About twenty years

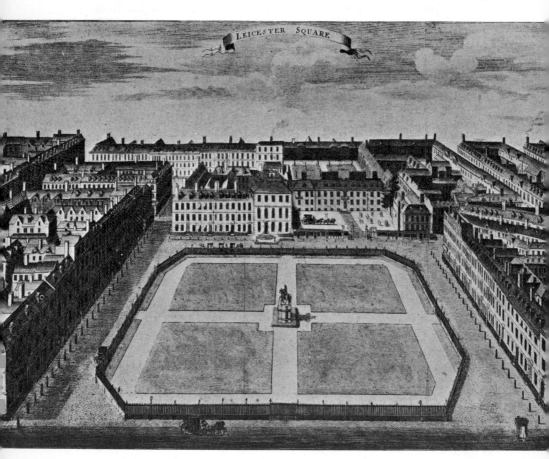

Leicester Square, 1754, when it was notable rather than notorious.

294

later, the same sort of quarrel had the same sort of result and the runaway's son ran away to Leicester Square. He eventually died there, so that his son had no father to quarrel with. Nevertheless when the boy became King George III, his succession to the throne was announced with full pomp in Leicester Square.

The garden in the center of the square fell into squalid neglect in the 1860's, and the family that owned it not only refused to put it in order, but successfully resisted court action by the authorities to take it over. Finally, in the 1870's it was bought, laid out much as it is today, and given to the public. The benefactor was strange. Known as Baron Grant, he had been born Albert Gottheimer in Germany, emerged from some picaresque adventures which gained him an Italian barony, and had come to England and floated companies profitable to no one but himself. He emerged as Albert Grant, publisher of the *Echo* and Member of Parliament for Kidderminster. Not long after his $140,000 gift of a renewed Leicester Square to London, the lawsuits began to catch up to him. One biographical note ends, "He died forgotten in Bognor in 1899."

When British soldiers marched singing "Farewell, Leicester Square!" this was the site of the Empire and the Alhambra (their names preserved by the cinemas which replaced them) the best of the London music halls. After the carnage of trench warfare had ground on for several years, Alfred Lester dared sing on the stage of the Alhambra:

> Send out the boys of the Old Brigade
> Who made Old England free,
> Send out my mother,
> My sister and my brother,
> But for Gawd's sake don't send me.

There are ten theaters within a stone's throw as one walks up toward Cambridge Circus along Charing Cross Road, one of the world dumping grounds for secondhand books.

Cambridge Circus, as readers of British spy stories know, is the headquarters of the Old Firm (British Secret Service). Which of these unprepossessing façades might hide such an organization? Nine streets empty into this circus, running harmlessly against a central asphalt island which conceals an underground men's lavatory (this, except for lady spies, would be the ideal spot). The corners are occupied by two banks, three pubs, the Palace Theatre,* a clothing emporium specializing in tropical and miltary kit, and Health Promotions, Ltd., home of the Great Restorative — Damaroids. Above street level behind the Victorian columns and flutings, are some flats and some offices. The general aspect is really too unobtrusive, too innocently outmoded and low-rental, but is it too real to be true or too real not to be true?

Although the existence of the Special Branch of Scotland Yard is acknowledged (they protect personalities, British and foreign, and keep an eye open for subversive plots), the existence of M.I.5 (counterespionage) and M.I.6 (British agents abroad) is not admitted, save in the most circuitous ways. For example, the memorial tablet to Sir Percy Joseph Sillitoe, K.B.E., put up in 1962 in St. Paul's Cathedral says, "Director General, Security Service 1946–53."

It all started when the War Office years and years ago labeled the doors on the corridor housing Military Intelligence from M.I. 1 to M.I. 13. The fact that domestic security reports were routed to M.I.5 and foreign reports to M.I.6 started the whole legend. Somehow, the domestic security agents eventually came under the Home Office (though they stayed physically in the War Office, now Ministry of Defence)' and some of the spies came under Foreign Office administration. In numbering doors at the Ministry of Defence, D.I.5 was purposely omitted from the integrated intelligence operation which starts at door D.I.1 and runs to D.I.88.

In Lord Denning's report to Parliament in 1963, he spoke of the domestic Security Service, and his remarks can apply as well to the Old Firm:

The Security Service in this country is not established by statute nor is it recognized by Common Law. Even the Official

---

* Built as the Royal English Opera House for D'Oyly Carte, who opened it majestically in 1891 with *Ivanhoe*, a grand opera by Sir Arthur Sullivan. In 1892 a new owner changed the name to the Palace Theatre.

Secrets Act does not acknowledge its existence. The members have no special powers of arrest such as the police have. No special powers of search are given to them.

Only one concrete fact is concretely ascertainable: Cambridge Circus does exist.

Up Earlham Street eastward one block is the hub of seven even seedier streets called Seven Dials, in the mid-nineteenth century the thickest part of St. Giles rookery, a sink of gin and poverty and crime. Seven Dials, its central Doric pillar hung with sundials, was planned in the late seventeenth century, and fully laid out by 1720. When Dickens looked at it something over a century later, he inquired — in one of his early Boz sketches, "Where is there such another maze of streets, courts, lanes and Irishmen?"

Shaftesbury Avenue, in the direction of Piccadilly Circus, was pushed through here in 1877–1886, and only in the 1960's began to get some newer buildings. The old ones, including several theaters and the Trocadero restaurant (one of Lyons's first experiments — about the turn of the century — in supplying luxury trappings for inexpensive meals) all seem dispirited. Wardour Street, which comes into Shaftesbury Avenue from the north, is the center of the film-distributing industry, and Great Windmill Street is the site of the Windmill Theatre. This house ran girly shows all through the blitz to boast for two decades, WE NEVER CLOSED. Then it closed, defeated by the striptease shops of Soho, which begins around the corner on Brewer Street. The new owners changed policy and reopened ("We almost never closed"?) as a cinema — showing girly films.

Soho, named from a hunting cry we are told (not very convincingly, but then no one seems to have contrived a better story), has no clearly defined borders, but its streets are clearly marked by a special tinhorn tawdriness which accompanies facsimile sin everywhere in the world.

Under the evident sadness rage seethes. The girls (smile, honey) in the lower depths of showbiz, the endlessly reproduced tourist on his last night in town are after something they secretly

Gin was the curse and surcease of the eighteenth-century working class. Hogarth's "Gin Lane": "Drunk for a penny. Dead drunk for two pence. Clean Straw for Nothing."

know they are not going to get. Under this exhibition of pathetic frustrations is the secret spread of dangerous ambitions: Soho has a high concentration of criminals.

A great many people think that Soho is still Bohemian, and, strangely enough, in spots it still is. There are painters and writers, artists and photographers who still hang out here, in whichever of the pubs or clubs is popular for the moment. Sprinkled around are some good pubs and quite a few good restaurants. The foreigners who congregate here (a few French still drawn to the original refugee settlement of 1550, replenished after the revocation of the Edict of Nantes, the original French Revolution and its nineteenth century successors; a few Greeks who echo the Greek colony established on Greek Street (of course) in 1677; a great many Italians (who have never ceased liking Soho) have their native restaurants and cafés and have even managed to denaturalize a couple of English pubs. Daylight sees honest businesses squarely plugging away among the shuttered night spots.

Londoners still go to Soho for fun, and there is fun to be had here, but like fun everywhere, it is almost entirely the kind you bring with you.

Shaftesbury Avenue was named for one of Britain's greatest philanthropists, Antony Ashley Cooper, Earl of Shaftesbury (1801–1885) and the fountain in Piccadilly Circus is a monument to him, to love in the evangelical, not the carnal sense. Sculptor Sir Alfred Gilbert, R.A., who used aluminum for this statue in 1893, meant it to represent the Angel of Christian Charity, a winged figure loosing an arrow from his bow while poised on the toes of one foot, but everyone calls it Eros.

The tall platform sits atop nine wide steps. Any hour of the day when the weather is not too bad, people from all over the world come and sit on these steps. Their expressions of deep content and their postures seem to signal journey's end. This, apparently, is what they have come from the ends of the earth to see. For them, Piccadilly Circus is the center of London and the heart of the Commonwealth.

They sit. Around them swirls one of the heaviest charges of traffic in town, the contents of six major arteries. Around them the painfully heavy Victorian and Edwardian buildings are in

299

large part screened by the giant electric signs that look so exciting on the colored postcards.

The Circus, which is not circular but rather triangular, has been kept as it is by this stream of vehicles: none of the rebuilding plans suggested up to 1965 was deemed proper to anticipated traffic increase in later years. So, this sentimental epicenter remained unchanged long after all the authorities agreed change was due. One suggestion was to abandon the Circus entirely to the motorcar and make an entirely pedestrian precinct of the adjoining Leicester Square area, from the top of Haymarket east to Charing Cross Road.

Where Shaftesbury Avenue enters the Circus is the London Pavilion, a movie theater, in its day a great music hall. In 1878 it virtually replaced the Foreign Office and featured a baritone named the Great Macdermott as temporary Foreign Minister.

Macdermott was awakened at the ungodly hour of eight o'clock one morning by a man drunk with inspiration. Having forced his way in, the man — a composer — croaked, "You must sing this tonight at the Pavilion!" Macdermott was actually hustled into listening to the song. The author, a Mr. G. W. Hunt, had read an article in the evening paper, rushed home, worked all night and here was the song, still wet.

That night the Great Macdermott sang it. He was a big man with a big voice booming out of big whiskers. He sang:

We don't want to fight, but by jingo, if we do
We've got the ships, we've got the men, we've got the money too!

It stopped the show. The audience wouldn't let him leave the stage, and he sang it over and over and over. Customers rushed from the theater and dragged in others from the street, from pubs, from other theaters. Overnight everybody in London knew the song. In Paris *Le Figaro* ran a special edition to print the song. The British fleet sailed and the Russians abandoned their threat to march on Constantinople. Turkey made a present of Cyprus to Britain. The word "jingoism" came into the language. And five pounds for the persistent Mr. — er — Hunt.

The Café Royal is still in Piccadilly Circus. The gilded caryatids were saved from the old building and put to work in the new grill room, pretending as of yore to hold up the gilded and painted ceiling. But even with red velvet upholstery, it is not Just Like the Old Days.

The café was founded by Daniel Nicholas Thévenon, a Parisian wine dealer whose royalist convictions had been stiffened by bankruptcy which he blamed on Napoleon III. He left Paris with an English capital of five pounds and an English vocabulary of zero. Within ten years he had altered Nicholas to Nicols and dropped the name Thévenon. His little coffee shop for other cross-Channel refugees had blossomed into the restaurant-café noted for its superb wines, cuisine and lush decor. Max Beerbohm in a single sentence as glittering and convolute as the interior, described it thus:

> There, in that exuberant vista of gilding and crimson velvet set amongst all those opposing mirrors and upholding caryatids, with fumes of tobacco ever rising to the painted and pagan ceiling, and with the hum of presumably cynical conversation broken into so sharply now and then by the clatter of dominoes shuffled on the marble tables, I drew breath and "This indeed," said I, "is Life!"

(It was this sort of observation which provoked Oscar Wilde, who deposed Whistler as king of the Royal, to remark that Max had been born with the incomparable gift of eternal old age.)

The time of the Café Royal was the time of Frank Harris and Bernard Shaw and the plush menace of private alcoves for female guests in the upstairs dining rooms (A little more of the wine, m' deah?). This Bohemia of best-selling playwrights and high-priced high priests of arts and letters petered off after the Oscar Wilde trial. It revived again on a less lavish scale in the roaring twenties, which roared as much in London as anywhere else without benefit of bathtub gin. Augustus John was one of the notable figures in the parade of notables. Lord Kinross has written, "There were Sitwells, Trees, Huxleys, Stracheys. . . . The aspiring and arriving writers, critics and artists of the 1920's — Harold Acton, Robert Byron, Cyril Connolly, Peter Quennell, John Betjeman, Alan Pryce-Jones, Osbert Lancaster, Cecil Beaton, Oliver Messel, Evelyn Waugh, Anthony Powell and the characters they were putting into their novels."

And in 1966? The Café Royal is part of the Forte restaurant chain (though *hors série*) and is noted for its unending stream of business banquets. The Queensberry Suite is reserved for the National Sporting Club whose dinner-jacketed members watch boxing matches under the Venetian chandeliers. The eighth Marquess of Queensberry was the man who brought down Oscar Wilde. There is no Wilde room or suite or broom closet in the Café Royal.

The notion of a circular space at Piccadilly was conceived by John Nash, a great architect and planner whose reputation is the victim of Victorian vengeance. He was too restrained, too refined, too old-fashioned for the builders of the age of the railroad, the steamship and the electrical telegraph. The Victorians liked soaring iron and great wrenching masses of mastered material, and their heirs followed like pygmies following in the tracks of an elephant. In Nash were all the attributes of modernity (the modernity of the 1960's, to be sure), startlingly clear in his metropolitan planning.

His great plan was the Via Triumphalis, starting at the edge of St. James's Park and moving north through the city to Regent's Park. Because the Regent was impatient and because His Royal Highness could not order a straight right-of-way which would tumble landmarks and rip through existing squares, Nash had to work his way around some troublesome problems.

The Regent lived in Carlton House. Behind it Nash redesigned St. James's Park, and before it opened out Waterloo Place. From here he ran Lower Regent Street northward and then found himself blocked. The longest stretch of straightaway lay before him, but three blocks to the west. How could he link it to the crossroads of Piccadilly and his new Lower Regent Street? He made Piccadilly Circus and from the top of it, he led the next portion of roadway in a magnificent sweep around a quarter-circle, the Quadrant of Regent Street.

From the end of the arc for almost half a mile the street ran straight ahead. Then came the awkward jog to go around Lord Foley's mansion and into the already existing Portland Place, built by the Adam brothers. He got around this frustration by making his focal point All Souls' Church, which he designed with a circular portico, carrying the passerby serenely around the otherwise ungainly corner.

At the entrance to Regent's Park his avenue spreads into two arms at Park Crescent, and the park itself is surrounded by magnificent terraces of classical houses. He not only laid out the park himself, but beyond his luxurious colonnaded terraces for Persons of Quality — i.e., money — he built Park Village East and Park Village West as ideal suburbs. These villages, precursors of the Garden Suburbs which were to make such impact later on, are still models for today. Nash made compact communities with a sense of space and air and privacy and yet of community. They had all the essentials for their own sustenance, plus unmatched

Nash's spectacular Quadrant leading Regent Street out of Piccadilly Circus.

amenities for leisure. And they are deeply pleasing to look upon. The houses are varied in scale and architecture, and while some experts today patronizingly term the bigger villas "picturesque," only a snob or a bigot can sneer at a fairytale cottage which is neither arch nor vulgar.

The whole work — a work of genius — was completed in 1816, and it did not endure. The Regent got bored with the plan and in 1829 had the source for the whole project, Carlton House, pulled down. Nash rushed in with Carlton House Terrace and the steps to St. James's Park and the Duke of York column (which he did not design). The magnificent colonnade along the Quadrant was hated by the shopkeepers whose shop fronts were sheltered behind the columns, and by 1848 they won. The columns were ripped out. Nash's adopted (and illegitimate?) son and student, Sir John Pennethorn strung balconies along the denuded façade in an effort to keep the horizontal sweep of the curving mass of buildings. But it was still too much in good taste for an over-stuffed age, and by 1900 it was largely rebuilt. By 1923 it was entirely rebuilt.

Oxford Circus, since tunneled by traffic engineers, was stuck in long after Nash. In 1877–1886 Shaftesbury Avenue came nosing in to spoil the circular outline of the Circus. And the grand terraces around Regent's Park were scheduled for demolition by the Crown Commissioners after World War II (they had also scheduled demolition of Carlton House Terrace just before that war). Appalled by the results of German bombing, and the devastating effects of wartime use by requisition, the Commissioners were also discouraged by postwar shortages of all that was needed to restore the houses. So they opted for destruction. As in the earlier case of Carlton House Terrace, these terraces were saved by the pressure of public opinion. They are now not only beautifully restored, but also beautifully rented at high prices.

"Nash transformed this part of London into a panorama of enchantment which grows rather than lessens with time," noted Walter H. Godfrey in his London architectural history. Nash used oil-painted stucco to cover his buildings. It was a surface easy to keep clean and bright despite London's vengeful air. But architects grew to loathe it.

Augustus of Rome was for building renowned
For of marble he left what of brick he had found.
But is not our Nash, too, a very great master?
He found us all brick and he leaves us all plaster.

The Regent for whom Nash labored was the son of George III, whose reign, 1760–1820, saw the end of the Seven Years' War with France, the loss of the American colonies and the start of a new war with the revolutionary government of France, and then with the Empire of Napoleon. George III's bouts of madness became more serious, more frequent, more enduring and when it was finally decided he was too crazy to carry on, son George was made Regent.

Tastefully, the Prince celebrated his Regency with a dinner party for two thousand at Carlton House. Historian E. S. Turner later observed, "The British taxpayer was privileged to maintain two major courts — one for an incurable madman and one for an incorrigible spendthrift."

The Regent, bawdy and capricious, became King George IV in 1820 and died ten years later. During his span as Regent and King much of London was built — Belgravia and Pimlico were the most notable sections — and much of the building followed the Nash notion of stuccoed exteriors.

Down Lower Regent Street from Piccadilly Circus, Charles II Street leads to St. James's Square. When this was the most fashionable square in London, a man named Samuel Travers bequeathed "sufficient money to purchase and erect in St. James's Square an equestrian statue in brass to the greater glory of my master, King William III." The pedestal was installed and stood empty for eighty-two years. An audit of unclaimed dividends rediscovered the 1724 endowment and the statue was commissioned. Completed in 1806, it shows the mounted monarch and the molehill on which the horse stumbled, throwing the king, who died from the effects of a broken collarbone. Since William had come to the throne of England by chasing his father-in-law James II off it, Jacobites for some time after William's death made a practice of offering a toast to "the little gentleman in black velvet" — the mole.

The garden in which the statue stands is locked, and only tenants have keys. That is the way it has been since Henry Jermyn, first Earl of St. Albans, had it laid out in 1664. The patrician air of privacy remains although the perimeter of the square has been invaded by institutions and even by office buildings.

When the Guinness family (including Lord Iveagh, who has a flat there) wanted to put modern offices in Nos. 10 and 11, from which they control their vast brewing fortune, they were obliged to retain the façades of 1736 (No. 11) and 1836 (No. 12), the fronting rooms, stairways and hallways. The requisite office structures went up at the back of the garden, invisible from the Square.

Next door is Chatham House, Nos. 9 and 10, also from 1736. These are, thanks to the generosity of two Canadian members, the headquarters of the Institute of International Affairs. Three Prime Ministers lived here — William Pitt, Earl of Chatham, Mr. W. E. Gladstone and the Earl of Derby.

Number 14, which looks like a small public library, is in fact a large private library. This is the six-hundred-thousand-volume London Library, founded in 1841 at the instigation of Thomas Carlyle, who interested Gladstone, Dickens, Thackeray and Macaulay in the idea, and who was possibly the most assiduous user of its books.

Number 15 was the home of the Duchess of Richmond, whose head appears as "Britannia" on copper coins. Also a 1763 house. The East India and Sports Club occupies the next two houses, in one of which (No. 17 from 1725) the unfortunate Queen Caroline lived during her divorce hearing, and in the other of which (No. 18, remade 1865) lived Lord Castlereagh, the Foreign Secretary involved in the proceedings.

King Street off to east is the location of Christie's, one of the world's great art auction salesrooms.

Robert Adam designed No. 20 and No. 21 has been transformed to match it. No. 31 was perpetrated in 1939 as a replacement for the 1723 town house of the Dukes of Norfolk and still bears the name Norfolk House. General D. D. Eisenhower, as Supreme Commander, Allied Forces in Europe, used this building to plan the North African and Normandy invasions. Next door in No. 31 the Bishops of London lived from 1771 to 1919.

In the northeast corner No. 4 houses the Arts Council of Great Britain, a post–World War II government cultural body in a 1676 house. A few steps away Duke of York Street leads northward and shelters a vintage Victorian pub, all cut-glass and polished wood with plasterwork ceilings, mirrors and ferns and that endemic name, the Red Lion. At the top of the street is the church of St. James's Piccadilly. By Sir Christopher Wren in 1676–1684, it was touched up and added to over the years until severely subtracted from by German bombers. Restored, 1954. The reredos was carved with rich garlands of fruit and flowers by Grinling Gibbons, who also incised Adam and Eve and the Tree of Knowledge on the font. Lord Southwood, before his death in 1946, provided money to make the churchyard into public gardens honoring the fortitude of Londoners during the blitz which wrecked this church.

Between the church and the top of Duke of York Street, parallel to Piccadilly, runs Jermyn Street, one of those West End streets designed to make the passerby feel ill-clad unless he stops in one of its shops for some object of hand-picked, hand-loomed, hand-cut wearing apparel.

There are also several expensive shops which do haircutting to order, while you wait. And at No. 50, corner of Duke Street, is Dunhill's, where anxious ladies buy those gold lighters and platinum cigarette cases, gifts so eminently hockable, in spite of those engraved indiscretions.

The Cavendish Hotel in Jermyn Street was a hive of indiscretions husbanded with impenetrable discretion by Rosa Lewis, the "Duchess of Jermyn Street," from 1906 until her death in 1952. Evelyn Waugh transformed her into Lottie Crump in *Vile Bodies*. As the years reel by, it becomes increasingly possible to believe that the Cavendish never existed.

Composed entirely of suites often furnished with family antiques by long-term tenants, it saw three generations of all the Puggies, Piggies and Pookies who later emerged as Admirals, Statesmen, Board Chairmen (and sometimes poets). Prince Tum-Tum had a place there, even after he became Edward VII. So did "The Ancestor," which is what chums dubbed Lord Ribblesdale because he was one of the rare ones who looked archetypically aristocratic (Rosa called him "Lordy" and called his kilted commando grandson, Lord Lovat, "young Shimi").

It was champagne and brandy and a squealing romp all the way. Rosa saw to it that those who could not pay were paid for through the padded bills of those who could pay. Rosa was reputed to be a superb cook as well as the sort of family retainer who adored her superiors but feared not to thwack them with her broad wit. She was also an exceptionally competent caterer and made a great deal of money at that.

The important thing about the Cavendish was certainly Rosa, who once berated a too-forward guest, "You are treating my house like an hotel!" The whole area was plastered with bombs in the blitz, and the damaged Cavendish was pulled together long enough to outlive Rosa by a little. It was the last of the inside-out Borstals where the upper classes were taken off the streets to perform their juvenile delinquencies. Yet, it was a respectable address, and for many guests a respectable place, where people stayed on honeymoons and had their mail sent.

Across the street from the site of the Cavendish is the rear of Fortnum & Mason's, whose front has graced Piccadilly since 1707, and "graced" is the word. The store is one of those commercial enterprises which by some magic becomes as distinguished as its clientele. William Fortnum had an intimate knowledge of the upper classes as a footman in Queen Anne's Household. His perquisites included candle ends from the many chandeliers and he sold them from a Piccadilly stall in his free time. When he married, he left the Queen's service and went into the tallow chandlery and grocery business with his landlord, Hugh Mason (Mason's Yard, where they ran a livery stable, still exists at the bottom of Duke Street).

Grandson Charles Fortnum at twenty-three entered service in the household of Queen Charlotte in 1761 and remained for twenty-seven years, his connections doing only good for the family business, which he administered for eighteen years after quitting the Household.

By 1788 Fortnum & Mason were selling potted meats, game and fowl in aspic, mince pies, Scotch eggs (hardboiled eggs in forcemeat), dried fruits. As a neighborhood grocery in the neighborhood of Piccadilly, Berkeley Square, Pall Mall and St. James's — including the palace — they served the Very Best People. Many clients were high officers during the Napoleonic Wars and the firms waxed even wealthier dispatching their specialties to the theaters of war.

During the Crimean War (1854–1856), Fortnum & Mason took their labels off shipping crates because cases marked with the name had a way of arriving at the final destination empty. Queen Victoria ordered 250 pounds of concentrated beef tea sent to Florence Nightingale in Scutari. The store created a special branch to handle dealings with clubs. Tinned goods began to sell well, especially Scotch salmon and beef stew. In those days a whole truffled pheasant was marked 15 shillings, real West Indian turtle they sold for 10 shillings the pound, a roasted duck with green peas came to 5 shillings and partridges were 2/6 each.

On Derby Day coaches and carriages began lining up at dawn to collect Fortnum & Mason food hampers. Charles Dickens wrote: "If I had a horse to enter in the Derby, I would name him Fortnum & Mason, convinced that with that name he would beat the field. Public opinion would bring him in somehow."

In 1908 the store set up a special department for customers going on expeditions or on yacht cruises. It all stayed pretty much the way it was — rationing in wartime was a bit of bother — until it was bought in 1951 by a Canadian bread-and-grocery magnate. The store then began to change subtly. More floor space has been given to clothing, gifts, and antiques. However, the clerks continue to wear morning coats, the floors remain carpeted from coffee grinder to bakery counter, the rich decor remains discreet. And last Christmas seventy thousand plum puddings were sent out to the furthest outposts of an Empire which remains attached to Fortnum & Mason if not to Great Britain.

A near neighbor, Jackson's of Piccadilly, remains firmly a grocery store and just as firmly a Piccadilly luxury establishment, though without morning coats or chandeliers.

Across Piccadilly, alongside the Royal Academy, is one of the splendiferous shopping centers of the world, the six-hundred-foot-long Burlington Arcade. It was installed on the grounds of the mid-seventeenth-century Burlington House in 1815, a sanitary-aesthetic device which incidentally brought in money. People were throwing garbage over the wall into the property and the Earl of Burlington wanted to stop them. The arcade was described by its designer, Samuel Ware, as "a Piazza for all Hardware, Wearing Apparel and Articles not Offensive in appearance or smell." For the title of first shopping arcade in England it contests with Nash's Royal Opera Arcade, Haymarket: the Burlington was started a year earlier, but was completed a year later than its rival.

Under a glass roof there are seventy-two tiny shops with bow-fronted chambers above. Throughout there is the restrained richness of the Regency. The original leases brought the owners about $6500 a year, and current annual rental value is estimated at more than $150,000. In keeping are the prices charged for lead soldiers, antique silver, cashmere sweaters, meerschaum pipes and other tempting nonessentials.

Since the beginning there have been beadles whose top hats and uniforms have altered little. They are there to enforce the

Luxurious Burlington Arcade was built to stop garbage coming over an earl's wall.

rules against singing, carrying open umbrellas or large parcels, and running.

On June 27, 1964, the beadles were baffled when, soon after they had opened the grilles at either end of the arcade, a dark blue Jaguar sedan mounted the pavement at 9:43 A.M. and roared down the nine-foot-wide central aisle, horn a-blare, lights a-glare. The car stopped in front of the Goldsmiths and Silversmiths Association. Five men in coveralls, gloves and black stocking masks leaped out, smashed the shop window with crowbars and sledge hammers, scooped up $150,000 worth of rings, brooches and necklaces and in sixty seconds were back in the car, already moving in reverse.

From upper windows employees of neighboring shops showered down chairs and heavy ashtrays. Bothered, the backing driver caromed off shop fronts, smashing more show windows in his frantic escape. By 9:45 — two minutes since it had driven in — the automobile had vanished. Up from the other end, from Piccadilly, rushed a police constable. He stopped a terrified witness and told her it was against the law to run in the Burlington Arcade.

The original Burlington House, more or less buried in additions put up to house learned societies, has been the home of the Royal Academy of Arts since 1869. It is, naturally, a stronghold of the academic in art, a position it is often strongly accused of holding. It surprises many that the Royal Academy Schools housed here have produced celebrated painters, including Constable and Turner, and continue to train some very lively youngsters.

From May to August 12 every year the Academy exhibits about 1500 works of British artists selected from about 11,000 pieces submitted. As an artistic event the Summer Academy is greeted politely, but as a social event it is capital. The private view, the Academy Soirée and the Academy Dinner are important society occasions to those to whom society and its occasions import.

The social season traditionally lasts not quite four months, from April into early August. Its duration was established some time in the eighteenth century when carriage roads were impassable in other seasons. Some time later a Little Season — September to Christmas — sprang up so that all of one's year's debutantes could fit in their dances.

A London debutante was originally the daughter of one of a very limited circle of ladies presenting their daughters to the Queen and introducing them to the children of other members of the circle. Queen Elizabeth II abolished presentation parties in 1958. Other than the debutante dances (ninety-five last season, many held in club ballrooms), the Chelsea Flower Show opening, Queen Charlotte's Ball, the Eton and Harrow cricket match, the Henley Regatta, Wimbledon champion tennis, Ascot and Goodwood Races and Cowes Yachting are all signal society events.

The whirligig stops in August because the grouse season opens on the twelfth (often and seriously called The Glorious Twelfth). Parliament does not sit at this period. "Everyone" is supposed to be off in the shires or in Scotland shooting at *Lagopus scotius*, smallest of the four species of ptarmigan. A week of this suffices to confirm one's orthodoxy. One investigator figured that such a week could cost in 1965, five hundred pounds, or about thirty-five shillings per grouse. Grouse can be bought at Fortnum & Masons for half that amount.

Before the days of paid vacations the masses depended on long weekends for release from travail, the occasions known here as Bank Holidays: Boxing Day, the day after Christmas when seasonal boxes are exchanged; Easter Monday; Whit Monday seven weeks after Easter, and the biggest, because of the likelihood of good weather, August Bank Holiday. In 1965, the government moved this holiday from the beginning of August until the end of the month in an effort to diminish the traffic chaos.

In this group of buildings along with the Royal Academy, whose forty members have R.A. after their names, are the Chemical Society, the Society of Antiquaries, the Geological Society and the Linnean Society. It may have been at a meeting of this last that T. H. Huxley listened to a speaker insisting that acquired characteristics could not be inherited, citing the fact that generation after generation had to undergo circumcision anew and Huxley was heard to murmur,

312

"There's a divinity that shapes our ends,
Rough-hew them how we will."

The Royal Astonomical Society is located here as well, and one of the most important scientific bodies in the world, with the extraordinarily simple name of the Royal Society. There are in all some forty-one royal societies. Many of these are in the arts, including Portrait Painters, Watercolorists, Sculptors, Engravers, Miniature Painters. Some of the other include the Royal Choral Society, the Royal Microscopal Society, and the Royal Toxophilic Society, an archery group.

On the east side of Burlington House is Albany Chambers, a 1770 brick house by Sir William Chambers, with 1804 additions by Henry Holland. It is set back from Piccadilly behind a forecourt, and in the rear, leading to Vigo Street, is a covered way flanked by suites of chambers. Lord Macaulay and Compton Mackenzie, who lived there, called it "The Albany," but Byron, who also lived there, called it "Albany," and his whim has prevailed — the "proper" name is simply "Albany."

Originally it was called Melbourne House, not after the noted nineteenth-century Prime Minister, but for his father, whose contemporaries did not credit him with the paternity. As was noted, "The honor was generally settled upon Lord Egremont but the number of candidates is considerable." It was said that Egremont had bought Lady Melbourne from Lord Coleraine for £13,000 and there were "various reports about Lady Melbourne's commission."

The Duke of York and Albany gave his Whitehall mansion by St. James's Park plus £10,000 to have Melbourne House. His Grace tired of it in a few years and departed, leaving one of his names behind. A builder named Alexander Copland acquired the property and had Holland lay it out as it is today. Women in recent years have been allowed to take chambers in what for so long was a male establishment (Lady Caroline Lamb called on Byron disguised as a pageboy).

Prime Ministers Canning and Gladstone lived here, but the reputation is largely literary. Both the *Saturday Review* and the *Yellow Book* were edited from Albany and here were written

The Second Mrs. Tanqueray, Sinister Street, The Last Days of Pompeii. It is firmly closed to the general public, who can gawk down the ropewalk from the Vigo Street gate.

Opposite this gateway is Savile Row, a street which has become a generic term for British bespoke (in the U.S., "custom") tailoring. About fifty tailors, most of them in this neighborhood, are the conservators of the cult of unobtrusive elegance based on fine materials and superb workmanship. Each house has its own basic notion of what a suit should be ("You wouldn't ask Rolls-Royce to change its front, and you shouldn't ask us to change our lapels"), but they will adapt themselves to customers' desires, narrowing trousers or padding shoulders or omitting cuffs. Their workroom ceilings are hung with the paper patterns cut for each customer and altered through the years as time has altered the customers.

Two things have changed in the bespoke world since World War II: credit and suiting weights. Big accounts which are never quite settled may still be run by families dressed by the same firm over generations, but the average buyer will be asked to pay about fifteen per cent down when he orders his suit and the rest on delivery. Suits start at $150 and can be delivered within three weeks.

Because tailors are no longer obliged to smile while bankruptcy threatens because of accounts outstanding, new customers are no longer expected to be presented via an introduction from an established client.

Suitings have become progressively lighter. Before World War II cloth weighing 22 to 24 ounces per yard were common, but by 1955 this had lightened to 16 to 17 ounces. Beyond this tailors were not willing to go because they couldn't get the drape and the shape they wanted out of lighter materials. But customers whose automobiles, offices and even homes were actually being heated for the first time, kept asking for lighter materials and finally the mill wizards found ways to "stabilize" cloth to hold the style tailored into it. In 1965 the cloth weight was down to 11 to 14 ounces per yard.

The tailors are a prideful lot, and one newcomer who said, "I want to buy a suit," was told, "We do not sell suits, sir, we make

314

clothes." Many of the establishments are not identified from the street as tailors or anything else: just a plate glass window with a screen behind it, and, somewhere in small lettering, the name of the firm.

Some houses have developed specialities over the years, so that a man may go to A for his dress clothes, B for his sack suits and C for his country tweeds. Adeney and Boutroy, 16 Sackville Street, do have a "civilian" clientele, but maintain the episcopal trade they have fostered since 1774, dressing half the bishops and both archbishops of the Church of England.

They have lately observed that the dark purple which was considered Roman Catholic and thus sparingly bought, suddenly found favor in the 1960's. Which leaves Adeney and Boutroy with a large stock of unsold bright purple and blue purple, yesteryear's favorites.

For one block at its Piccadilly end, Bond Street is Old Bond Street (built by Sir T. Bond, 1680), after which up to Oxford Street it is New Bond Street (built by the Earl of Oxford, 1722). For a long moment, the west side of the street between Grafton and Conduit was numbered as New and the east side as Old. Now that that has been adjusted, one finds that the numbers of New Bond Street go up the east side and down the west, so that No. 1 is across the street from No. 185.

Bond Street is a street of dreams: famous jewelers such as Cartier's, famous cosmetic houses such as Coty, famous art galleries such as Agnew's, and Sotheby's, where some people pledge fortunes for objects that other people wish to be rid of.

Sotheby's, whose name goes along with rival Christie's (in St. James's) is an auction house. Both places sell secondhand furniture, dishes, rugs, books and pictures. It is a good business (Sotheby's has been going since 1744 and Christie's since 1766) which can handle over a million dollars in sales in a good day and more than three million on a record day.

Most sales at these two institutions — except for gala evening events — start at eleven and are done by lunchtime. The goods are on view three or four days in advance and the catalogue is available three or four weeks before sale day. Vocal bidding is uncommon. In March 1965, Rembrandt's portrait of his son Titus went for £798,000 and there was a scandal at Christie's: the auctioneer forgot the secret signs deposited earlier by the winning bidder, closed the bidding and then had to reopen it.

Lord Nelson lived at 147 New Bond Street when the Hamiltons, Sir William and Lady Emma, lived at 23 Piccadilly, where little Horatia was born.

The Christmas card was born on Bond Street. Sir Henry Cole, one of the instigators of the Great Exhibition of 1851 and later of the Victoria and Albert Museum, was too busy to write his traditional Christmas letters in 1843. He had John Calcott Horsley design a card of which a thousand were lithographed, four hundred going to Sir Henry's friends and relations, the rest being put on sale for a shilling each in a shop in Old Bond Street. At the 1964 estimate, the British buy 640 million Christmas cards a year.

Cut west from Bond Street along Bruton Street and there is

Built on the grounds of a great house, Berkeley Square was originally a real estate speculation.

Berkeley Square. And on the corner is a big blah brick building occupying much of the east side and squatting on the site of No. 17 Bruton Street, where Queen Elizabeth II was born in 1926.

A similar big bashing block occupies the south side of the square. The only "Berkeley Square houses" left are on the west side. These are tall, or at least tall-seeming three-story brick houses. Several of them still have torch extinguishers alongside the entries: the link-bearers who saw people home at night doused torches by thrusting them up into these black iron cones. In general the exteriors, though pleasing in proportion, are quite plain, with no clue to the magnificence within.

The best of the houses is No. 44, a 1744 house by William Kent, architect of the Horse Guards in Whitehall. The splendor of its ceilings and fireplaces, the double staircase, the richness inherent in the bones of the building may be regarded by the public, but not freely, for since 1962 this has been the Clermont Club, chairman the Earl of Carnarvon. Of its four hundred members, one hundred are also members of White's and most of the rest are from Brooks's, Boodle's, St. James and from the Portland Club around the corner. The purpose of the Clermont is gambling and the *salle privée* provides the kind of absolute privacy, absolute liquidity and absolute dedication that world figures in gaming consider ideal working conditions.

Very near here, in Hill Street, which leads off the square, is another gambling club dating from the new gaming laws of 1962. This is Quent's, in an elegant eighteenth-century house. Like the others it provides superior food and drink for very low prices, and roulette, chemin-de-fer and the rest. Curzon House is a similar establishment at 20–23 Curzon Street (go down the steps at the south end of Berkeley Square and turn right) also housed in the proper period mansion, offering bridge, poker, chemin-de-fer all night and roulette until 2 A.M.

The other major private casino in London is across St. James's at 16 Carlton House Terrace. It bears a name long linked with gambling in London, Crockford's. The original 1828 Crockford's from St. James's Street was revived in 1928 after a lapse of some years and completely reborn after the change in gaming laws in 1962. There is a sliding scale of fees for play, since the law does not allow the house to take a share of the stakes, and this goes from £2 for a turn at a £40 bank with a £10 opening bet all the way up to £40 which entitles the player to half an hour's baccarat with an £800 bank.

Off-track betting has always been legal in Britain, and football pools were never illegal. The government itself revived a form of lottery in the 1950's with Premium Bonds, which paid prizes on lucky government bond numbers. When television began killing off neighborhood movie houses, the cinemas reopened often as bingo parlors. The slot machine — the "one-armed bandit" — is legal.

Altogether, with half the adults in the nation wagering in one form or another, gambling is one of the truly major industries of Britain. In 1964 the Customs and Excise Commissioners revealed that sixteen million gambling club memberships totalled thirty-five million dollars in membership fees alone, which was before anyone wagered a single penny. The one-armed bandits had a play that same year of more than 150 million dollars. The ten or eleven million Britons who play the football pools every week ante up with their very small bets, more than 300 million dollars a year. Two New York State investigators judged that bookie joints (quite legal, and referred to commonly as "betting shops") handle a billion pounds a year — $2,800,000,000.

Next door to the Cleremont, at No. 45, Lord Clive of India lived and — by his own hand — died. Number Six was for a while the home of William Pitt, Earl of Chatham. Lord Bute, another of George III's Prime Ministers, lived at Landsdowne House and there received Dr. Johnson's visit of thanks for the pension granted him. Lady Randolph Churchill occupied No. 16, and Charles James Fox, another Prime Minister, No. 25. Lord Brougham lived at No. 21. He is esteemed in the South of France as the *Milord* who popularized the Côte d'Azur among foreign tourists. Lord Brougham returned from his Cannes villa in 1894, where he had learned bridge, and resorting to the Portland Club around the corner for whist, dealt a bridge hand instead: this was the first bridge game in England.

The Portland Club at 19 Charles Street (the Guards Club is at No. 18), has attained the position in cards that St. Andrews has in golf: it is the arbiter of rules and fine points. In 1963 it produced its latest rules for bridge, the first official change since 1948. Founded in 1816, this is possibly the smallest of the gentlemen's clubs, with only a hundred members.

The oval garden in the center of Berkeley Square is open to the public. In the middle is an 1800 pump house with a Chinese roof, and it is one of the peculiarities of this part of the world that it doesn't really look peculiar. The opulent plane trees have been rooted here since 1780.

North from the Square, Davies Street runs to Brook Street, just where Claridge's happens to be standing in the same place where it used to stand in 1808 under the name of Mivart's Hotel. It spread from one house to another and occupied four by the time Monsieur Mivart sold out to Mr. Claridge forty years later.

After Mr. Claridge was safely buried in 1895, his heirs pulled down the old place which had sheltered so many impressive guests, persons who would not normally have condescended to stop at a hotel. For all its late Victorian pomposity the exterior of the present hotel is modest considering the high range of its registers, both guest and cash.

Down to the right at No. 25, Handel composed his *Messiah*, and died after thirty years of residence there. To the left at No. 69 is the Savile Club, which has a heavy prejudice in favor of writers. Past members include Rudyard Kipling, H. G. Wells, and Robert Louis Stevenson. The current roster includes many distinguished contemporary authors.

Brook Street goes serenely on into Grosvenor Square, whose six acres make it the largest in Mayfair. This development was one of the shrewd ideas of Sir Richard Grosvenor, who laid it out in 1725. A few eighteenth-century houses remain, conspicuous among the neo-Georgian apartment and office buildings which take up three sides of the square. The west end is entirely taken up with the 1961 United States Embassy by Eero Saarinen.

This great white glass-fronted structure topped by a gilded eagle with 35-foot wingspan is a good representation of America in the 1960's: big, open (but defended — there is a moat, a railing and a glacis), at base sure of itself but then again temporizing (unsuccessfully) in order to please. Which is to say that the

319

bottom portion of the building, inside and out, is forceful, individual and impressive. But the upper part tries to effect a Compromise Georgian doing its awkward best to fit in with Olde London. However, it does have three cardinal virtues as an embassy — it's clean, it's comfortable, and you can't miss it.

During World War II, with so much of the American military effort directed from here, U.S. servicemen called Grosvenor Place Eisenhowerplatz. The Supreme Commander had his headquarters for a while at No. 20. The park has been dedicated as a memorial to wartime President Franklin Delano Roosevelt. His statue, a gift from the English people, was unveiled in 1948 by Mrs. Roosevelt in the presence of the King and Queen. American attachment to this square started when John Adams, first Minister to the Court of St. James's, set up residence at No. 9.

A lot of the streets around here are named for the Grosvenors and their relatives. Hugh Audley, "a wealthy scrivener," bought this property from the Abbey. It stretched for two miles down to Millbank and included what long after became Belgravia.

His great-grandniece, Mary Davies, inherited it and married Sir Thomas Grosvenor in 1677. Her son Richard turned large parts of the holdings into huge housing developments, such as Grosvenor Square. Eventually, in 1847, the Grosvenors became the Dukes of Westminster, owning one-quarter of central London. The death duties (sixty million dollars) on the estate of the second duke, who died in 1953, have since occupied a separate subdivision of Inland Revenue and may have forced quiet disposal of some of the town properties.

The first Duke of Westminster lived two blocks west of Grosvenor Square on Park Lane. His place was called Grosvenor House, and as Lord Grosvenor in 1842, he let the public visit his picture gallery on Sundays, an uncommon act of generosity at the time. Among the pictures was *Blue Boy*. When the house was razed in 1930 and replaced by a Lutyens-designed hotel (called Grosvenor House), a colonnade appeared on the Park Lane side of the new house where the old house had had its columned picture gallery. The Dorchester Hotel, another swank hostelry replacing another town palace, also was built in 1930.

The same thing that happened to Park Avenue, New York,

320

has happened to Park Lane, London. The old mansions have been erased and hotels, luxury apartment buildings and "prestige offices" have been installed.

A piece of Hyde Park was chewed off to make Park Lane a dual carriageway, as it's called locally, a highway with a landscaped strip dividing north- and southbound trunks. At Upper Brook Street is the entrance to an 1100-car garage gouged under the Park, "Western Europe's largest parking garage."

When an American corporation erected a twenty-two-million-dollar, twenty-four-story hotel three hundred feet high at the Piccadilly end of Park Lane in 1963, Londoners objected that (a) it was to high for the area's prevailing proportions and (b) it permitted peeking into the garden of Buckingham Palace on the far side of Constitution Hill. But when during its first year the hotel lost about $15,000 a week, the most vociferous commentators refrained from comment.

Park Lane's Park is a great green parallelogram, almost three-quarters of a mile north to south and more than a mile and a half east to west. The eastern half is Hyde Park, the rest Kensington Gardens. Hyde Park is the one with Rotten Row and the Serpen-

Decimius Burton's screen at the entrance to Hyde Park Corner.

321

tine. It is supposed that Rotten Row is a corruption of *Route du Roi*, King's Road, and it is known that the Serpentine is the scooped-out bed of a stream called the Westbourne.

In the 1860's Rotten Row was the resort of the great English *cocottes*, who appeared in beautiful carriages drawn by handsome steeds, or in dazzling little traps pulled by ponies which the ladies drove themselves. It was then and is still fashionable for the ultra-respectable to ride horseback along Rotten Row, but since the disappearance of Skittles and her friends they have had little to be outraged about except the 1965 restaurant on the edge

Some ladies splendidly riding Rotten Row in 1897 were not ladies at all. Though muffled, laughter was not dead.

322

of the Serpentine, which they thought might bother the horses.

The mile-long Serpentine is not at all snaky. It is shaped more like a whale. Perhaps the name arose from the slippery fashion in which Prime Minister Walpole extracted from public funds the money to pay for this whim of Queen Charlotte's without King George II hearing about it.

There is boating on the lake and swimming from a public beachlette called, with English irony, the Lido. Every year since 1865 the Serpentine Swimming Club has staged a 100-yard swimming race on Christmas morning.

The whale tail of the lake curves upward through Kensington Gardens to a corner made into an Italian garden of marble and water. This formal assemblage of balusters and statues, fountains and pools, conch shells and damp demigods is startlingly — and pleasingly — un-English. Inside Kensington Gardens the lake is

La Dolce Vita in Kensington Gardens, the Serpentine Italicized.

323

not called the Serpentine, but the Long Water. The round pond nearer Kensington Palace, is called, with English irony, the Round Pond. Here children play with sailboats and adults test miniature yachts, although without being an expert it is difficult to tell which is which (to separate the ships from the boats?).

Both Hyde Park and Kensington Gardens began as hunting grounds, and Charles II in the 1660's put a brick wall around Hyde Park. In 1789 the Board of the Green Cloth awarded a yearly pension of £18 to Sarah Gray in lieu of her husband, killed in Kensington Gardens by groundkeepers hunting a fox. Up to the Broad Walk were the private gardens of Kensington Palace, open to well-dressed members of the public on Sundays when the Royal Family was absent. That was the mid-eighteenth century; a century later the gardens were extended and open to the public from spring until autumn. Kensington Gardens is still

Marble Arch, at the northeast corner of Hyde Park, was once the entrance to Buckingham Palace.

324

the exercise ground for some infants of the wealthy, and pram-pushing nannies nattering may still be seen there, as well as little boys with hoops and — perhaps they are the children of rich foreigners — white gloves.

There is no city park anywhere like this one (or, rather, these two): only in rare segments is it identifiably a city park, otherwise it is a sequence of meadows, shaded walks, bowers, flower gardens, the many moving aspects of the grounds of some stately home in some rural shire.

The areas bordering the park(s) are as various as London can provide. At the top of Park Lane, Marble Arch — which gave its name to the adjacent quarter — is isolated in a maze of highway construction. Inside the park behind it is Orators' Corner where cause-pushers shout against hecklers, an ancient freedom enjoyed as early as 1875.

Across the way, at the corner of the Edgeware Road, a stone disc is sunk into the pavement, marked with an X and lettered "The Site of Tyburn Tree." For more than five hundred years this was a principal place of execution, the last hanging carried

For the populace of all ranks, death was a holiday at the "Tyburn Tree."

325

out in 1783. It left us a word, derrick (name of the first hangman), and a phrase, "You're pulling my leg." Hanging at Tyburn was by strangulation. They drove off the cart on which the haltered prisoner stood, and he was left to dangle to death. To save him further torment, his friends would run up and hang on his legs so that he would die quickly.

From here westward along the top of the park, the Bayswater Road. The district of Bayswater has always been respectable, its many garden squares girt with tall houses, many of them now small hotels and higher class boardinghouses. Somewhat déclassé for a while, it has, like other neighborhoods, been much restored as a Good Address by new building and by the housing shortage which compels many to find new chic in old neighborhoods.

After the edge of the Gardens is passed, the Bayswater Road becomes a street named Notting Hill Gate, which was redeemed from slumhood only in the 1960's, when the place was razed and rebuilt in modern terms. But north of here the remaining slums of Paddington and North Kensington commingle, stabbed here and there with newly rebuilt streets. Some of the smarter new streets were the scandal of London in the early 1960's, when the word "Rachmanism" came into the housing vocabulary. Polish-born Peter Rachman came to Britain in 1946 when he was twenty-seven, and when he died sixteen years later he was worth a quarter of million dollars gained through slum real estate operations.

He bought old houses in which the apartment rents were frozen as long as the occupying tenants remained. He persuaded them to leave by making life an absolute hell, providing no upkeep or repairs, filling vacant rooms with prostitutes and with colored immigrants with little knowledge of multiple housing piled ten to a room, and in the end, using strongarm tactics. When he had broken all the rent restrictions, he bounced the worst tenants and sold the properties to serious developers at a fat profit. There were other landlords like Rachman, but not with such big holdings or such small morals.

A 1965 housing report to Parliament said that 190,000 London families needed rehousing, that of the half-million households living in subdivided houses nine out of ten either "shared or lacked at least one of the basic domestic facilities." (Heating is not on the list — cooking stove, sink, hot and cold water, bath and lavatory.)

More than 70,000 out of 200,000 multiple dwellings lacked a fixed bath. One six-apartment building visited had a whole family in every room, a total of eighty-five persons. The bad landlords were out of the worst scenes painted by Dickens. Conditions, said the report, were "akin to those prevailing in the middle of the nineteenth century."

The shortage of living space persists in spite of the energetic development of housing all over London which provided hundreds of thousands of new units in the fifteen years between 1950 and 1965. People were marrying earlier and dying later, founding new households and preserving the remnants of old. Slum clearance drove the occupants of condemned buildings into competition for available inexpensive housing. While the Location of Offices Bureau labored to persuade firms to move twenty thousand jobs a year out of London, new high-rise office buildings were attracting forty thousand new jobs to the area (A provisional stop to new office construction was ordered in November 1964).

Among the worst sufferers from bad housing have been colored immigrants. In London, "colored" means "non-white," and prejudice and exploitation affects Indians, Pakistanis and other Orientals as well as Negroes. After World War II, immigrants from Commonwealth countries began streaming into Britain and by 1965 there were more than two million of them. About one million of these, two per cent of the population, were non-white. Although they have taken on the menial jobs the white natives reject, as hospital orderlies and subway sweepers, for example, there is a flourishing prejudice against them. Some public houses refuse to serve them, rooming house landladies put up "Sorry, no coloured" signs, and good Socialist world-brotherhood union members refuse to work alongside them. It crept into politics in 1964: "If you want a nigger neighbor vote Labour," was a slogan disowned by the winning Conservative candidate at Smethwick.

It was considered an act of daring, if not of downright democracy, when a Pall Mall club, unable to replenish its stock of comfortably rude old family retainers at low wages with no tips,

327

actually hired Negroes as servants. The club custom of granting honorary membership to Ambassadors serving in London was curtailed with "little republics sprouting like mushrooms in all directions, but particularly in Africa."

The area around Notting Hill is remarkably piebald, very good and very bad neighborhoods scattered with no apparent reason. Notting Hill Gate becomes Holland Park Avenue, off which rise Campden Hill and Holland Park, containing some of the best housing in all London. Campden Hill clings to the rustic, with many gardens and with cottages clinging to the hillside, some occasionally pink or blue, with artists' studios and professors' studies, picturesque, reposeful and expensive. The street named Campden Hill, with its nineteenth-century mansions, was once known as "the Dukeries," owing to a surfeit of authentic coronets in the neighborhood.

There is a park called Holland Park here, its northern reaches really quite wild and opening onto the lawns of Holland House. Although Hitler's bombers left only one wing standing, that wing is part of a Jacobean country mansion, built in 1607 by James I's Chancellor of the Exchequer and Keeper of Hyde Park. The Chancellor's son-in-law was the first Lord Holland. The widow of the third earl married Joseph Addison, who brought to the gabled house such friends as Swift and Pope and enough brandy to kill him, which it did.

Henry Fox bought the house from the family in 1768, and when elevated to the peerage revived the lapsed Holland title. In a notoriously corrupt time, Fox was notorious for corruption. Struck but amazingly uninjured in a pistol duel, he cried, "Egad, sir! It would have been all over with me had we not charged our weapons with Government powder."

When this first Lord Holland (the originals were earls, Fox was a baron) lay seriously ill, George Selwyn came to call, but was turned away. Selwyn loved executions and deathbed scenes, and Lord Holland gave instructions that if Selwyn called again he was to be shown up at once. "If I am alive I shall be delighted to see him and if I am dead he will be delighted to see me."

The wife of the third Lord Holland (second set) ruled as a commanding hostess from the reign of George III on into that of

Victoria. Her guest list was quite overwhelming, including Metternich, Talleyrand, Humboldt, Canova, Sydney Smith, Wordsworth, Sir Walter Scott, Tom Moore, James Fenimore Cooper, Madame de Staël. Macaulay described her as "a bold-looking woman with the remains of a fine person and the air of Queen Elizabeth."

At her dinner table a cross-eyed lady asked Talleyrand how political affairs were going. He replied, "*Comme vous voyez, Madame.*"

The London municipal government bought the house and its grounds in 1951, restored the wing, and tucked into a nearby corner a Youth Hostel. At the bottom of Holland Park is Kensington High Street and the Commonwealth Institute. The Institute is an 1887 commemoration of Victoria's Golden Jubilee in a 1962 building. Under its copper-sheathed roof ("five interconnected hyperbolic parabolas"), films on the Commonwealth are shown daily. There is an exhibition gallery, a reading room and a restaurant, and admittance is free.

Southward and eastward from here stretch hundreds and hundreds of acres of gentility, a good deal of it shabby, a considerable part of it architecturally pompous and embarrassing, bits of it extremely elegant. Around Earl's Court Road and Edwardes Square, the young of the Commonwealth can be seen in relaxed garb, gabbing and guzzling, sometimes even at outdoor cafés. Antique shops, curio shops, bookshops proceed up Kensington Church Street off which are lanes (Church Walk, Duke's Lane) full of little shops and little cottages of great charm, age, and decorum.

Where Kensington Church Street meets Kensington High Street are several large department stores. One of these, Barker's, has nobly forborne shoving its bulk any further down Young Street, thus preserving Thackeray's two-and-a-half double-bow-fronted brick house. Here he wrote *Vanity Fair*, *Pendennis* and *Esmond* before moving on to the glories of Palace Green. Kensington Square was planted here about 1700 in the midst of open fields to create an urban adjunct to the Court of William III in Kensington Palace. Many of the houses, though altered by time

329

and owner's whim, are original. Talleyrand lived at No. 11 from
1792 to 1794, and at No. 18 John Stuart Mill lived 1837–1851.

> John Stuart Mill
> By a mighty effort of will
> Overcame his natural bonhomie
> And wrote *Principles of Political Economy.*

At the edge of Kensington Gardens is Palace Green, which
changes its name but not its style as it runs (not the best word for
it) to meet Notting Hill Gate. This is the street most suburbanites
eventually persuade themselves that they live on, a street of little
traffic, broad lawns, noble trees and well-kept mansions. It is in
fact a private street laid out in 1843 and there are gates and gatekeepers at each end.

The house Thackeray designed for himself is an 1860 one-man
Georgian revival before the fashion began. Next to it is a low cottage with painter's studio attached, the property almost hidden
from the road by a sprangly wall of wild bushes. The name
changes to Kensington Palace Gardens and the long row of Edwardian mansions begins. Most of these big houses are occupied
by diplomatic offices and diplomats' residences. The English scene
is livened by the sight of sari-clad women carrying shopping
bags to market and of Eastern European men possibly bent on
the same errand, but looking tense and mysterious. The gates
have not kept out the change sweeping London: No. 8, a glass and
concrete structure, opened in 1965 as the nearly most expensive
flats in London.

From the private street across a mowed field appears the homey
façade of Kensington Palace, provisional home of the London
Museum and also the home of Princess Margaret and her family.
The palace contains portions of the original 1661 mansion built
for a man who was later the Earl of Nottingham, but who at the
time bore, with equanimity, the name of Heneage Finch.

William III bought the place in 1689, had it enlarged by Sir
Christopher Wren, and after him George I had it enlarged again,
by William Kent. The 1704 Orangery, very likely a Wren work,
is architecturally more handsome than the palace, but the palace
is a warmly handsome old place.

This is where Victoria lived when she learned that she was Queen. As a mere princess she used to take democratic but supervised strolls along the Broad Walk in the gardens. The statue of Victoria at the path to the park is by her daughter.

Opposite the south side of the Gardens, between Palace Gate and Queen's Gate, is a little nest of curved streets called Hyde Park Gate. The architecture along these pleasant lanes ranges from bulky apartment buildings to small country cottages. Sir Jacob Epstein, the sculptor, died here in 1959 and Sir Winston Churchill, the warrior, died here in 1965.

East of Queen's Gate the eye is fatally drawn to a monument in the park: the Albert Memorial. Sir William Eden was never Foreign Minister nor Prime Minister nor even a peer like his son Anthony, but he made his contribution: he wished to see all the bad architects of Britain burned at the foot of the Albert Memorial.

The seventeenth-century engraver tried to make something grandiose of homey Kensington Palace.

It is probably the best-known work of art in Britain, if for no other reason than the loud loathing which so many twentieth-century beholders have expressed for it.

Built 1863-1872, it is 175 feet high with 175 figures at least life-size. Two dozen 200-foot-wide steps lead up to a Gothic spire sheltering a gilded gunmetal statue of Prince Albert (seated, but nonetheless 14 feet high) reading a book. The tome is neither the Bible nor the *Almanach de Gotha*, but one of the four volumes of the catalogue of the Great Exhibition of 1851. There is lots of marble, gold, enamel and general glitter. The whole thing, despite the snickers, is an impressive memorial and one contemporary in every way to its time, "improving" on the past, rapt with progress but cognizant of heritage.

A true Wonder of the Age, the Crystal Palace in Hyde Park.

The memorial marks the site of the Great Exhibition, the very first World's Fair, an idea of Albert's. Queen Victoria wrote to her uncle Leopold of Belgium of ". . . the triumph of my beloved Albert . . . It was the *happiest*, *proudest* day of my life . . ."

The remarkable iron and glass building created by Sir Joseph Paxton to house the Exhibition was rightly called the Crystal Palace. After the exhibition closed it was moved to the outskirts and reerected at Sydenham Hill, which then became known fairly generally as Crystal Palace — and is still, although Paxton's marvelous contraption was destroyed by fire in 1936.

The Exhibition was more than just a successful show, though that it certainly was: it had far-reaching cultural success and stimulated international exchange of ideas and design. It also provoked imitation exhibits, notably by Napoleon III in Paris.

It also made money, lots of money, almost a million 1851 dollars' net profit. The Exhibition Commissioners used some of the money to buy Gore House and a surrounding eighty acres, which they still own, and which is a cultural center any modern town planner can admire. It contains five colleges, four museums and a concert hall.

The elliptical Albert Hall (Royal Albert Hall of Arts and Sciences), which can hold eight thousand spectators under its dome,

When the Great Exhibition opened, Victoria wrote of "the triumph of my beloved Albert."

is on the site of Gore House, whose ménage would have affronted Queen Victoria had anyone told her about it. The lady of the house was Lady Marguerite Blessington, initially Maggie Powers of County Tipperary.

She came to Gore House at the age of forty-seven, the widow of the first Earl of Blessington and the patroness of Albert Guillaume Gabriel, Comte d' Orsay, age thirty-five. The Count was the husband of Lady Blessington's stepdaughter. He lived in a cottage next door, but had a painter's studio in Gore House. A big gambler at Crockford's and a Continental dandy ("resplendent as a diamond beetle," said Jane Welsh Carlyle).

To the dinner parties of this couple came the Duke of Wellington, Lord Brougham, Sir Edwin Landseer, Tom Moore, Walter Savage Landor ("who never used and/or"), Thackeray and Dickens as senior lions. When the Blessington fortune was finally gone, the Count began doing paintings and drawings for money.

As the bailiffs moved in, the Count moved out. In 1859, Lady Blessington auctioned off what she could and followed him to Paris, where she died in 1852, the year the Commissioners of the Exhibition bought the house.

The Albert Hall is the scene of concerts (especially the Promenade Concerts), boxing matches, political rallies, balls.

Profits from the Great Exhibition of 1851 provided the land for the Albert Hall.

To the right, facing the hall, is the 1964 building of the Royal College of Art, gray, solid and uncommunicative as a dropped boulder, and behind it, still as pert as a pansy is the Royal College of Organists, the name of which is lettered shop-fashion in gold leaf on the transom. The door itself is pale blue, and two dozen red panels are stuck on to the pale cream stucco of the façade. On the red panels are sgraffiti in blue and cream and across the top of the building a frieze of happy Arcadian musicmakers dance. Out of this delightful confection — designed by a Lieutenant of the Royal Engineers in 1875 — organ music vibrates into the open spaces among the buildings.

The main open space is a sort of *cour d'honneur* behind the Albert Hall with yet another memorial statue of the Prince Consort (ermine collar courtesy Albert Hall pigeons) looking out over a very grand staircase. To the left is one of the first apartment buildings constructed in London, the 1879 Albert Hall Mansions. Again the impulse that produced *Alice in Wonderland*, solid but slightly daft, highly personal and anti-stuffy.

At the foot of the grand staircase, in Prince Consort Road, are the Royal College of Music, the Royal School of Mines, and some of the buildings of the Imperial College of Science. The street running past the Albert Mansions makes a downhill S passing the rear of the Royal Geographic Society (museum open to public). Between curving cliffs of red brick, it is a Victorian futuristic landscape. South toward Cromwell Road are the museums of Natural History, Geology, Science, and the Victoria and Albert Museum. There is a whole school of buildings completed in the late 1960's for the Imperial College of Science and Technology, incorporating other colleges, affiliated with London University, and one of three British Special Institutions for Scientific and Technological Education and Research (which, archly, spells SISTER). As such, it receives special funds and facilities from the government, with emphasis on graduate study and advanced research.

Back up atop the slope where the park runs, Kensington Gore has meanwhile turned into Knightsbridge and is going smartly past the Household Cavalry Barracks toward Hyde Park Corner. Not long after passing the barracks, it encounters Knightsbridge

Green, where Sloane Street and the Brompton Road wait to meet it ("Daaaaahhhling!"). The Green itself has been reduced to a small grass patch with fountain. Tattersall's horse room, a landmark for generations, has given way to a modern pub boldly called Tattersall's. Until mid-1966 Tom Hill carried on the sale of classic riding gear (including Tattersall waistcoats) just as if the horsy set still thronged the streetcorner.

The entrance to Hyde Park passes under ungainly Bowater House of 1959. Oxford students thought this building so crass they left their cloisters to come here and picket against ugliness. Since those days so many offensive erections have appeared in London that the combined student bodies of Oxford and Cambridge would not suffice to man the picket lines.

Editorial comment in 1964:

> The British are a visually uneducated people. The developers and the planning committees are genuinely blind to the horrors they promote or permit, and the public often seems indifferent.
> — *Guardian*

> Commercial buildings are dull when they are not ugly. . . . The appearance of perhaps ten per cent of postwar council housing is admirable, the rest indifferent to poor. Nor is private building much better. . . . In towns new housing is extremely expensive and generally without distinction.
> — *Sunday Times*

This crossroads and its branches, like those in the City, smell of money. But this is a different perfume: it is the smell of money being spent, not made. Of course, the luxury shops which here abound do make money, but with great art do so invisibly and odorlessly.

Symbolic of Knightsbridge is Harrods' turn-of-the-century pink terra-cotta emporium. Writer Beatrice Bishop calls the store "an object lesson in opulence without ostentation." Remarking the women shoppers who all seem to be tall and elegant, "with tall, somewhat gauche daughters," she observes, "but they are merely ideal and do not exclude the rest of us."

The cable address of the store is EVERYTHING, LONDON, and for families of its category, that is just what it is. Buying or selling a house? Harrods run a real-estate agency. Storing or shipping household goods? Theater tickets? A nice juicy steak to cook at home? A grill to cook it on? A safe deposit for valuables? Reservations for wintering in the Canary Islands? Canaries for your winter garden? A family portrait to restore? They'll do it.

One women's editor gushed, "They will locate a school for you, provide your outfit, take you there, and later will design your trousseau, arrange your wedding, give your entertainments for you, bank your money, buy your shares, dress you, cater for your recreations . . . and erect a monument to you when you are no longer in this world." Cheap it isn't. This general department store began in 1849 as a tiny Brompton Road grocery operated by Digby Harrod.

Stretching away from here are the residences of a good many customers of Harrods and the other impressive shops. These persons reside around elegant and beautifully kept squares, in small soigné lanes and mews as well as on regal avenues. This is the Good Life for thousands of well-off Londoners.

Down the Brompton Road on the way to that marvelous national attic of precious odds and ends — the Victoria and Albert Museum — one can perambulate Trevor, Montpelier and Brompton Squares, all small and enviable in the extreme, heavy with trees and lined with small, distinctive houses where, from the outside at least, nothing would ever seem to go wrong.

The way of life can be glimpsed on a stroll from Knightsbridge through Rutland Gate (some rather forbidding mansions at first and then, after a wasp-waist, more of Rutland Gate, a right turn into Ennismore Garden Mews, which leads into the hidden churchyard of Holy Trinity. The walk through the churchyard leads into a cobbled lane called Cottage Place, which leads timidly out of calm and curried byways into the bustling Brompton Road.

THE LONDON OF
THE LAST BUTLERS

*Belgravia — Pimlico — Smith Square, Archer's church, La-
bour and Conservative Headquarters — The Tate*

BELGRAVIA is still an impressively impressive address.
True, most of the palatial residences are occupied by clubs
or institutions or else are cut up discreetly into apartments.
There are but few families able to occupy whole houses with the
platoons of servants essential to the order and ease consonant
with such grandeur.

The borders, as much mental as physical, are south from
Knightsbridge to Eaton Square, west from Grosvenor Place to
Sloane Street. The area is not quite believeable: some thirty streets
interspersed with garden squares and crescents, almost solidly
lined with mansions and their dependencies.

Belgravia's history favors the idea of unreality too: in 1824 it
was all fields and bogs, and in 1826 its squares were laid out
and several buildings already occupied. London owes much of its
lofty socio-topographic heritage to the building speculator, which
today is an unkind thing to call anyone, considering prices and
building standards. This acreage belonged to Lord Grosvenor,
whose second title was Viscount Belgrave, and who became,
thirty years later, Duke of Westminster.

When Lord Grosvenor obtained permission from Parliament
to develop the site, the contract for the work went to builder
Thomas Cubitt. It was not a promising site, but being the man he
was, Cubitt made it both desirable and lucrative. Cubitt had gone
to India as a ship's joiner when he was nineteen, and on his return invested his savings in a London carpentry shop. He prospered, expanded and went into the building trade on a scale

338

which would be considerable even today. He undertook the development of early Bloomsbury squares, and when he embarked on the Belgravia project, was engaged in making the St. Katherine Docks just below the Tower of London.

Cubitt scooped the squishy clay off the Belgrave bogs and made bricks of it. Over the gravel the scoops had exposed he then dumped earth, brought by barge from his dock excavations downstream.

The most imposing set piece in this movie-set corner of London is big (almost ten acres) Belgrave Square, all pillars, pilasters, balustrades and stucco. At each corner of the square an especially overpowering mansion is set cater-cornered, facing the center of the garden. The other houses run in long ranges, much on the Nash principal, given a sense of variety within a stated unity.

The Austrian, Norwegian, Portuguese, Spanish, Turkish and German Embassies are on the Square, along with the Spiritualist Association, the Royal College of Veterinary Surgeons, the Nature Conservancy, the Forum Club, the Society of Chemical Industry, the No. 10 Club and the residence of the Maharajah of Cooch-Behar.

Among those who lived here when the staying was good were the Duke of Norfolk (No. 14), the Duke of Bedford (Nos. 15–16), the Duke of Kent (No. 3) and the Earl of Shaftesbury (No. 5).

The back streets are in their way as fascinating as the noble groves of aristocracy in this quarter. Those who duck into the first opening to the right off Wilton Place will discover what so many Londoners think they have found in Shepherd Market. This is Kinnerton Street, virtually hidden, not widely known, a long alley whose charm is not obliterated by the chintzing up of its little two-story houses, most of them former stables with stablemen's quarters above the carriage room.

For pub-studiers Kinnerton Street has two *trouvailles*. The Nag's Head (locally called Len Cole's) has its main bar below street level. The upstairs bar, with a comfortable capacity of three, seems capable of absorbing half the neighborhood, a thing for which every good local must develop a facility. The beer pulls are made of real Chelsea China. The other Kinnerton Street pub

339

is really in Groom Place and is called the Horse and Groom. Its layout hasn't changed since it served grooms (despite the name, horses waited outside).*

At the bottom of Kinnerton Street is Motcomb Street, containing two buildings especially cherished by Belgravians. One has giant Doric columns standing sentry across its façade, the other is less austere, with even more Graeco-Roman decorations on it. Both are from about 1830, both are sober, monumental buildings and both are furniture storage houses.

It is two long blocks from the bottom of Belgrave Square to Eaton Square. This distinguished (by its lofty rents and titled tenants) oblong might be considered one of the biggest in London if King's Road didn't run smack through the center, somewhat like a bowling alley down the middle of a ballroom.

The borders of Belgravia can be stretched a few blocks further south, say as far as Ebury Street, beyond which lies Pimlico, built by Cubitt right after Belgravia, and in much the same style. But after the Grosvenor Canal was drained and became the railroad right-of-way, Pimlico became "the other side of the tracks." It dwindled toward slumdom. Its population was, however, working, not starving class. Since the housing shortage Pimlico has been rediscovered by the sort of people for whom it was originally built. In this period London land prices have risen somewhat (from $24,640 an acre in 1951 to $173,040 an acre in 1965). The newcomers have the money to restore the old houses and inject modern plumbing and heating. The very best houses in Pimlico have beautiful river views, balconies, parks, and they are not opened to the rich newcomers. These are council flats built for the longtime neighborhood folk by the Westminster City Council on bombed sites. The project, named Churchill Gardens, was begun in 1946, the first British effort at a planned community with some buildings as high as eleven stories and some single houses, all heated by surplus hot water from the Battersea power station across the river. Population about 5500. Twenty years later, the development remains a model of its kind and one of the best in London.

* In Wilton Row, on the other side of Wilton Crescent, is another ex-coachmen's pub, rather gussied-up, but cozy and full of rather grand neighborhood folk. This is the Grenadier.

The name Pimlico? One group of explainers endorses a drink whose recipe is lost; another supports a tavernkeeper, Ben Pimlico, and another contends the name was imported along with native mahogany from Honduras. At any rate, the London meaning of Pimlico is changing at this time.

Between Belgravia, Pimlico and Westminster (officially, it is all Westminster, of course) Victoria Station stands, only about five blocks from Buckingham Palace. One Londoner commented, "Here railway architecture met its Waterloo."

Beyond the station, Victoria Street is rebuilding, eliminating a good deal of scurf which has accumulated over the years, making a less distressing setting for the 1903 Westminster Cathedral, the chief church of Roman Catholicism in this country. Red brick, with bands of stone, it is a Byzantine church with a soaring (284 feet) campanile. It has been called "the finest church that has been built for centuries," and it grows in importance and beauty as the embellishment of its interior with marbles and mosaics continues. In other words, one is privileged to experience the growth of a great monument.

That modern tower rearing almost directly south on the river bank is the 34-floor Vickers building, for a moment in 1963 the tallest structure in the country. With concave and convex walls (not at the same time on the same wall), decorative elements surrounding the tower at different levels, and good landscaping, it is exciting (for London), contemporary, and a decoration rather than a desecration.

Eastward past the tower and first turning on the left after Lambeth Bridge is one of those public places concealed from public view which Londoners assume that absolutely everybody must be familiar with: Smith Square. Most of those who do know all about Smith Square pretend that no one knows who Smith was, that perhaps it was somebody famous enough to name a square for, but who preferred to go under the name of Smith. Unfortunately, somebody does know who Smith was, because Smith, Sir James J., built the square early in the eighteenth century and named it for himself.

The north and west sides contain some winsome original houses, the other two sides have been rebuilt in the current century. This is one of the smallest London squares and the center of it is "filled — one might say stuffed" with the second of Queen Anne's fifty churches.

Designed by James Archer, it was built 1713–1728, a daring piece of British baroque. Its originality, especially its four towers, wasn't the sort that Victorians liked and they quite successfully implanted the idea that the whole thing was a bad joke. The utterly false anecdote of its design is still ho-ho-ho-ly repeated: Queen Anne, rejecting Archer's plan, kicked over her footstool and said, "Make it look like that!" Such folk were not prostrated at the news that the Germans had wrecked the church. Since 1941 it has stood derelict, its steps moss-grown, its clock hands pointing to seven, marking the hour it was bombed, and its few friends out raising money for its restoration.

In one corner of Smith Square stands Labor Party headquarters, and in the other, 20 yards away, stands the Conservative & Unionist Central Office. The Laborites have Victorian brick with a broad porch of double columns, the Tories have a severe neo-Georgian of much paler brick. The Conservatives are content with a small brass plaque outside the door. The Laborites are content to say nothing. However, the pediment of Labor's temple is inscribed in large letters TRANSPORT HOUSE, indicating that the building is property of the Transport and General Workers Union, the world's largest. With this group the Labour Party shares premises both political and physical.

There's a traffic sign outside Transport House which says "Turn Left One Way Only." But this apt instruction is supplemented by an arrow pointing toward Conservative Headquarters.

The riverside from here on upstream to Vauxhall Bridge is known as Millbank, there having been a mill on the bank. Between the Queen Alexandra Hospital and the Royal Medical Corps barracks stands the Tate Gallery, a pushed-about little bastard which finally grew to be big — and legitimate.

In 1890 sugar magnate Henry Tate gave sixty-five paintings to the nation. After making a tremendous fight to have the building approved, he then paid the construction costs himself. He added new galleries in 1899, and between 1910 and 1937, the Duveen family paid for the construction of three more galleries.

342

The National Gallery and the Royal Academy made life as hard as possible for the poor Tate and when anything really good showed up that the National wanted, the National got it. Finally in 1955 the Tate became master of its own fate. In the first fifty-eight years of is existence it received less than one thousand pounds a year for new purchases. The public reacted as coldly as the authorities, and in the 1930's the first duty of the guards after opening the doors was to spin the turnstiles to clock fictitious attendance.

In the 1960's, especially, for such exhibits as the Picasso retrospective, the turnstiles didn't turn fast enough for the eager public. The collection in 1965 included four thousand British paintings, more than three hundred modern foreign works and three hundred and sixty pieces of sculpture. The oldest painting dates from Henry VIII, and the newest is hardly dry. With its tremendous range and its talent for making friends, the Tate is one of the liveliest and one of the biggest museums of art in the world.

It is, in fact, too big a museum to stay within its walls, and its Trustees asked for proposals in 1964 for an extension. The best

The Tate Gallery now occupies the site of this Thames-side penitentiary.

solution seemed to be to rip off the Edwardian façade and push toward the river, but there were outcries from artists and architects that today's bore is posterity's treasure. Approval for any plan by the Ministry of Public Building and Works was not forthcoming by mid-1966.

The site was formerly occupied by another dream come true. This was the Millbank Penitentiary completed in 1821 to the plans of Jeremy Bentham, who among his other interests included advocacy of prison reform. It was certainly big — eleven hundred single cells on eighteen acres of ground, six pentagonal courts around a central hexagonal court. It was demolished in 1890 and traces of the old walls can still be seen in the streets around the Tate.

THE LONDON OF
OSCAR WILDE

Chelsea origins and geography — Cheyne Walk and Row, notable residences — "Yacht Basin" — Physic Gardens — Tite Street — Royal Hospital — The King's Road, the Chelsea Kick — Sloane Square and Street

AT FIRST sight Chelsea seems to be all pubs and private addresses. However, there are some public sights much worth seeing, and there is the curious Chelsea beat which one might be able to discern — Chelsea through its history has been a parade ground for the avant garde.

The southern boundary is the Thames. The river view is lovely and its river walks uncrowded. The riverside has Wren's Royal Hospital, several groups of large and more or less historic houses, the Apothecaries' Garden, three nice pubs (people bring their drinks out of doors on sunny Sundays), three nice bridges and a covey of houseboats. It has a heartwarming summer view, especially at night, of Battersea Park across the water with its lights and occasional breeze-borne snatches of music. The river is wider here than anywhere else above the Pool of London. It rises high along the Embankment walls, flowing deep and swift and bearing an entertaining variety of water traffic.

Chelsea got its name through the Saxon word *ceosol*, referring to the gravel of the river banks. In the thirteenth century these banks were fraught with bishops in their episcopal palaces (Fulham Palace, just upstream, is still there).

After the bishops, a saint came to Chelsea, Sir Thomas More. Son of a Judge of the King's Bench, More was a page to the Archbishop of Canterbury, and at age seventeen was sent to Ox-

345

ford, then to Lincoln's Inn. In 1501, at twenty-one, he became a Member of Parliament, where he so eloquently opposed a subsidy requested by Henry VII that the Commons actually refused the money. In 1516 he wrote *Utopia*. In 1520, he became Speaker of the House, in 1523, Chancellor of the Exchequer under Henry VIII (and moved to Chelsea). In 1529 he became Lord Chancellor in place of Cardinal Wolsey, and in 1532 was beheaded.

In spite of his duties of state, More's life in Chelsea beside the Thames was idyllic, with his family, his garden, his menagerie and guests such as Erasmus and Holbein. There remains behind only one souvenir, his chapel in Chelsea Old Church. When the clearing crews removed the rubble from the bombed church, they found the 1528 chapel unharmed. Around it, the church was restored.

Henry VIII took over the Manor of Chelsea and built a large country house on what is now Cheyne Walk when Elizabeth was four years old (1537). Anne of Cleves, the wife who got away from both Henry and the headsman, lived out her life here until 1557. And Henry's widow, Catherine Parr, lived here during the regency of the Duke of Somerset for young Edward VI.

The single medieval structure left in Chelsea isn't a Chelsea building at all. Moved from Bishopsgate in the City to this Embankment in 1910, it was the Great Hall of Crosby Place. Crosby was a fifteenth-century baronet, London Sheriff, and City Member of Parliament. The elegant hammer-beam roof of his hall now shelters dining members of the British Federation of University Women (the hall is open to the public before and after lunch).

Long after Sir Thomas More, his manor house was occupied by Sir Hans Sloane, who bought the Lordship of the Manor (and the manor of Chelsea itself, of course) from William Cheyne in 1712. As a young man Sloane studied in the Chelsea Physic Garden and then went to both the Sorbonne and Leyden in the same year, 1683, emerging with his medical degree. From 1694 to 1730, he was Physician to Christ's Hospital, and since he had a wealthy wife, always returned his salary to the hospital. He was the first physician to be made a baronet. As owner of Chelsea, he gave the Apothecaries the land on which their garden of medicinal herbs grew (still grow). His private museum of antiquities, gems, ores, botanical specimens and stuffed animals became the nucleus of the British Museum.

Sir Hans's daughter married the second Baron Cadogan of Oakley. (Oakley Street runs to Albert Bridge. There is a Cadogan Gardens, Square, Street and Lane, a Hans Crescent, Road, Place and a Sloane Square, Street, Terrace and Avenue.) The manor house was demolished in 1740; Beaufort Street runs across its site.

At the far western end of Chelsea is a modest white waterfront cottage at 119 Cheyne Walk. Here a Mr. Booth — neighbors called him Admiral Booth — lived from 1846 until his death in 1851. Later people learned the Admiral was really the great British painter Joseph Mallord William Turner, who had taken the name of the lady into whose house he had moved.

Between the late Admiral's and Battersea Bridge the fleet of houseboats is moored. The boat dwellers, who love telling stories about each other's eccentricities, report only one drawback in their riparian existence: when the tide ebbs power on the telephone line is apt to do the same.

On the inland side of Cheyne Walk (Nos. 95–100) is Lindley House, dating from 1675, although the roof was put on in the eighteenth century when Count Zinzendorf bought it for the headquarters of the Moravian movement in England. Whistler, when he first came to England, lived here for a few years. Whistler lived up and down the block in several houses for a few years each, rather like the six-year-old who is running away from home but isn't allowed to cross the street by himself. The two great engineers Sir Marc Brunel and son Isambard Kingdom Brunel also dwelt in Lindley House.

East of Beaufort Street begins the stretch of fine houses which the breadth and serenity of the river has provoked. Chelsea Old Church is here, and after Lawrence Street (Tobias Smollett lived in Lawrence House 1749–1765, the street passing over the buried foundations) there is what the British call a block of flats. In flat 21 Henry James died in 1916. In 1965 one of the doormen was certain that this was not at all the house: "Been here all me life. Know all the gentlemen including the foreigners, and never heard of no Mr. Jymes." The building is called Carlyle Mansions and is just about as crusty in appearance as the old historian was in manner.

Cheyne Row (pronounced chain-y) comes down into Cheyne Walk just here, and in the Row at No. 24 Thomas Carlyle lived for almost fifty years (1834–1881), and died at the age of eighty-six. The house was built in 1708 and Carlyle thought it "eminent, antique," but one of his visitors, a philosopher named Frederic Harrison, noted, "He seems to live in a very dismal corner of this foul city . . . in that alley where one might expect to find one's washerwomen." One found Dickens, Chopin, Tennyson and Emerson visiting, at any rate. In search of light and quiet, Carlyle had a skylit double-walled room built in the attic. The house is open to visitors, having been bought by public subscription in 1895, now in the hands of the National Trust. It was Leigh Hunt, living in Upper Cheyne Row at the time, who found the house for the Carlyles, and when embraced by Jane Welsh Carlyle for bringing some happy piece of news, fluttered home and wrote "Jenny Kissed Me."

Most of the houses along Cheyne Walk here are early Georgian (1718). At No. 4 George Eliot (who remembers her name was Mary Ann Evans?), after almost a quarter of a century of Living in Sin (and in St. John's Wood) with G. H. Lewes, who died in 1878, came here as a respectable married woman. In 1879 she married Mr. Lewes's best friend, J. W. Cross. The couple moved into the house in November, went to a Covent Garden concert the first night. Mrs. Cross caught a chill and died three weeks later.

At that time Dante Gabriel Rossetti was living up the Walk at No. 15, with his wombat and Brahman bull in the overgrown garden and Fanny Cornforth, awkwardly titled Mrs. Hughes at the time, as his hostess. Whistler lived at No. 21 and at No. 74, where he not only lived, but died too.

After the Walk ends, the river road is called Chelsea Embankment. The embankment was made in 1871 and its houses date from then. Most of this stretch is a tour-de-force by Norman Shaw, possibly the most interesting and enduring of the Victorian London architects.

The Chelsea Physic Gardens, four acres rented from the Cheynes in 1673, later deeded to the Apothecaries by Sir Hans Sloane, appear here. Every year somebody makes an astonishing discovery about this walled garden. It is always the same discovery — seed sent from here was planted to start cotton-growing in the American South. The garden still operates as a botanical research station.

Along its eastern edge Swan Walk runs inland, for the second half of its length one of the hypnotic streets in London. Here two eighteenth-century cottages sit at the bottom of their gardens refusing to admit that the town has changed at all since the time those people across the street sent those cotton seeds to the colonies.

Tite Street is the next to make its way to the Embankment. It comes down from Tedworth Square, where Mark Twain lived in a house just about like the ones in Hartford, Connecticut.

Tite Street is Oscar Wilde's street, and it couldn't have been all that comfortable for him even before the scandal because of all the noise of the new buildings going up, especially the Victoria Hospital for Children immediately across the way. Most of the houses are quite romantic, designed around big painting studios, open and easy (Whistler lived in three of these at various times, including a few months in No. 35 which was built for him), but wife and child and Wilde lived, from 1884 until his trial in 1895, in one of a row of identical, tall, thin brick houses. When Mrs. Wilde was obliged to sell off the contents of the house, people bid ridiculously low prices on most items and stole a good many others. John Singer Sargent died at No. 31, where he had lived for twenty-four years.

After Tite Street eastward along the river the grounds of the Royal Hospital stretch for more than a quarter of a mile to Chelsea Bridge.

Charles II, taking example from Louis XIV, established the hospital in 1682 to care for invalid pensioners of the recently formed Regular Army. The broad lawns and the tree-guarded gardens are peopled by pensioners in bright scarlet coats designed in Marlborough's day. The pensioners rightly regard themselves as retired warriors with the complete freedom of the community, including the odd free pint in the pub; the people of Chelsea regard them more as large, responsive household pets, elderly but still decorative.

The grounds are as immaculately kept as the pensioners and are open to a public which makes itself genteelly at home. From the Embankment, the buildings seem very pleasant, but seen close up they are rich and rather monumental. They should be impressive, since they are the work of Sir Christopher Wren and Robert Adam. Grinling Gibbons added some touches, including the statue of the founder. Every May 29 the four hundred pensioners (or as many as are fit) muster in the forecourt to honor Charles II. The day is known as Oak Apple Day (Americans would call it Acorn Day) to mark Charles's escape from Cromwellian troops who searched below while he successfully hid in his oak.

The grounds are annually transformed by the Chelsea Flower Show, held here under canvas, and usually opened by the Sovereign. It is not only a major social event, but since almost every living Englishman is at heart a gardener, it takes on an importance somewhat stunning to the visiting foreigner.

Running opposite the top of the hospital grounds is St. Leonard's Terrace, one of the best of Chelsea's Georgian house rows (1765). From here Royal Avenue thrusts northward, broad and tree-lined. With its four rows of plane trees it was planned in 1692 to link the Royal Hospital with the Royal Palace of Kensington.

Alas, it never got further than the King's Road, one block away. Today it is privately owned and its regal pretensions come to an end facing a shop emblazoned with the royal coat of arms. The shop window is filled with bathroom fixtures. Beneath the gilded and enameled Lion and Unicorn the legend reads: "Thomas Crapper, by Appointment to His Majesty George V, Sanitary Engineer."

King's Road, a series of footpaths and lanes through the farm fields, was made into a carriage road to give Charles II a decent route to Hampton Court Palace upstream, and the King's Road it remained, reserved to the King, his men and his friends, until 1830. It is the Main Street of Chelsea, and there are plans to rescue it from the seediness which prevails in spite of its bright shop windows and traditional pub façades. The side streets and the squares leading off King's Road go from the artist's atelier to the Victorian cliff dwelling. Chelsea was badly bombed, and many of the local working folk subsequently found modern housing in council flats erected on bombed sites. Into the former workmen's cottages, cracked and peeling two-story affairs, have moved increasingly wealthy (or spendthrift) tenants. Though the buildings in themselves are devoid of charm, they have had charm energetically appliquéd all over them. There is a powerful lot of "cute" — what some Britons call "twee" — in Chelsea.

There are also stretches of individual brick suburbia and here and there rows of Georgian and Regency, broken by apartment buildings from various vacuous periods of the twentieth century. There are occasional grand dwellings and some rare post-Bauhaus constructions. There are some genuinely winsome corners to be discovered as well as some genuinely gruesome ones. All of which makes for good exploring, since if it is not around this corner it will be around the next, the sight worth stumbling upon.

However, the important factor in Chelsea is not its distinctive and occasionally distinguished appearance, but its people. Not only those who make their homes here but those who reside elsewhere and come here to the pubs and restaurants and coffeehouses to live.

It is a mélange of arts, letters, theater and those liberal professions which give play to a flair for self-dramatization and vanity inflation. And there are always those not really in the swim but who almost participate by standing on the banks proffering warm towels and cool drinks.

In the 1960's the commercial world of fashion was important to Chelsea — designers, retailers, models and photographers — and out of it came an electric effect on national dress similar to that *les Incroyables* had in Paris a hundred and fifty years earlier.

British commentators were happy that the inventive Chelsea young were giving something fresh and gay to the appearance of the whole Western world. In reality, what was happening was that they were catching up to the rest. The traditional dowdiness of the British female was attacked largely through adoption of bases long ago laid in America and Scandinavia: meticulous

351

cleanliness mated to a chic casualness of dress. Plus a recognition that girls were not all necessarily cylindrical in shape. The British variation on these basic but hitherto alien themes did find world acceptance.

It was not in dress alone that the Bright Young Things pushed up standards. By their own demands they created a market and with their designs, and their shops and restaurants, they supplied a new market for better food, lighting, furniture, fabric. In the new push for freer, brighter, newer design, sculptors and painters found sudden appreciation for their new departures as well.

The impetus behind the push was different from the optimism of the Victorians which was based on scientific advance and colonial exploitation, and it was different from the feverish patterns of the Lost Generation swimming toward hope through a sea of hopelessness. It was primarily a simple explosion of joy, an innocent rejection of Fog Gray. It was individual enthusiasm sustained by general prosperity.

Certainly, not all this work was done exclusively in Chelsea, but the kick came from a small group of Chelsea folk, and Chelsea remained the center for the new leaders in the new version of the good life. Their enterprise, originality and sharp practical sense had not, by 1966, penetrated to politics or to heavy industry.

King's Road terminates at Sloane Square, where Pimlico and Belgravia lap at the Chelsea borders. Down in the Underground station there is a pub with its entrance on the train platform. It is called the Hole in the Wall. One expert cautions, "At closing time it is advisable to avoid walking too far across the platform . . ."

Also in Sloane Square is the Royal Court Theatre, always the home of the coming revolution which will save the expiring theater. Here Harley Granville-Barker produced the early (1904–1907) plays of George Bernard Shaw. Here, after World War II, the plays of the Angry Young Men opened the eyes and added to the discomforture of what was then called the Establishment.

And also in Sloane Square is the Peter Jones department store, a building which in 1936 gave the mistaken impression that the

London of the future was going to be full of interesting and handsome buildings.

Sloane Street leads from here up to Knightsbridge. Sloane Street is neither Chelsea nor Belgravia nor Brompton nor Knightsbridge but a rich mixture of all four. Rich, as in "money." On the right about halfway up is Cadogan Place, the largest private park in London, about a quarter-mile of sylvan walks, gardens and tennis courts for the tenants of the tall, graceful old houses on the east side of the Place.

From the west emerges Pont Street, noted for its gabled and fretted terra-cotta fantasies, constructed in the 1880's and labeled in the 1930's "Pont Street Dutch," which should be seen, if not believed. On the corner of Pont and Sloane Streets is the Cadogan Hotel, which has spent all the years since 1895 rising above the unfortunate arrest on these premises of Oscar Wilde. Not that the arrest of this person was unfortunate, you understand. But at the Cadogan Hotel! Well . . .

THE LONDON OF
SHERLOCK HOLMES
AT HOME

*Oxford Street shops — Portman Square, horse racing —
Baker Street, Sherlock's homes — Hospitals public and pri-
vate — Harley Street — Regent's Park, Terraces, Canal, Zoo
— Little Venice — Lord's Cricket Ground — Portland Place
London's tallest — Bloomsbury, topographic and intellectual,
a suite of squares, Dickens House, British Museum, London
University, RADA — St. Pancras Station*

SOMEHOW, St. Marylebone (pronounced Sin Marlebun)
has managed to preserve a good deal of its village coherence.
In spite of being officially part of Westminster, and in spite
of the fact that its entire southern border constitutes the biggest
shopping street in the kingdom.

Oxford Street (and Regent Street, which runs off it) accounted
for thirty per cent of all the retail trade of London at last count.
The impetus for all this came from an American, Gordon Sel-
fridge, who opened a grandiose department store here in 1909.
Having sold out to his partner, Marshall Field, in Chicago, the
forty-five-year-old merchandiser found himself idling in London
with an idle fortune. To revive some of the lost Chicago excitement, he built a palace of commerce in a shabby, neglected stretch
of Oxford Street while the rest of London's retailers hummed and
looked discreetly into the middle distance. But the ornate emporium drew crowds of customers, and his Bargain Basement
was a sensational innovation.

The big store towers over Orchard Street, which leads into
Portman Square, named for Lord Portman who owns the ground

and who, until bombed out, lived in what was an eighteenth-century house on the northwest corner. Next to it No. 20 still stands, built by Robert Adam in 1777 for Elizabeth, Countess of Home. Her neighbor, Mrs. Montagu, gave her an additional title, Queen of Hell. Her house has been since 1932 the Courtauld Institute of Art, London University. The interiors are superb eighteenth-century preservations, and the stables at the end of the garden remain as originally built. The house on the other side, No. 21, was designed to make one gentle composition with Home House. The north side of the square retains several of its original eighteenth-century houses, but the east and most of the south side were invaded in the 1920's and 1930's by hulking new buildings.

The installation in Portman Square of an accounting firm, Weatherby's, which moved from Cavendish Square in 1965, marked a major change in a major British preoccupation, horse racing. For 213 years English horse racing had been conducted under the auspices of a private club, the sixty-member Jockey Club, to which Weatherby's acted as Secretary. In 1752 a race was announced in the little market town of Newmarket "for horses the property of the noblemen and gentlemen belonging to the Jockey Club, at the Star & Garter in Pall Mall." The group built its clubhouse, the Coffee Rooms, in Newmarket High Street in the 1750's (they are still there), and used Weatherby's as its London headquarters.

Weatherby's also acts for the National Hunt Committee, keeps the Match Book, the General Stud Book, publishes the Racing Calendar and registers trainers and horses for racing. In 1965 a new control body was established and named the Turf Board, on which the Jockey and National Hunt are members along with representatives from the Betting Levy Board and the government. The Turf Board makes all the policy decisions regarding racing, but their rulings are carried out, as before, by stewards of the two clubs who govern the country's race meetings. Sample policy decision: all horses are one year older on January first, no matter what the date of their actual birth.

After passing down the east side of Portman Square, Orchard Street becomes Baker Street. Sir Edward Baker, a country neighbor of Lord Portman's, helped in developing the property. Until the 1920's, Baker Street went only as far as Marylebone Road, and the remaining leg to Regent's Park was called York Place. When the whole street was renamed Baker Street, the house numbers were changed, which led to conflicting theories about the exact location of mythical 221B, Sherlock Holmes's place. The evidence seems to favor the block between Dorset and Blandford Streets, on the west side, a block that was literally flattened by Hitler's bombers.

Baker Street was for a long time a distinguished address. Mrs. Siddons the actress lived here, Cardinal Wiseman died at No. 15 in 1865, and at No. 120 William Pitt the Younger died. Now the street is almost wholly commercial, but how it looked when Holmes stalked the street can be judged from early nineteenth-century Gloucester Place, which runs parallel one block west.

The High Street of this respectable village is Marylebone Road, running east-west, but the original Marylebone High Street is still to be found, running in quite the opposite sense, and still bending here and there to accommodate commons and farm entrances of the seventeenth century. This was then the village of St. Mary-le-Bourne (the bourne, brook, was the Tyburn).

Buildings began to spread over the fields early in the eighteenth century, and within seventy-five years the whole district was pretty well covered. Cavendish Square was laid out in 1717, and the surrounding streets were named for the daughter of landlord John Holles, Duke of Newcastle, and the family into which she married. Thus Henrietta Place and Holles Place and streets bearing the names and titles of Edward Harley, Earl of Oxford and Mortimer. Their daughter Mary Cavendish Harley married William Bentinck, second Duke of Portland, whence yet more names.

Just east of Baker Street along Marylebone Road is Mme. Tussaud's waxworks, which, when the old lady came over from Paris in 1802, were originally in Baker Street. Next to the waxworks, the London Planetarium. Across the way is the entrance to High Street and on its northwest corner a 1960 office building bearing a plaque struck with characters from Dickens. The building they knocked down in 1958 to erect this new thing was the house where Dickens lived 1839–1851 and wrote *David*

Copperfield, The Old Curiosity Shop, Dombey and Son, A Christmas Carol, Martin Chuzzlewit, Barnaby Rudge.

In the next street, at No. 2 Devonshire Place, Dr. Arthur Conan Doyle had his consulting room. He used to walk here from his lodging in Montagu Place, just behind Baker Street off Dorset. While he waited for patients who rarely came, he began writing the Sherlock Holmes stories, including this sentence from "The Norwood Builder," which sounds like a parody of the Holmes works:

> "You mention your name as if I should recognize it, but beyond the obvious facts that you are a bachelor, a solicitor, a Freemason and an asthmatic, I know nothing whatever about you."

and the famous

> "Excellent!" I cried. "Elementary," said he.

Devonshire Place melts into Upper Wimpole Street as it goes south, and Upper Wimpole descends into plain Wimpole. Tennyson called this bottom part "a long unlovely street," and Elizabeth Barrett, who lived at No. 50 (original house no longer there) described it as "like Newgate turned inside out."

To the contemporary eye Wimpole Street looks dignified, ancient and aesthetically worthwhile. It is an overflow container for medical and dental specialists from Harley Street, the next street east. Its entrance from Marylebone Road is appropriately guarded by the London Clinic, a building which does its best not to be there. Most hospitals discharge an odor of swill and iodoform, and their goods delivery boys are unsightly. Not so with the Clinic, severe and unobtrusive as an haute couture house, one of the most private of private hospitals and one of the most expensive.

Its close neighbor, the small (fifty beds) King Edward VII Hospital on Beaumont Street, is open to former British officers and "distressed gentlewomen." It was probably under the first category that in 1964 Princess Anne and her grandmother, the Queen Mother, were among the patients, along with former Prime Minister Harold Macmillan and Field Marshal Lord Montgomery.

There are other hospitals in the neighborhood which are not only public, but, under the National Health Service, entirely free. National Health cost more than a billion pounds in 1964, or about twenty pounds per head of population. More than half this money went to hospitals, many of which were termed by inspectors and staff members overcrowded, understaffed and out of date to the point of peril. Nevertheless, the record of the NHS since its inception in July, 1948, is impressive, and the health of Britain continues to improve statistically. Not only hospital care, but all medical care, health devices and prescription drugs are supplied free to Britons. Most Harley Street men are specialists, who give, as all doctors do, much of their time to unpaid work, but here in their consultation rooms charge as if no one ever heard of the National Health Service.

Doctors do collect in the area: the General Medical Council in Hallam Street, the Medical Council in Chandos Street, the Royal Society of Medicine in Henrietta Place, and on the edges of Regent's Park the Royal College of Physicians and the Royal

Saved from "improvers" after World War II, Nash's terraces around Regent's Park still grace London.

College of Obstetricians. And this was of course, the home ground of Dr. Watson. And Dr. Conan Doyle.

A block east of Harley Street is the formal entrance into Regent's Park. John Nash's terraces of houses around three sides of this huge park are unique. The grouping of palatial façades around a landscaped park exists nowhere else. The urban residents can have the impression of living in their own stately homes and looking out over their own ancestral acres (with the added fillip of eccentricity, in Cumberland Terrace, of a nightly concert from the Zoo lions). The groupings of colonnaded façades, all in buff stucco, some with friezes and roof-perched statuary, give views from within and vistas everywhere from without. They are distinguished, lofty, civilized. They define the word patrician. They are all on Crown lands, and public outcry prevented the Crown Commissioners from pulling them down after wartime damage, just as public outcry prevented 1930 Crown Commissioners from destroying Nash's Carlton House Terrace.

Nash built only eight of his projected twenty-six villas inside

One of Nash's villas in Regent's Park, fragment of a vast piece of city planning.

the park, and since 1818, four of these have disappeared and been replaced. St. John's Lodge and the Holme just outside the Inner Circle, and Grove House and Hanover Lodge in the northwest corner remain as they were. The American Ambassador lives in one of the newer houses.

Nash did get to install a serpentine lake and a romantic stretch of the commercial Grand Union Canal in which the architect had a more commercial than romantic interest. The trip along this canal is one of the great delights of London (this portion is called Regent's Canal). It is different from any other canal trip, say in Venice or in Amsterdam, and different from anything else one can do in this city. There is a modest sybaritic tingle in being so entertained while being so reposed.

There is one serious risk on this still voyage, however: one might emerge a member of that small band of enthusiasts who want to save the canals of England. At their peak, before railroads came, and then motor highways, there were almost five

The Limehouse entrance from the Thames to the Regent's Canal.

thousand miles of canal in Britain. Now there are two thousand miles, many of them derelict. This canal, made in 1820, bends above central London to emerge at the Thames at Limehouse, six and a half miles away. There are eleven locks, the first of them ninety feet above Thames level, and there's a tunnel under Islington three-quarters of a mile long. The trip offered by the traditional narrowboat *Jason* runs from Little Venice in Paddington, through a tunnel under Edgeware Road (a road best seen from the underside), through the Park, past the Zoo (you can see the animals) up to the locks of Camden Town. The scenery includes noble avenues, woodland scenery, slums and industrial waterfront in a round trip which takes an hour and twenty minutes and which in 1965 cost four shillings.

Little Venice, where the trip begins, is an overlooked happy corner of London (its residents, with a heavy admixture of artists and peers, are grateful for the general oversight). It is easily reached on foot from the Warwick Avenue Underground station, one stop past Paddington Station and fourth from Baker Street on what is, alas, called the Bakerloo Line.

At the cruise departure point off Bloomfield Road are clustered several canal boats, decorated in the fierce folk fashion which has always prevailed among Britain's inland merchant mariners. At the end of the outbound trip, in Cumberland Basin, there is a barge-borne restaurant called the Barque and Bite. On a Little Venice gate is the sign, "Beware of the Doge." In *The Ring and the Book*, which Browning wrote in his years as a widower here, there are similar bits of tinsel. Perhaps this is the effect of the unaccustomed (for London) calm and sense of spaciousness of this so-pleasant corner from which the municipality keeps beating back the slums.

The Zoo is really the Gardens of the Zoological Society of London, a private organization. The Gardens contain, the guide says, "the finest and most representative collection of animals in the world, with over 5800 inhabitants." It is certainly a great zoo. It introduced the non-fence compounds for animals in 1913. It is varied in architecture and landscaping, some of the original Decimus Burton buildings still serving, and the newest aviaries designed by Lord Snowdon, who before his marriage to Princess

Margaret was photographer Anthony Armstrong-Jones (behind every successful man there is a woman).

The Zoological Society was started in 1826 by Sir Stamford Raffles and Sir Humphry Davy. The zoo opened two years later and in 1831 received the animals from the Tower of London Royal Menagerie. The first chimpanzee seen in Britain was seen here in 1835 and the first hippopotamus in 1859.

In March 1965 the temporary escape of Goldie, an eagle, dominated local headlines. One dispatch to the rest of the world began: "A golden eagle that escaped from a nearby zoo two days ago attacked a dog in Regent's Park today. A bystander beat it off with a rolled-up copy of *The Times*."

The park has a big lake for boating, an outdoor theater for Shakespeare, and Queen Mary's rose garden, for which fanciers have a fancy. A children's village is planned with kiddy-sized houses, roads, and tricycle jams.

Possibly the most famous playground in the Commonwealth is to the west of the park in St. John's Wood, which is a sort of in-town suburb. This is Lord's Cricket Ground, repository of the Ashes, the game's greatest international prize, and is also headquarters for the MCC (Marylebone Cricket Club).

The name of the grounds does not refer to their paradisiacal nature, but to their founder, Thomas Lord, who in 1814 brought his own turf with him from a previous location in Dorset Square. Bereft of the sacred turf, Dorset Square keeps something worth contemplating: house No. 1, from which volunteers of the Free French movement with their false identities and real dreams departed to be parachuted into Occupied France. Lord's makes the rules of cricket, the way the Jockey Club makes the rules for racing.

Into Nash's grand entry at Park Crescent comes Portland Place, designed by the Adam brothers. The landlord had promised tenant Lord Foley that nothing would be built between the house and the then-wild park. So the line of sight directly north from the house was kept rigidly unencumbered — it became a wide street, lined on both sides by Adam houses.

Their superb street lasted almost a hundred years before the greedy got at it, starting with the erection of the Langham Hotel (still there, but a BBC office building now) which Dr. Pevsner calls "a High Victorian monster." Flats began to push in about 1900. The Royal Institute of British Architects is here in a 1934 building which at least respects the original Adam scale. In 1931 the British Broadcasting Company put up a building which, if it represents nothing architecturally, does reflect the BBC in being big, dull and cautious.

Cowering away from this amorphous threat is the small church of All Souls' with which Nash contrived to turn the final stem of Regent Street into Portland Place and the park. The whole district was overwhelmed in 1965 by the completion of two of England's tallest structures a few blocks eastward along Tottenham Court Road, a street badly in need of rehabilitation.

The highest of these, both on the map and in the air, is the 620-foot-high General Post Office Tower on Howland Street. The other is a 35-story building at the bottom of the road, where it crosses Oxford Street at St. Giles Circus.

The tower beams TV programs and telephone conversations by microwave. It looks perhaps like a torch turned upside-down, with the flame part turned to the bottom. Its observation tower proposes an unrivaled view, and for those not unduly sensitive, meals "in what is probably the highest revolving restaurant in the world."

The other building is made of precast concrete scallops and, aside from this and its height, lacks any other distinction.

Having edged this far east, one has left Sherlock Holmes's London and entered that of Virginia Woolf — Bloomsbury. This singular district lies between Euston Road (north), Southampton Row (east), New Oxford Street (south) and Tottenham Court Road. One of the remarkable things about Bloomsbury ever was the Group, a handful of young, generally lovely, extraordinarily talented Londoners who decided to change the world and who, in stunning measure, succeeded.

They included the two Stephens sisters, painter Vanessa, who married art-critic and theorist Clive Bell, and writer Virginia, who married writer-editor-political-thinker Leonard Woolf; Lytton Strachey, who passed new frontiers in biography; E. M. Forster; painter Duncan Grant; and John Maynard Keynes, who redirected the mainstream of economic thought. Their personal fire crackled most fiercely, burning new paths in arts, letters, politics and economics, between 1911 and 1921. Some died (mad Virginia by her own hand) and others came, others such as Aldous Huxley and David Garnett.

A reviewer of Leonard Woolf's 1964 volume of autobiography oberved, "The crack Cambridge intellectuals, of whom Mr. Woolf is eminently one, were never to have it so good again." They tilted against windmills, which when dead proved to have been dragons after all. They did it, and it is one of their secrets, perhaps *the* secret, that they laughed a great deal.

Bloomsbury exists not only as an adjective, but despite officials who no longer understand the name, it exists as a place. A place of marvelous sheltering garden squares and a bright hope and the habit of achievement. It is the home of the British Museum, London University, the Royal Academy of Dramatic Art and the Slade School of Art. Plus a multiplicity of other organizations, such as the international headquarters of the YMCA, YWCA, Rotary International, the Trades Union Congress and the Central Council of Physical Recreation.

When the monarchy was restored in 1660, the Earl of Southampton celebrated by rebuilding his town house and south of it having constructed the first London square to be so called, Bloomsbury Square. Down Bloomsbury Way westward is a Hawksmoor church of 1720–1731, St. George Bloomsbury. The steeple was based on the Mausoleum of Halicarnasus, one of the Seven Wonders. Atop the church sits a small classic temple and atop that a skinny pyramid of tapering steps. The bottom step is embellished with the Crown, originally supported by the Lion and Unicorn, the top step is embellished by a statue of toga-wrapped George I of England (not the George referred to in the name of the church). At the time someone commented:

> When Henry the Eighth left the Pope in the lurch
> The Protestants made him the head of the church;
> But George's good subjects, the Bloomsbury people,
> Instead of the church made him head of the steeple.

From Bloomsbury Square northeastward is the procession of squares for which the district is admired. At first, in 1800, vast Russell Square, the Russells being the Dukes of Bedford, owners of Bloomsbury through marriage to the heiress of the last Earl of Southampton. Next, Tavistock Square, the Dukes being also the Earls of Tavistock.

From here the long, slender Woburn and Torrington Squares lead into Gordon and Tavistock Squares. In Torrington Square two brothers dueled over a woman who was there and saw them both die. The marks of their forty footsteps remained, the story goes, and grass would never grow in them. In this square the British Medical Association building (done by Lutyens, 1922–1929, for the Theosophical Society) sits on the site of the house where Dickens lived (1851–1860) and wrote *Bleak House*, *Little Dorrit* and *Hard Times*. The Dickens residence chosen in 1924 to be his museum is a quarter-mile east of Russell Square along Guilford Street, at 48 Doughty Street. Here the young author lived from the spring of 1837 until late 1839. Here daughters Mamie and Kate were born, the *Pickwick Papers* completed, and *Oliver Twist* and *Nicholas Nickleby* written. This very simple house in a bare street of similar structures is a reduced copy of the grander ones around the big squares.

To the left of the train of squares, on the site of seventeenth-century Montagu House, is the British Museum, its entrance in Great Russell Street. The nucleus of this almost incomprehensibly rich treasurehouse was already the property of the government before the Museum existed.

In 1794, finding itself possessor of the Cotton collection of state papers, the Harleian manuscript collection of the Earls of Oxford, the library and natural history collection of Sir Hans Sloane, and the Royal Library dating back to Tudor times, presented by George II, the authorities looked to house them.

The government ran a lottery and for £100,000 bought Montagu House, opened in January 1795 as the British Museum, open, that is, to fifteen persons at a time three days a week.

The classic colonnaded structure we see today was constructed, starting in 1823, by architect Robert Smirke. The famed Reading Room was added later by putting a dome over the central courtyard. The library, which receives a copy of every book printed in the United Kingdom, has more than six million volumes, including a sterling collection of foreign books. The manuscript collection ranges from Greek Papyri (Aristotle's *Constitution of Athens*) through *Beowulf* through *Alice in Wonderland*. The Print Room is world famed. But out of the endless objects of wonder, there are at least two objects the most hurried of visitors should not fail to see: the Rosetta Stone, which enabled moderns to decipher Egyptian hieroglyphics, and the Elgin Marbles brought home from Greece by the British Ambassador to Constantinople (1801–1830), who either rescued from further deterioration or by the same action pillaged a national treasure in taking sculptures from the Parthenon frieze and the Erectheum.

In the British Museum Reading Room, founded by an Italian refugee, German refugee Karl Marx wrote Das Kapital.

Lord Elgin paid £75,000 to get them to London intact and sold them to his government for half that sum.

To fashion a fitting precinct for the Museum, which they proposed enlarging, the Royal Academy right after World War II suggested razing the bookstores, publishers' offices and curio shops standing between the Museum and Hawksmoor's church. In 1964 the Ministry of Public Works, embracing the project, presented plans to the various planning and housing authorities concerned. It envisages an open way between Museum and church, the open space flanked by two modern block-wide seven-story buildings to rehouse inhabitants and businesses. Only pedestrians could penetrate the immediate Museum area. This would put Bloomsbury Square at the east end of the enclave and Bedford Square at the west end. Bedford Square, built about 1775, is for many the finest of the Bloomsbury squares. Dr. Pevsner, who has scrutinized them all, says it is "without doubt the most handsome."

It has remained unspoiled, standing as designed by its original architect, who was probably Thomas Leverton. The middle houses on each side are grouped together to make a single composition of pedimented, pilastered, stuccoed façade (this almost fifty years before John Nash). The central garden is especially lush, and still boasts its original railing. When the railings around other Bloomsbury squares were uprooted for the scrap-metal drive during the war, their owner, the Duke of Bedford, assented. But about Bedford Square he was inflexible in defense of his railings. It was learned much later that much of the old iron patriotically ripped out all over Britain was a century or more too old to be of use in modern manufacture.

From Bedford Square toward Euston Station goes Gower Street, which both Ruskin and George Gilbert Scott agreed was the nadir of street architecture. On the basis of such sage counsel, there is an immediate tendency to disagree. Alas, Gower Street *is* ugly. Since the buildings of London University run along the right-hand side, the comment is rather sweeping. The 1939 plans for expanding some parts and rebuilding others of the agglomeration may be put in action (after drastic revision) in 1967.

Still, there are two doorways worth gawping at, not for any aesthetic thrill, but because they are the doorways to the Slade

School of Art and the Royal Academy of Dramatic Art (pronounced Rah Dah). Both of these academies have produced and are producing outstanding artists. While they have not resisted hardening of the artistic arteries over the years, they have both in the 1960's cured it.

By 1966 Euston Station will have been entirely improved, together with Euston Square alongside it. This means that the stone hymn to the iron horse, Philip Hardwick's 1837 great granite Greek Revival arch, with columns 44½ feet high, and flanking gatehouses, has been destroyed.

For this loss one can be comforted but hardly consoled by the continued existence of St. Pancras Station five streets east along Euston Road. Where Euston's lost façade was a paean to man's conquest of time and space, St. Pancras is a Song of Myself, a dithyramb to Sir George Gilbert Scott, Victorian gentleman and architect. It is a Rhinemaiden's erotic dream. Everything in this 1870 creation is arched, paneled, mullioned, diapered, even the ticket booths. Under all the encrusted decor and the pinnacles and finials, there is a building which preceded modern architects by several generations in applying the free grouping principle, as well as in such details as the drive-in carriage ramp.

Attached to this structure is another, the train shed itself, a typical piece of honest Victorian problem-solving executed with the dash and daring of the period's engineers. This one, W. H. Barlow, flung a glass and iron roof across an unsupported span of 243 feet. The roof is almost 700 feet long and 100 feet high.

THE LONDON OF
SHERLOCK HOLMES
AT WORK

*The East End — Slum Clearance and rebuilding — Former
glories and iniquities — Limehouse — Music Pubs and River
Pubs — Judge Jeffreys — Jack the Ripper*

SHERLOCK HOLMES wouldn't recognize the East End,
nor would Jack the Ripper. Nor would Baroness Angela
Burdett-Coutts and George Peabody of Massachusetts, who
tried to solve East End problems through charity, nor Arnold
Toynbee, who tried to solve them through education and community action, nor General Booth, who tried to solve them
through evangelism.

Of all those who dedicated themselves to effacing the horrors
of East End slums, perhaps only George Lansbury, Labour Party
fighter and once mayor of Poplar, would recognize the place
now, and he would recognize it as the place he had seen in his
dreams.

Along the Thames for six miles and to a depth of three miles
inland, the East End groaned and festered for more than a century, one of the worst slums in the Western world. Philanthropists put up model housing, and late in the nineteenth century
the municipal government began taking strenuous sanitary measures and started ripping out the worst of the rookeries.

Slum clearance was energetically undertaken between the
twentieth-century wars. But the rot was so deep and so much
money was being spent simply keeping citizens alive that little
headway was made. The unemployed could have been put to work
clearing their own slums, but the British system at the time was
the dole system.

369

It was said at the time that the only way to handle this Herculean task (and for once, the cliché has meaning) was to flatten everything and begin anew. Over wide stretches, the German bombers undertook the demolition process.

After the war many of the residents who had been evacuated or rendered homeless did not come back to the East End. Other families were happy to get out of battered London into the newly built satellite towns. The population of Stepney went down from more than 300,000 to less than 90,000, that of Poplar from 155,000 to 74,000. Some of the frightful pressures were relieved.

The national government, the London County Council and the individual boroughs got to work rebuilding and rehabilitating the slum areas. The poverty which was at the root of the rags and filth and hopelessness was banished. Employment rose, wages rose, social services were extended to all, educational opportunities enlarged. Parks appeared among the new buildings. The work goes on, and in 1965 further clearance schemes costing six million dollars were announced, more than half of the sum to remake ten and a half acres in Bethnal Green. The figure did not include a project centering around a 25-story apartment house in Poplar, which cost another three million dollars.

Before World War II it was possible to know an East Ender just by looking at him. His dress, his demeanor, his generally undernourished or overworked aspect identified him. Not in the 1960's. Some of the old neighborhoods remain, most of them drab in gray brick, but no longer sordid. Outside the barrackslike buildings new automobiles are often parked, and television aerials spider across the roofs. It may not be nifty but it isn't nasty.

In an earlier day not long gone the children were abnormally silent and wizened or sly and destructive, but today they are healthy and decently clad and schooled very much like any other normal kids anywhere. Which is not to say that the children of the East End no longer grow up to be thieves and murderers — they do, for the old networks and folkways have not been totally erased. Some of the most prosperous criminals in the country are East End boys who have clawed their way up through criminality to a sort of sham respectability.

Almost the whole of the East End was grouped under the

Greater London Council into one borough, Tower Hamlets. This means that in official nomenclature there is no more Stepney (which included the ex-village neighborhoods of Whitechapel, Spitalfields, Mile End, Wapping, Shadwell, Ratcliff and Limehouse), no more Bethnal Green, no more Poplar (including Stratford-le-Bow and Blackwall).

One relaxed way to have a glimpse of almost the whole area is via the pub crawl. The London-loving, London-prowling Londoner has his private list of pubs suitable for a variety of moods and occasions. Sherlock Holmes had his list, of course, and in "The Man With the Twisted Lip" he resorted to the Bar of Gold — really an opium den — which had a balcony over the river at Limehouse.

Probably there aren't any more opium dens left in Limehouse, there being hardly any Limehouse left either, and no more Chinatown. It has even left the popular imagination. West End people directing others to this year's preferred Chinese restaurant say it's in Stepney: it's really in Limehouse, but since there is just about no more Limehouse . . .

The music halls are just about gone, too. In the first place they expanded from pubs, and have now shrunk back into pubs again. Usually the performance, purely musical, goes on in a barnlike room with the pub appurtenances shoved into a corner or behind a partition. These musical pubs are principally in the East End and the music is usually not "Knees Up Mother Brown" and "Knocked 'Em in the Old Kent Road." It is what's called (this year) Pop Jazz, and the pubs are often a rough nursery for budding talent.

The Rising Sun is on Globe Road in Bethnal Green, a few streets east of the scraggy Green along Roman Road. The Iron Bridge is at the east end of the East India Dock Road, just above Poplar. It sits between the Gas Works and the old East India Dock. Down in the Isle of Dogs (another name for Poplar, if one smudges the fine local distinctions a bit) by the South Dock entrance of the West India Docks is the Gun, an early nineteenth-century house where the oceangoing steamers steam past the river balcony. There is no big musical effort at the Gun, but about a mile south on the same peninsula, there is music at the

Victorian-decorated Waterman's Arms on Glengarnock Avenue.

Upstream one comes to Limehouse and the Grapes on once-notorious Narrow Street. It is a small house, peaceful and cozy, with a sliver of a balcony. Off Narrow Street is a street called Ropemaker's Fields, with the Black Horse. It has no view on anything but the clientele and the interior, both of which are pure waterfront. The tables are scrubbed, the benches narrow, and the paint an honest Pub Brown.

Narrow Street goes toward Tower Bridge, passing the King Edward Memorial Park. If one goes along with it that far and then turns right down Glamis Street, one is at Wapping Wall and the Prospect of Whitby, an honest and ancient riverside pub turrible tarted up for the tourist trade. The upper room with the water balcony has become, for example, A Smart Restaurant.

Further along is Wapping High Street, and in a corner by Oliver's Wharf is another old pub, not afflicted with touristitis. It is called the Town of Ramsgate and they'd like you to think it was originally called the Red Cow, where they spotted Judge Jeffreys in 1688.

The Lord Chancellor was disguised as a sailor, and a drunken sailor at that. After a meteoric rise in his twenties, George Jeffreys became an ardent drinker and was once reprimanded on his knees before the Speaker of the House of Commons. He became Charles II's tool in the king's power struggle with Parliament and was rewarded in 1683 — he was thirty-five — with the Chief Justiceship. Two years later, his principal patron, the Duke of York, became James II and made Jeffreys Baron of Wem.

Then James's bastard elder brother, the Duke of Monmouth, invaded England from across the Channel. It was a stupid operation, quickly quenched. But the frightened King took terrible revenge. He sent Jeffreys and four Judges to Winchester, Dorchester, Exeter and Taunton in a series of trials known since as the Bloody Assizes.

A total of 1381 were found guilty, more than 800 sentenced to transportation, about 300 hanged, and even more than that died in jail of smallpox and jail fever. On the bench Jeffreys exhibited the ferocity for which he was noted and hated:

I hope, gentlemen of the jury, you will notice the strange and horrible carriage of this fellow, and withal you cannot but observe the spirit of that sort, what a villainous and devilish one it is, Good God!

After the Assizes, Jeffreys was made Lord Chancellor at the age of thirty-seven. When James fled at the approach of William of Orange's fleet, Jeffreys arranged to slip down the Thames aboard a sloop disguised as one of the crew. But waiting for the tide at Wapping, he absolutely had to have a drink. At the Red Cow he was recognized by a man who as a witness had been humiliated in court by the judge. A few months later Jeffreys died in the Tower of London at the age of forty-one, of drink. It has since been learned that he suffered agonies from gallstone, and that he drank to kill the pain which made him so vicious.

Another way to see other parts of the East End is to follow the invisible footsteps of Jack the Ripper. Before that nineteenth century moment when so many scores of thousands were jammed so miserably into Spitalfields and Whitechapel, Shelley wrote:

> Hell is a city much like London,
> A populous and smoky city;
> There are all sorts of people undone —
> And there is little or no fun done;
> Small justice shown and still less pity.

Dr. Jekyll made his first appearance in 1886, Sherlock Holmes was noticed by the public in 1887, and in 1888 Jack the Ripper came.

Behind the street frontages were alleys and courtyards crammed with smaller buildings and sheds. Back doors, areaways and passages led from one warren to another.

There were 63 brothels, 1200 full-time prostitutes, 233 common lodging houses capable of sheltering 8600 persons in this district. There is no record of the number of grogshops and cellar dives. Notorious gangs of thieves were headquartered here. Sailors from all over the world came through. There were the tough butchers and porters from Spitalfields Market. There were "good" streets where the merchants lived and kept shop. And

373

there were thousands of Jewish refugees from Polish and Russian pogroms. Cholera was not infrequent. Brutality was banal. Poverty was universal.

And then came murder. It lasted three months, August to November 1888 and cost six lives. It troubled the world, shook England (Queen Victoria sent a sharp memo to the Home Secretary on how to catch the killer; the Commissioner of Metropolitan Police resigned), and terrified London.

Between 11 P.M. and 4 A.M., silently and within a few feet of detection, Jack the Ripper did his murders in a world waiting and

Cockfighting is illegal today in London, but losing at other forms of gambling is no

watching to pounce on him. He operated always within a circle not more than six blocks from the meeting place of Whitechapel Road and Commercial Road. All the victims except the last and most thoroughly dissected — she was twenty-four and pretty — were middle-aged women drunkards who walked the streets for dram money when they could not come by it otherwise.

Various superior officers of the London police named the murderer after the murders had ceased. But each of them named a different man. The only suspect whose character and conduct precisely matched the crimes and the fragmentary descriptions was known to the London police as Mikhail Ostrog.

To the police of other countries he was known as Alexander Pedachenko, Wassily Konovlav and Andrey Luiskovo. He arrived in London on the run from French police who suspected him in the killing and mutilation of a Parisian girl. At the time of the Ripper murders he worked in the Walworth district as a barber-surgeon (the murderer had had some sort of medical training) and assisted a doctor in Camberwell, next to Walworth, where four of the victims were said to have received treatment.

Ostrog disappeared from London in 1888 and was arrested in St. Petersburg following a Ripper-like murder there, and died soon after in the madhouse. The Russian police organ *Ochrana Gazette* named him as "wanted for the murder of five women in the East Quarter of London in 1888."

This is the tour of Jack the Ripper's crimes, all except the last committed out of doors without a sound:

Gunthorp Street, where Whitechapel and Commercial Roads meet, August 7. The victim was Martha Tabram, thirty-five, on the first landing of the outside staircase of the since-demolished George Yard Buildings. She had thirty-nine stab wounds on all sides of her body.

Durward Street, then called Bucks Row, the other side of Whitechapel Road from London Hospital. Victim, Mary Ann Nichols, forty-two. Lying partly in the gutter, partly on the sidewalk, she was raised up by a policeman who thought her another drunk. "Her throat was cut almost from ear to ear," *The Times* reported. "The woman had terrible wounds in her abdomen." August 31.

Hanbury Street, in the back yard of No. 29, just east of Spitalfields Market, "without a cry of any kind, under the window of light sleepers." The victim, Annie Chapman, forty-seven. Head almost completely severed, body disemboweled, uterus removed and carried away. Around the feet, arranged in a semicircle, the few coins and trinkets from her pockets. September 8. Vigilante committees formed.

Berners Street and *Mitre Square*, two murders the same night. A school now stands at Berners and Fairclough Streets, four blocks from the Commercial Road crossroad and one down. The victim, "Long Liz" Stride, a Swede, was killed in a courtyard under the windows of the International Workmen's Educational Club, where members were singing. Only her throat was cut, the killer apparently frightened away by a horse and cart entering the court at midnight. Long Liz had been seen alive fifteen minutes earlier.

As the first victim lay dying, the second victim, Catherine Eddowes, was at the police station, detained for drunkenness. She was released at one A.M. and at two A.M. her body was found in Mitre Square, just over the border inside the City. When the patrolman had passed on his rounds twenty minutes earlier, the tiny square was empty. The square watchman saw and heard nothing unusual, but Catherine Eddowes, forty-three, had her throat hacked, her face gashed, part of her right ear cut off, and internal organs removed. About twenty-five minutes later, half the victim's apron, used to wipe blood from a knife, was found five blocks away.

Duval Street, where Miller's Court once ran off what was then called Dorset Street. The last crime, November 9, 1888. The victim, Mary Kelly, twenty-four. Neighbors in the surrounding buildings heard her singing in her tiny courtyard house. The song was "Sweet Violets," and it was one o'clock in the morning. After her candle guttered out, Jack the Ripper burned Mary's clothes in the fireplace so he could see to work. He cut the features off her face and his mutilations on her body were meticulous and terrible.

He did much to promote the cause of slum clearance, as a stroll through his old neighborhood clearly shows.

376

THE LONDON OF
GEOFFREY CHAUCER

Greenwich, architectural wonders, museums, the Cutty Sark, *the observatory, parks and pervading beauty — Blackheath — Deptford — Rotherhithe, the* Mayflower *— Guy's Hospital — George Inn — John Harvard — Southwark Cathedral, Elephant & Castle — South Bank   Old Vic — St. Thomas's Hospital — Lambeth Palace*

IN Chaucer's day (he died in 1400) Greenwich was a tiny fishing village. But not long after, it became fashionable, out in the country but only six miles from London Bridge. Of course, the number of fashionable persons in London at the time was limited. The Duke of Gloucester built a house there in 1428 and began collecting books, thus unwittingly starting Oxford's Bodleian Library. Bequeathed to his royal relatives, the mansion was enlarged and named Placentia, from the Latin for "to please." Henry VIII was born here, as were his daughters Mary and Elizabeth. Charles II had the park of the house redone in 1664 by Le Notre, Louis XIV's landscape man, and ordered a new palace begun. This eventually blossomed into the noble assembly of buildings standing there today.

The most entertaining way to reach Greenwich is to follow in the wake of Henry VII *et seq.* and take a boat downriver. The half-hour cruise from Tower Pier — there's a longer one starting at Westminster Pier — is available only in the summer. One can alternatively cruise through the East End atop a bus as far as West Ferry Road, change to a 56 bus which chugs around the bulbous peninsula of the Isle of Dogs. Those descending at Ferry Street at the bottom of the Isle can loll in Island Gardens, the lit-

tle park at the tip and there drink in the waterfront aspects of
Greenwich (pronounced Gren-nidge) across the river.

The view is one of the rare ones of northern cities, a Canaletto
scene of order and majesty, with balanced buildings poised between a moving river and a moving sky. To each side is a twin-
faced palace, four pediments, four colonnades. Between the end
pieces, set further back, twin towers face each other across a
lawn, each tower topping its own colonnaded palace. Still further
back (later one learns it is indeed across a road and at the far
edge of a broad lawn) is a little jewelbox of a palace, the "Queen's
House," whose wings are hidden from this viewpoint. Behind this
rises a wooded hill out of whose massed greenery pokes a glass
crown, the Greenwich Observatory, author of Greenwich Mean
Time and the zero meridian. In a single glance one has seen the
principal monuments of Greenwich in their superbly impressive
unity.

There is the temptation to walk bodily into this *trompe-l'oeil*
picture. To succumb to it, one has only to walk across the river.
Not on top of the water, at least not most of us. Most of us will

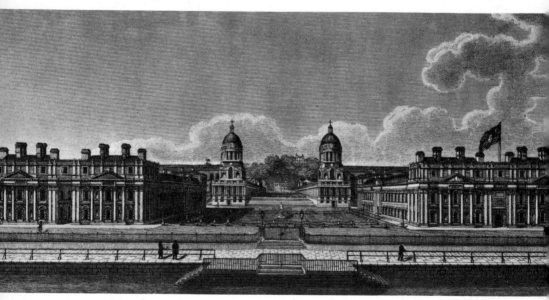

*Some of England's greatest architects — Webb, Wren, Hawksmoor,
Vanbrugh — wrought this noble prospect.*

walk underneath, through the 1902 Greenwich Foot Passenger Tunnel.

As a tourist site Greenwich is splendidly endowed. It is beautiful, historic, airy, spacious, understandable and filled with fascinating things to see. And the fact that all this is literally educational as well as entertaining gives additional glow to the day of the conscientious tourist.

At the exit of the tunnel on dry land sits the tea clipper *Cutty Sark*, launched at Dumbarton on the Clyde in 1869 and here established as a maritime monument and merchant marine educational unit in 1954, crammed not only with nostalgia and tradition, but also with figureheads, marine prints and seagoing artifacts.

One of the pleasant walks in London is the river walk fronting the grounds of the Royal Naval College and leading from the dry *Cutty Sark* to the non-dry Trafalgar Tavern on the river.

The Royal Naval College is the Navy's staff college and welcomes visitors only to its chapel (a burned-out Wren unrecognizably rebuilt) and to its Painted Hall (an okay Wren). Its build-

The birthplace of Henry VIII and his daughters Mary and Elizabeth vanished in the late seventeenth century.

ings served as the Royal Naval Hospital from 1752 until 1873, and there is still a small hospital in the grounds and the relaxed wanderers in the red jackets are convalescents.

Across Romney Road is the National Maritime Museum, whose center building is the unique Queen's House, by Inigo Jones. It is matchless by the testimony of all those houses which have aped Jones's work but which have lacked that "x" factor which graces works of genius.

The museum contains the history of the British maritime tradition, of some importance to an island state. It is here recounted in pictures (including some masterpieces), uniforms, scale models, weapons, prints, documents, furnishing. There is one tiny room devoted to Horatia Nelson, daughter of Lord Nelson and That Woman. The uniform he wore at Trafalgar (yes, the bullet hole is there) is also on display. And there are some state barges, in which the Queen of England proceeded up the Thames in a red and gold cockleshell ship, like a Chinese Empress.

The park behind slopes upward to the now decommissioned Observatory, whose buildings date from 1676 to 1897. In 1950 the Astronomer Royal complained he couldn't see the sky

The hilltop observatory in the righthand corner is the home of Greenwich Mean Time.

through the over-rich London atmosphere and the observatory was shifted to Herstmonceux Castle in Sussex. But when the staff departed, they left the meridian behind them. It is there in the courtyard, a brass strip several yards long. There is nothing to impede the straddling of this line and standing with one foot in each hemisphere.

Outside the observatory, a bronze General Wolfe looks from the hilltop. A gift of the Canadian nation, it was unveiled in 1930 by the Marquis de Montcalm. The General's boyhood home, Macarteney House, is by the west gate of the Park, and his tomb is in the crypt of St. Alfege's Church below in Greenwich Church Street.

Over the crest of the hill is Blackheath, where the Danes camped in 1011, the Kentish rebels in 1381 (Wat Tyler) and in 1450 (Jack Cade), the Lancastrians in 1452 (Henry VI) and the Cornish rebels in 1497 (Lord Audley).

By 1608 the grass was pretty well trampled, and here Scottish James I showed the English how to play golf. Later, highwaymen lurked along the Dover Road and, after their black deeds were done, scampered off across Blackheath.

Just beyond, Blackheath Village has nests of good houses from the seventeenth, eighteenth and early nineteenth centuries, including a crescent on the heath's southeast corner called the Paragon and Wren's Morden College. The college is a set of luxurious almshouses for "decayed Turkey merchants" (nothing to do with people who have gone broke trying to sell spoiled poultry, but rather elderly and needy men who once traded with the Levant).

Upstream on the riverbank is Deptford (pronounced "Detfurd") where the mothballed Royal Victoria Victualling Yard is all that is left of an English glory. This was the Deptford dockyard founded by Henry VIII — and there are still some Tudor buildings in there somewhere — where many of the "wooden walls" of England were built. Queen Elizabeth was thrilled to the depths of her exchequer by Francis Drake's exploits in the *Golden Hind*, came to the Yard to welcome him home in 1581, and then made him a knight. The business with the Armada was seven years later. It was also here that Sir Walter Ralegh laid his cloak across the mud puddle for the Queen. (There is no proof that he ever did any such thing, but happily there is no proof that he did not.) The Yard was shut in 1869 as a shipbuilding center, but continued to operate for one purpose and another until 1961.

In Deptford Green by the river is the Church of St. Nicholas, in whose churchyard Christopher Marlowe was buried in 1593, knifed to death in a nearby tavern. The dark tales still persist of this dark genius and the true story of his death has not been told.

The Surrey Commercial Docks are next along the waterfront, with names such as Lady and Lavender and Albion and Stave dock and Canada, Quebec, Greenland and Norway docks. The dividing line between Deptford and Rotherhithe is a spot named Cuckold's Point, a name often omitted from today's maps of London. It used to be marked by a pole topped with a big set of horns, in memory of the miller of Charlton — a village east of Greenwich — who found his wife giving her all for her king. The King (John, it was) offered the injured miller all the strip of land he could see, provided he would walk annually over it wearing buck's horns on his head. To Rotherhithe from Charlton is three miles and the river crosses the line of vision twice. So the story can't be true, but that hasn't stopped a good piece of gossip even after 750 years.

Rotherhithe Street begins just west of the docks, leading past St. Mary's Church, a 1715 replacement of a medieval structure. The old register shows that Christopher Jones is buried here, master of the *Mayflower* and a Rotherhithe man. Mayflower Street is nearby, and so is Clark Orchard, named for the first mate. The ship, though registered at Harwich, was "of London" during the years of her New England voyaging.

There is a Mayflower on the other side of Rotherhithe Street, a pub with a balcony above the water (or the mud, depending on the tide) and a good view of Wapping on the opposite bank, including customers on the balcony of the Prospect of Whitby looking at customers on the balcony of the Mayflower looking at them. The Mayflower is the only pub in London permitted by law to sell postage stamps.

Upstream, but still in Rotherhithe, is another pub with a river balcony, the Angel, near Tower Bridge, noted for its meals to the point where phoning ahead for a table is a wise precaution.*

Rotherhithe, which Swift picked as the home port of Gulliver, has a name which persists in spite of official nonexistence. For generations it has been included in the borough of Bermondsey, which itself has since been included in the super-borough of Southwark. People who live and work in Rotherhithe don't call it Rotherhithe: they call it Redriff.

At London Bridge there is a railroad station which has wine cellars (not public) underneath. On the river side of it runs Tooley (originally St. Olave's until bent out of shape by the Bermondsey tongue) Street, and on the land side, St. Thomas Street. St. Thomas's Hospital stood here from 1213 until the railroad put its station on the spot in 1871. Using the compensation money, the hospital moved into a new set of buildings (Florence Nightingale, adviser) upstream above Westminster Bridge, where it still functions.

Across St. Thomas Street, is another hospital, Guy's, one of the nation's great teaching hospitals. It was founded in 1721 by Thomas Guy who, because he did leave a monument of living charity behind, is today called "frugal" instead of "miserly." He was a bookseller in Lombard Street whose biggest item was Bibles, through a deal made with university authorities who held the monopoly on Bible printing and distribution.

A bachelor, Guy lunched on his shop counter with a newspaper for a tablecloth. His economies he put into South Sea stocks and saw them swell preposterously into an overnight fortune. Before the bubble burst he sold out at a vast profit and lived to see the roof put on the first buildings of his hospital.

The original buildings are still standing along St. Thomas Street, partially rebuilt after bombing. There are later blocks behind this, including a 1963 eleven-story surgical tower. This latter rather shocked people at first, but now other hospitals are hoping to solve space problems by building upward. Guy's hopes to add by the early 1970's a new wing about thirty stories tall.

---

* In Britain reserving a seat is called "booking." Box offices are called "booking offices." If a headwaiter inquires, "Have you booked, sir?" he is asking about reservations, not poking into your personal history.

Although many noted surgeons and physicians have been trained here, the most celebrated student continues to be one who was here 1814–1816, John Keats, a dropout.

East of the hospital Borough High Street begins. We are in Southwark, pronounced "Suth-uck," which locals call "the Borough," pronounced here as in faroff Brooklyn, U.S.A., "burra."

Through a gateway into an alley at 77 Borough High Street is the entrance to the George Inn, the last of London's galleried coaching inns. After centuries of trade, the original George burned in Southwark's own Great Fire of 1667. It was rebuilt instanter, keeping its U form with two wooden galleries running

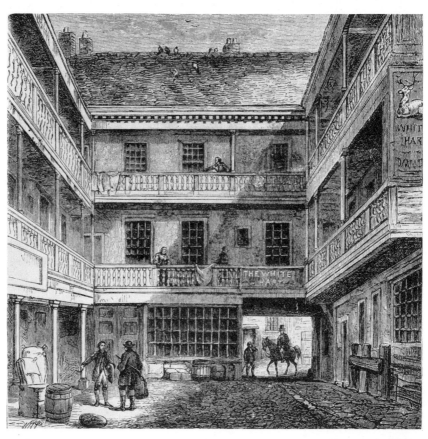

Only part of one galleried inn — the George, Southwark — remains today in London.

all the way around. Thus it remained until 1889 when the greedy railway chopped off all but the southern leg of the U. Now the National Trust stands guard over what is left, and what is left is extremely enjoyable. The cheery, bustling coaching atmosphere still bubbles in the swaybacked inn, and hearty waitresses deal out hearty portions of inexpensive and edible food.

White Hart Yard (mentioned in Shakespeare's *Henry VI* and Dickens's *Pickwick Papers*) marks the site of the White Hart Inn, as the site of the Tabard is indicated by Talbot Yard. (Yes, Talbot. Odd, isn't it?)

> By fel that in that season on a day
> In Southwark at the Tabard as I lay
> Ready to wenden on my pilgrimage
> To Canterbury with full devout courage,
> At night was come into that hostelcric
> Wel nyne and twenty in a compainye.

The Tabard was one of many inns here just without the gates of London Bridge on the main route south. The sale of one of them, the Queen's Head, provided John Harvard with some of the money he left to the college in New England which in gratitude called itself by his name.

John was born in the parish and baptized in Southwark Cathedral, where there is a Harvard Chapel. This church, standing since the thirteenth century — not without major changes — became a cathedral only in 1905. Officially it is the Collegiate and Cathedral Church of St. Saviour and St. Mary Overy (or Overie, which means over the water). The beauty of its ancient portions glows all over the cathedral. So does its modesty and its poverty. It manages to give concerts for those in the neighborhood who need more than food at noon, and it does find volunteers to help visitors. The 1947 gift of the Vancouver, B.C., branch of the Dickens Fellowship to the cathedral was an oaken iron-strapped poor-box. It is a rare cathedral indeed that moves one to sympathy rather than awe.

Just down from the cathedral, which is hemmed in by warehouses and London Bridge, is Borough Market, which was originally held in the 1200's on the Bridge itself. Still offering fruits and vegetables, it has been in its present location only since 1765.

Romantics who can adjust the smells and noises to fit an earlier century and who people the stones with friendly shades will enjoy making their way from the market to Clink Street. The Liberty of Clink, attached to the Bishop of Winchester's palace, was free of interference from outside authority. This is what attracted theaters, which also served as bull- and bear-baiting pits, and the brothels, which were called "stews" in the sixteenth century. The prison eventually erected here was called the Clink.

Southwark had a curiously large number of prisons: the Compter, the King's Bench, the Marshalsea, the White Lion (all these near the present St. George's Church), and the new King's Bench, where Dickens's father was jailed for debt.

At the sight of the plaques indicating where the debtors' prisons stood, many a visitor gives a little shiver of self-congratulation that those bad old days are done. Which is undeserved, according to a government committee reporting in March of 1965 that "about 7000 people are in prison at any one time for non-payment of debt." The committee was charged to inquire into the law and possible changes.

Another 1965 government project sought to establish a commission to clarify and update the laws of the land, some of which have been in force since the thirteenth century.

Cobbled, clattery Clink Street threads between brick cliffs of warehouses where bars of sunlight glow wanly through the dust, and emerges from under a railroad bridge into Bankside. Dead ahead is a bright, inviting pub, the Anchor, which has the use of a pierhead sticking out over the river. The pub has secret rooms they think were used to hide fugitives from the Clink. Pub specialist Alan Reeve-Jones observes, "At the Anchor you can still see the very handy Shakespeare Room, so called because Shakespeare used to drink in another pub nearer the Globe Theatre."

Bankside was certainly the London theater district of Shakespeare's day. Now it is a street making its slender way along the river's edge under Southwark Bridge almost to Blackfriars Bridge. The site of the Hope Theatre is in an alley called Bear Gardens; the Rose, in Rose Alley, is now an office parking lot.

The Swan site is in the yard of some vacant warehouses. The Globe is inland, near Park Street, under Barclay's Brewery (which Dr. Johnson auctioned off for the widowed Mrs. Thrale).

In 1965 a band of the faithful were trying to raise $250,000 to build a new Globe. They were looking not only for the money but for a likely spot somewhere near the original to build.

Bankside Nos. 49–52 are houses rather than warehouses, and date from the seventeenth and eighteenth centuries. They might, however, fall down any day. Yesterday, perhaps. This is one of the few streets in London where it is still possible to be run over by a horse-drawn dray (and watch out for the swinging cranes).

Opposite the respectable City, the roistering theater district of 1638, with Shakespeare's Globe on the right.

387

The street makes a turn at the power station and passes the 1752 Hopton's Almshouses, twenty-six two-story brick cottages.

If one follows Borough High Street instead of Bankside — not an enviable procedure — after a mile one comes upon the Elephant & Castle. And what is Elephant & Castle? It is the center for roads to seven bridges, twenty-six bus lines, two underground lines, a railroad station and five country bus lines. The Germans destroyed about fifty per cent of the district, creating a vacancy planners were quick to seize upon, but not all that quick to act upon: the first part of the rebuilding was completed twenty-two years after the bombing.

Why is it called Elephant & Castle? This tangle of crossroads was so complex that no one street could dominate the rest, and so the whole thing was called after the leading pub, which disappeared in the general dust cloud which hung over the place in the

Shakespeare's Globe Theatre being viewed,
apparently, by a gigantic public.

blitz. But why Elephant? And Castle? There is a perfectly simple explanation, which is that the Worshipful Company of Cutlers and also the African Company (something like the East India Company) used this as their symbol. The howdahs on early pictures of elephants — and perhaps on early elephants themselves — resembled castles. This intriguing badge could easily have been used as a tavern sign. But no. This simple explanation is too simple to please Londoners. They must have it that when Charles I was engaged (it never came to anything) to the Crown Princess of Spain, some publican dubbed his dram shop L'Enfanta de Castille. This is Spanish and means, as any Iberian will tell you, Elephant and Castle.

There is a new (1965) shopping center with escalators, under-

A horsecar ride in the 1870's was a purely middle-class venture.

ground garage, 115 shops, two new pubs and a place of honor for the old bronze castle-carrying elephant which stood atop the late lamented pub. Office space in this privately built center is occupied by the Ministry of Public Building. The Ministry of Health over the way is housed in what seems to be a group of heroic autoclaves named for the late Sir Alexander Fleming, discoverer of penicillin.

One of the new pubs here installed is called the Charlie Chaplin for a fellow who almost starved to death in the neighborhood as a boy. After he had made his first million as a movie star, he returned to London, Mr. Chaplin records, took a taxi to the old district, was stricken with fear it might suck him back down again, and was glad to get back across the river.

But since World War II, slowly but perceptibly, the derelict districts of Kennington and Lambeth are being rebuilt.

Out of Elephant & Castle, London Road leads to Waterloo Road and the railroad station and bridge of the same name. Underneath the bridge spreads one of the most notable changes of postwar London, the South Bank. Cleared of a nasty, moldering industrial tangle, it was filled with goodies for the 1951 Festival of Britain. Color, excitement, new uses of materials, new ideas bubbled out of this riverbank plot. The phoenix seemed to be rising from the ashes of the blitz. But after a while, it seemed clear that the phoenix had crashed on takeoff.

In the 1960's, however, there was a new beating of wings. A seven-and-one-half-acre complex of high office buildings rose behind the river park, crested with a 26-story tower, which, being 351 feet high, pokes quite a sore thumb up into the skyline. The 1951 Royal Festival Hall was enlarged and more public amenities (riverfront restaurant, for example) added. At the same time (1965) the side was removed from the 500-seat National Film Theatre under the railroad bridge, and then put back on again after money for enlargement could not be raised. The long-planned National Theatre (replacing the Old Vic) and Opera House (replacing Sadler's Wells) seemed imminent. There was also considerable governmental anguish over granting or not granting building permission for a 440-foot-high hotel with attached conference center and art school.

Meanwhile the National Theatre group carried on at the Old Vic on Waterloo Road behind Waterloo Station. A Frenchman was astonished to find "so many places in London named for defeats." In a way, he was almost right: the man who loses "meets his Waterloo," just as if Waterloo had not been a victory for the British.

Starting as a melodrama house called the Coburg in 1816, the theater was renamed in 1833 for the young Princess Victoria. In 1880 it was taken over and remodeled by Emma Cons who wanted to bring low-priced, high-class culture to the unmoneyed, undercultured masses. It was a success. Her niece, Lillian Bayliss, carried on after Miss Cons died in 1912. From the Old Vic, starting about 1930, emerged the greatest actors of the English stage. One of them, Laurence Olivier, returned to the Old Vic in 1964 as director of the homeless National Theatre.

Also looking for a home in 1965 was the 12½-ton Coade Stone red-painted lion which stood atop the Lion Brewery from about 1820. When the South Bank was cleared in 1950 and the brewery razed, King George VI intervened to be sure the lion would keep his lair. New construction in 1965 forced the beast to seek new quarters. His brother, yellow (in color, not character), waits in the basement of County Hall.

The South Bank gardens stretch as far as Westminster Bridge, where the open space along the water's edge is continued across the front of St. Thomas's Hospital, facing the Houses of Parliament.

The St. Thomas celebrated here was St. Thomas a Becket, murdered at the instigation of his dearest friend, King Henry II. The Augustinians founded the hospital in Southwark in 1173. Edward VI changed the dedication to the more tactful St. Thomas the Apostle. At this period the hospital was run by the Matron, the Clerk, and the Hospitaler, with the surgeon listed below the shoemaker. There was no physician on the staff until 1566. Difficult patients were confined in the stocks and nurses were disciplined at the whipping post. He who did not rise for church on Sunday got no dinner.

The oldest buildings here date from 1868, most of them scheduled for replacement by a new, larger (1000 beds) hospital on which work began in 1963. To pay some of the costs, the hospital built an office building on the west end of its choice river property and rents the space for useful sums of money.

Standing in its own park on the riverfront is Lambeth Palace, one of the most ignored ancient monuments in London. The Archbishop of Canterbury chose this site in the twelfth century for his London palace because while it was isolated from the court, it was readily accessible across the river. Viewed from the water, it looks more like a fortress than an episcopal palace, but it has an enormous dignity, and time has mellowed its hostile countenance. Wat Tyler's rebels looted the palace and burned its library in 1381. And while Laud was Archbishop, mobs unsuccessfully attacked the building twice, a momentary respite for the primate who in 1644 was beheaded by the Puritans on charges of Popery. In all, its buildings range amiably over eight hundred years of different kinds of buildings well worth a history-alerted prowl.

A few blocks inland stretches Lambeth Walk, a fifty-acre area severely bombed and rebuilt with housing, although the shops in the Walk itself were replaced. But what could not be built back in was the old spirit which cocked a snoot at a hard life.

Lambeth Palace, London seat of the Archbishop of Canterbury, chief prelate of the Church of England.

392

THE LONDON OF
JOHN KEATS AND FRIENDS

*Hampstead village — The Heath — Community Pride —
Noted natives, the Keats House, the bountiful Baroness —
— Celebrated pubs — Kenwood House — Highgate Ceme-
tery, necropolis extraordinary, tombs of Karl Marx and others.*

HAMPSTEAD is only a mile and a half north of Regent's Park, a good deal closer to the center of town than say, Greenwich or Twickenham. Yet it is still referred to as "London's most residential suburb." Those who live there consider themselves not Londoners, but Hampstead folk.

The reason for this (superior) sense of separation is that Hampstead grows around London's highest hill, and the dome of St. Paul's and the tower of Big Ben seem blessedly remote. The steepness of the hill reinforced the local exclusivity until the automobile became prevalent.

The Hampstead considered here is the old village around the hill, across the heath from the twin village of Highgate which sits on a similar hill. Officially, when Greater London came into being, the word Hampstead became vague, melted into a general blob covering a huge expanse of North London stretching to the far end of Bloomsbury, all under the title of Camden.

Hampstead has always attracted writers and artists of note, especially those with strong personalities and fat wallets. These individuals have always enjoyed the sense of community, the pleasures of village life provided with hot and cold running urbanity, and they have joined in civic activities and supported community projects. One of the biggest projects is the continual preservation of the village.

One of the longest struggles was against the Lords of the Manor, the Wilson family, who owned a good bit of Hampstead and the whole rolling heath. The Wilsons made a good thing out of digging fine red and silver sand used on pub floors in preference to sawdust. Some of the water-filled hollows on the slopes of the road between Spaniards Inn and Hampstead Village are vestiges of this digging.

When Hampstead residents objected, Sir Thomas Maryon Wilson contended that since it was his heath he could do with it as he jolly well pleased. This was in 1856. The sniping went on for a whole decade when Sir Thomas unlimbered his big guns; he began building on the heath. The Hampstead Heath Protection Society haled him into court and kept up guerrilla activity until Sir Thomas lay down and died in 1870. His surviving brother unloaded the manor rights to the Metropolitan Board of Works for £45,000. Twelve years later the Board was in court as land-

Many corners of Hampstead retain the rural charm of yesterdays.

394

lord *v.* the people of Hampstead, who wanted the right to play cricket and football on the heath. The Hampstead justices refused to hear a test case against a father and his two little wicket-defending sons. The Court of Queen's Bench refused to order the magistrates to hear the case, and that was that.

In 1964 British Railways announced the closing of the branch line serving Hampstead. There was an immediate protest from an immediately formed committee which issued what the *Guardian* called "a cogent, 50-page booklet by Hampstead intellectuals." When the local council proposed the installation of parking meters, there was another protest directed by another committee.

Thus Hampstead preserves much of its coherence. It supports a theater, an art movie house and the kind of pubs and restaurants which draw non-hill dwellers to N.W.3.

In addition to its personalities, the hill is so traced and laced with lanes and connecting walks and terraces and setbacks following the contours of the hill that Hampstead must be explored rather than just visited. The emotions such exploration are most likely to produce are envy and greed.

The land prices which have risen all over London have in Hampstead soared grotesquely. Cottages in Flask Walk, humble Georgian cottages for humble Georgian villagers, were sold at auction in 1953 for as little as £125 each. Ten years later they were valued at about £15,000. Building land sold in 1964 for £70,000 an acre — in dollar terms, about $75,000 an acre more than the London average. Large houses with gardens were going for up to $300,000 each.

There's hardly a street in the village which has not housed at some time in its history someone interesting and — in his circle — important. There are so many streets with houses either beautiful or antique or curious or all three at the same time, and there are surprises which escape classification. A quick quote from Dr. Pevsner gives a hint:

In East Heath Road Nos. 14–15, two cottages of two storeys and only two bays each, with two most improbably tiny balconies, one of them at the corner, the whole like a piece of whimsical stage design for an 18th Cent. play.

While it is undoubtedly pleasant to be a connoisseur of Hampstead and to gloat over one's favorite spots, it is also a pleasure to be a stranger and to get lost. Here one is not lost and desperate nor lost and damned; here one is lost and enchanted, lost without loss.

The local authorities have handily changed the name of John Street to Keats Grove, which makes it easier to ask the way and find the house in which Keats passed so many tortured and so many exalted hours. This was not his first Hampstead home, and the whole story is so fictitious in all its aspects save one: it is true.

On Sunday, December 1, 1816, the *Examiner*, edited and published by Leigh Hunt, printed "On First Looking into Chapman's Homer." That day John Keats went to Hampstead, to that strange tribal encampment in the middle of the wild heath, the Vale of Health. He went there to thank Hunt. It was, after all, the first recognition the young man had received as a poet.

When, about four months later, his first volume of poems appeared, Keats was living in Well Walk with his brothers Tom and George, at the house of Bentley, the village postman. In December 1818 Keats and the painter Charles Armitage Brown moved into the east half of newly built Wentworth Place on John Street. In April, Mr. and Mrs. Brawne and their daughter Fanny moved into the other half of the pretty stuccoed house. In six weeks Keats struck off gem after gem — "La Belle Dame Sans Merci," "Chorus of Faeries," "To Sleep," and the first of the odes, "Ode to Psyche." One May morning after breakfast he sat under a tree in the garden and wrote "Ode to a Nightingale." In the same month, "Ode on a Grecian Urn."

Then Keats's suspicions were confirmed. He had it, the tuberculosis that had killed his mother and his brother Tom. He tried to break with Fanny. She refused. He moved out of Wentworth Place. He came back only to move away again and then come back again. Finally September 13, 1820, Fanny Brawne wrote in her diary, "Mr. Keats left Hampstead." He went to Italy and there, five months later in Rome, "in that little room with the gold roses on the ceiling, that overlooks the Spanish Steps," he died.

Wentworth Place is a museum now, with the furnishings and

literary exhibits one would expect, and a lock of Keats's hair. In 1920 Thomas Hardy wrote a poem there:

> O poet, come you haunting here
> Where streets have stolen up all round,
> And never a nightingale pours one
> Full-throated sound?

Charles Dickens lived in Hampstead fleetingly, on different occasions, for the first time in 1837. He had gone to school lower down in the borough at Wellington Academy, Hampstead Road. He was a prodigious walker and used to drag friends along the heath in his wake. He also came often to visit that homely woman with the beautiful soul, Baroness Angela Burdett-Coutts, who consulted him about her projects for improving the lot of London's poor.

Her story opens some years before she comes onstage. Thomas Coutts, son of an Edinburgh banker, came to London in the 1750's with his brother to set up a bank, which flourished. The no-nonsense Scot married one of his brother's servant girls and had three daughters who nevertheless married rather well. They became the Countess of Guildford, the Marchioness of Bute and the Lady Frances Burdett. When Mr. Coutts found himself a widower, he married a small actress, Harriot Mellon, with whom he blissfully lived the remaining seven years of his life. With a million-pound estate, Mrs. Coutts married the Duke of St. Albans, who refrained from taking a penny of her money, so when she died she was able to leave two million pounds to her granddaughter Angela Burdett.

Angela's father, Sir Francis, was the last political prisoner in the Tower of London. He fought in the Commons for the release of a debating club chairman who printed an announcement of a debate on Parliament's exclusion of the public from sessions and possible curtailment of press freedom. The man, John Galen Johns, found himself in Newgate for Breach of Privilege of the House. Sir Francis claimed the detention was illegal and made a motion for his release.

Defeated in the House, Sir Francis began crusading through the columns of Cobbett's *Political Register*. After long debate and defense of his actions, Sir Francis was ordered arrested and confined to the Tower, again for Breach of Privilege.

Although the culprit remained in his Piccadilly house thereafter, the Serjeant at Arms took four days to find him. The London mob, identifying a rare friend to common man, blocked access to the house and were finally scattered by the Guards. But Sir Francis kept his door closed to the summons-server for three more days. Then, to stop the riots, he voluntarily rode to the Tower, and the mobs tried to rescue him from his own coach.

No sooner had Sir Francis presented himself to the Governor than Parliament, its power honored and honor vindicated (this in 1810) ordered his release. Sir Francis sneaked off to quake in Wimbledon: he had developed a horror of crowds.

Dickens later wrote admiringly of Sir Francis's stand in this unedifying business and came to know the family. He helped Miss Burdett-Coutts plan her Bethnal Green slum clearance project, writing, "I have no doubt that the large houses are best. You can never, for the same money, offer anything like the same advantages in small houses." So the heiress cleared more than four acres of big city horror and put up two projects in 1860. The first was a housing group called Columbia Square, four five-story units, and the second was Columbia Market, a million-dollar Westminster Abbey of petty commerce, an indoor market to protect the poor against gouging, street accidents, bad weather and the general mess engendered by pushcarts in clogged streets. The housing, though not nearly so elaborately bossed, pinnacled and groined as the market, was given some gothic decoration. The market was an immediate failure (the LCC gave it back to the Baroness) but the buildings remained standing until, with a good deal of strenuous labor, they were torn down in 1964. The moral seems to be that you can't throw a silk purse into a pig sty. Slum clearance is but one segment of general social reform.

Another Lady Bountiful, whose real name was Lady Gainsborough, for a while made a society spa of Hampstead. In 1698 she granted six acres of land near the heath for "the benefit and advantage" of the local poor, and put the ground into the hands of fourteen trustees.

These gentlemen arranged for the waters of a mineral spring

on the property (they preferred to call it "chalybeate" rather than "iron") to be piped to a Hampstead tavern, where it was put into flasks and dispatched daily to a Fleet Street apothecary, faintly appropriate inasmuch as the source of the Fleet River is Hampstead Pond. When this business proved profitless, the property was leased to men who put up a Great Room, an Assembly Room and a Pump Room to which a tavern, gardens and a bowling green were added to make a resort. But after the supervising physician died, the trustees took it over and the business evaporated.

Flask Walk is a souvenir of Hampstead Spa and in Well Walk the spring is still marked. The sign at the wellhead says: NOT TO BE USED FOR DRINKING WATER. For those suspicious of water in any form, the Wells Hotel was constructed in Well Walk in 1830 and is still dispensing refreshment. Unlike most other pubs which have inherited the name Hotel, this one actually has rooms for rent. In New Square, facing Well Walk, is the 1703 Burgh House, erected for the spa's first doctor.

Constable remained ten years in Well Walk, the longest of his many stays in Hampstead. One of his earlier dwellings, a two-story cottage at No. 2 Lower Terrace, is still intact. Constable painted the heath, and under the title *The Romantic House in Hampstead*, painted a picture of the Admiral's House in Admiral's Walk, down the street from Lower Terrace.

Romantic it is, a mid-eighteenth-century white-painted house which obviously grew on the hillside to the owner's fancy. Sir George Gilbert Scott, he who wrought St. Pancras Station and the Foreign Office, lived in the large but essentially simple house for eight years with nary a narthex nor an ogee to keep him company.

Attached to the house is the more modest (but not all that modest) Grove Lodge where John Galsworthy lived from 1918 until his death in 1933. Around the corner in the Grove, George du Maurier lived from 1874 to 1895, and while few people today could name the three novels he wrote here, many will recall his most celebrated character, Svengali.

The National Trust owns Fenton House, which means that visitors may snoop through the rooms and the grounds. The house dates from 1693 and has a walled garden.

399

The local for this neighborhood — the handy pub in a locality is called "the local" — is the Holly Bush on Holly Mount, a pub which has resisted change for many generations. Three famous pubs mark the boundaries of Hampstead Heath: Jack Straw's Castle, part of which dates from the 1700's, although its history is supposed to go back four hundred years before that; the Bull and Bush, a remodeled eighteenth-century farmhouse, about which Florrie Ford introduced a song in 1910 that everyone in England seems to know, "Down at the Old Bull and Bush"; the Spaniard's, also built in the eighteenth century, is much more a country inn than a pub in appearance, both inside and out.

Just past the Spaniard's is Kenwood, which was in 1780 the country house of Lord Chief Justice Mansfield. The Gordon "No Popery" rioters burned his Bloomsbury town house and swarmed up to the heath to destroy his Adam-built retreat. The landlord of the Spaniard's invited the whole mob in for drinks on the house, and there they stayed swilling until a detachment of soldiers who couldn't drink on duty came and carted them off.

Thus majestic Kenwood House was able to endure. In 1927 Lord Iveagh (Guinness brewing family) bequeathed it to the nation along with a sensational collection of British eighteenth- and early nineteenth-century portraits (Gainsborough, Reynolds, Romney, Raeburn, Lawrence) and other fine paintings (Rembrandt, Vermeer, Turner). The London Parks Department offers a full summer season of weekly symphony concerts from a shell by the lake in Kenwood, and other concerts and poetry readings up at the house.

The heath itself offers playing fields, hiking trails, golf, swimming, and on Bank Holidays the noisy joys of the Hampstead Fair. In the old days the principal activity on the heath, aside from poaching and al fresco amorosity, was highway robbery. The Fair, by the way, takes place in a hollow near the odd hamlet called the Vale of Health (the Black Death always passed it by) where there is also a pub, further evidence that heath-wandering is thirsty work.

Across the heath toward the southeast lie the Highgate Ponds, and from there the way is more or less open to Swain's Lane which goes whistling through the Highgate Cemetery. Some visitors to

London peek quickly at a couple of principal monuments, and then hurry to this burial ground to honor the grave of their prophet, Karl Marx.

However, there are other notables lodged here. If one has already seen the extreme measures taken to memorialize some of Westminster Abbey's dead, the monuments here may not seem extraordinary, but they do demonstrate that British authors who have profitably snickered at California cemeteries are overlooking a goldmine in their own capital.

The original cemetery lies higher up on Highgate Hill, on the east side of Swain's Lane. Its narrow roads wind around the contours of the slope, some corners of which are completely overgrown by brambles and distractedly entangled weeping trees. Finding some of the graves means parting long, matted grasses or poking through resentful underbrush.

The entrance is at the bottom of the slope, forbidding, deep stairways let into a stone wall, a promise of the climax reached at the top of the rise. At the top is the Columbarium, an Egypto-Transylvanian necropolis with trees forcing their way out of the masonry, as at Angkor Wat. It is an open-air, drive-in crypt. Dug into the crest of the hill, its ramps take the visitor into a circular theater lined with little stone cottages for the dead. Visible through the grilles, these permanent residents occupy wooden boxes ranged on stone shelves. The gateway into this sunken circle is Egyptian, as are the tombs on the inner side of the circle. Above, growing out over the core and level with the rest of the cemetery above, is a well-nourished cedar tree.

There is a reason why British film-makers have not used this setting in horror movies: it is not believable.

Somewhere in the old cemetery is the grave of Lizzie Siddall, Dante Gabriel Rossetti's red-haired model, whom he married. When she was buried in 1862, Dante Gabriel put into her coffin the manuscript of his poems.

> Rossetti in a gesture brave
> Laid his verse in Lizzie's grave.
> Seven years passed by, and then
> He went and dug them up again.

401

He did, oh but indeed he did. Or rather his friends did, by the light of a huge midnight bonfire. They reached among the death-grown russet tresses and fetched back the not very good poems.

Another grave reopened, this one by the authorities, was that of Mr. Thomas Charles Druce, whose shop grew into an important Marylebone store. Some forty years after his interment in 1864, his daughter-in-law, Anna Maria Druce, became persuaded that the late draper had led a double life and had been in reality William John, fifth Duke of Portland. She insisted no one was buried in the grave, but that the Duke, an eccentric who had appeared only at night with muffled face, had shammed the Druce death to be free to resume his ducal occupations, which included digging tunnels. One of his tunnels, she contended, had led from the Druce store. In 1907, possibly at the urging of the sixth Duke, the authorities corrected her mistaken impression by disinterring Mr. Druce.

A mid-nineteenth-century menagerie man is buried beneath the carved figure of a sleeping lion, and more than one grave bears the effigy of a favorite dog. A concert pianist is laid away beneath a marble piano. The tomb of Lillywhite, the cricketer, shows Death bowling his wicket.

George Eliot, Michael Faraday, Herbert Spencer, the Dickens family (Charles is in the Abbey) and Pierce Egan, first of the world's great sports writers, are buried here. So is Christina Rossetti, undisturbed.

Karl Marx was moved from the old sloping cemetery to the new flatter one, sharing a family plot where also lies the daughter who committed suicide. There are always flowers on Marx's grave, over which, on a low block of granite, is posed a massive head of Marx, almost all hair and beard. The inscription reads "WORKERS OF ALL LANDS UNITE."

And a further quotation —

> The philosophers have only interpreted the world
> in various ways. The point however is to change it.

NOTE TO THOSE WHO HAVE
READ THIS FAR

THERE is one corner of London in which the author of this book has never set foot. And when the book was decided upon, he refrained from going there in order to leave it for the reader to discover for himself.

This is Red Lion Square, just north of Lincoln's Inn. At No. 17 the young pre-Raphaelites rollicked in 1856. Dante Gabriel Rossetti was twenty-eight, Edward Burne-Jones was twenty-three, and William Morris was twenty-two. The housemaid was named Red Lion Mary. Ruskin came often to call. They painted and wrote and argued and visited famous friends (such as the Brownings) and the Zoo.

Burne-Jones wrote:

There was a year in which I think it never rained, nor clouded, but was blue summer from Christmas to Christmas, and London streets glittered, and it was always morning and the air sweet and full of bells.

And perhaps it still is, in Red Lion Square, in Holborn. It isn't too far to go and see, as nothing really is in London.

SOURCES OF ILLUSTRATIONS

British Museum: 22, 30-31, 49, 108, 154-155, 162, 187, 210, 240, 259, 285, 292, 303, 310, 316, 325

Folger Shakespeare Library: 4, 19, 21, 27, 33, 39, 50, 62, 109, 124, 127, 128, 151, 169, 379, 384, 387, 388

Museum of Fine Arts, Boston: 80 (Harvey D. Parker Collection), 125 (Harvey D. Parker Collection), 214 (Gift of Miss Ellen Bullard), 217 (Gift of Miss Ellen Bullard), 242 (Gift of Miss Ellen Bullard), 298 (Harvey D. Parker Collection), 374 (Harvey D. Parker Collection)

New York Public Library: 16, 24-25, 36, 41, 42, 43, 44, 46, 47, 64, 68, 70, 72, 73, 79, 87, 96, 98, 99, 103, 106, 108, 116, 122, 130-131, 132, 135, 141, 142, 161, 166, 173, 178, 180, 189, 199, 216, 218, 221, 223, 225, 227, 229, 230, 232, 234, 235, 241, 243, 245, 247, 249, 252, 255, 257, 260, 263, 266, 271, 273, 274, 283, 284, 287, 289, 294, 321, 322, 323, 324, 331, 332, 333, 334, 343, 358, 359, 360, 366, 378, 380, 389, 392, 394

INDEX